BOMBER HARRIS

THE STORY OF SIR ARTHUR HARRIS, MARSHAL OF THE ROYAL AIR FORCE

By the same author:

The Bomber's Eye

BOMBER
HARRIS

The story of Marshal of the Royal Air Force
Sir Arthur Harris, Bt, GCB, OBE, AFC, LLD,
Air Officer Commanding-in-Chief, Bomber Command, 1942–1945

DUDLEY SAWARD

Foreword by Sir Arthur Bryant, CH, CBE

Doubleday & Company, Inc.
Garden City, New York
1985

Library of Congress Cataloging in Publication Data
Saward, Dudley.
Bomber Harris: the story of Sir Arthur Harris,
marshal of the Royal Air Force.
1. Harris, Arthur Travers, Sir, 1892–
2. Great Britain.   Royal Air Force—Biography.
3. Marshals—Great Britain—Biography.   I. Title.
UG626.2.H36S29   1984   940.54′4941   84-21196
ISBN 0-385-11258-0

Contents

Illustrations

Maps

Dedication

I dedicate this book to all those who served in Bomber Command during World War II, and to their parents, their wives, girlfriends and families, many of whom were bereaved of their loved ones in order that Britain, her Commonwealth, and the Western World might remain free from the tyranny of Nazism. Those who survived and those who died can be eternally proud of their inestimable service to their Country and its Allies.

Foreword
by Sir Arthur Bryant, CH, CBE

At the beginning of World War II, Nazi Germany, regardless of all considerations of humanity and morality, by a ruthless exercise of air power against civilian centres of population, gained total control of the Continent. Her bombers flattened Warsaw and Rotterdam, though, thanks to the Battle of Britain, they failed to flatten London. Thereafter, first alone, and then with her American allies, by exercising command of the sea and the air over the sea, Britain, as in earlier wars, put a ring of salt water round the aggressor who had overrun Europe, and kept him in that ring until the reviving forces of liberation were strong enough to enter that ring and throttle him. Yet, attacking as they were, from the outside of an immense sea circumference, they had first to overcome an enemy with the advantage of interior lines and quick communications and of everything that ran on wheels in a vast continental fortress. In the wars of the past for this reason the attack from the outside of the sea circumference had taken a long time. Owing to our adversary's initial advantage of being able to strike back in superior and overwhelming force, we had always had to launch it at some remote spot far from his heart where his communications were most strained and difficult—in the mountainous peninsula of Spain and Portugal in the wars against Napoleon, and in the mountainous toe and spine of Italy in 1943, before we could build up sufficient power to strike on land anywhere nearer his heart.

  But in 1944 we did make good our foothold within striking distance of his heart and, by doing so, cut many years off the length of the War. We were able to do so by virtue of our use of a new weapon—one which Hitler's own moral obliquity had put into our hands, the terrible weapon of air bombardment of industrial centres and communications. Those ceaseless battles fought by Bomber Command over the Rhine, Ruhr and Berlin, beginning in the days of our utter weakness in 1940, and steadily and inexorably mounting in strength—battles attended by greater comparative losses than in any sustained victorious operation in human history—were imperceptibly driving the heart of German war industry eastwards, away from the future D-Day beaches.

When the Germans blitzed us in the winter of 1940–41 it did not vitally matter, because, thanks to our command of the sea, they could not follow up their attack in person and we were not having to fight a major war on land and supply our armies for it. The delay caused to the flow of our war production was not therefore vital. But when, two, three and four years later, we and our American allies visited on Germany an infinitely greater weight of air bombardment, the Germans were having to fight and supply a major war on land – in the east, in the south and, after D-Day, in the west too. It was that combination of the ceaseless hammering from the air of the enemy's supplies and supply-lines which finally broke the will and power of the German Army to go on fighting.

In that great and sustained operation of war, when nightly the crews of Bomber Command went out on their perilous missions, suffering losses in proportion to their strength unparalleled in any sustained successful operation known to history, it was 'Bomber' Harris, who, by his fortitude, patience and persistence, and by his power of evoking from the brave men under his command a capacity for endurance and devotion to duty which has seldom been equalled and never surpassed in the annals of war, who won and retained for the Allies that stranglehold on the aggressor's production centres and communications without which D-Day could so easily have been a shambles and disaster, and London itself might have been destroyed by German rockets and flying bombs.

To anyone who lived through those years when, night after night, our bombers were passing overhead on the way to and from their dangerous, but ultimately decisive missions, it is an honour to be associated, in however humble a capacity, with Group Captain Saward in his noble tribute to this great commander, for long the last survivor of the little group of supreme captains who together delivered the *coup de grâce* to our enemies in the year of victory 1944/5. I remember so well on the night before D-Day standing on the lawn of a little Midland village, watching, as I had so often watched before during the past four years, 'Bomber' Harris's bombers passing overhead: not now the forlorn, doomed and gallant few of earlier days, but hundred after hundred of mighty planes, the throbbing of whose engines made the earth shake beneath my feet, whose lights were like the heavenly host on the march, the march of avenging might and doom, like great Birnam Wood marching to high Dunsinane Hill. The stars, it seemed that night, were moving, and they were all moving in one direction to one appointed place. It was the subject and hero of this book who, with the brave men he inspired and led, played so essential a part—a part that has for some time been forgotten—in that victory.

ARTHUR BRYANT, 1980

Author's Preface

During World War II I served on Sir Arthur Harris's staff from February 1942 to the end of the war in Europe in May 1945. In the following years I watched, with dismay and profound disgust, not only the official indifference to the immense contribution of Bomber Command to the winning of the war, but to the flood of literature, television programmes and so on decrying its policy and denigrating the name of perhaps the greatest commander to emerge from World War II.

With Harris's continued silence, and encouraged by my wife and the late Air Marshal Sir Robert Saundby (Harris's Deputy from 1942 to 1945), I at last plucked up courage to persuade Harris to entrust me with the task of writing his biography. When he finally agreed I was, I confess, apprehensive, for I realised that I had committed myself to writing a vitally important chapter of history. I decided to drop all other activities and devote my entire time to the project. As I had just finished a task in Liechtenstein and New York, I returned to England with my wife in July 1971, bought a cottage in Wiltshire about an hour and a quarter's drive from Sir Arthur Harris's home, and retired completely from business activities in order to devote all my time to research and writing.

Nevertheless, I could not have accomplished my task without the help I received from many people and many sources. From Sir Arthur and Lady Harris I received indispensable assistance. Sir Arthur made available to me all his personal correspondence with Ludlow-Hewitt, Portal, Churchill, Archibald Sinclair, 'Boom' Trenchard, Harry Hopkins, Averell Harriman, 'Happy' Arnold, Eisenhower, Brendan Bracken and others. In addition he permitted me to tape-record more than fifty hours of conversation with him. Lady Harris helped me to sort much of his correspondence and also allowed me to tape-record several hours of conversation. Many days were spent by my wife and myself at their home, and it is impossible for me to measure my indebtedness to them for their cooperation and hospitality.

Next I have to thank Clifton Child, the former head of the Historical Section of the Cabinet Office, who constantly encouraged me in my endeavours, guided me, gained access for me to Churchill's papers, Chiefs of Staff minutes and War Cabinet minutes, and introduced me to the heads of the historical sections of the services. Equally, I must thank Group

Captain E. B. Haslam of the Air Historical Branch of the Ministry of Defence for all his help in enabling me to trace various important documents and letters contained in pre-war and wartime Air Ministry files. Both Clifton Child and Teddy Haslam read my original typescript and made important suggestions for certain modifications and additions to the text.

I received considerable help from several members of the Royal Air Force, but in particular I must mention Marshal of the Royal Air Force Lord Elworthy and the late Air Chief Marshal the Hon Sir Ralph Cochrane. Both devoted much of their time to assist me with information for various parts of the book. The main help I received from the USA was from Lieutenant-General Ira C. Eaker, to whom I am also deeply indebted.

I am profoundly grateful to the late Earl of Avon for his invaluable help in connection with various items of diplomatic history during the 1918 to 1939 period. In addition he was kind enough to ensure that I secured full cooperation in my researches into 1939–1945 documents associated with the Cabinet Office.

Another major source of assistance, particularly with my researches into World War I and the period between the wars, was from the Public Record Office. I must especially thank Mr Jeffery Ede, the former head of the Public Record Office, for he personally saw to it that I had the maximum assistance in obtaining access to the most relevant and important documents. He was also kind enough to read the typescript and make valuable comments.

Further help came from Leonard (Frank) White of the Cabinet Office, who helped me to search through many of Churchill's papers, as well as minutes of the Chiefs of Staff and the War Cabinet.

At the War Office Historical Branch I had much assistance from Colonel Ben Neave-Hill, to whom I am truly grateful.

Next I must turn to my researches abroad. From Herr Albert Speer I received a wealth of cooperation and help for which I can never thank him enough. He provided me with access to all his private papers, and guided me in my search for other vital German documents. He permitted me to spend many hours at his home in Heidelberg to study reports, production records and letters in connection with the armaments situation in Germany from 1942 to 1945, and the impact of the bombing by the Royal Air Force and the USAAF. In addition he allowed me to tape-record many hours of conversation. My thanks also go to Frau Margarete Speer, his wife, who so kindly entertained me in their home on those many occasions and saw to it that my stomach was well sustained whilst my brain was being filled with facts and figures. Neither must I forget Bello, their St Bernard, who after my first visit greeted me like an old friend.

I am also particularly indebted to General Johannes Steinhoff, who kindly received me at NATO Headquarters in Brussels, where he was chairman of the North Atlantic Committee, and, despite the pressure under which he was working, devoted much time to my enquiries.

In Switzerland I am grateful first and foremost to the late Herr Hans Hausamann, the founder and wartime head of Büro Ha in the Swiss Intelligence Service. He kindly searched out many official on-the-spot assessments of bomb damage caused by Bomber Command and the American Eighth Bomber Command on specific towns in Germany and German-occupied territory. These assessments numbered some 500 sheets of closely typed information, all of which he copied for me. He also provided me with other relevant facts about the deteriorating state of the German economy resulting from the Allied bombing. I will always be much in his debt.

The others I must thank for their considerable help are Dr Geoffrey von Meiss, formerly a Colonel Divisionnaire in the Swiss Air Force, and Colonel Divisionnaire Peter Burckhardt, later the General Direktor of Oerlikon-Bührlé Holding SA, who from 1942 to 1945 was the Swiss Military and Air Attaché in Berlin.

For much of my information on Harris's activities in Rhodesia, particularly those in connection with his East African cruise in 1932 and his attachment to Southern Rodesia in 1936, my sincere gratitude goes to the late Mr Clifford Dupont, the former President of Rhodesia, and at one time my senior when we were at school at Bishop's Stortford College. He provided me with copies of a number of important documents from the Rhodesian archives which related to the Harris story, information which was invaluable in emphasising the breadth of Harris's vision in all stages of his romantic life. For information on his earlier life in Rhodesia, my sincere thanks go to the late Mrs Pollock.

From Liechtenstein I received valuable help from my good friend Walter Alicke who, as a boy, survived the Dresden raids. He provided me with a number of German wartime publications relating to bombing raids, Goebbels' speeches, Dresden, etc.

Other sources of assistance were Sir Arthur Bryant, the late Air Marshal Sir Robert Saundby, the late Lord Renwick, Colonel Juan Hobbs and Mr George Thomson, who was Harris's rigger from 1922 to 1924 in Mesopotamia. I also received help from the Wiener Library and from Mr E. M. Boyle, ALA, the reference librarian of the Salisbury Divisional Library, Wiltshire Library and Museum Service.

To my former secretary in Liechtenstein, Frau Martha Negele, go my sincere thanks for all her help. She typed the entire manuscript from my handwritten version—no easy task. In addition she worked on many German documents for me, making numerous translations where the contents were too complicated for my limited knowledge of the language.

When the first typescript was completed, Raleigh Trevelyan read it for me and then, with his considerable professionalism, advised me how I might improve the final script by rewriting sections for greater interest to a wider readership. His help was invaluable, given in the most tactful, albeit persuasive manner, and even though he caused me an extra three months' hard work I shall always be most grateful to him.

To my wife go my very special thanks. She helped me in my searches through many documents, listened to me reading the manuscript aloud in bits and pieces, criticised, encouraged me, fed me—and protected me from interference from outside sources.

Finally, I have to thank Gerald Pollinger, my agent, my guide and my friend—and the one who wielded the proverbial stick and kept me hard at my task for nearly four years. Without his constant encouragement I think I might have thrown in the towel.

11th October, 1976   DUDLEY SAWARD

Marshal of the Royal Air Force Sir Arthur T. Harris died quietly at his home in Goring on 5 April 1984, just a few days before his 92nd birthday. Under my agreement with him, this biography, begun so long ago, may now at last be published.

30th April 1984   DUDLEY SAWARD

The real importance of the air war consisted in the fact that it opened a second front long before the invasion of Europe. That front was the skies over Germany. The fleets of bombers might appear at any time over any large German city or important factory. The unpredictability of the attacks made this front gigantic; every square metre of the territory we controlled was a kind of front line. Defence against air attacks required the production of thousands of anti-aircraft guns, the stockpiling of tremendous quantities of ammunition all over the country, and holding in readiness hundreds of thousands of soldiers, who in addition had to stay in position by their guns, often totally inactive, for months at a time.

As far as I can judge from the accounts I have read, no one has yet seen that this was the greatest lost battle on the German side. The losses from the retreats in Russia or from the surrender of Stalingrad were considerably less. Moreover, the nearly 20,000 anti-aircraft guns stationed in the homeland could almost have doubled the anti-tank defences on the Eastern Front.

Albert Speer, Spandau: The Secret Diaries

Introduction

It is recorded at St George's Church, Agra, in the Diocese and Archdeaconry of Calcutta, that Arthur Travers, the son of George Steel Travers Harris and Caroline Maria Harris, was baptised at Gwalior on 11 December 1892, and 'said to be born' on the 13 April 1892.

Fifty years later, Hitler and his Nazi Germany were in no doubt as to whether Arthur Travers Harris had or had not been born. A nation which had begun the indiscriminate extermination of the Jews, ransacked Czechoslovakia, ravaged Poland, razed Rotterdam, sacked much of Western Russia, overrun Belgium and France, and added the verb 'to Coventrate' to the dictionary of war, but had, itself, remained inviolate against the horrors of the 'Blitzkrieg', suddenly found itself in the front line of battle. In February 1942, Air Marshal Arthur T. Harris was appointed Commander-in-Chief of Bomber Command and immediately proceeded to mount the first offensive against the very vitals of Germany, an offensive which was to grow to such proportions that it contributed largely to the final destruction of Germany by the Allies. In April 1942, Cologne and the Ruhr had a foretaste of what was to come. On Harris's birthday Essen and other parts of the Ruhr were attacked by 327 bombers. At the end of May he launched the historic 'Thousand Raid' against Cologne, a milestone in World War II which marked the turning-point for the Allies from the defensive to the offensive.

What kind of man was Sir Arthur Harris? Was the course of his career a matter of chance? Was it by accident that he was entrusted with the only weapon of war that was capable of carrying the offensive into the homeland of the enemy until the Allied armies were ready to invade Europe and march to victory? The more one studies Harris's life the more convinced one becomes that he was groomed by destiny to undertake the task of saving this nation from the ignominy of defeat and the loss of its freedom.

Goebbels, Hitler's Minister of Propaganda, described him thus: 'Brutality, cold cynicism and an undiluted lust for murder are his chief characteristics ... You have only to look into his eyes to know what to expect from such a man. He has the icy-cold eyes of a born murderer ... He has accepted a task which many others have declined—the total war against the Huns, as they call us.' Goebbels, however, was not destined to look into

Harris's eyes, for after killing his own wife and six children he committed suicide rather than face the penalty for his crimes, which included a major responsibility for the murder of more than five million Jews.

His fitter in No 45 Squadron in Mesopotamia in 1924, Corporal George Thomson, wrote in a letter to the author: 'We called him "Blood" Harris— I'm talking about the riggers and fitters—because he was inclined to be red-haired. It was nothing to do with his temperament, though he could be irascible, as we all were, because it was one hell of a climate. We'd do anything for him—we loved him . . .' At the end of the War, Marshal of the Royal Air Force Viscount Trenchard wrote these words to Harris: 'I know no man that could have been more determined to carry out what you did. I know no one who could have combined such determination with technical and operational knowledge. I give all credit to your staff and your wonderful air crews and maintenance crews. But it was your leadership and knowledge that made the Bomber Command the magnificent force it was. The world should thank you.'

Truly a controversial personality. Certainly, with Montgomery, one of the two greatest operational commanders to emerge from the war. Unquestionably unorthodox as a professional military man. Indisputably a man of integrity and courage and one who has that understanding and knowledge of what motivates people which makes a great leader.

Can one write a conventional biography about such an unconventional individual? No. His life is a vibrant, warm and exciting story, and it is this story that I try to tell.

I
The young Harris

Arthur Harris was born at Cheltenham on 13 April 1892, when his parents were on leave from India. His family's background was predominantly military. His great-grandfather was a Captain R N, but his grandfather was a colonel, and most of his numerous uncles also attained the rank of colonel in the late nineteenth and early twentieth centuries. Indeed, Arthur Harris complains that in his youth he suffered from such a surfeit of colonels that he decided at a very tender age that soldiering was not for him at any cost. His father, who had wanted to follow a career in the Army, like his numerous brothers, had been thwarted in his ambition due to extreme deafness from early youth. Rather than allow his disability to destroy his youthful hopes—one being a fervent desire to serve the British Empire in India—he studied civil engineering and architecture, qualified, and went out to India as a Civil Servant in the Public Works Department, where he achieved notable success in designing and erecting a number of magnificent buildings.

The newly arrived Harris, the youngest of a family of four boys and two girls, accompanied his parents on their return to India. He remained with them until the age of five, when it became necessary for him to begin his education. Due, as Harris says, to the 'damned snobbery' of that era, it was essential for the children of the white officer and official classes in India, as a matter of Victorian propriety, to be sent home to England for their education. There were, of course, perfectly good schools in the hill-stations, such as Simla, but it just was not done to send children to these centres of learning, which were regarded as suitable only for the offspring of those engaged in trade and somewhat contemptuously known as box-wallahs. So, perforce, the child Harris had to return to England when he was barely five years old, to be left parentless and effectively homeless in order to receive an education in keeping with the official status of his family. This meant that he was thrust into the care of so-called baby farms which, run by impecunious generals' daughters and vicars' wives, catered for the infant sons and daughters of the official classes serving the Empire abroad. Amongst the baby farms that were his 'homes' in these formative years was one he remembers vividly and with resentment. 'It was run', he says, 'by a female religious maniac—and believe me, the female version is infinitely worse than the male.' She thought the best way to spend a holiday was on one's knees, a view which I somewhat vehemently disputed. And that didn't exactly produce the most harmonious relations.'

India seemed a long way away at the turn of the century, so his parents became almost total strangers to Harris in his boyhood. In fact, he remembers only one occasion during his schooldays when his father came home on leave with his mother, and two occasions when his mother came to England on her own for several weeks to be with her sons. Of the families to which he was sent only one stands out in his mind and conjures up happy memories—clergy folk called Graham-Jones. After his primary education at a Cheltenham kindergarten Arthur Harris entered a preparatory school as a boarder at the age of seven. It was the same school which his two elder brothers—the third had died as a child—had attended earlier and went by the rather pretentious description of 'Preparatory School for Eton'. It consisted of two or three villas converted into one house at Upton Park, near Slough, but later moved to a magnificent manor house called Gore Court, near Sittingbourne in Kent, and was run by a family by the name of de Winton. There appears to have been little individual attention to boys from an educational point of view, but with the beautiful setting, including its own nine-hole golf course and a farm, there were distractions that appealed to the young Harris. 'They realised,' he says, 'that I could handle horses and ponies and animals—something of a discovery for myself too— so I got the chore of rolling the golf course with the horse-drawn roller, riding a nice old booted pony called Topper. I set off on him on many occasions, sometimes driving him on errands in the dog-cart. These opportunities whetted my appetite. One of the proudest days of my life was, when on holiday with the Graham-Joneses, I was allowed to drive the governess cart down to the station to fetch a guest. I don't know what the guest thought of being entrusted to a ten-year-old, but as far as I was concerned it was a great occasion.'

Education at this stage of his school life was, however, minimal. The only individuals to receive anything like real teaching were those favoured by the headmaster. The younger of his two elder brothers won a scholarship to Eton, thus proving that the school might well have some right to its description. This brother was very good-looking, and Arthur Harris believes this weighed greatly in his favour in the matter of getting individual teaching attention. His eldest brother went to Sherborne, and both brothers went on to Cambridge. But when Arthur Harris's turn to move on came at the age of twelve, 'There wasn't much money left in the kitty,' he says, 'so I was despatched to Allhallows at Honiton in Devon, which then consisted of three or four houses scattered on either side of the main Exeter road, and a large meeting hall and common dining-room. Despite that dining-room, I remember being mostly cold and hungry. In fact, my memories of schools are primarily something almost approaching starvation, which was probably the common lot of all schoolboys in those days.'

At Allhallows Harris did not receive anything which by the widest stretch of imagination could be called an education by today's standards. There was an examination known as Matriculation, but this was really only for those who wanted to be doctors and barristers and, as Harris says: 'Those who went in for that sort of luxury were specially coached.' During his five years at Allhallows from 1904 to 1909 he was still the boy with no family except the Graham-Jones' to go home to in his holidays. But his loneliness did not turn him into a shy recluse or a youth lacking in confidence and initiative, as might have been expected. Quite the reverse. He became self-reliant at an early age, developed the equanimity and stoicism of one much older than his years and, as he progressed to maturity, displayed an unselfish nature and a tremendous sense of integrity and justice. His courage as a youngster was also great, but it was always tempered by plain good sense. Talking of the bullying of small boys at the beginning of the century, he says: 'I can never understand how any boy got away with bullying. If a number of you got together, however much smaller, you could always give any bully a hell of a time—and he left you alone.' One has the impression that the young Harris organised his own defence forces at an early age and recognised that attack is always the best method of defence. In growing up on his own and becoming independent he also found satisfaction in protecting and caring for others less able to look after themselves.

In his last year at Allhallows something happened which had a marked effect upon the next stage of his life. The lessee of the Comedy Theatre was at that time a benefactor of Allhallows, and it was his practice to give the boys tickets to the plays which were put on. Harris received one and in his holidays went to see the play. 'The show I went to,' he says, 'was about a Rhodesian planter who came back to England to marry his very society fiancée, but fell out with her because she was so damned snooty. He finished up by marrying the housemaid, a Scottish yeoman's daughter, and taking her out to Rhodesia instead. She was far more suited to be a farmer's wife. I was so intrigued with the whole of this damned play, about a country where snobbery was out and where you became what you were by what you did, that I decided I would go to Rhodesia.'

Harris's father retired in 1909 and he and his wife returned to England. His inability to make his career in the Army had left him determined to foist his youthful ambitions upon his sons. His two elder boys failed to gratify his wishes, although the eldest had got as far as passing the entrance examination to the Royal Military Academy at Woolwich and gaining a place. At the last moment, however, this son turned down his chance and left home, coming back a few years later to join the Levant Service, a separate side of the Consular service in the Middle East and which the other son had entered on leaving Cambridge. At least this was some consolation, but Harris senior was to be grossly disappointed and somewhat annoyed that his youngest son should not only decline to take up the Army as a career, but should even scorn Government service. And for what? To go farming in Rhodesia! But he agreed. 'He paid the passage out, but he never dreamt, mark you, that I would really go. He bought me a second-class passage to Beira on a tuppenny-ha'penny steamer of the Rennie Line called the SS *Inanda* and covered my fare up to Umtali—and he came to see me off at Tilbury. Even then my old Pa thought I'd never go. When I did, he relented. I'll never forget. When we stopped off Weymouth to drop the pilot, he sent a message aboard to have me moved into the first class, which was jolly decent of him.'

That was on 24 February 1910, just two months before Harris's eighteenth birthday. The young boy was on his way, on his own, to a new world where he hoped to make a life for himself, a life in which success would depend upon his own abilities, his own determination and his own courage.

2
Rhodesia grooms a youth

The voyage to Beira took five weeks and, as Harris described it, it was a whale of a trip. 'I fell desperately in love with a girl on board—she was a niece of the owner of the line. He was on board too with his wife. This girl was several years older than I, as lovely as a picture, and I fell—and by golly, at that age how it hits one. She's still alive, but I've never seen her since. We've corresponded and we exchanged Christmas cards.'

The girl, a widow* in her late eighties when the author visited her, remembered the time well. 'I was going out with my aunt and uncle to see something of Africa and to stay in Durban. I don't remember exactly how I met Arthur on the boat ... We used to call him Peter. One day he appeared in a kind of boiler suit. No one else had anything like it—and someone christened him Peter Pan, so the name stuck. There was another young man on board and the three of us were always together—we sat together and did everything together all the time—but I liked Peter best. I remember when Peter first spoke to me, he said he had been watching me walk about for several days and that I had a very conceited walk—but he said it so nicely I had to laugh ... He had a lovely sense of humour. There were some very odd females on board, who were a constant source of amusement to us, and Peter made up the most droll rhymes about them. But of course he was always awfully nice to them. He would never willingly hurt anyone ... We disembarked at Beira—Peter too—and from there we went on by train. I remember the compartments had two sleeping bunks; my aunt and uncle had one together, and I found myself sharing another with a woman who had been on the boat and whom I very much disliked. I told Peter about it and he said he'd go and see the guard to find out if something could be done. Well he came back and said he'd found me an empty compartment I could have to myself. He was only one night on the train, and the next day we said goodbye to each other when he got off at Umtali. It wasn't until later that day that I discovered he had given me his own compartment and had slept in the guard's van. And I've never seen him from that day to this.'

Arthur Harris said: 'When I waved goodbye as the train pulled out, my heart just about hit the deck. It was the end of my world. How it hits one—that first time, at that age!'

At Umtali Harris went to the British South Africa Company's Premier

*Mrs Pollock, who died on 15 July 1973.

Estate, where they had accommodation for half a dozen young men like himself and training arrangements so that they could learn the language, something about the country, and what they could do to earn a living. The charges were reasonable—about £10 per month, which included accommodation and food. He stayed there for three months and then started his wanderings in search of work.

One of his first jobs was to help a farmer build a house. There were no building contractors: in that land of pioneers men and women found their own salvation or went under, and he found himself completely on his own, except for native labouring help. He was quite undaunted, even when he was told that he would have to make his own bricks. After he had been duly instructed in the art, he found himself enjoying the task immensely and eventually be became a proficient brick-maker. During his several jobs in Rhodesia he undertook a considerable amount of building on different farms.

For a while Harris went into the transport business. This was the era of horse-drawn transport, and the great problem was the life span of a horse in that part of the world. Rhodesia then was afflicted by a horse sickness for which there was absolutely no cure and no known inoculation. Mules were not much better off, but lasted a bit longer. Harris says that to keep 5 per cent of your horses alive throughout a year was good going. 'The first cars to arrive were called Colonial Models. The first Colonial Model that I remember was a Napier, and the irritating thing about it was that the starting handle wound the opposite way to all other cars, which made it very awkward to swing. Damned fool design. I can never think why they did it. Too many people make things which they never bother to try out for themselves and discover what damned idiots they are. The only difference I could find between that model and the old English taxi was that you had a wash basin in the back—a sort of open tonneau with a folding basin. I can't think what for—especially when the last thing you could ever find on the road out there was water. Then came the Model 'T' Ford. At first the back wheels had a habit of coming off, but once they put this right it was a marvellous car—face anything, any country—and it won the war in Europe, Mespot, and Africa in 1914–1918.'

From 1910 to 1913 Harris undertook a number of jobs which, apart from those already mentioned, consisted of working on agricultural and livestock farms, growing some of the first tobacco in Rhodesia for a planter called Gibson, building tobacco barns, and going on shooting expeditions in the Bundu to supply meat to miners in the small mining concessions. Throughout these years he had learnt to stand on his own feet, do things for himself, improvise when and where necessary, turn his hand to almost any trade, live rough when required, which was not infrequently, and enjoy living by his wits and his own labour.

During this time he had not forgotten his first love and had corresponded with her regularly both during her visit to Africa and after she had returned to her home in Ireland. 'In one of his letters,' she recalls, 'Peter mentioned that he didn't very much like the job he was in at that time and was looking for another. Well I had some great great friends called Crofton Townsend who had a big farm not far outside Salisbury. She was especially a dear friend of mine. So I just told Peter to go and see them—I didn't write to them myself—which he did, and they gave him a job. In fact they made him farm manager when they came home to Dublin in 1914 on a year's leave. Then one day I remember them contacting me in a frightful state—it must have been just about the time war broke out. They told me they had just received a cable from Peter telling them he was going to join up so they had better come back quickly to look after the farm themselves. They were livid! But I remember later—it must have been when Peter came back from the German South-West African campaign—Ethel Townsend told me he had been to see them a couple of times and had grown into a fine man. Apparently he escorted their daughter to a dance on one occasion—she was only seventeen and rather shy, and so proud of being escorted by such a good-looking man. So all was forgiven.'

The time Harris spent on the Crofton Townsends' farm was important for many reasons. It was well equipped and he had plenty of experience with steam and traction engines and mechanisation, so far as it went in those days. But most important of all, he had to manage quite a big enterprise on his own—and he was then only twenty-one years old. At the time, he was hoping the experience would stand him in good stead for managing a farm on which he was planning to take up an option. But war broke out, and that was that. Nevertheless, these first few years in Rhodesia had been vital in the training of the man for his future life.

In August 1914, 'like all the other damned fools' he signed up in the 1st Rhodesian Regiment, which completed its formation in October with 500 European volunteers. 'By the time I applied,' says Harris, 'I was told there were only two vacancies left, one for a machine-gunner and one for a bugler. So I said I'd be the machine-gunner. But the machine-gun officer soon put a stop to that when he discovered I didn't know which end of the gun was the spout! And that was lucky for me, because the guns we had were some odd things called Rexers, and I don't think they ever fired more than two consecutive shots at a time without jamming. Anyway, I went to my friend Hope-Carson, who was the adjutant, and said okay, I'll be the bugler—and he said he supposed I knew as much about a bugle as I did about a ruddy machine-gun. I told him that as a matter of fact I had been pretty hot on the bugle when I was in the O T C at school, and I picked up a bugle and nearly blew his head off! So there I was, signed up as the bugler. I must admit I got fed up with the thing banging around my knees, so I buried it in the end in the trenches outside Swakopmund—after all, they were never used in serious warfare.'

There was no training of any consequence and the volunteers, who joined up patriotically to fight the Germans in South-West Africa, received only an elementary preparation for war. The colonials, many of them farmers and farm workers, were put through a short course of square-bashing, forming fours, arms drill and marching, and then sent straight off to war. They only had their first chance of firing practice when they were already marching to do battle with the enemy. They were given five rounds each to fire at a few square paper targets set up at 500 yards' range. Since the regiment consisted of 500 men, some 2,500 rounds were fired, but Harris recalls there were not many more than half a dozen hits in all. Harris and one or two other old lags deliberately fired their rounds at the rocks well away from the targets, so that they could see from the spurts of dust how far off they were from the point of aim. 'We had Canadian ·303 rifles,' Harris says, 'and they were fantastically bad until you got to know which way the barrel was bent!'

What Harris remembers about this campaign, however, is the marching. The regiment left Salisbury on 14 November 1914 to go to Bloemfontein, where it formed a garrison until the South African Rebellion was put down. It was only there a short while before it went on to Cape Town to embark on 21 December for South-West Africa, landing on Christmas Day at Walvis Bay. There it joined 4 South African Brigade and moved on to Swakopmund, which was taken and occupied with only a few skirmishes and little opposition, by 14 January 1915. The stay at Swakopmund was of relatively short duration, and then the marching began in earnest—'living on biscuits,' Harris says, 'which you had to bust with your rifle butt, and bully beef which in that climate was almost liquid in the can.' From Swakopmund they moved up the Swakop River in the direction of Nonidas, which had previously been occupied, without opposition, by 3 South African Brigade. From there they went into the Namib Desert, where they spent three months protecting personnel who were reconstructing the railway that had been dismantled by the retreating Germans. The railway was important since it was the supply route from Walvis Bay to the advancing South African Army under General Botha. The brigade was three months in the desert, following the progress of the railway to Arandis. From there it marched to Trekkopjes where, on 26 April, a battle took place. It was Harris's second taste of warfare, but he describes it, as does history, as only a small engagement.

After this they marched again. 'And how we marched! We marched and we marched and we marched, and, God knows, as far as I was concerned I'd already marched too far! Talk about "Angels of Mons." Certainly under those conditions of exhaustion you do get hallucinations. I remember in the depths of the night we saw the lights of what seemed to be a magnificently illuminated city. We thought, well now we're getting somewhere—what is this? It's certainly quite a place. When we got up to it—do you know what it was?—a waggon with half a dozen Africans sitting round a fire in the bush. Just the reflection on the scrub trees and on the clouds in the pitch dark. And we thought it was a big town!'

On the march towards Ebony, Harris recalls another incident. 'We were slogging on our flat feet when a Boer commando unit rode past us, and as they went by they shouted in their best English, "Trek you boggers, trek!"

I thought to myself, we'll march your horses off their hind legs—and sure enough, some weeks later, we passed them dragging what was left of their horses, or just marching because their horses were dead. As we passed them we shouted in our best Afrikaans, "Trek you boggers, trek!" So you see, a man can outmarch a horse.'

From Ebony they continued marching until they joined up with 1 South African Brigade at Orange on 17 June. From here they went to Kalkfeld expecting to engage the enemy, but the Germans had departed. Finally they moved on to Otavi, which they reached on 30 June and where they remained until the German South-West African campaign ended victoriously at the beginning of July. This part of the war being over, the 1st Rhodesian Regiment returned to Cape Town and was disbanded.

'We'd had enough of war by that time,' Harris said, 'and as for marching—well I swore I'd never walk another step. We'd been marching pretty solidly from January to the end of June. Six ruddy months. We'd had enough and we didn't care if the bottom fell out of the Empire. Anyway, they bunged us on a train and sent us back home to Rhodesia, so I went back to the farm I had been running—the Crofton Townsends'—to pick up the bits and pieces. But I was restless and, like the others, I thought I ought to do more. You see, everyone thought the whole thing would be over in a year—but instead, it was going from bad to worse. So I went into town and there I found many friends from the old regiment, all with the same thought that they'd better get on with the job. Well, the Government asked us if we'd join up with the 2nd Battalion of the Rhodesian Regiment, which had gone to East Africa to help clean up the Boche there. But about 350 of us said nothing doing—we'd had our share of "bush whacking!" We decided we'd go back to England and do something there, but that was easier said than done. All we got out of the shipping company was a horse-laugh when we said we wanted passages for about three hundred back to England. But that didn't put me off. I went along to a friend of mine who was in the Union Castle offices and told him he'd better get on to his principals in Cape Town, or wherever they were, because the boys were getting wild. I told him they'd start taking his bloody office down if he didn't get us back to England—brick by brick, beginning with the chimneys.'

Whether or not this threat was responsible, Union Castle turned over the *Cluny Castle*, a small freighter of 5,152 tons built in 1903, to undertake the voyage. This ship only had accommodation for twelve passengers, so 'monkey cages' were built up in two of the holds to accommodate the numbers. After embarking the men at Beira it called at Durban, whence it sailed on 21 August 1915, arriving at London on 7 October, having first disembarked the volunteers at Plymouth. Rhodesia paid the fares of £10 a head.

3

He tucks his feet under his wings

Some time before Harris returned to England, he had read an advertisement in an English paper about joining the Royal Naval Air Service (RNAS) or the Royal Flying Corps (RFC) and learning to fly. But when he arrived back from Rhodesia in 1915 he first tried to get into the cavalry, partly because of his love of horses and partly because he was determined henceforward to fight 'sitting down'. As there were no vacancies in this already somewhat outdated arm of the British forces, he next turned his attention to the Royal Artillery, only to discover that they were full up and accepting no more recruits. Now it began to look suspiciously as if he was once more to be a footslogger in the infantry. It was at this point that he remembered his interest in the flying advertisement and, ready to pursue any course that would prevent him from using his feet again, he applied to join the RFC. He went to the War Office where he was seen by what he now describes as a supercilious individual who asked him, in a rather offensive manner, what he wanted, and when told by Harris that he wanted to fly, replied that there were six thousand other young men who wanted to fly, so would he like to be the six thousand and first? So back went a very depressed Harris to his parents' house to relate the sad news of yet another rejection.

'"I'm not going to walk," I said to my Pa. "I must find something to sit on." And then my Pa said he'd give me a note to my Uncle Charlie—he was one of the surfeit of colonels—who was on Kitchener's staff. This he did and back I went to the War Office the next day. The supercilious young man I'd seen the day before took the note and disappeared. Well, I never did get to see my Uncle Charlie because he was at some meeting or other, but the person who had taken my note returned in quite a hurry—he was a little more polite, too—and gave me another note to take down to an old medico, who conducted the usual "trousers down, cough, and say ninety-nine" examination. But when he saw my legs he asked me where I'd got all that suntan. So I told him—in South-West Africa. "Oh," he said, "were you in that show? What were you doing?" When I told him I had been in the infantry and had marched for six ruddy months, mostly in the desert, he said if I'd got through that he didn't need to see any more of me! So he just passed me as fit for flying, and that same evening I was down at No 2

(Reserve) Squadron at Brooklands, where I had my first taste of the air in a Maurice Farman Longhorn.'

Harris received his main flying instruction in the last week of October and the first week of November, his principal flying instructor being an officer by the name of Lywood. This instruction consisted of being told about the controls, followed by less than half an hour's dual instruction leaning over the pilot and watching him handle them. That, apart from being taken up in a BE2C and looped by a Corporal Ryder, who was an American and 'quite a hot' pilot, was the total flying training Harris received before going solo.

From the Longhorn Harris graduated to a Shorthorn and, with a total of up to an hour and a half's solo flying, qualified for his Royal Aero Club Certificate as a civilian pilot. On 6 November 1915 he was advised that he had been appointed a Second Lieutenant, Special Reserve, RFC, and was to report in uniform to the Central Flying School, Upavon, on the following Monday. A hasty call at Alkit's produced the necessary RFC 'maternity jacket', breeches, boots and cap to go with the British Warm he already had.

At CFS he received further instruction and undertook more solo flying, and qualified for his Service Certificate and wings. (This certificate No 915, was signed by Lieutenant-Colonel Duncan Pitcher and dated 29 January 1916.) Harris says: 'I completed the Long Course and qualified for service. The Long Course, ye Gods! I don't know what they'd think of it today. I suppose it must have been about ten hours—certainly not more—on four different types of aeroplane, starting with the Bloater with the 50 HP Gnôme engine. This was a warp wing biplane and was the original BE type aircraft. From that I went to a super Bloater, the BE8A. Then for my third I went on to the four-wheeled Martinsyde Scout with a Gnôme engine. This had what was known as the bedstead undercarriage, and with four wheels it was a difficult machine to land. The front wheels were small and weak, and if you landed mostly on them they broke off, the skids dug in, and you turned over. You couldn't land on the tail skid, because there wasn't one—so you had to land on all four wheels at once with the rear wheels just touching down first. I never crashed one—though I did crash a Bloater. Then my last type was another Martinsyde—the same machine virtually, but with the more conventional V undercarriage. And that was that.'

On 29 January 1916 2nd Lieutenant Arthur Travers Harris passed out of CFS a fully qualified pilot of the RFC. The man who was perhaps to be the greatest commander in the Royal Air Force during the crucial years ahead had won his wings and was ready to accept the challenge of the air.

After taking a week's leave he reported to the adjutant of the RFC station at Northolt in Middlesex, for active service. 'He was quite a well known character called "Pongo" Barker, who after the war became the Chief Game Warden of the Sudan,' Harris says. 'He looked at me rather quizzically and asked if I could fly in the dark. To which I replied that I couldn't fly in daylight, so maybe I could in the dark!'

Harris was then told that he belonged to No 39 Squadron, which had its headquarters at Hounslow and detachments of two or three aircraft based at various airfields round London, including two aircraft at Northolt for which Harris was to be responsible. His duties were those of the Official Anti-Zeppelin Night Pilot, which required that he be on standby every other night, the pilot for the alternate nights being supplied from the station. The two aircraft allocated for these duties were a BE2C and a BE2A, which were kept in the 'end hangar'.

No 39 Squadron had been charged with the task of the defence of London against the Zeppelins—Germany's latest development in air warfare for carrying the offensive right into the civilian heart of England. The war on the Western Front was already doing much to break down the morale of civilian populations as the massive German war machine rolled forward, blasting cities, towns and villages with its artillery. But the Channel had hitherto preserved England from the horrors of war. The advent of the Zeppelin caused an uproar in Parliament, and a number of squadrons already in France, or destined for France, were reallocated to the defence of Britain. If the German bombing efforts were puny by modern standards, they certainly created sufficient concern for the defence of London and other industrial cities to be put into the hands of one man, Sir Percy Scott. Forty aircraft were assigned to the London area for the defence of the city, as well as extra guns and manpower. In point of fact the Germans, with their 'city-busting' techniques,* achieved some of the success they had been looking for—the diversion of aircraft and guns away from the Western Front. The diversion was not that great, but had the bomb loads of Zeppelins and aircraft been heavier, and the radius of action greater, they might well have drawn away enough essential armaments from the real battle zone to have been disastrous for the Allies. As it was, the Zeppelins earned a handsome dividend for Germany. Although the raids were, in essence, unsuccessful, by the end of 1916 17,340 officers and men were tied down in the home anti-aircraft services, and twelve RFC squadrons, consisting of 200 officers, 2,000 other ranks and 110 aircraft, were stationed in England despite the urgent need for them in the Somme battles.

Harris's aircraft were in fact two of the forty spread around London on call for patrol or whenever a Zeppelin was heard or sighted approaching the shores of England. Night flying in those days of inadequate instruments was, however, a pretty hazardous affair, and the casualty rate extremely high. On his first evening at Northolt, a dark and drizzling night, the War Office ordered all duty defence pilots into the air. Conditions were completely impossible. The station CO, Penn-Gaskell, was on duty as

---

* General Johannes Steinhoff, a well known Luftwaffe pilot in World War II and later chairman of the North Atlantic Committee of NATO, discussed bombing tactics with the author in Brussels in January 1972. He said that criticisms of RAF Bomber Command for indulging in area bombing in World War II should be viewed with suspicion. He went on to say that 'city-busting'—his term—was invented and first employed by the Germans with Zeppelins in 1915.

night pilot and he crashed on take-off within the aerodrome boundary just beyond the last flare. The aircraft went up in flames and, although he was pulled out of the blazing machine, he died shortly afterwards. Two nights later, Harris went up on a night exercise to try to spot a small airship which had been sent up by the Army to cruise in the London area. Harris says: 'I was the only one who found it. By pure luck I saw the damned thing silhouetted against the lights of London. It was my first night flight—the first of my life and I'd had no training. Following the crash two nights before—and probably others which had occurred before that—the Army had been called upon to supply searchlights to help us land, the idea being to direct the beam along the ground so that we could see where we were landing. That morning a searchlight with its detachment had arrived at Northolt, and when I got back to make my landing the searchlight team hurriedly went into action to help me down—by the simple process of pointing the damned thing straight at me so that it was shining slap in my eyes as I made my approach. How I got down, God only knows. Into the bargain I discovered the next day that the first flare was thirty to forty yards from eighty-foot elm trees. Anyhow, I remember the new CO of Northolt, who had already arrived and went by the delightful name of Boddam-Whetham—and you can imagine what the troops called him, although he was a nice old boy—on the blower to headquarters after I'd reported spotting the airship, telling them I'd made a marvellous landing. Well, of course I hadn't. For most of the flight I hardly knew which county I was over, let alone where the ruddy aerodrome was. But it was a good lesson. From then on I used to go up in the evenings and fly around and around, landing time and time again as it grew progressively darker, until I'd got this flying thing at night weighed up.'

Shortly after, it was decided to concentrate the aircraft of the Anti-Zeppelin Force by flights, instead of being dispersed in twos and threes around London. Harris, to his surprise, was given command of the new flight formed at Sutton's Farm (now Hornchurch), and the first thing he did was to introduce practice night flying based on the training he had designed for himself. Indeed, it was this early experience of being expected to do the most impossible things without any semblance of instruction that set his mind thinking about the value of proper training, a matter that was to become a fetish with him in his later life, and to which Bomber Command in World War II was to owe a great deal of its success. It was also at this time that the possibilities of the use of the aircraft by night as offensive weapons were first sown in his mind—but they were to germinate much later. For the moment there was a war on hand, and little time to think of anything else but fighting it in an entirely new medium for which there was virtually no historical experience to draw upon.

Lieutenant W. Leefe-Robinson, who was in Harris's flight, was the first pilot to bring down a Zeppelin over England, and for this he was awarded the V C. Later, two more Zeppelins fell to the flight but, by then, Harris had been posted to Castle Bromwich to start a new defence squadron in the

Midlands. From there he was posted to France to join a squadron at St Omer, flying first Morane Parasols, then Morane Bullets, both monoplanes, and finally the Sopwith 1½-Strutter in which he crashed when making a forced landing, 'busting myself up a bit and finishing in hospital.' When he recovered, he applied to go overseas again and was posted to No 45 Squadron at Marie Cappel, commanded by Pierre van Ryneveld, a South African.*

This squadron was also equipped with Sopwith 1½-Strutters, but in 1917 it was re-equipped with Sopwith Camels, which Harris describes as among the best of the early aircraft to be produced. There were two versions of the Camel and the ones No 45 Squadron had were those fitted with the Clerget engine, which unfortunately lost power at altitudes above 6,000 feet—and in those days the fighting height was between 10,000 and 15,000 feet. However, Harris says: 'Although it was underpowered at heights, it was very manoeuvrable, even above 6,000 feet, and with its twin machine-guns it was quite an aeroplane.'

A short time afterwards, van Ryneveld was shot down and very seriously wounded. Harris said: 'He was stalking a German when he was shot up. Although he had bullets all round his heart, he got his Camel down at Bailleul. How the hell he lived, I don't know. I dashed over to see him in hospital and there he was, propped up and hardly able to breathe. I remember the only thing he said to me was, "They all think I'm dying— well, they're ruddy well wrong!" He was a tough fellow. I learnt a lot from him.'

Harris, who was by now a captain and the next senior to van Ryneveld, took command of the squadron until a replacement arrived. But if Harris's command of this squadron was to be short-lived at this stage, it was only to be delayed, for just after the war he was to command it again, and with it to develop a technique of bombing which was to revolutionise the military control in Mesopotamia.

At this period he had the impression that no one knew what they were doing in the air. For example, he says of his time in No 45 Squadron: 'We just flew about, got shot at by Archie (anti-aircraft guns) from both sides and shot up by all the German fighters, who thought we were easy meat— which we were, particularly when we had 1½-Strutters. And our contri- bution? Bagging an occasional German fighter with our rear guns and photo- graphing enemy trenches. There didn't seem to be any plan.' In fact Harris was already wondering if the aeroplane was being used as a plaything, a kind of new toy, by the Army and Navy, when with a proper plan for its coordinated use it could be a major military arm in modern warfare. If Harris's thinking was immature at this time, it was not out of line with that

---

*Later General Sir Pierre van Ryneveld, KBE, CB, DSO, MC, head of the South African Forces. Van Ryneveld made the first flight from the UK to South Africa, starting from Brooklands, with Quintin Brand as his co-pilot. A great personal friend of Sir Arthur and Lady Harris, he died in 1972.

of two men for whom he was to develop the greatest respect and admiration, and who had a tremendous influence on his ideas and opinions in later years. These two were Jan Smuts* and 'Boom' Trenchard.†

Up to 1917 the Royal Flying Corps and the Royal Naval Air Service had remained quite separate services, the only link between them being an Air Committee, later named the Air Board, which signally failed to control inter-service rivalries or to produce any coordinated use of this new dimension of war. The German raids on England, which began in 1915 with the Zeppelins and increased in 1916 and 1917 with the use of aircraft—in particular Gothas—had turned into something very serious with the enemy operating from bases in Belgium. The raids in May, June and July of 1917 forced Lloyd George, the Prime Minister, to take urgent action. Through the Imperial War Cabinet, he formed a committee of two, consisting of General Smuts and himself, to review the air situation. He shrewdly left the task to Smuts, who submitted his report on 17 August. He recommended the appointment of Major-General E. B. Ashmore as Commander-in-Chief for the defence of London, with full control of observers, anti-aircraft guns, balloon barrage and fighter squadrons. But his most far-reaching recommendation was:

'That an Air Ministry be instituted as soon as possible, consisting of a Minister with a consultative board on the lines of the Army Council or Admiralty Board, on which the several departmental activities of the Ministry will be represented. This Ministry to control and administer all matters in connection with aerial warfare of all kinds whatsoever, including lighter-than-air as well as heavier-than-air craft... That the Air Ministry and Staff proceed to work out the arrangements necessary for the amalgamation of the Royal Naval Air Service and the Royal Flying Corps and the legal constitution and discipline of the new air service, and to prepare the necessary draft legislation and regulations... That the air service remain in intimate touch with the Army and Navy by the closest liaison, or by direct representation of both on the Air Staff, and that, if necessary, the arrangements for close cooperation between the three Services be revised from time to time.

A later part of the report was so prophetic that Smuts might have been issuing a directive to Bomber Command to prepare for World War II:

'Air power can be used as an independent means of war operations. Nobody that witnessed the attack on London on 7th July, 1917, could have any doubt on that point. Unlike artillery an air fleet can conduct

---

* General Jan Christiaan Smuts, the senior South African statesman, who in May 1917 became a member of the Imperial War Cabinet. Later Field-Marshal Jan Smuts, PC, OM, CH, DTD, Prime Minister of South Africa.

† Major-General Sir Hugh Trenchard, later Marshal of the Royal Air Force Viscount Trenchard, GCB, OM, GCVO, DSO, DCL, LLD, the first Chief of the Air Staff.

extensive operations far from and independently of both Army and Navy. As far as can at present be foreseen there is absolutely no limit to the scale of its future independent war use. And the day may not be far off when aerial operations with their devastation of enemy lands and destruction of industrial and populous centres on a vast scale may become the principal operations of war, to which older forms of military operations may become secondary and subordinate.

Trenchard, who was at this time the Commander-in-Chief of the RFC in France, was opposed to the formation of a separate air arm, but he put forward a recommendation that a large strategic bomber force should be created to bomb deep into Germany. This was entirely in line with his long-held opinion that the aeroplane was as much a weapon of offence as defence. His opposition to a separate air arm was due to his belief that the temporary disorganisation which could result might add to the considerable difficulties already besetting Field-Marshal Haig, the Commander-in-Chief of the Army in France.

In fact the views of both Smuts and Trenchard were upheld. The Royal Air Force (an amalgamation of the RFC and RNAS came into being on 1 April 1918, under the control of the Air Ministry. A strategic bomber force, called the Independent Air Force, was formed in 1918 under the command of Trenchard. Some attacks were carried out against the Ruhr and Rhineland, but the war finished before it could be used to much effect. The curious thing about these forces was that Trenchard not only commanded the Independent Air Force, but he also became the first Chief of the Air Staff when the Royal Air Force came into being on 1 April.

As Harris says: 'Boom was not the father of the Air Force—Jan Smuts was. But Boom was the protector of the Royal Air Force through the years between the wars, when the admirals and generals, if they could, would have torn it apart and taken the pieces back under their own care, to ensure that this newly created service could never become a force which was independent of their influence and control in the future.'

Late in 1917, Harris was posted back to England to command a mixed flight at Joyce Green consisting of Sopwith 1½-Strutters and DH5s. In the short time he was there he showed his technical interest in the behaviour of aircraft—and his considerable courage. The DH5 was a peculiar machine with a back-staggered top plane, the pilot sitting in front of the leading edge. The aeroplane was designed for ground strafing, but it had a well-earned reputation for spinning into the ground and killing many pilots. 'Rather fancying myself,' Harris relates, 'I took one up over the Thames to see if there was anything in this story of spinning, and to find out what was the matter with the aircraft. There had been the same story about the Camel, which also killed many pilots, although we had no problems with ours in France. Anyhow, I put the thing into a spin—and had the devil of a job getting it out. I was scared stiff, I don't mind telling you! But I got out in the end by opening up the engine, which taught me that the back-staggered top plane blinded the tailplane in a spin, and until you put the engine on and got that bit of extra draught under the elevators you couldn't get out of the spin.'

This was typical of Harris. It is an early example of his inquisitive mind and his determination to know as much as possible about the aircraft he and his men had to use.

In 1918, he was promoted to the rank of major and posted from Joyce Green to Marham to start up and command a night flying training squadron, No 191, consisting of DH6s and FE2Bs. The pilot who had once had to teach himself to fly at night was, for a short time, to teach others how to master the hours of darkness in the air. Interestingly, the FE2Bs were used as night bombers in France so he was, in fact, to command an early blueprint of a bomber Operational Training Unit—OTU. But, again, he was only in this post for a relatively short time, for he was posted, late in 1918, to Hainault's Farm, near London, to command No 44 Squadron and form another night fighter squadron, equipped with Camels, which he was to take to France. During this appointment, he went across to France to spend two weeks with the only other night fighter squadron which, under the command of Major Brand, later Sir Quintin Brand, was operating on the Western Front. There he studied at first hand night fighter tactics. He was ready to move his squadron by November, and was actually due to fly it out to France on the 11th. However, with the signing of the Armistice, Harris and his squadron never left England. As Harris says: 'That was the end of my war.'

In fact, his war was yet to come.

4
Of Admirals and Generals . . .

Harris was a major when the war ended. It had been his firm intention to go back to Africa as soon as the war was over, but to his astonishment he was awarded a permanent commission in the newly created Royal Air Force. A permanent commission with no demotion was too good to pass up and he elected to stay on. His rank was changed from major to its equivalent of squadron leader. When the Royal Air Force was formed it introduced its own ranks and badges of office, choosing titles which were more appropriate to the type of formations that made up this new service. Harris regards the retention of his rank as an extraordinary miscarriage of justice in his favour, because many people senior to him were given their permanent commissions in ranks junior to his. 'I don't know how true it was, but the story put about at the time was that in the printing of the *Gazette* two sets of names somehow got transposed and having been gazetted they couldn't ungazette you, so to speak. All they could do was to hasten the promotion of the poor devils who got into the wrong paragraph!'

During 1919 and 1920 he had the depressing task of closing down squadrons, the first being No 50 Squadron at Bekesbourne. He went there straight from Hainault's Farm to discover that demobilisation riots were his first problem. On arrival he found the adjutant standing on the table in the NAAFI being heckled by the men who wanted to get demobilised at once. The truth was that the demobilisation schemes were working most unsatisfactorily and unfairly, with little information being available to the men as to when they would be released. As a result there were riots all over the place, not just in the Royal Air Force, but in the Army and Navy as well. Harris says: 'One of the troubles I met was the men taking the motor transport without any authorisation and parking it in London with the idea of having a party—but their excuse was that they were going to protest in Trafalgar Square about not being released quicker. Well, the first thing I did, with the aid of my adjutant and Transport sergeant, was to remove all the magnetos from the vehicles and lock them up in the squadron safe; then I'd only issue a magneto when a vehicle was required for service purposes. At the same time I formed a demobilisation committee on which the men were represented, and told them that the priorities as to who was demobbed first were laid down by the Government and we had a list made out according to those priorities. I said I hadn't the power to alter the priority system, except that anyone who misbehaved would automatically be put down to the bottom of the list. Well that stopped the riots.'

Harris found the disposal of aircraft one of his most distressing jobs. He collected dozens of Sopwith Snipe aircraft at Bekesbourne and had to burn them—even new aircraft that were still arriving from the manufacturers, for the Government would not stop production until there were other jobs for the men from the greatly expanded aircraft industry. And so the post-war waste was begun.

From Bekesbourne Harris went to Brooklands and, ironically, closed down the very place where he had first learned to fly. From there he went on a navigation course at Andover from which he passed out top, although, 'this was some miracle,' he says, 'because I never could make two and two make four!' But his navigation course did not save him from returning to the job of wielding the axe, and back he went to closing down more squadrons and stations, this time in Lincolnshire. From Digby he closed down a number of R N A S units and organised the equipment to be sold by the Disposals Board. All this time there was virtually no serious flying for Harris, beyond occasional 'joy rides'—it was a bitter pill, as he had become totally dedicated to the air and was uncomfortable and restless in any job that denied him plenty of flying. Indeed, one of the most interesting aspects of his service career is that it was dominated by squadron and station experience, with relatively few staff appointments, except for those which involved operational command.

The hasty demobilisation of the Royal Air Force, as soon as the Armistice was signed, was part of the general disarmament of the forces. But the emphasis of the cut-back was on the Royal Air Force, because the Admiralty and the War Office thought of it as nothing more than a wartime expedient and confidently expected that the Air Ministry and its air force would disappear. In fact, both the Navy and the Army showed a strong desire to kill General Smuts's creation and have the flying forces revert to the organisation that existed up to April 1918—that is to say, a Royal Naval Air Service and a Royal Flying Corps firmly under the thumbs of the Admiralty and the War Office. This boded ill for a future air arm in the event of a future war. Indeed, in the case of a reversion to a Royal Flying Corps it could have been disastrous, particularly if it were to be subjected to the fate of the Tank Corps, which was already suffering cut-backs and appalling neglect. The tank and the aircraft could well be regarded as the greatest innovations applied to military operations in World War I, and they had had a decisive effect upon the outcome. But as Harris observes: 'When I went to the Army Staff College in 1927, they almost asked me to leave after the first year because I used to say frankly what I thought of their ideas. At the time, the Army had just abolished the Tank Corps; they had also thrown out the Machine Gun Corps, which—with the Tank Corps— were the only real essentials to emerge from World War I that could help reduce cannon fodder. That is, apart from the aeroplane. As the only airman on the course, I was asked my views of the tank. I said that I gathered from what had gone on during the week when we had studied tank warfare, that the Army would never select a tank as suitable in war until it could do exactly what a horse did—including eating hay and making the appropriate noises thereafter! You can imagine how popular I was.'

Whatever the ideas of the Navy and the Army, the first Chief of the Air Staff, Boom Trenchard, held other views very strongly, and during those first years after the war he fought hard for the continued existence of the Royal Air Force as a separate service. He was assisted in his successful endeavours by two situations, one not of his making. This was the fact that the Admiralty and the War Office, even before the 1914–1918 war, had neither the experience nor the desire to cooperate with each other—and after the war remained just as insular. The result was that first one attacked the continuance of the Royal Air Force and then the other, and too often their arguments were contradictory and tended to cancel each other out. Had they made a concerted attack they might well have been successful. The other situation arose from the policing requirements overseas and Trenchard's skill in proving that the Air Force could undertake some of these more economically than the other services.

Trenchard relentlessly pursued the view that air forces must be consolidated under one central control in order to achieve concentration at any place and at any time, as and when they are needed. He recognised that the greatest assets of an air force are mobility and flexibility in both its defensive and offensive capacities. The Navy and Army were, however, totally unconvinced of the offensive capability of air power, and derided Smuts's opinion—in which he was strongly supported by Trenchard—that the day would come when, in war, the roles of both Navy and Army would be subordinate to that of the Air Force. For the moment, however, Trenchard's immediate task was to find a way of showing how the Royal Air Force could take over some of the responsibilities of the other two services, and thereby permit reductions in land or sea forces, making overall economies in the policing of areas in India, the Far East and the territories formerly administered by the Ottoman Sultans and now mandated to Britain by the League of Nations.* Trenchard's problem was, in fact, to prove to the taxpayer that the Royal Air Force could undertake tasks which were previously the responsibilities of the Army or Navy, at lower cost.

The Mandate was a new concept, giving a Great Power responsibility for the defence, internal security and political and economic development of a new state until it was fit for independent status, when it would then become a member of the League of Nations and the Mandatory Power would withdraw, leaving the state to govern itself. It was, however, hoped that the new state and the former Mandatory Power would maintain relations by a

* The areas removed from Turkish rule were formed into the new states of Palestine, Transjordan, Mesopotamia (Iraq), Syria, the Lebanon, the Hejaz and the Yemen. Syria and the Lebanon were mandated to France, and Mesopotamia, Palestine and Transjordan, inter alia, to Britain.

treaty of friendship and mutual assistance. All of these countries mandated to Britain and France were backward and economically weak—oil, at this time, had not been exploited anywhere in the Middle East. These new states, however, were unacceptable to Turkey and Saudi Arabia—Egypt at this period was a protectorate of the British Empire—and the policy of establishing a Jewish colony in Palestine aroused the hostility of the Arabs. This boded ill for peaceful development.

The British public were, in essence, opposed to such commitments, for they recognised that a large part of the British forces would be occupied with the task of defending hundreds of miles of disputed frontiers and maintaining law and order amongst wild peoples, who, with their new-found liberty, were ready to indulge in insurrection, murder and every other form of lawlessness. This involvement they saw as a heavy cost to their pockets with no worthwhile return. In fact, the cost to Britain was very considerable, and the rebellion in Mesopotamia early in 1920, which put the British forces in a position of great difficulty and danger, created an outcry in Britain and a demand by the public to the Government to withdraw from the mandated territories and hand them back to the League of Nations. The Government, however, knew that withdrawal would certainly result in the whole area being submerged in bitter interstate feuding and warfare and an attempt by Turkey to impose its rule, yet again, throughout the Middle East. Not wishing to expose these new countries to such a fate and, in particular, unwilling to permit the growing Jewish settlement in Palestine to be annihilated at the hands of the Arabs, it resisted home pressures for withdrawal. The dilemma was nonetheless serious and Winston Churchill, then Secretary of State for War, and temporarily for Air as well, chaired a conference in Cairo in March 1921 'to investigate the situation, examine costs, consider economies that could be made without reducing the ability to control effectively, and make recommendations.'

Trenchard had already seen a way out of the dilemma, and a way, at the same time, of going a long way towards securing the future of the Royal Air Force. Air Vice-Marshal Sir Geoffrey Salmond,* the Air Officer Commanding, Middle East, who at Trenchard's instigation had studied the possibilities of exercising an air control of Mesopotamia, resulting in great savings in troops, equipment and cost, had just completed his report and made detailed recommendations. These he submitted to the General Officer Commanding, Mesopotamia in May 1920, with a copy to Trenchard. The Army in Mesopotamia was bitterly opposed to the proposals and did everything possible to suppress the report. Trenchard, however, as a result of discussions with Churchill had already submitted to the Cabinet a preliminary scheme for the military control of Mesopotamia

---

* The brother of Sir John Salmond, who succeeded Trenchard as Chief of the Air Staff in January 1930. Sir Geoffrey succeeded Sir John in March 1933, but died six weeks later.

by the Royal Air Force, and Geoffrey Salmond's report gave great strength to his proposals. Churchill saw significant savings in them and took a bold decision at the Cairo Conference of March 1921 to give responsibility for law and order in Mesopotamia to the Air Ministry, who planned to exercise it with eight squadrons and a small force of ground troops. The decision was violently opposed by the Chief of the Imperial General Staff, Sir Henry Wilson, who even went so far as to refuse to allocate the necessary troops to the new command. His somewhat childish attitude was to no avail— Trenchard proceeded to raise the Royal Air Force's own Assyrian levies and armoured car units.

The Mesopotamia experiment, which was immediately extended to Transjordan, proved to be a great success and, in due course, the Royal Air Force responsibility was increased, yet again, to cover the Aden Protectorate, saving the British taxpayer some £35,000,000. But before that happened, Trenchard made his next move to consolidate the position of the Royal Air Force as an independent service. He reckoned that what was being done in Mesopotamia and Transjordan could be achieved on the North-West Frontier of India. However, the tradition of the Army control of the North-Western Provinces was deeply entrenched from the time when it first operated in India as a private army of the East India Company. Whereas elsewhere throughout the Empire the RAF had, since 1918, been a separate autonomous service with its own budget introduced to Parliament by its own Secretary of State, in India it was firmly under the thumb of the Army, its budget being merely one of the cost centres of army expenditure in the Military Services Budget, which was controlled by the Commander-in-Chief in India as Army member of the Viceroy's Council. It was not even shown in a separate section, as was the expenditure on the Royal Indian Marine. Trenchard ultimately got his way. Coincidentally, Harris found himself in the midst of this political battle.

In 1921, Harris applied for service overseas and was posted to India to command No 31 Squadron at Cawnpore. His first year there was a great shock to him. 'I was incensed by the appalling conditions, lack of spares and unserviceability of aircraft,' he says. 'It made me realise what happens when air forces, or any other forces equipped with new weapons for that matter, are put under the control of another and older service and subordinated to archaic methods and weapons. We lacked everything in the way of necessary accommodation, spares and material for keeping our aircraft serviceable. The only thing there was no shortage of was demands for our service when trouble blew up on the Frontier. It was shocking. It was almost as if the Army wanted to ensure that we were proved to be a useless service and, by making it almost impossible for us to operate, because they held control of our supplies and requirements, they ruddy well nearly succeeded.'

In fact, when Harris arrived in India the Royal Air Force there consisted of six squadrons, each with an establishment of twelve aircraft divided into three flights. Four of the squadrons were equipped with Bristol Fighters with aerodromes at Quetta, Parachinar, Kohat and Peshawar, and two with DH9As and DH10s at Risalpur. Harris's squadron* was at Cawnpore when he arrived, but moved to Peshawar shortly after he took command. But of the combined total of seventy-two aircraft it is doubtful whether a dozen could have been put into the air at any one time.

According to Harris it was not unknown for aircraft to take off on operations on wheels with naked rims, because there were no tyres available, and with axles lashed on with doubtful locally made rope, because there was no rubber shock-absorber rope. Moreover, aircraft were still fitted with single ignition system engines, which had long been discarded as obsolete and unsafe. Despite the vast number of dual ignition engines available at home, which the Disposal Board were selling off as scrap for a few pounds, the Army in India, on whose financial vote the RAF was dependent, refused to supply them. Naturally Harris was incensed at having to send out his crews in aircraft that were far from airworthy. During one of the expeditions on the Frontier one of the less pleasant types of General visited Harris's squadron at Miranshah, when it was operating with its last four aeroplanes that were in flying condition—the last four in the whole of India! The General told Harris that he was to stop operating until he received further orders from Headquarters. Harris thereupon said he would take his machines back to Peshawar, get them under cover and 'nurse' them until they were wanted again. At this, the General went off the deep end and made some uncalled-for remarks that airmen could never do anything unless they were coddled to the point of living in the lap of luxury, adding: 'I suppose you must get back to your spare parts before you can do any more.' Harris replied: 'Yes, it's high time we got back to our ball of string—and that's about all the Army and the Indian Government have ever supplied for our use!' The General reported him to Air Force Headquarters for his insubordinate remarks, but nothing came of it. But Harris was furious. 'We had hardly an aircraft that would fly or a motor vehicle that had any tyres. With our single ignition Bristol Fighters falling to bits in our single RE hangars—the covers of which had rotted, leaving only the metal frames with a few rags flapping around—that was our lap of luxury!'

It is Harris's opinion that even if the RAF had been well equipped, air power would never have been used intelligently under the control of the Army at that time. Bombing, the main task of the RAF, was usually made part of a combined operation. The Army's idea was to control the Frontier with troops supported by long and vulnerable lines of communication, the

---

* No 31 Squadron was the first squadron in India and its aeroplanes were the first flying machines, outside the legendary flying machines of the Lord Krishna, ever to be heard of or seen in India. Its crest is the Star of India and its motto, '*In Caelum Indicum Primus*'—'First in the Indian Sky'. Some years after Harris commanded it the squadron moved to Quetta where, in 1935, it suffered devastating casualties in the Quetta earthquake as well as having most of its machines destroyed. The author was, at the time, serving with No 31 Squadron as a pilot officer.

convoys being given air escorts. Seldom was the RAF given the chance to operate independently to reduce a tribe to submission by bombing, thereby saving lives of soldiers on the ground. No effort was made to take advantage of this new weapon which could offer substantial economies in men and equipment if used properly.

It was at this stage that Harris became disillusioned with the services and decided to return to farming in Rhodesia. In early May of 1922 he sent in his resignation. But fate was to intervene. Following Churchill's support for the use of air control in Mesopotamia, giving the Royal Air Force responsibility for imperial policing of this area, Trenchard selected Air Vice-Marshal Sir John Salmond for this new command. Salmond, who had succeeded him in commanding the RFC, and then the RAF, in France, and was now one of his closest and most trusted colleagues, was due to take over in Mesopotamia in October 1922, at a time when the Turks, under Kemal Ataturk, were determinedly attempting to drive the Greeks out of those Turkish areas that had been invaded and occupied by them at the end of the war. Earlier in the year, the appalling situation of the RAF under the Army in India had been exposed in a letter to *The Times* by Lord Montagu of Beaulieu. Trenchard, who already had plans to extend his air policing methods beyond the Middle East, but was thwarted in India by the fact that the RAF was still financially and operationally under the control of the Army, saw his opportunity to have this control broken. If there was a scandal about the conditions of the RAF in India, then he would quickly have it investigated and rub the Army's nose in the dirt they had created. He therefore decided to send Salmond to India to make a detailed enquiry into the situation before taking up his appointment in Mesopotamia.

Salmond left England at the end of May 1922 and arrived in Bombay at the end of June. He completed his tour and studies of the situation on 27 July 1922, when he reached Simla prior to his return to England to prepare for his move to Mesopotamia. From Simla he wrote a personal letter to Trenchard telling him of his findings and recommendations, in advance of his official report to the Viceroy of India. 'The Royal Air Force in India,' he had to state, 'is to all intents and purposes non-existent as a fighting force at this date.' His recommendations included the reorganisation of the Air Force units in India with specified increases in establishments, the provision of adequate barracks and technical buildings, the move of Air Headquarters from Ambala to Delhi and Simla, where it would be alongside Army Headquarters and the Government of India, increased status of the Air Officer Commanding in India to that befitting the head of an autonomous fighting service, and a proper system of budgeting and accounting for RAF expenditure independent of the Army's budget.

During his investigations, Salmond received scant, if any, cooperation from the Army and met with dogmatic opposition to his recommendations for the increased use of the air arm on the North-West Frontier. But the recommendations were, over a period of time, forced through because the value and economy of exploiting the use of the air arm soon became apparent and its importance and necessity was, even if reluctantly, accepted by the Army. On the other hand, Salmond did have plenty of cooperation from the RAF officers, in particular from Harris, who had served under him in France in the war and afterwards. Salmond had known Harris when he was in No 45 Squadron, which had been under his command in France. Harris, who had already sent in his resignation in disgust, was very explicit in his opinions about the situation and made sure that Salmond saw for himself the disgraceful conditions. He had nothing to lose by being outspoken, a characteristic he learnt to develop throughout his life, to good effect. Salmond, who knew of his resignation, had no wish to see the Royal Air Force lose a promising young officer and persuaded him to withdraw it. Before he left Harris's squadron he told him, in confidence, that he was going to take over Mesopotamia in October, and he promised to have Harris transferred to his command if he agreed to stay on. 'Well,' Harris says, 'I'd always enjoyed working under Sir John Salmond, so I said yes. And I went to Mespot that same year. I'm sure that because of my personal knowledge of the shocking technical conditions of the RAF in India under the Army, the Army was glad to see the back of me! Anyway, I was given command of No 45 Squadron, which was moved from Egypt to Mespot as part of the new Royal Air Force control scheme.'

The hand of destiny must again have been at work. If Salmond had not gone to India, Britain might never have had available the only man capable of devising and directing the sustained bomber offensive against Germany in World War II. Moreover, in commanding No 45 Squadron in Mesopotamia, which was equipped with Vickers Vernons fitted with twin Rolls-Royce engines, he was to have the experience of the heavier type aircraft and the opportunity to exercise his ability to improvise, in the face of necessity, by turning a troop-carrying squadron into the first real heavy bomber squadron of the RAF. Lastly, in his new squadron he was to meet, as his two flight commanders, the two men who later played leading roles alongside him in the bomber offensive against Germany; Flight Lieutenants R.H.M.S. Saundby and the Hon R. A. Cochrane. These two were to become Air Marshal Sir Robert Saundby,* the Deputy C-in-C Bomber Command, Harris's right-hand man from 1942 right through to the end of the war, and Air Vice-Marshal the Hon R. A. Cochrane,† Air Officer Commanding No 5 (Bomber) Group.

The method of air control, which was being applied for the first time to maintain law and order, differed considerably from the old Army method. In brief, under the old method, when there were disorders which could not be handled by the local police forces or military posts in the area, a column

---

*Air Marshal Sir Robert Saundby, KCB, KBE, MC, DFC, AFC, DI, who retired after World War II and died in November 1971. He wrote *Air Bombardment, the Story of its Development*.

† At the end of the war he became Air Chief Marshal the Hon Sir Ralph Cochrane, GBE, KCB, AFC, C-in-C Transport Command. He died in 1978.

of infantry was sent from the nearest large garrison to the trouble spot. Such an expedition was always costly, and action was thus invariably postponed until the disorders reached dangerous proportions. These columns frequently met with opposition in the areas through which they had to pass, partly because the inhabitants in any case feared that the troops were on their way to punish them, and partly because they just enjoyed fighting for the sake of it.

The troops' progress therefore became well advertised, as well as slow, and by the time they arrived at the offending area, usually a village, those inhabitants who were to be punished for raiding other villages, stealing livestock, looting and kidnapping, had already flown, leaving houses empty and everything of value removed. The only means of punishment left to the Army would be to burn or destroy the empty houses. The column then had to fight its way back again and any miscalculation of ammunition or food supplies in the planning of the expeditions, which was not infrequent, could result in disaster. Harris recalls the occasion when many men of one battalion were captured, stripped naked and made to march back in the sun. There were few survivors.

With the air control method, as soon as the police or local political officer reported unrest, action was taken immediately and at little cost. The offenders were ordered to submit themselves for trial in a court of law, and if they obeyed no further action was necessary. If they refused and committed further outrages, warning leaflets were dropped telling them that on a certain day and at a certain time their village would be bombed, that they should evacuate it, and that it would be unsafe for them to return until they were prepared to yield themselves to the law. At the appointed time the village would be attacked, care being taken to inflict as little damage as possible. But the house or fort of a persistent trouble-maker would be selected for definite destruction, and this required a high degree of accuracy. After this there followed what was termed an air blockade, which consisted of light bombing attacks around the village to prevent the inhabitants from reoccupying their houses and cultivating their land, until such time as they agreed to surrender to the process of law. This nearly always worked and at the point of surrender a small body of police or troops would be flown in, accompanied by medical staff, to restore order, distribute food, rehabilitate the area and apply fines or appropriate punishments to the main offenders.

The air control method was successful. But more important, it never built up the bitter rancour or hostility that the old Army method seemed to engender. Indeed, as Saundby said:* 'The opponents of air control predicted that the use of the bomb would leave a legacy of hatred and ill-will. In fact nothing of the sort happened and airmen were held in great respect. No airman who fell into tribal hands during such operations was killed or ill-treated.' Equally important, it resulted in an enormous saving of money.

* In his book *Air Bombardment, the Story of its Development* (1961).

When Harris arrived in Mesopotamia he had to await the arrival of No 45 Squadron at Hinaidi for about a month, whilst it was moved from Cairo by its two flight commanders, Saundby and Cochrane. Cochrane says: 'We had heard various things about Bert Harris from India and when we knew that he was going to take us over we thought, "My God what is going to hit us!" But we found, to the contrary, that he was an excellent CO with plenty of ideas and lots of drive—which we had sorely lacked up till then.'

No 45 Squadron was a troop-carrying squadron. It arrived at Hinaidi and was taken over by Harris at the time when Kemal Ataturk, triumphant with his success in recovering Constantinople and virtually all Eastern Thrace, was seeking more gains by belligerent activity along the Kurdistan frontier and trying to win Mosul for Turkey. Harris's task was to take supplies up to the troops and squadrons operating on the frontier under Sir John Salmond's command and bring back the casualties for hospital treatment in Baghdad. 'We literally took beer up to the troops,' said Cochrane, 'and brought back casualties. But this wasn't at all in accord with Bert Harris's idea of what he wanted to do.'

Indeed Harris had already worked out the bomb load that one Vernon could theoretically carry, and this was the equivalent of the entire load of one whole squadron of DH9As, the aircraft which were doing the bombing on the frontier. What was needed, however, was the installation of bomb racks and bombsights. With the aid of Saundby and Cochrane and his squadron fitters and riggers, bomb racks were improvised and fitted. The DH9As used a sight on the side of the fuselage for bomb aiming; and an untrained aircraft hand in the rear cockpit dropping the bombs with the guidance of this haphazard instrument. Harris, who had already formed his own ideas on bombing methods, had holes cut in the nose of the Vernons so that the bomb aimer could lie prone and look down, forward and below at the approaching target. A crude but effective bombsight was developed and installed in this nose position, together with an improvised automatic bomb release gear, consisting of a long piece of rubber shock absorber cord combined with a trigger to operate the bomb release cables, which ran back to the bomb racks under the wings, singly or in salvo. Thus the bomb aimer could watch the target coming up into his sights and trip the trigger mechanism at the appropriate moment.

So far so good. But there was another major problem. Cochrane takes up the story. 'We realised that in the heat of Mespot the Vernon, when fully loaded, could only just get off the ground and wouldn't climb to much more than a hundred feet unless you got into an up-current. So the problem was to find the up-currents. Well, the engineering officer—a chap called Rope who was later killed in the R31—an excellent fellow—and I developed an up-current indicator on the lines of ones we had used in airships—we had both been on airships. With a two-gallon petrol tin, some tubing and a disused turn-indicator on the instrument panel, we had what we needed. We used the petrol can with a pinhole bored in the cap as the pressure chamber and with this connected up to the instrument on the cockpit panel, up-currents were indicated by the needle. When you got into an up-current the needle went hard over. So when you took off and got to a hundred feet or thereabouts, there you stayed until the needle went hard over and indicated you were in an up-current—then you proceeded to circle, to stay in the up-current, and to climb at the same time until you were a thousand feet or more and out of the super-heated thin air.'

Harris was nearly ready, but not quite. Practice had to come first—practice to achieve perfection. Corporal George Thomson, Harris's rigger, says: 'We would land on the "blue", as we called all that flat desert land, and we'd make a circle with the tail skid and stick a red flag in the middle. That was the bombing practice target. Then the squadron would practise bomb dropping, using 28-pound Coopers. The CO would often do the bombing from his aircraft himself, with Flying Officer Ragg* at the controls—we called him "Bones", it was the CO's nickname for him. The CO would get down on his stomach and use his own bombsight. He was very keen on bombing and he was good.'

According to Cochrane they practised in the early hours of the morning when it was quiet. Flying upwind at between 1,000 and 2,000 feet, they got their bombs to within ten or fifteen yards of the target. With a ground speed of not much more than forty miles an hour—the maximum air speed of the Vernon was only about eighty miles an hour—it was not too difficult to be accurate. When Harris was satisfied with his squadron's performance, he went and had dinner with Sir John Salmond in Baghdad, discussed his ideas, and said his squadron should do the bombing and that the DH9A and Bristol squadrons should deliver the beer! Salmond agreed to the extent that there should be an immediate bombing competition, and if No 45 Squadron was successful, then it should change its role. The competition took place, and the DH9As and Bristols were shown up so badly in their accuracy that the change was made immediately and No 45 Squadron took over the bombing role.

Harris, with his flight commanders Saundby and Cochrane, had laid the keel of the long-range heavy bomber of the future; and he also gave Salmond the major assistance he needed by successfully bombing the Turkish columns as they attempted to cross the border from Turkey into Mesopotamia in the Mosul area. More importantly, he materially assisted Trenchard and Salmond to demonstrate to the politicians that the Royal Air Force could successfully undertake a campaign of this nature at a fraction of the cost in lives and money that would be incurred by the Army. Indeed, the bill for the five months' campaign, or expedition as it was perhaps more accurately called, was a mere £100,000.

Although Turkey renounced all claims to sovereignty over Mosul on 6 August 1923, under a Treaty of Peace ratified at Lausanne, the truculent and warlike tribes that occupied large areas of Mesopotamia remained a continuous source of trouble. It was, in fact, in the quelling of these local

---

* Later Air Vice-Marshal R. L. Ragg, CB, CBE, AFC.

rebellions and inter-tribal strife that air control was exercised more and more successfully.

Harris, who remained in Mesopotamia until the end of 1924, was not entirely content with converting his Vernons from troop-carriers into heavy bombers. His flying experience had, almost *ab initio*, involved him in night flying. Those first hours, early in 1916, when he found himself having to fly by night without any instruction, were never forgotten. That episode at Northolt had not, as might have been expected, deterred him from exploiting the hours of darkness. On the contrary, he had decided that the dark could be a great asset to offensive bombing, if the navigation was good enough and if the target could be located and accurately bombed. It also occurred to his ingenious and droll mind that night operations could have a most salutary effect on the superstitious minds of the tribesmen. It had been a big enough shock to them to discover that some men could fly in machines in daylight like birds, but at night they had been free from the watchful eyes of these aerial monsters. As Harris says 'You could just imagine what they would think if they heard us over them in the darkness—you know, "By Allah they can ruddy well see us in the dark too."' And so night flying was introduced and Harris trained his squadron to a high degree of efficiency in night operations. But first he discovered that for really effective night bombing a marker bomb was required, which should be dropped by the most expert night crew. 'We made our own marker bombs,' Harris says, 'by the simple process of screwing two pieces of bent tin on to the back of a twenty-pound practice bomb, into which we clamped a white Very light. Between the clamp and the Very light we inserted a striker so that when the bomb hit the ground the Very light was detonated and shot up into the air, illuminating the surroundings for a few moments and leaving a trail of smoke from the point where it had hit. Of course, the nights were very clear out there and visibility was excellent—and we flew at only one or two thousand feet—never more than three thousand—couldn't get higher. So you see, target finding was not too difficult. And our crude marker bombs were very effective under those conditions.'

Harris continues by saying: 'Within a year of taking over No 45 Squadron we were night flying and doing active bombing by day and by night. Most of the bombing was done with baby incendiaries. We didn't want to hurt people if we could avoid it—except for the Turks who were invaders. No, after the Turkish war it was a matter of keeping the tribes in order by air control, and we found that by burning down their reed-hutted villages, after we'd warned them to get out, we put them to the maximum amount of inconvenience without physical hurt, and they soon stopped their raiding and looting of the quieter and better behaved areas.

Even more than laying the keel of the future long-range heavy bomber, Harris had already conceived the principle of long-range night bombing, employing pathfinding and target marking techniques.

5

Mostly on safari

When Harris came back from Mespot at the end of 1924, he first went on a course at the Army Senior Officers School at Sheerness, and from there he was sent to Worthy Down in Hampshire to command No 58 Squadron, which was in the process of forming with Vickers Virginias—'another job of picking things up from zero.' In those formative days they did some *ab initio* training for direct intake pupils; and they did night flying from the start. 'In the three or more years I was there,' Harris recalls, 'I reckon we did more night flying than all the rest of the air forces in the world put together.'

This night flying fetish stemmed from his assessment that even the Virginias, which at this date were relatively modern, would never survive in daylight against a World War I fighter, let alone the fighters that might well be developed by foreign powers in the near future. He was well aware of the weaknesses of the Royal Air Force's front-line bombers—unprotected fuel tanks, two Lewis guns as armament, and these not even as tail and nose turret defence,* and a very slow speed. Night was therefore the only possible defence and because of this he concentrated on night flying training. He says, however, 'I couldn't say that I had any serious ideas about forming a strategic bomber force at this stage. It was just that I thought the aircraft of any air force ought to be able to fly at night. But I had in the back of my mind that the larger and therefore slower aircraft—as was the case in those days—with a heavier load to deliver, would have better chances of escaping the fighter, and reaching its destination, if it could have the cover the darkness.'

Success for night operations was dependent, however, not just on skilled night-flying pilots but also on blind-flying instruments and other navigational equipment which were essential for accurate navigation to the target area and safe return to base. Harris had a constant fight to get good instrumentation developed and supplied, and he fought tenaciously, for he knew from practical experience the absolute necessity for proper instru-

---

* Harris persuaded Vickers to produce either a tail gun position or, as an alternative, two gun positions on the top plane of the Virginia. The former went into production on the Mark IX Virginia.

ments if a night bomber squadron was to be able to get airborne, let alone succeed in its operational task. And No 58 Squadron was, after all, the first heavy bomber squadron to be reconstituted after the war and to get back to training for night operations. 'I don't like to criticise the old men in the Services too much—but all old men are a pest when things have got to keep pace with progress,' he remarks. 'It's always a case of we didn't have it in our day, so what do you want it for? I can remember what a prolonged and bitter fight it was—and at the risk of incurring the grave displeasure of my seniors—to get blind-flying instruments. I hadn't forgotten the difficulties and dangers of night flying in the war, and again in Mespot, without such things as horizon and turn indicators, and those other instruments essential to flying in darkness. I remember on more than one occasion when I damned nearly crashed in Mespot through not having a horizon in the dark and no instrument to tell me whether I was flying straight and level. Today, of course, no one but a lunatic would expect a pilot to fly in cloud or at night without a very comprehensive set of instruments.'

But Harris's early pioneering of the principle of night flying, and his constant demands for proper equipment to be developed and manufactured, slowly had their effect. Throughout his career, in all his appointments at all levels, he kept himself constantly in touch with flying techniques by remaining a practical pilot. Even as C-in-C Bomber Command he always flew himself when he had to visit distant stations or headquarters. His extensive personal experience of flying undoubtedly enabled him to view the future use of the aeroplane in warfare with rare prescience.

He was not alone among the men of his generation who saw, even if hazily, what the future requirements of an effective fighting force would be, but he was one of the very few. Strangely enough, two of the others were Saundby and Cochrane, who had been with him in Mesopotamia. Now, in No 58 Squadron, chance had given him Saundby once again as one of his flight commanders. Cochrane, into the bargain, was on the Area Staff.

Trenchard, their leader as Chief of the Air Staff at this time, was quite clear about the future of air power, and certainly his views influenced the thinking of Harris and Saundby. But Trenchard was still a lone voice at the Chiefs of Staff level when preaching about the major role the aeroplane would play in any future war. In a memorandum for the Chiefs of Staff sub-committee on 'The War Object of an Air Force,' dated 2 May 1928, he wrote:

The object of all three Services is the same: to defeat the enemy nation, not merely its army, navy or air force. For an army to do this it is almost always necessary as a preliminary step to defeat the enemy's army ... It is not, however, necessary for an air force, in order to defeat the enemy nation, to defeat its armed forces first ... This does not mean that air fighting will not take place. On the contrary, intense air fighting will be inevitable, but it will not take the form of a series of battles between the opposing air forces to gain supremacy as a first step before the victor proceeds to the attack of other objectives. Nor does it mean that attacks on air bases will not take place. It will from time to time certainly be found advantageous to turn to the attack on an enemy air base, but such attacks will not be the main operation ... The stronger side, by developing the more powerful offensive, will provoke in his weaker enemy increasingly insistent calls for the protective employment of aircraft. In this way he will throw the enemy on to the defensive, and it will be in this manner that air superiority will be obtained and not by direct destruction of his forces.'

This thinking was truly prophetic, but Trenchard went even further when considering objectives of aerial warfare.

Such objectives [he wrote] may be situated in centres of population in which their destruction from the air will result in casualties to the neighbouring civilian population, in the same way as the long-range bombardments of a defended coastal town by a naval force results also in incidental destruction of civilian life and property. The fact that air attacks may have that result is no reason for regarding the bombing as illegitimate, providing all reasonable care is taken to confine the scope of the bombing to the military objective. Otherwise a belligerent would be able to secure complete immunity for his war manufactures and depots merely by locating them in a large city which would, in effect, become neutral territory—a position which the opposing belligerent would never accept.

This view of future aerial warfare, which did not go quite as far as that of Smuts in 1917, was to be the foundation of Harris's strategic thinking and practice in World War II. But Harris, with Saundby's able assistance, took it further—he went much nearer to Smuts's concept of the air role. This is discussed later.

For the moment, the future thinking and structure of RAF Bomber Command was only in its embryo stage. But the future commander, who was to make it the most devastating weapon history had ever known, was in the process of being groomed for the task which lay ahead. For the moment Harris was commanding a Virginia squadron, based on a grass airfield that dipped to a valley from north to south on one side, and sloped from the hangars at such an angle that when the aircraft were wheeled out half the flight personnel had to hang on behind to stop the machines from running away, there being no brakes in those days.

'58 Squadron was a darn good squadron and we did a lot of work—and flying—and we had a lot of fun. Worthy Down was practically useless as an aerodrome, but it had its interesting aspects. It was on the site of an ancient Belgic settlement and the local archaeologists, some of them bearded old guys—well old to us, because we were still young—used to come out on Wednesday afternoon and nose about the airfield. There was no flying on Wednesday afternoons—it was a half day for sports in those days. We used to let them dig wherever we could permit it—of course they couldn't dig up the whole aerodrome, though they would have liked to. I was a bit interested in this sort of thing too—I suppose it was being in Mespot, where you come across a lot of Biblical relics. I remember after one of our annual sports days we noticed the ground rang a bit hollow where we'd had the marquee. So we opened it up, and we found a deep chamber, about twenty feet by fifteen feet, cut into the chalk. As the archaeologists were coming the next day I had it fenced off so that they could get on with it. We lowered bundles of blazing straw down to see if the air was all right, and so on and so forth. Then these old boys went down by ladder. They were fearfully interested in it. There were marks on the walls of the pit—"probably made with antlers as picks," said one. "And this left-handed one," said another. "You can see the man must have been left-handed doing it that way." And so it went on—most interesting. And whilst I was watching, a rather adenoidal old boy was sniffling away behind me and trying to butt in. Well, he turned out to be the camp sanitary man, a civilian labourer who ran the camp sewage farm. So I asked him what he wanted. He said: "Well Sir, do these gentlemen want to know what this place is?" I told him they did, and I asked him if he knew what it was. "Yes Sir," he replied. "I should do—I dug it! We had a German prisoner of war camp 'ere during the war and this was the soakaway for the latrines." So that was the end of that discovery. The joke was on us—but did we laugh!'

In 1927 Harris was sent to the Army Staff College at Camberley where he spent two years. They left him somewhat disillusioned as the course progressed, for he discovered that the Army was still thinking in terms of trench warfare and cavalry charges, and was almost determined to ignore the development of modern weapons, and quite unprepared to concede that the next war would be fought on any other lines than the last. But he was full of admiration for the type of young Army officers who went through the course, whom he describes as first class men whose problem was that of being heavily sat upon by top brass which was still apparently fighting the last war.

'I was the only airman on the course and I came in for a good deal of attack. Not that that worried me. I was so critical of some of the Army's ideas that I was almost asked to leave during my first year. I remember one occasion when the then CIGS, the Earl of Cavan, after giving a lecture, turned to me and said rather sarcastically something to the effect: "Of course, we hear a lot about bombing. What percentage of bombs dropped do you think would hit, say, Gibraltar?" Mark you I don't remember a word of what else he said in his lecture, but I doubt if I missed much. Anyway, I said: "In reasonable weather ninety-nine per cent—that's allowing for one per cent hang-ups on the racks." He thought I was being facetious, but of course it was absolutely true—you couldn't miss the place in reasonable visibility.'

Harris is critical of some of the instructors too, but not of one, an army officer he met for the first time and learnt to respect enormously—a respect which was mutual—and who was to be, perhaps, the greatest army commander in World War II. His name was Bernard L. Montgomery. 'Monty was first class,' he says, 'although at that time he obviously had to mind his Ps and Qs. As a lecturer he was precise and extremely lucid, and he was very advanced in his ideas on motorised warfare and armoured vehicles and the general probabilities and conduct of future warfare. But his views were not popular with the powers that be and were even regarded as heretical, though they seemed to me to be sound and reasonable. As a stranger in the house I kept my own counsel, but I was convinced at the time that we had a great soldier of the future in Monty.'

Despite Harris's forthright views on the air strategy of the future and his blunt opinions on the stagnant and even reactionary thinking of the Army and Navy at this period, he was, to his surprise, asked to stay on at the Staff College for another two years as an instructor. However, the idea of spending two more years away from his own service and, in particular, from flying, horrified him; so he declined the invitation. Even so, the invitation indicated the impact he had made on the Army and the College's senior staff.

After leaving the Staff College, Harris, now a wing commander, was posted to command a flying-boat squadron at Plymouth, but he had barely arrived at his new station when the posting was cancelled and he was sent instead to Egypt as Senior Staff Officer to the Air Officer Commanding Middle East Command, then Air Vice-Marshal Scarlet. This was Harris's first real staff appointment. He was there from 1929 to 1932 and the period was relatively uneventful. However, after Air Vice-Marshal Cyril Newall* took over the Command, Harris managed to land himself one major flying task before returning to England in the latter half of 1932.

It was the practice for a flight of aircraft from Middle East Command to undertake a 'showing the flag' cruise to Cape Town or the west coast of Africa in alternate years. Harris proposed that instead of these more or less straight through flights they should, on this occasion, fly half way down through East African territories and then fly all around the areas, visiting as many places as possible and thus open up the air to many people who had scarcely heard of aeroplanes. Cyril Newall was impressed with the idea and sent Harris as his personal representative to command the expedition, which came to be known as the 'East African Cruise—1932,' and which visited Kenya, Tanganyika and Uganda. It consisted of a flight of three Fairey 111Fs from No 14 Squadron in Amman, Transjordan, which were led by its flight commander, Flight Lieutenant Richard Atcherley,† and Harris flying his own Fairey 111F. The flight set out from Heliopolis in

---

* As Air Chief Marshal Sir Cyril Newall (1886–1963), he became Chief of the Air Staff from 1937 to 1940. Later, Marshal of the RAF Lord Newall, GCB, OM, GCMG, CBE, AM, and Governor-General of New Zealand.

† The well-known Schneider Trophy pilot and later Air Marshal Sir Richard Atcherley, KBE, CB, AFC (1904–1970).

January and first made for Nairobi via Khartoum and Entebbe. After a short stay at Nairobi, they flew to Moshi via Mombassa, where, at the request of the civil authority, Harris made an attempt to fly over Mount Kilimanjaro. Unfortunately it was smothered in cloud, but Harris did manage to obtain a photograph as he flew over the top, when the summit appeared momentarily through a gap in the cloud. From Moshi they proceeded on a series of visits to different places in East Africa, including Tanga, Zanzibar and Morogoro, before returning to Nairobi.

During these visits they took provincial commissioners and officials on flying tours round their districts, an innovation never before attempted. The passengers were immensely enthusiastic about the new view over their domains and the seed of the idea that the aeroplane had enormous civil applications in these areas of vast distances and difficult terrain was successfully sown. One interesting outcome centred around the Earl of Onslow's complaint, when presiding at an annual meeting of the Society for the Preservation of the Fauna of the Empire, that airmen flying in East Africa had, because of their aeroplanes, frequently stampeded herds of game, separating the young from their mothers and causing many to die or be injured in the stampede. Harris had heard of this complaint and had read similar allegations in an article in *The Field*. Having observed the reactions of animals in his youth in Rhodesia, he was sceptical of these claims and, since the East African Cruise passed over the most famous game reserves during its itinerary, he decided to make his own careful observations and report on the matter.

In an interview with a representative of the *East African Standard*, Harris emphasised that if one deliberately set out to chase an animal herd one could undoubtedly terrify the animals, but the same effect could be produced by a motor car driven by a person who desired to create this kind of senseless havoc. From his own careful experiments he reported that an interesting feature was that the effect of high-flying aircraft lasted longer than that of low-flying aircraft. This he suggested was due to the fact that the low-flying machine came suddenly upon the animals, passed over them and was gone in a matter of seconds, in which case the game normally reacted with a quick stampede which ceased immediately the aircraft had passed on. They then continued their grazing. He considered this type of flying produced approximately the same effect as that produced on animals by natural means, such as that on a herd of zebra when approached by lions. When machines were flying higher, however, he noted that the stampede lasted longer, because the animals appeared to hear and to see the aircraft over a longer period of time and therefore their defensive manoeuvre lasted longer. He was emphatic that at all heights an aircraft making a straight flight caused a stampede no greater than the periodic stampedes to which animals were subjected by day and by night from entirely natural causes. Indeed, he said that whilst flying at varying heights he had never seen animals gallop more than a comparatively short distance, nor had he seen any signs of panic likely to cause injury to the animals or signs of the young being deserted. His conclusion was that wild life would become so used to the passage of aircraft on regular routes that they would, in the end, completely ignore them. He was right. Later, the animals became a menace to aircraft on the airfields, in particular at Nairobi Airport.

During one flight he took the Governor of Tanganyika from Tabora to Moshi and back, flying at different heights over game areas and through the Ngorongoro Crater, the most famous of all wild game haunts. They saw every conceivable animal on the trip. Describing the reaction of animals, Harris said: 'The lion just lopes away. We passed over a large pride of lion—they just stopped and adopted their usual defensive attitude. But when we looked back after we'd passed about half a mile beyond them we saw they had reformed their single file and were proceeding happily on their way. The wart-hog,' he said, 'will not budge from anybody or anything and merely becomes exceedingly truculent, but the wildebeest and zebra gallop away.' However, they saw a solitary bull wildebeest which, Harris said, 'seemed to prance around in a circle waving its head and tail. From the marks on the ground it appeared to be doing it on its regular stamping ground.' He went on to say that the only animal that appeared to be in a state of extreme panic, at whatever height we flew, was the hyena. 'He just tore across the plains at full belt waving his head from side to side, and you could almost imagine him howling blue murder as he went.'

Undoubtedly Harris's views on the effect of passing aircraft on game, and the practical experience he afforded the Governor of Tanganyika, had a material influence on the Governor's approach towards any future legislative restrictions against aircraft flying across game reserves and areas.

Another highlight of the East African Cruise was the cooperation given to a Mr J. H. Lieb of Fox Movietone News. Mr Lieb was granted permission to film areas of Kenya from an aircraft for publicity purposes. The main objective was Mount Kenya. His film equipment was fitted into the rear cockpit of Harris's machine and Harris himself flew him on this expedition, the other three aircraft of the Cruise accompanying them in formation. They left Nairobi aerodrome at 06.05 hours on Monday 21 March, and flew straight to Mount Kenya, making height en route. By 07.00 hours they were at 18,500 feet over Mount Kenya, and there began for Mr Lieb an unforgettable experience. Harris led the flight over the summit of the mountain and then circled down so closely that they were able to see clearly the snow and ice, the lakes in the hollows, and the contours generally. Mr Lieb secured a movie film that excited him immensely, including shots of the other three aircraft with the mountain as their background. They were over Mount Kenya for the best part of an hour and, at that height without oxygen, Mr Lieb said he found it very exhausting moving about in the cockpit and operating his camera equipment. He also found it very cold. But the sheer grandeur of the scene more than compensated for his bodily discomforts. He said: 'In the course of my travels I have done a good deal of flying, but this trip over Mount Kenya in one of the RAF bombers was the most outstanding. I shall never forget the fine pilotage of Wing Commander Harris and his courteous and useful assistance.' Some of this film formed part of the prelude to the Noël Coward film *Cavalcade*, which was shown all over the world.

The East African Cruise left for its journey back to Heliopolis on 23 March, the day after the Mount Kenya filming expedition.

At the end of Harris's tour of Egypt he was, to his horror, posted to Baghdad yet again to command a Vernon squadron. Having done two and a half years in that part of the world, he had no intention of repeating the dose, so he protested to Newall, the AOC. Newall told him that he could not argue against a posting, and that, in any case, the Air Ministry were insistent; to which Harris replied that he was not going back to the same job he had done for three years eight years before. 'I'd rather have resigned and gone back to Rhodesia,' he says, 'and I would have done too. But Philip Babington* saved me—he was "P" Staff, Cairo, and he found a regulation which said that all postings to and from Iraq must be to and from England. So he told the Air Ministry they should refer to their own ruddy regulations.' Harris, as was his wont, got his own way, although he had to go to Baghdad for two months to write their defence scheme. He returned to England after this, where at the end of 1932 he was given command of a flying-boat base and No 210 Flying-Boat Squadron at Pembroke Dock. This posting pleased him, for he had long wanted to have a boat squadron in order to clear the black magic out of what was known as the flying-boat trade union. He was also keen to help solve some of the difficulties they were having with night flying. In fact, he had impressed on almost every other part of the Royal Air Force the need for and advantages of being able to operate at night, and now he felt it was time for flying-boat squadrons to fly in the dark.

According to Harris, the flying-boat branch of the service had succeeded in surrounding itself with an esoteric atmosphere based on largely spurious nautical lore, and wished it to be understood that there were so many difficulties in the way of taking up a flying boat by night that for an ordinary mortal to attempt this feat was suicidal. However, helped by such stalwarts as Jack Woodin† and Donald Bennett,‡ he soon discovered that the only difference between flying in the dark in a flying-boat and an ordinary aeroplane was that it was in every way much simpler and safer. 'The sea landing areas,' he says, 'provided "aerodromes" of comparatively unlimited extent and a flying-boat could be "felt" down onto the water, blind, in conditions in which no land based aircraft could, at that time, be landed.'

However, the time allotted to Harris to spend what he described as an enjoyable period sailing boats and flying flying-boats, for which he developed a great affection even though he regarded them as having no future, was strictly limited. He was in any case wasting his talents, and it

* Later Air Marshal Sir Philip Babington, KCB, MC, AFC.

† Later Group Captain J. H. Woodin, OBE.

‡ Later Air Vice-Marshal D. C. T. Bennett, CB, CBE, DSO.

was just as well for the country that he should spend only one year in this appointment. Even so, two things of great importance happened in that year which make it clear that destiny had a purpose in sending him to Pembroke Dock. First, he met some people with whom he became friends and through whom he was later to meet his wife, Jill. Secondly, he had as one of his flight commanders Don Bennett, who was later to become his Air Officer Commanding the Pathfinder Force (No 8 Group) in World War II.

6
Air Ministry

In 1919 the War Cabinet, as part of an economy campaign, instructed the service departments that their financial estimates should be based on the assumption that the British Empire would not be engaged in any major war for the next ten years. This dictum came to be known as 'The Ten-Year Rule'. At much the same time the Government also gave an undertaking that the Royal Air Force would possess a first line strength equal to that of any other air force within striking distance of Britain. But, in fact, the Royal Air Force, which at the end of the war had been the most powerful air force in the world, had by 1923 dwindled to insignificance. In his book Saundby states that the total strength of the Royal Air Force in the United Kingdom in the period 1923 to 1925, apart from training schools, was five army cooperation squadrons, and that there was not a single fighter or bomber squadron in Britain at that time. Whilst Saundby's figures do not agree with those quoted in the official records, he was probably factually correct. The records indicate that in 1925 the Royal Air Force in Britain consisted of fourteen squadrons of which four were designated as fighters and the rest as bomber or army cooperation. Analysis, however, reveals that the squadrons consisted in most cases of only one flight, or an aircraft or two, as nuclei for the formation of complete squadrons.

Overseas the Royal Air Force had fared better, thanks to Trenchard's successful and highly economic policing of the mandated territories and areas of the Empire. Even so, the overseas strength was no more than two fighter squadrons and twenty other squadrons equipped with Vernons and light bombers or army cooperation type aircraft. These covered duties in Iraq, Egypt, Palestine, Transjordan, the Sudan, Aden and Singapore.

Despite the recommendations of a committee, set up in 1923 under Lord Salisbury to examine the country's needs for an independent air force, that a substantial home defence air force should be created, absolutely nothing was done. In 1925, however, following the French occupation of the Ruhr in 1923 and a later realisation that the strength of the French Air Force exceeded the strength of the Royal Air Force by some one hundred squadrons, political pressure was brought to bear upon the Government to implement its promise that Great Britain should possess a force equal to any of its potential enemies—and France was now the greatest. The result was that Trenchard's proposal that the new Air Defence of Great Britain (ADGB) force should have a total of fifty-two squadrons, one third or seventeen squadrons to be fighters and two thirds or thirty-five squadrons to be bombers, was finally accepted. But progress was slow and although the intention was that the total force should be completed in five years from 1925, in 1930 there were seventeen fighter squadrons in existence and only twelve of the thirty-five bomber squadrons. Of the bomber squadrons eight were short range light day bombers and four were longer range twin-engined bombers.

The reasons were manifold. Lack of money was one. Then any real threat to Britain from the air was difficult to discern—the German Air Force had ceased to exist due to disarmament; the Italian Regia Aeronautica and the Russian Air Force were out of range, even if they had been serious threats; Spain had no air force; and most people, when they considered the matter seriously, could not bring themselves to believe that the French would really attack Britain. But perhaps the most potent reason was 'The Ten-Year Rule', whose really pernicious effect was that as each year passed it was still maintained as a period of ten years rather than being reduced year by year. The result was that it was still assumed in 1930 that there would be no war for another ten years. Two years later the strength of the RAF was still no greater, with the bomber squadrons equipped with short range and obsolescent types of aircraft that were useless for modern warfare. Whilst the rule was, in fact, officially abandoned on 23 March 1932, it remained psychologically effective for some considerable time.

The change in attitude towards 'The Ten-Year Rule' was brought about by Hitler, whose rise to power in 1933 brought British politicians to earth with a bump. Germany's rearmament programme quickly resulted in the break up of the League of Nations Disarmament Conference in the spring of 1934, and it was only then that the Air Ministry was allowed to prepare and issue requirements for high performance long range bombers, capable of carrying bomb loads far in excess of anything previously visualised.

The strength of the Royal Air Force at this stage was 850 first-line aircraft, and the Air Estimates of March 1934 provided for an increase of four new squadrons, bringing the first-line strength up to a pitiful 890. Then, on the 20 July 1934, the National Government proposed an additional forty-one squadrons, an increase of approximately 830 aircraft including reserves, to be completed in five years. This was a considerable improvement, but still inadequate. Even so, it was opposed by the Labour Party with the support of the Liberal Party, both of whom were hell-bent on pacifism and leading the way to world disarmament in the face of a resurgent Germany which was openly arming itself to the teeth.

It took another year, Italy's invasion of Abyssinia in 1935 and her resignation from the League of Nations, and the alarm created by the report of Sir John Simon* and Anthony Eden† on their return from a visit to

* Then Foreign Secretary in the MacDonald-Baldwin National Government of 1931–35.
† Then Lord Privy Seal in the MacDonald-Baldwin National Government.

Germany in March 1935 (when Hitler had stated to them that the German Air Force had already reached parity with the Royal Air Force and now planned expansion to 2,000 first-line aircraft), before all the bells were ringing in panic in Whitehall. As a result a new scheme for the immediate expansion of the RAF was approved by the National Government headed by Ramsay MacDonald, leader of the Labour Party and an avowed pacifist. Fortunately for the country, MacDonald could no longer command a majority in the House of Commons. In fact, the leader of the Conservative Party, Stanley Baldwin, took over as Prime Minister of the National Government on 7 June 1935 and went to the country in October 1935 for a triumphant General Election in which he received a majority of 247 seats over all other parties combined. From this point onwards, the expansion of the services received a real degree of priority, but there were only four years left, as it transpired, to make good the depleted armed forces—a length of time which nearly proved to be disastrously inadequate, particularly in the case of the Royal Air Force.

So far as the Royal Air Force was concerned, several plans were considered, the first being to produce by 1937 sixty-eight bomber squadrons with a total of 816 aircraft, which together with fighter squadrons and other first line aircraft would give the Air Force a total home strength of 1,512. This scheme was the one approved by the National Cabinet after the Eden–Simon visit to Germany. In February, 1936, this scheme was upgraded by the newly elected Conservative Government, increasing the number of bombers from 816 to 990 and making smaller additions to the number of fighter aircraft. The expansion in bombers was to be applied to the planned sixty-eight squadrons rather than for the purpose of creating a greater number of squadrons. Importantly, the upgraded scheme allowed for heavier bombers carrying much bigger bomb loads and for the provision of adequate reserves to back this new front line strength. In essence, the Government was now aiming at parity with Germany.

It was into this politically charged atmosphere that Harris was pitched when he was posted to the Air Ministry to undertake the first major Staff task of his career, a task that was to prepare the blueprint of the bomber force which he was to command from 1942 to 1945. He was promoted to group captain in July 1933, and posted Deputy Director on 11 August to the Directorate of Operations and Intelligence (DOI). Then, on 3 April 1934 he was appointed Deputy Director Plans (DD Plans) in the same directorate. At this time Air Marshal Sir Edgar Ludlow-Hewitt* was Director of Operations and Intelligence and Deputy Chief of the Air Staff (DCAS).

* Sir Edgar Ludlow-Hewitt, KCB, CMG, DSO, MC, was DCAS from February 1933 until January 1935. He was one of the very few high-ranking practical airmen and encouraged and supported Harris in his developing views on bomber aircraft. After a tour of duty in India, he was C-in-C Bomber Command from September 1937 to April 1940.

It was Harris's job to assist in forming Air Staff policy and to prepare specifications for the type of aircraft required. He also had to advise on and prepare proposals for the best methods of utilising the air forces in the event of war, either independently or in conjunction with the Navy and the Army. In addition, in his capacity of DD Plans he was the Air Staff representative on the Chiefs of Staff Joint Planning Sub-Committee, which consisted of one Naval, one Army and one Royal Air Force member.

The task ahead was not an enviable one.

Thanks to Trenchard, and later Sir John Salmond, the Royal Air Force still existed as a separate service, but thanks to the politicians, particularly the pacifist Labour Party, it had been so reduced in size, and its equipment had become so obsolete, that it was no more than a paper tiger. Although the Ten-Year Rule had been abandoned in March 1932, still no action was being taken to build up the Royal Air Force to a size and quality necessary for the security of the country. Stanley Baldwin, who as leader of the Conservatives was serving in the National Government under Ramsay MacDonald until he took over as Prime Minister in June 1935 and won the election in October, was subjected to much criticism for his inactivity on defence matters and, therefore, for this state of affairs. Harris, however, takes a more tolerant view. 'Baldwin,' he says, 'couldn't have worked any faster with rearmament, otherwise he would have irretrievably damaged the chances of his party winning the election of October 1935. No one really believed war was possible in the near future, until they saw Germany rearming and Italy invading Abyssinia. Some people say he was putting party before country by not pressing for rearmament earlier, but there are two ways of looking at it—he may have put party before country in the hope that in this way he wouldn't be putting into power a party which would be disastrous to the country's interests. No, I think it's unfair to blame Baldwin for our lack of preparedness—he did most of what he could do in the circumstances.'

In 1934, as Harris puts it, the RAF was suffering from a 'General Purpose Aircraft disease', which had persisted throughout the period of the Ten-Year Rule and had provided types of aircraft that could, with modest changes to the basic design, be called bombers, or reconnaissance aircraft, or fighters, but which could never adequately fulfil these roles in modern warfare. The famous Hawker series was a good example, with the Fury, a single-seater open cockpit fighter biplane, the Hart and Hind, two-seater open cockpit bomber versions, and the Audax, the two-seater Army cooperation version. They were virtually indistinguishable from each other. Of the larger bombers there were also the Wellesleys and Harrows which, like the Hawker series, were hopelessly out of date. But the thinking remained in terms of the light bomber that could also be a fighter bomber, a medium bomber or a general reconnaissance type. The pure fighters of the future went little further than the Hawker Fury, the follow-up being Gloster Gauntlets and Gladiators, again biplanes of little better performance than the Fury and with no better armament. Fortunately, however, as a result of the successful partnership of the Royal Air Force and Vickers Supermarine in developing the high performance Schneider Trophy low-wing monoplanes, replacements beyond the outmoded biplane fighters had been specified by the Air Staff. These gave the RAF the metal low-wing multi-gun Hurricanes and Spitfires only just in time for the Battle of Britain in 1940, and only in barely sufficient quantities. In March 1939, when Hitler invaded Czechoslovakia, only six months before Britain was at war with Germany, the RAF possessed less than one hundred Hurricanes and only six Spitfires, with weekly production rates that would not have been adequate to meet wastage rates had Britain been forced into war at that stage. For the rest of its effort Fighter Command was dependent upon wooden biplanes with totally inadequate performance and armament.

But for the generosity, and possibly the foresightedness of a remarkable woman, Lady Houston, Britain might well have been denied the Hurricanes and Spitfires at a crucial moment in her history. The Labour Government had decided against giving financial support to a British entry for the 1931 Schneider Trophy high-speed flying contest although in 1929, and in previous years, governments had supported an entry by the RAF for this international race. The Under-Secretary of State for Air had told the House that the race was in the nature of a sporting event, and it was thus undesirable that it should be supported by public money. In the face of this bitter blow to British aviation, Lady Houston stepped in with an offer of £100,000 out of her own pocket to finance the British entry—a prodigious sum in those days. This was gratefully accepted by the Air Council, and Britain was enabled to defend her title and win the trophy yet again. But the important outcome of the Schneider Trophy contest was its influence on the design of high-speed aircraft under Mitchell of Vickers Supermarine, the designer of the Schneider Trophy low wing monoplane seaplanes and later the famous Spitfire. Perhaps the most significant spin-off, however, was from the Rolls-Royce 'R' series of racing engines, used in Mitchell's Schneider machines, from which emerged the Rolls-Royce Merlin and Griffon engines that not only played a vital part in the defence of Britain, in the Spitfire, but also a notable part in the destruction of the German war effort, in the Lancaster bomber. As Harris says: 'Lady Houston, ably backed by Fighter Command, won the Battle of Britain.' For good measure she also helped Bomber Command to win the Battle of Germany.

At this time the Air Staff requirements for the bombers were an improvement, with specifications for the Whitley, Hampden and Wellington twin-engined aircraft,* but these designs were, to Harris's way of thinking, almost certain to be obsolete by the time they came into service. In fact, by the end of 1934 he was becoming more and more convinced that

---

* In March 1939, there were less than fifty of these twin-engined bombers available. The rest of the bomber force consisted of single-engined Fairey Battles and twin-engined Bristol Blenheims, which were of such short range that they were unable to attack Germany except from Continental bases, and then only with an insignificant bomb load.

the bombers that were being planned were barely adequate to meet the long-range bombing task. The deterrent to correct specifications was, he now firmly believed, the desire to design aircraft that could be Jack of all trades and master of none.

Two memoranda to the DCAS from Harris, dated 1935, are of interest. On 16 January he wrote that the light bomber was outmoded and he strongly advocated a policy of seeking maximum range and bomb capacity. The term fighter-bomber, 'came into use,' he stated, 'solely to satisfy the demand for a fighter in certain stations overseas, when we ourselves did not wish to provide fighters but preferred bombers.' He went even further by suggesting that the medium bomber should also be abandoned in favour of a long-range bomber with a large bomb capacity.

In November 1935, in response to a request by the Admiralty to consider a requirement for a general reconnaissance aircraft, inspired and based on the principle of developing an aircraft that could be used for naval reconnaissance or bombing, Harris minuted the DCAS with characteristic bluntness: 'We cannot afford to specialise a large proportion of our limited total strength in reconnaissance, which is purely a negative contribution to war winning and an impossible drain on our limited resources.' Referring to the continual attempts by the other two services to fritter away the already inadequate resources of the RAF and to dampen the resolve to build up an offensive bomber force in addition to a defensive fighter system, he went on to say:

> These matters are assuming such vital importance and becoming so urgent that a decision will be required in the near future on which will depend, in my opinion, not only the question of whether we shall or shall not succeed in protecting our sea communications in the event of war, but also whether we shall succeed in retaining more than one third of our national air forces under our control, as opposed to Admiralty control;* whether we are to fritter away our resources in defensive ancillary types, or whether we are to have an ubiquitous force with, as the primary requirement, the maximum offensive potential. This is what Germany intends to have and, in spite of extra commitments perculiar to our situation, it is Germany that we have got to meet when it comes to a show down.

Harris concluded by stating the minimum required range and speed necessary for a bomber, and emphasized that even this was only suitable for a medium bomber. 'As for performance,' he said, 'anything less than 1,000 miles' effective radius at 250 mph will not compete with our requirements and will be hopelessly out of date by the time we get it. It is in fact no more and no less than the contemporary medium bomber requirement.' In this

---

* The 'one third' was a reference to the Trenchard proposal accepted in 1925, that there should be an Air Defence of Great Britain force home based, consisting of fifty-two squadrons of which one third was to be fighters and two thirds bombers. Harris was hinting in his minute that the RAF was in danger of being reduced to a fighter defence force and nothing more.

context, the medium bomber requirement referred to the specifications already set down for the Whitley, Hampden and Wellington.

It was not until 1936, however, that Harris's pressure for a truly strategic bomber began to bear fruit and the Air Staff began to think in terms of far heavier bombers than had previously been considered. The idea of developing the ability to attack Germany from home bases resulted in two new specifications emanating from the Air Staff, via the medium of the Directorate of Plans, for a twin-engined and a four-engined bomber with performance, range and bomb-load greatly increased over any earlier specifications. These specifications were the blueprint for the twin-engined Avro Manchester, the four-engined Handley Page Halifax and the four-engined Short Stirling. The Avro Manchester effectively became the prototype for the famous four-engined Lancaster. So Harris became one of those largely responsible for planning the giant bombers that were to comprise the force under his command from 1942 to 1945. Indeed, it is more than evident that the two men who contributed most to this foresighted planning were Harris and Saundby, who was then a wing commander and who had joined Harris in the Directorate of Operations and Intelligence in December 1936—again a strange coincidence! But more than this, it was Harris, in conjunction with Captain T. S. V. Phillips, R N* and Colonel R. Forbes Adam,† the three of whom comprised the Joint Planning Sub-Committee of the Chiefs of Staff Committee, who produced the revealing 'Appreciation of the Situation in the Event of War against Germany in 1939—Provisional Report'. This report was submitted to the Chiefs of Staff on 26 October 1936. But more about this later, for there had been two other events of importance in Harris's life.

On 4 October 1935 Harris was invited for drinks at a London hotel by friends he had met whilst he was stationed at Pembroke Dock. The girl who invited him also invited a great school friend, a young and lovely girl called Therese Hearne. Unfortunately Miss Hearne was suffering from a bad cold. Harris took pity on her and seeing how miserable she was with her streaming nose he offered to escort her home when the party was over. For his courteous efforts the young Miss Hearne almost threatened him with her umbrella. As Harris said: 'She had been brought up in a convent and taught the facts of life by a Jesuit priest who, no doubt, was an expert, and she was obviously quite certain that if she even got into a taxi with a strange man she would wake up in an Argentine brothel. Typical convent training!'

But despite her defensive attitude Harris persuaded her to lunch with him a few days later. In the course of the conversation he had discovered that she worked not far from the Air Ministry, which was at Adastral House in Kingsway, so he asked her to join him for lunch at Rules, the well-known

---

* Later Vice-Admiral Sir Tom S. V. Phillips who went down with HMS *Prince of Wales* when she was sunk with *Repulse* off the Malayan coast on 10 December 1941, by Japanese bomber aircraft.

† Later General Sir Ronald Forbes Adam, Bt, GCB, DSO, OBE.

restaurant in Covent Garden. 'Well,' says Harris, 'I didn't think she looked properly fed and I asked her to lunch again and again—and from then on we never looked back. I've never regretted one second of our married life. She's as sweet a person as ever lived on this earth—she really is a saint.'

Therese Hearne, known as Jill, or Jillie by Harris himself, confirms that she used to be very nervous about going out with strangers, even when she had met them through friends. She, like Harris, had had a very limited family life, her mother having died when she was nine years old and her father when she was sixteen. Her guardian was an old aunt who was very kind but not very worldly. Jill's fears were bred from what she describes as the awful school leaving speeches about white slave traffic: 'Never help someone across the road because they might give you an injection. Don't go to pyjama parties, and never smell a bunch of flowers or accept a chocolate from someone on a train—it'll be sure to be doped. When I got a job in London I was absolutely terrified! But Bud [her name for Arthur Harris] was so kind and patient, I always had that protected feeling when I was with him.'

Although, as Jill Harris says, he proposed to her several times, they were not married until June 1938, nearly three years later. Being so much on her own with no parents to talk to, she found it difficult to make up her mind. Also Harris was forty-three and there was therefore an age gap of twenty-three years between them. But if Jill Hearne was in any doubt, Harris was in no doubt whatsoever. He loved her and he knew she was the only girl for him, so he continued his courtship with great persistence and the utmost patience. It was, however, to have an enforced but short interruption only a few months after it began.

Arising from a generous offer by Southern Rhodesia to make an annual contribution towards British Imperial Defence, the Committee of Imperial Defence decided that the money would most usefully be expended in providing for the training of pilots in Rhodesia and the establishment of a Rhodesian Air Force Unit. Harris, as the RAF member of the Joint Planning Sub-Committee of the Chiefs of Staff Committee of the Committee of Imperial Defence, was selected to study the problem in Rhodesia. He left for Salisbury in the middle of February 1936 and after meetings with the Prime Minister of Southern Rhodesia, G. Martin Huggins (later Viscount Malvern), and his Minister for Justice and Defence, the Hon V. A. Lewis, he commenced his task based on the following intentions which he had already outlined in London:

A. To provide ab initio flying training and technical training for an annual intake of Rhodesian personnel.
B. To provide Service training as and when Service type aircraft could be made available.
C. To provide a Rhodesian Air Force Unit as a striking force.
D. To maintain in training the reserve of personnel eventually built up.

His plan was that these steps should be undertaken progressively, as and when funds and equipment could be made available. His aim was that the Air Force Unit finally created should, in conjunction with the other branches of the Rhodesian Forces, provide for defence against external aggression and for the preservation of internal security. In addition, he aimed to make the Rhodesian Air Force, and the reserve of trained personnel, effective enough to be regarded as a real contribution by Southern Rhodesia towards Imperial Defence, either by relieving Britain of the necessity for providing the equivalent forces for the direct defence of Rhodesia or, in certain circumstances, by making this force available for Imperial Defence outside Southern Rhodesia. He assumed the goal to be an air force organised on normal lines, consisting of the required number of squadrons and supporting units with the necessary administration of command and supply to maintain them. In fact, he had at the start of his task visualised for this country an air force that could stand on its own feet and operate with a considerable degree of independence.

To back his programme, Harris went into considerable detail on technical training, *ab initio* and service flying training, repair facilities, choice of aerodrome sites, provision of aircraft and reserves, requirements for Royal Air Force seconded personnel in initial stages, development of Rhodesian personnel, and even the constitutional position of the Officer Commanding the Southern Rhodesian Air Force in relation to the Minister of Defence, the Officer Commanding the Defence Forces and the Director of Civil Aviation. He also prepared the ground for the training of technical apprentices at the RAF Engineering Apprentices' School at Halton Bucks, in England, and he negotiated with the Air Ministry for service type aircraft, which were new, albeit now becoming obsolete in the RAF for £100 each, plus four complete sets of servicing equipment and spares for £300 per set. Moreover he arranged for more up-to-date types of aircraft to be provided on similar terms when available.

Harris's report, and recommendations, dated 13 March 1936, which he submitted to the Minister for Justice and Defence, requested provisional agreement in principle with the procedure outlined, so that he could investigate, in more detail, the practical moves to put the plan into action. The approval was duly given.

Harris's knowledge of East Africa, and Rhodesia in particular, together with his technical skill, flying experience, and sound common sense, made a tremendous impression on V. A. Lewis, the Defence Minister; so much so that whilst he had Harris on the spot he decided to ask him to make a survey of Southern Rhodesia and to advise on those points in the country that were vulnerable to attack. For this purpose W. S. Senior, the Minister for Mines, loaned his Hornet Moth to Harris. Harris's report is a remarkable document, so far-sighted that it could almost be applicable to today.

Harris left for England on 25 March 1936, having completed his task in six weeks. He had laid the firm foundations of the Southern Rhodesian Air Force which, with the other Rhodesian military forces, played such a gallant part in World War II. But if his immediate task was finished, he certainly did not forget his newly conceived child. Back at the Air Ministry he continued to assist in every way possible the growth of the Southern Rhodesian Air Force.

To appreciate Harris's urgent duties at this period, it is necessary to review briefly what had happened just before and after the Eden–Simon visit to Germany in March 1935. On 9 October 1934, the Chiefs of Staff decided that it had become expedient to consider Britain's defence preparations in relation to the possibility of war with Germany. For this purpose their Joint Planning Sub-Committee, of which Group Captain A. T. Harris was the Air Staff member, was furnished with appropriate terms of reference. There were four reports, headed 'Defence Plans for the Event of War Against Germany', the last being submitted on 31 October 1935. With the Eden–Simon report on the German Air Force now at hand and very much on everyone's mind and with memories of the Zeppelin and Gotha attacks on London in 1916 and 1917, opinion was forming that German strategy would be aimed at a quick knock-out, either by direct attack from German air bases or after an invasion of Belgian bases. Targets were expected to be government and military establishments, London docks, other South Coast ports, and industrial areas, inevitably involving the civilian population. If such attacks were successful it was believed that the effects would be catastrophic. The Army and Navy, fighting for their own estimates and still trying to dissolve the RAF, found these views unacceptable and decried the power of the bomber, enemy or otherwise. The Air Staff opinion was, however, that in the event of Britain being isolated, a defence fighter force alone could not save the country from defeat; but, in conjunction with an offensive strategic bomber force, it could hold the enemy offensive whilst the bomber force mounted an offensive against the enemy's bases, war industry, communications and various targets of economic importance. The strength of the Air Staff view lay in the fact that, if Britain were isolated, there was no other means that the Army or Navy could offer for mounting any offensive at all against Germany. Consequently their view began to prevail.

The sub-committee's next effort, 'Appreciation of the Situation in the Event of War Against Germany in 1939,' dated 26 October 1936 brought things to a head and resulted in the Joint Chiefs of Staff formulating a plan which gave prominence to the necessity for a strategic bomber force. These plans were approved by the Committee of Imperial Defence and the Cabinet in May 1937. The 'Appreciation' which was prepared by Harris, Forbes Adam and Tom Phillips, is a document of great foresight, and was completed with no signs of the inter-service rivalries and bigotry that existed at higher levels.

Under the heading 'Probable Attitude of Powers', the writers foresaw that the likely belligerents would initially be Germany against France, Belgium and Britain, with Holland remaining neutral unless Germany attempted to move troops through her territory. They assumed that Italy would be sympathetic towards Germany and might enter on German's side. They felt that Britain could not rely on Russian intervention on the side of Britain and her probable allies but, at the same time, they believed Germany would find it necessary to be prepared for active Russian hostility at short notice. They counted upon the support of the Dominions and Colonies, but felt that in the Far East Japan would take every opportunity of pursuing her ambitions. Lastly, they were of the opinion that the United States of America would remain neutral and impose an embargo on the export of arms to the belligerents.

This comprehensive document contained a detailed comparison of the estimated strengths of the naval, military and air forces at the expected date of the outbreak of hostilities. In discussing the preparation for war it drew attention to the great differences that existed between a democratic and a totalitarian state in conditions of international tension.

> In the past [they wrote], it has been after the outbreak of war that a nation's industry had been adapted and expanded to war requirements, her man-power organised for war and the morale of her people artificially sustained. In Germany, as in other totalitarian States, these processes are now being perfected in time of peace. The dragooning of the populace and their submission to economic hardship to a degree previously only associated with wartime, or acceptable under war conditions, is being enforced during the peace period preceding the actual campaign ... The German people can be made to submit to this system under the stern discipline of their totalitarian regime, but in no way does democracy lend itself to the experiment.

They concluded that the problem was how to prepare an equivalent war potential to that of Germany under the democratic conditions which prevailed within the British Empire. Whilst it was not their task to solve this problem, they drew attention to the fact that when war broke out Britain could find itself in such a state of unreadiness that, even if Germany's expected onslaught on the country could be contained, the military and industrial development to mount a counter-offensive might be too slow to be effective, and Britain might be forced into a negotiated peace to her disadvantage.

Whilst the comparison between naval strengths was in Britain's favour, ignoring the contribution of the French, and that between army strengths, including the French, was reasonably well balanced, the big question mark was the air forces. France had already announced her intention of building a metropolitan force of up to 2,000 first-line aircraft in two years, but Harris thought that the French aircraft industry was in a state of chaos. The view was therefore adopted that France would have great difficulty in achieving its proposed strength even by 1939. Moreover, it was agreed that, at best, she would not achieve better than 50 per cent reserves, which was totally inadequate to support such a strength in war. In Germany, Hitler had already stated that he would maintain air parity with France, so the assumption was made that Germany would also build up to a 2,000 first-line strength. But the members of the Committee believed that fear of Russia would cause Germany to exceed this figure substantially. Even so, they felt that the best Germany could achieve by 1939 was 2,500 first-line aircraft, backed by 100 per cent reserves. Since all reports and information indicated that the German aircraft industry was exceptionally well organised and already changing over to war production, as well as being dispersed to reduce vulnerability from attack, Germany's ability to achieve such figures was not held in doubt.

The strength of the RAF at this time was barely 1,000 first-line aircraft. It was only fifth amongst the air forces of the world and yet the promise had been made, years before, that it would be maintained at a level equal to that of any power within striking distance of Britain's shores. In the committee's 'Appreciation' Harris therefore planned an essential build up by 1939 to 2,204 first-line aircraft, of which 1,736 would be metropolitan aircraft, the remainder being for service in Britain's overseas territories. He also proposed that the metropolitan force should be backed by 200 per cent reserves. Of this force 420 first-line aircraft were to be fighters and 990 were to be bombers. This was in line with the bomber strength put forward earlier in 1936 by Harris as DD Plans.

In the case of Germany's 2,500 aircraft, the view was taken that this would include 1,700 first-line bombers and 270 fighters. France's Air Force of 2,000 was planned to include 775 bombers and 500 fighters, so that her bombers, combined with Britain's 990, would constitute a force of 1,765 bombers. But the general opinion of the Committee was that France would fall short in her air rearmament programme and that her bomber force would fail to mature. In fact, Harris, Forbes Adam and Tom Phillips displayed a grave lack of confidence in France's ability to wage war in the event of hostilities with Germany, and they were proved more than justified.

This feeling is very much evidenced in their consideration of Germany's likely strategy at the outset of hostilities. Indeed, under the heading 'Germany's Choice of Initial Objective', they were positively prophetic:

> By concentrating her main offensive against France, Germany would be able to employ her army and her air force, in co-operation, with a single object. Germany might well consider that her best prospect of breaking through the French fortifications might occur during the first few weeks, when her attacks would have the advantage of initiative and surprise. A rapid success against France might give Germany control of Holland, Belgium and Northern France and so place her in a strategic position from which she might hope to dominate the United Kingdom. An offensive against France would be popular in Germany, where France is regarded as the hereditary enemy rather than Great Britain.

Nevertheless, they considered the alternative, which visualised the initial main strategy being directed against Britain:

To carry out a main offensive against Great Britain, Germany could only employ her air force and naval forces. Complete concentration against Great Britain would entail a defensive role for her army which would be very unpopular in Germany and would prejudice the prospects of German success in attacks against the French fortifications, if they were eventually to be undertaken. The vulnerability of Great Britain to air attack is, however, so apparent that Germany would not lightly dismiss the possibility of concentrating at once on this form of attack. She realises the extent to which the power of the British effort can develop as the war progresses, and, by attacking us at the outset with the advantage of the initiative, she might hope for decisive success before our country could be organised for war. If such an offensive were postponed Germany could hardly hope to obtain such great results.

With the achievement of the 1,736 first-line metropolitan aircraft (of which 420 were to be fighters), it was assumed that the German air attacks would be contained, and that the German losses would prove to be a powerful deterrent to the continuance of the attacks and have a cumulative effect upon the morale of pilots. However, it was estimated that within a week of such German air attacks civilian casualties could be as high as 150,000, and disorganisation of communications and food supplies could be extremely serious. It was the opinion of the three writers of the 'Appreciation' that a high standard of organisation of local authorities and their services would be essential, together with great fortitude on the part of the population, if order was to be maintained and loyal support given to the Government.

The question of counter offensive in the air was also dealt with in the 'Appreciation', but it was only a whisper compared with the space given to the defence necessary for survival. The 'Appreciation' finished by assuming that the ultimate defeat of Germany would have to be a counter-offensive by the Army on land.

Harris says of the 'Appreciation' that it was largely academic to talk in much detail about the air offensive against Germany, since the Royal Air Force had little hope of receiving any reasonable number of medium bombers such as the Whitley, Wellington and Hampden before 1940/41, and no hope of seeing the long-range four-engined bombers, the Air Staff specifications for which were duly laid down at the time of the submission of the 'Appreciation', before 1942. Therefore the problem was one of survival long enough to build for a counter-offensive, with the form of the offensive being considered in general, if not vague, terms of bombing economic targets that would reduce Germany's war potential. Bombing was still, even in those days, very much a dirty word, and the idea of causing casualties to civilian population by any means other than by starvation by naval blockade, naval bombardment of coastal towns, army artillery bombardment, and invading armies, was viewed with horror, except by the Germans who were more realistic and regarded the bomber as an extension to the range of their artillery.

All in all, however, the 'Appreciation' was, as Harris says, a very accurate appraisal of the line-up of allies and of the course the war would take. Whilst the collapse of France was not actually predicted it was anticipated as a possibility. Admittedly the eventual entry of the USA on the side of the Allies was not anticipated, but then, as Harris says, 'Neither did we predict the incredibly stupid mistakes the Germans would make.' The important fact is that the 'Appreciation', backed by a 'Review of Imperial Defence', dated 26 January 1937, prepared by Harris, Phillips and Colonel E. L. Morris (who had replaced R. Forbes Adam on the Joint Planning Sub-Committee), was accepted by the Chiefs of Staff. This meant that the lines of strategy in the event of war were now to be translated into effective plans, which, in turn meant that the build-up of the Royal Air Force could proceed with more speed. The principle of a strategic bomber force had been conceded by the Navy and the Army, even if reluctantly.

It is interesting to note here that Generalfeldmarschall Erhard Milch* made some pertinent comments on this planning in a speech to a meeting of Gauleiters on 6 October 1943. He said of the British, using the unusual expression 'Der Engländer', which can be construed as a mark of respect:

They have already in the years 1936/37 considered the development of four-engined bombers. The Engländer planned right from the beginning to use these bombers by night and not by day, because the speed and height of these planes were not suitable for daylight attacks in the face of our day fighter defence ...

The types of planes the Engländer has are of different performances. There are three main types. The best is the Lancaster, the worst the Stirling, and then there is the Halifax. These are the three types which are frequently mentioned in the German reports of planes shot down over German territory ... Germany has certainly not observed this method of war well enough and has not been able to disturb the build-up of the forces of the Engländer ...

The attempt in our country to construct four-engined planes was started in 1934 and continued in 1935 and 1936, but on the basis of a tactical decision of the authorities in charge, this was given up in 1937 in favour of twin-engined planes ... It is regrettable that this development [four-engined bombers] which we started, and which seemed to be fruitful, was not continued and was abandoned in order to have available a great number of planes as soon as possible. The two-engined planes were preferred because they could be constructed quicker and more easily.

Milch went on to admit that the night attacks of RAF Bomber Command were proving so disastrous that urgent action was necessary.

The 'Appreciation' produced action and a sense of urgency which was

---

* Generalfeldmarschall Erhard Milch was State Secretary in the German Air Ministry, and Armaments Chief of the German Air Force.

long overdue, but it did not completely stop the Navy and the Army from trying to divide a large part of the Royal Air Force between themselves. The truth is that they were never really able to accept the principle of an independent offensive and defensive Air Force. But of these two services, it was the Royal Navy which was the greatest opponent to the expansion of the Royal Air Force.

An example of the Navy's attitude at this time occurred in connection with a relatively small but not unimportant matter. On 2 June 1936, Harris put forward a proposal for the development of a new type of anti-ship bomb, which he called for reference purposes the 'H' bomb. In his proposal he wrote:

> The H bomb would be dropped to *miss* the ship in harbours, anchorages, channels and in any shallow waters frequented by ships. No great accuracy would be required. It would lie on the bottom. It would be fitted with a delay action fuse, the functioning of which would only make the bomb 'live'—and would not explode it. Once the bomb was 'live' the bomb would be fired by the magnetic field created by any ship passing over or within a predetermined distance of the bomb.

Harris went on to explain the likely targets for this bomb, which was in fact the first concept of the magnetic mine that was used to such great effect during World War II, and to point out the difficulties in 'sweeping' it, because '... it should prevent the effective use of "magnetic sweeps" for exploding H bombs lying in a given area; only those bombs rendered live by expiry of the time fuse would be so exploded. There would be no guarantee that more bombs would not become "live" immediately or shortly after the "sweep" had passed.' He also made proposals for preventing successful diving operations to recover the bombs.

Out of his suggestion came an Admiralty proposal for a mine to be used from aircraft. This was in February 1937, and it drew from Harris a minute in praise and support of the proposal. This minute was dated 2 March 1937 and one point he made was that apart from use in open seas there were other aspects of its use that tended to prove that the investigation and development of this weapon should be a joint responsibility between the Navy and the Air Force in so far as it might well be put to use by either of the two services for their own separate ends or by both, conjointly, for a common end. Harris mentioned inland waterways as an independent Air Force target, and German Baltic ports as Air Force targets in conjunction with the Navy as an extension of their blockade plans, such ports being ones which the Air Force alone would be in a position to mine. Another example he gave was the Kiel Canal.

From the start of Harris's proposal, however, the development of this mine, which was regarded as an excellent weapon and entirely feasible, was held up by inter-departmental bickering instigated by the Admiralty. Almost as soon as the suggestion was put forward by the Air Ministry, the Admiralty adopted an awkward attitude. On 30 September 1936 they wrote: 'My Lords are strongly of the opinion that although capable of being laid by aircraft the weapon is indistinguishable in function from a mine. They therefore hope that the Air Council will agree that its development should be undertaken by the Admiralty ...' And again on 8 October 1936 an inter-departmental meeting of the Admiralty stated that the Admiralty was of the opinion that: 'The operational control of this weapon, affecting as it does the movement of all ships, whether friendly or hostile or neutral, must rest with the authority responsible for the maintenance of sea communications.'

The Air Ministry did not accept the Admiralty view, but despite Harris's minute of March 1937, the Admiralty continued its dog-in-the-manger attitude. This finally drew a more than usually pungent minute from Marshal of the Royal Air Force Sir Edward Ellington, the CAS, to the Secretary of State for Air, dated 24 June 1937. In it he wrote: 'The whole affair is an outstanding example of the deplorable result of inter-departmental bickering, and provides further proof of the Admiralty's determination to maintain naval "autarky" at all costs. It is very probable that the Admiralty realises quite well that the "bomb-mine" will normally have to be used by shore-based bomber squadrons, and that their claim for "operational control" over the weapon is therefore yet another attempt by back-door methods towards the attainment of a separate Naval Air Force.'

Ellington also enclosed an Air Staff note which had been prepared by Harris. This included a delightful comment upon the Admiralty's claim to operational control over the weapon because the medium in which it was to be used was water. Harris had written: '... in this particular connection it is pertinent to point out the fallacy of claiming that the element in which a projectile explodes must govern the Service responsibility for discharging it. If this were really so, then the Admiralty ought to control all coast defence batteries, the War Office all ships engaged in the bombardment of shore batteries, and the Air Ministry all anti-aircraft guns whether ashore or afloat!' However, with greater levity, Harris went on to describe the various uses of the weapon and emphasized the fact that the use of the 'bomb-mine' seemed to be pre-eminently a matter for inter-Service cooperation and fully coordinated direction. It has a dual nature, combining the functions of a bomb, an air weapon, and a mine, a naval weapon. It is to be carried and dropped by aircraft with the object of destroying ships. It can be used against ports, harbours and shallow coastal waters and also against internal communications in the form of rivers and canals far from the sea. If there is any question of exclusive operational control it would seem at first sight that this should rest with the Air Ministry. The weapon is to all intents and purposes a bomb until the moment when it strikes the water.' He went on to point out that it had to be carried by an aircraft which would have to adopt air tactics to reach its target, face air opposition, and use air-trained bomb-aimers with a bomb sight for delivery. Even so, he stated that there should be no question of exclusive operational control by the Royal Air Force any more than by the Navy.

The Air Ministry won the day in the end, and this proved to be of the utmost importance, for Harris, who had conceived the bomb-mine, became the greatest exponent of its use, first in No 5 (Bomber) Group when he was the Air Officer Commanding from 1939 to 1940, and generally in Bomber Command when he was the C-in-C from 1942 to 1945. In fact the greater part of all sea mining in and around the enemy and enemy occupied territories was undertaken from the air by Bomber Command under the code name of 'Gardening'. But that is another story which follows later.

7
Two years to war

At the beginning of June 1937 Harris was promoted to the rank of air commodore, and on the 12th he was posted to Bomber Command as Air Officer Commanding No 4 Group in Yorkshire, which was at that time just forming. Shortly after his arrival, Air Chief Marshal Sir Edgar Ludlow-Hewitt arrived back from India to take over as C-in-C Bomber Command, and Harris was thus to serve again under a man for whom he had the greatest respect and admiration. He says of him: 'Ludlow-Hewitt was a first class pilot and a first class brain in every way. When he was DCAS, he really saved the ship. He pressed continually for the long-range four-engined bombers, and we would never have got them if it hadn't been for him. You could talk technicalities to him and you knew he knew what you were talking about. With a lot of other top Air Force brass, I'm sorry to say, it was just hopeless. They just didn't know which end of an aeroplane went first, because they hadn't used the ruddy things since the First World War! But Ludlow-Hewitt—he was a thoroughly practical airman.'

In No 4 Group Harris had the first of the new twin-engined heavy bombers, the Whitley, though not until the beginning of 1938. As with so many of his commands, he found himself starting from scratch, and following his old fetish he immediately entered upon a programme of intensified training for the crews of the newly forming squadrons, including cross-country flights by night and night bombing practice. Whilst he was desperately short of proper equipment, and faced with every conceivable kind of trouble and opposition when he tried to get training areas allotted for bombing practice, he was not deterred. With backing from Ludlow-Hewitt, he got what he wanted.

During his time at the Air Ministry Harris's friendship with Jill Hearne had developed. He had taken her out regularly, and when he was in Yorkshire he maintained the campaign to win her hand. Every possible weekend he could get away, he travelled to London to be with her. On the occasions when he could not leave Yorkshire, he arranged for her to come north to stay in York. Then, early in 1938, she succumbed and they became engaged, with plans to marry in the summer.

No sooner were they engaged than Harris heard that he was to be posted to Jerusalem as Air Officer Commanding Palestine and Transjordan.

Almost immediately, however, the posting was delayed, as the Air Ministry selected him for a mission to the United States in April 1938 to investigate the possibility of purchasing aircraft and equipment at an early date. The Air Ministry had suddenly become much concerned about the progress of the programme for the build-up of the Royal Air Force, in particular Bomber Command. The idea appears to have been to relieve the aircraft industry from production of training aircraft and certain other types, such as anti-submarine patrol aircraft, so that more capacity could be made available for the production of bombers and fighters. Oddly enough, this decision was taken when the whole programme of expansion of the Royal Air Force was being put in jeopardy by the politicians, in particular Sir Thomas Inskip, the Minister for the Coordination of Defence, who was appointed to this newly created post in the middle of 1937. The mounting cost of rearmament had frightened the Chancellor of the Exchequer, and the Cabinet demanded a review of the needs of the three services with the intention of making savings. Inskip, in short, achieved cuts in the Royal Air Force by abandoning the principle of parity with the German Air Force, increasing the number of fighter aircraft at the expense of bomber aircraft, because fighter aircraft were cheaper to produce, cutting back the planned number of heavy bombers in favour of light medium bombers, again to save money, and by substantially reducing reserves. The Air Staff was totally opposed to these plans, as was the Foreign Office, but on 22 December 1937 the Cabinet accepted Inskip's proposals, despite the Air Staff's warnings that the decision could lose Britain the war with Germany if it should come within the next two years. And, in the event, the Air Staff's assessment came dangerously close to reality in 1940 and 1941, even though Germany gave Britain a longer breathing space to prepare for real war than was anticipated, by failing to mount the blitz on Britain until the middle of 1940. As it was, the period before Britain could strike back after miraculously surviving the blitz, was so long delayed that the duration of the war was extended far longer, and therefore at greater cost to Britain, than it need have been if proper preparations had been supported and made. This view is strongly held by Harris.

On his buying mission to the USA he took with him an engineering officer from the Aeroplane and Armament Experimental Establishment and a test pilot. Mr J. G. Weir, a director of the Bank of England and industrial expert, accompanied them, to advise whether the factories to which orders might be given were industrially and financially competent to undertake them. In addition to the buying task Harris was instructed to investigate American methods of navigation, including assistance given from the ground, blind flying methods, quality and effectiveness of navigational and blind flying instruments, aircrew policy and training, runway construction, fog and night landing equipment and many other items in connection with modern flying techniques. Also he was to find out as much as he could about the American views on military requirements for aircraft such as weapons, bombs, turrets, armoured protection for crews and so on—but above all, in this category, to discover what he could about America's latest bombsight, the Norden Sight, and negotiate, if at all possible, for information about it in exchange for information about Britain's own bombsight.

Harris was much impressed by American business efficiency and the youthfulness of the men running important enterprises. One of the biggest orders the mission gave was to a comparatively small firm, the Lockheed Aircraft Company. This was for the famous Hudsons, which proved so invaluable on anti-submarine work in the Battle of the Atlantic. When the mission visited Lockheed to see an aircraft that was thought to be basically suitable for coastal reconnaissance work, Harris was struck by the ability and energy of the young men running the show. He says: 'When I told them that I could not very well give them a large order when I had only seen a civil version of their aircraft and had to take their word for it that it could be converted to meet our military requirements, they prepared a mock-up for us within twenty-four hours. Not only did they cover our own requirements, but they prepared an alternative showing their idea of how the conversion could best be done. It was, in fact, their version that we chose and the order was placed. I was entirely convinced that anyone who could produce a first class mock-up in twenty-four hours would make good all his promises—and this Lockheeds most certainly did.'

After the buying mission had completed its task, Harris remained in the USA to undertake his investigation into American military aviation. But he did more than that. He made some invaluable contacts and friends who were to be important to Britain both before the American entry into the war and after. Most important of all these was General H. H. Arnold, later the Commanding General of the US Army Air Forces. He gave Harris every possible assistance on this trip, and it is clear that these two men liked and respected each other from the start. However, there was one item upon which Harris obtained no information whatsoever from General Arnold, and that was the Norden bombsight.

Harris's study of the American Air Force was a remarkably comprehensive one, conducted in a short space of time, but completed efficiently by dint of working at great pressure. The survey and the extremely informative report he produced were only possible because he himself was such a highly experienced practical airman and so well versed in all the technicalities associated with modern aircraft. His final conclusions were, however, shattering:

In summary, neither in its equipment nor organisation can the American Air Force be counted amongst the first class air powers, an opinion in which I am supported wholeheartedly by the present Air Attaché, and I am at a loss to understand where the myth of American air power and efficiency arose.

They may be able to produce a first line of from 200 to 300 indifferent aircraft with much impractical equipment and no reserves.

They have money, enthusiasm and enormous potential industrial resources, together with a vast reservoir of potentially efficient personnel. They have one or two 'stunt' units which can, and occasionally do, put up 'stunt' performances. They are making a dead set at competency in celestial navigation and they are certainly getting there—almost as fast as we are, but on a limited scale. They have excellent group (ie station) navigation schools, but little else which we might well copy. They also have ideas, although their major obsession is that all their geese are swans, and that everybody else's are, at the best, ducks.

They could certainly have a magnificent Air Force if they decided to. At present they possess only an elaborate and expensive piece of window dressing which comes perilously near to being little more than a jest when judged by the standards of any first class air power.

Finally, I suggest that we further investigate the items mentioned below. There is nothing else for us to learn from the American Air Force.

There followed eleven items of equipment, mostly associated with radio communication equipment and navigational instrumentation.

A number of the criticisms Harris made in his report he also made verbally to American officers he met during his visit, including Colonel Olds, who commanded the Boeing Fortress Squadron, and General Andrews, Commander of the Independent Headquarters Air Force, and his staff. He was also frank with General Arnold. Unquestionably, his comments were noted, and it is certain that action was later taken to remove the reasons for his criticisms and follow his advice in many matters. Certainly the American Air Force began to build itself up and to modernise itself to that of a top power, but it nearly left it until too late. It was not until 1943, a year after it had entered the war, that it made any worthwhile contribution to the prosecution of the war in Europe. But as Harris observes: 'War seemed a remote possibility to the Americans. They had no intention of being involved in a European struggle, and they never foresaw an attack upon them by Japan—and neither did anyone else for that matter. So there was no urge to build up large military forces. Even in 1941 they didn't see it coming. Even with the possibility of a German victory over Europe they thought it could be "business as usual" for them. But Roosevelt didn't.' Harris was, in fact, to return to the USA on another mission in 1941 and was present when Japan made her devastating attack on Pearl Harbor. It was on this second mission that he proved himself a great ambassador as well as a great commander, for he made friends with Roosevelt and Harry Hopkins and won from them considerably more help than was strictly permitted by the American official position of neutrality before that country actually entered the war. He also, at that time, strengthened his friendship with General Arnold.

When Harris arrived back in England at the end of May to get married and then to go to Jerusalem with his bride, and take up his new post in Palestine, he found himself in for a shock. He was informed by Newall, who was now Chief of the Air Staff, that his posting had been cancelled and instead he was to go to Fighter Command as Senior Air Staff Officer (SASO) to Air Chief Marshal Sir Hugh ('Stuffy') Dowding.* But true to form, Harris argued. 'My heart went into my boots. I had had lots of rows with Stuffy when he was Air Member for Research and Development and I was in Plans. I had had a major fight to get him to agree that our aircraft needed to be far better equipped with instruments for navigation and blind flying—and I couldn't afford to be polite on these matters when he started laying his ears back and being stubborn. Stubborn as a mule, but a nice old boy really. He was just out of touch with flying. But we'd had those rows and I told Newall this and I said I thought it was unfair to give me one of the top commands and then stop it and give me a staff officer's job. I was damned angry. I told him quite frankly I had had so many differences of opinion with Stuffy that I doubted if he'd even want me, any more than I wanted him—and that I thought a much better suited SASO could be found. Newall was a bit annoyed and said: "You're always arguing against your postings". Well, of course, there had been that time when Newall was AOC in Egypt and I'd been posted to Baghdad for a second time, and I had argued my way out of that one with the help of Philip Babington. But I said: "I'm not arguing against my posting this time—I'm arguing for it!" And he said he didn't think he could alter it. So I shrugged my shoulders and told him I was just getting married and my wife-to-be's trousseau was all tropical and I'd have to tell her it was all cancelled. Then he shrugged his shoulders and said rather irritably: "All right have it your own way." So I went to Palestine! But I always liked Newall. I owe him a lot—and so does England.'

Within a matter of days Harris received a letter from the Air Ministry, dated 15 June, informing him that it had been decided anew that he would succeed Air Commodore R. M. Hill* as Air Officer Commanding Palestine and Transjordan, with effect from a date in July 1938.

On the 17 June 1938, Air Commodore Arthur Harris married Therese Hearne, and almost immediately they sailed for Palestine. Their first home was a magnificent house just outside Jerusalem, set in the midst of olive groves with the most superb views. 'It was,' says Harris, 'far beyond the sort of official residence one would normally expect from the Air Ministry, who were never exactly noted for their generosity, and I couldn't think why. But then I discovered it was only four hundred yards down wind from the leper asylum, so the rent was cheap! The world expert on leprosy, a German doctor, lived nearby, so I asked him if it was all right, and he said yes, although he wasn't too sure about sharing mosquitoes with them.'

---

* Air Chief Marshal Sir Hugh Dowding (1882–1970), GCB, GCVO, CMG, ADC, C-in-C Fighter Command from 14 July 1936 to 24 November 1940. Later Marshal of the Royal Air Force Lord Dowding.

* Later Air Marshal Sir Roderic Hill, KCB, MC, AFC, C-in-C Fighter Command from 15 November 1943 to 13 May 1945.

When the Harrises arrived in Palestine, the Arab revolt was smouldering and, in parts, becoming very active. The troubles arose from the old Arab-Jewish controversy. The Arabs, from the very beginning of the plan to create a Jewish settlement in Palestine after World War I, had been bitterly opposed to the scheme. The British task of policing this mandated area was, therefore, primarily one of keeping the Arabs from raiding, plundering and slaughtering the Jews, and to prevent retaliatory action by the Jews. The revolt was, in effect, a civil war.

With some cynicism, Harris comments: 'The rules for rebellion in Palestine appeared to me to get simpler every day. For the British Forces they amounted to the rule that you must not get rough, no matter how rough the enemy gets. If you get rougher than the enemy at any time and kill a noticeable number of his men, even in protection of your own men, then it's just too bad for you. My advice to all young commanders in all services is whenever you see any prospect of being called out in aid of a civil power, in any part of the world, get to hell out of it quickly and as far as you can! If you fail by being too soft you will be sacked; if you succeed by being tough enough, you will certainly be accused of being too tough and you may be for it. So take long leave, or get transferred, or retire and buy yourself a farm. Do anything, in fact, sooner than get involved in aid of a civil power, for there are only two things you can get for helping—brickbats or blame!'

Air control, as applied in Iraq in the 1920s and in the early 30s was not used in Palestine. Indeed, there was no question of it, since the Palestine problem at this stage was essentially a police task. The problem was insufficient police to maintain law and order, and so the Army and the Air Force had to be used extensively to assist the civil forces. Invariably the problem was to flush out trouble-makers, apprehend them and convict them where found guilty. The trouble-makers were in the habit of making raids on each other, seizing property, beating each other up and killing each other, although the activity was more from the Arabs against the Jews than vice versa—and against those who collaborated with the Jews. Then the rebels would retire to the mountain villages and take refuge there until the next raid was planned. The Police and Army relied on their own intelligence information, often obtained from the villages themselves, about intended raids or the whereabouts of rebel operators. Then, overnight, the troops would move out over the mountains, making a laborious encircling approach, surround the suspect village and make a thorough search for arms and trouble-makers. Invariably, however, the progress of the army was well announced, and when they arrived the birds had flown, together with their arms.

When Harris arrived he thought up another system, which came to be known as the 'Air-Pin'. With this method the Air Force flew out to the suspect village with just a few minutes' notice, and dropped messages saying that no one would be hurt provided they stayed put in the village, but that anyone trying to run for it would be shot. The village was then continually circled by aircraft until the army and the police arrived. As Harris says: 'The Army were then able to have breakfast before they started, and travel by daylight in buses in a civilised fashion.' Although Harris's suggestion was viewed with mild suspicion at first, it was adopted and proved to be very successful, and the army was assured of far larger hauls of rebels and arms with greater speed and less physical effort.

The General Officer Commanding Palestine and Transjordan was General Sir Robert Haining,* who had only taken over in April of that year. He, unlike many senior army officers, had a high opinion of the Royal Air Force and this in turn was reflected in the attitude of his officers. The result was that cooperation betweeen the two services, in this area, became exemplary, and a very profound mutual respect for each other rapidly developed. In fact Harris's desire to operate in cooperation with the army as much as possible, and his ideas on simplifying the army's task whenever and wherever possible, were greatly appreciated at all levels. Indeed it was Haining who gave him one of his Mentions in Despatches.

Whilst Harris was in Palestine he met Montgomery for the second time in his life. Montgomery arrived sometime after Harris and took command of a division at Haifa. Harris, who remembered him well from the time when he was on the Army Staff College course, met him at General Haining's headquarters at a meeting to discuss the military aspect of the rebellion. Harris says: 'He greeted me with his usual clipped intonation and said, "Aircraft, aircraft, this is no job for aircraft." I said, "No—and it's no job for troops either. It's a job for police, but there ain't none—or rather there aren't enough." I pointed out to him that the strength and determination of the rebels and the weakness of the police in arms and numbers demanded the use of all military resources available. But I said that if he himself did not require air assistance I should be only too pleased to allot the share we should otherwise have held for him to the other army commanders—their calls for assistance from us were by this time incessant and their appreciation of its value unqualified. But Monty picked up ideas fast—he appreciated realities quicker than most people and it didn't take more than a week or two before he was even more insistent for help than most of the others! I always pride myself that Monty, who was always only too willing to learn anything new—and he learnt at speed—got his first real understanding of air cooperation from me during his very short term of office in Palestine in 1939.'

Montgomery's tour of duty was cut short because he was taken seriously ill with a patch on his lung within months of his arrival, and he had to be invalided home. 'He was carried on to the ship on a stretcher,' Harris recalls, 'and I thought he was a goner. I remember thinking to myself, there

---

* In June 1941, Churchill appointed General Sir Robert Haining, KCB, DSO, Intendant-General, Middle East, to relieve the Army C-in-C of detailed control of rearward administrative services and supply arrangements.

goes one of the liveliest generals in the British Army, probably the best we've got.'

During Harris's tour of duty, he found many things of interest outside his service activities, although sometimes associated with them. For example, he remembers how he went to investigate the shooting up of a Jewish convoy bringing potash from the works in the Dead Sea. They had been ambushed and badly mauled at a bend in the road from Jericho to Jerusalem. 'I had my interpreter with me, a Levantine, and he told me that the ambush had occurred on the actual corner where another incident had happened more than 2,000 years ago, when the good Samaritan had rescued one of the victims of the local bandits. And, he added, the bandits had come from the selfsame village   and he pointed it out to me.'

But there was much in Jerusalem that disgusted him. 'I was repulsed, utterly repulsed, by the financial finangling in places like the Holy Sepulchre. All those greasy priests of all sorts and different denominations, all hating the sight of each other, with the Holy Sepulchre falling about their ears, running the thing like an exhibit at a fun fair. You would see a party of some type of orthodox churchmen holding a service in one part of the Sepulchre, and there would be a line drawn between that part and the next. On the side where they were holding the service it would be packed solid with people chanting, moaning and groaning away, and on the other side of the line not a soul in sight except for an awful looking brigand swinging a censer. And you could see the look in his eyes—"One foot across into our preserve and you get a wallop with this." And it really was the attitude. With candles too—the priests made you buy a candle, because all the things worth looking at were concealed in the darkest places, so you couldn't see them without a candle. But as soon as you'd seen one of the things of interest they'd take the candle away from you and put it out. Then when there was something else you wanted to see they'd sell you back the same candle again! They had to eat, granted, but it really does knock religion out of you. Palestine, of course, is just a factory of religions, and always has been. It's spilled out and spewed out religion after religion, and all variations have fought each other and cut each other's throats for centuries. I remember when we were there the Abyssinians, who had been beaten up by the Italians, couldn't pay their whack for their square yard in the Sepulchre, so they were banished to black-hair tents on the roof.'

In June 1939, Harris was promoted from Air Commodore to Air Vice-Marshal and in the latter half of July he received a personal letter from the Chief of the Air Staff, dated 7 July:

> I am writing to give you an indication of the date when you will be relinquishing your command in Palestine and Transjordan, which, it is at present intended, will be about 1st January, 1940. I am not yet able to inform you of the post which it is intended you shall subsequently assume.

This time he did not argue about his posting. In fact, he was invalided back to England shortly after receiving this letter, having been taken ill with a duodenal ulcer. He arrived home about a month before Britain's declaration of war on Germany on 3 September 1939, following Germany's invasion of Poland.

8
The calm before the storm

Harris and his wife were staying with friends in Norfolk on a convalescent holiday at the time of Neville Chamberlain's announcement over the radio at eleven o'clock on the morning of 3 September 1939.

The declaration was no shock—it was expected. It was now only a matter of time before the real strength of the German military forces would be displayed, and the form of their strategy revealed. It was only a matter of time before the Harris, Phillips, Forbes Adam predictions on the line-up of belligerents would be proven correct and their doubts about the effectiveness of France as an ally justified.

As Harris sat listening to the historic broadcast many things went through his mind. His confidence in the French was even less than it had been in 1936. He knew that France had nothing that even resembled a modern air force, and that the numbers of her first-line aircraft were far below the strength she had planned three years earlier, and that into the bargain what aircraft she had were hopelessly obsolete. He recalled his long held opinion that the French did not want to fight at any cost, and would not fight when faced with battle conditions imposed by a competent, disciplined and well equipped mechanised army such as the Germans possessed. In fact Harris was already convinced that Britain would soon find herself left on her own to face Germany and her Axis allies, and in this context he was still firmly persuaded that the only hope of a British victory, indeed of survival itself, would lie in an effective, bomber offensive.

'I knew as I sat listening to Chamberlain that the bomber offensive would only be undertaken after older methods of warfare had failed. Considering the state of France I saw no hope of successful military operations on the Continent. But it never entered my head that the Germans would succeed in crossing the Channel. What I feared was a complete stalemate, with the politicians eventually deciding to call it a day and Germany, after defeating France and the Low Countries, being left to refresh herself for the next step. I had faith in a bomber offensive, if we could build up our force before the Germans could find effective countermeasures. I was convinced that the surest way to win a war was to destroy the enemy's war potential, and all that I had seen and studied of warfare in the past led me to believe that the bomber was the predominant weapon for this task. What I wasn't sure of was the time we would be given to muster ourselves for the battle. If the war began at the tempo that we expected, I knew we would certainly run out of aircraft and crews in a matter of weeks, if not days. As I said to a good service friend of mine: "Every time you pass a lamp post take your hat off, because if war starts seriously the blame is going to be put on us and that is where we shall finish." '

But the tempo of war at its outbreak was not as expected. There was, first of all, the 'Phoney War', which lasted until first light on 10 May 1940, when the Germans launched their blitzkrieg against Belgium, Holland and France, defeating all three countries and driving the British out of France by 18 June. Had the 'Phoney War' not happened, Harris believes the Germans would have got into France without any real resistance and would have caught the British on the hop, and it would have been the end of the war. Hitler could then have turned against Russia, unhampered by any front in the west and with no threat from Britain from across the Channel. 'Why we had that long pause I will never understand,' comments Harris. 'Of course, he may have had more in the shop window than he had behind, but he had a damned sight more behind than anyone else, and a hell of a lot in the shop window!'

So, completely unexpectedly, Britain was given that vital breathing space which preserved her admirals, generals and air marshals from hanging from the nearest lamp post. The breathing space became the time for preparation, first to survive the Battle of Britain, and then to fight, initially alone, the Battle of Germany.

When Chamberlain's speech on the radio was over, the convalescing Harris got up and went straight to the telephone. With some difficulty, because all telephone lines to the Air Ministry were engaged, he managed by invoking the magic word priority, backed by his rank, to get through to Air Marshal Portal, who was Air Member for Personnel. When they were connected Harris simply told him that he was now out of the hands of the service doctors and that he wanted a job, preferably in Bomber Command, whose Commander-in-Chief was then Ludlow-Hewitt. A few days later Portal telephoned Harris to tell him that Ludlow-Hewitt wanted a Group Commander for No 5 Group and was enthusiastic at the idea of having Harris. So, ulcer and all, Harris left with his wife to take up his new post at the headquarters in Grantham.

The Harrises' new home was a pleasant old place by the name of Elm House, which the Air Ministry had rented for the Air Officer Commanding. It had an ornate entrance in a narrow lane and, as Harris describes it, a magnificent view across the lane to the back of a cinema displaying two large notices, 'Ladies' and 'Gents', and a regular evening queue for both conveniences, with the 'Gents' entrance also disgorging its clients too often defying that well worn injunction: 'Please adjust your dress before leaving.' Harris presumed that the Air Ministry's choice of residence was again due to obtaining a bargain because of the outlook. However, the Air Ministry later relented, and a new residence was acquired, a very comfortable house by the name of Norman Lees, which was on the Great North Road just outside Grantham. But even this gave Harris and his wife a good laugh, for they were told shortly after they moved into occupation that it had once been notorious as one of the really fancy *maisons de rendezvous* on the Great North Road.

Elm House, however, has one very special memory for Arthur and Jill Harris. On 13 October 1939, a month after they had moved into their new home, their daughter Jacqueline was born.

When Harris took command of No 5 Group, Bomber Command consisted of a front line force of thirty-three squadrons comprising 480 aircraft, a figure pitifully below the figure of 990 first line bombers, backed by 200 per cent reserves, which had been planned in 1936/37 when he was DD Plans and Air Staff member on the Joint Planning Sub-Committee of the Chiefs of Staff. In the last month of peace the strength had been fifty-five squadrons, but on the outbreak of war Ludlow-Hewitt had wisely withdrawn twenty-two squadrons from the front line to cover initial war wastage and to provide for the urgent needs of operational training. Ten of the remaining thirty-three operational squadrons were immediately despatched to France to form the Advanced Air Striking Force. These were equipped with the totally obsolescent single-engined Fairey Battle, which was slow, ill-defended and so short-ranged that it was quite incapable of bombing Germany from bases in England, with its puny bomb load of 1,000 lbs. The twenty-three squadrons left in England were, however, equipped with rather better material, six being armed with the twin-engined Bristol Blenheims and the remainder with twin-engined Wellingtons, Whitleys and Hampdens, all slower than the Blenheims but all capable of carrying a much greater bomb load to a greater range.

As France had failed, even more miserably than Harris had pessimistically predicted in 1936/37, to attain her much vaunted first line strength of 2,000 aircraft, of which 775 were to be bombers, Britain was clearly going to be out on a limb. In fact, by September 1939 the French had no bombers worth mentioning; indeed, their Air Force was disastrously inadequate. The Germans, however, had a medium range offensive force of some 1,500* bombers, which was fully capable of reaching all vital targets in

---

* Erhard Milch, in his speech of 6 October 1943, said: 'When the Air Force [Luftwaffe] entered this war it was the second great war in which the Air Force was also at the front. The question of what the Air Force would contribute in this war, and what could be expected, was so different compared with the experience in the 1914/18 war that one can say that the Air Force entered this war for the first time as a force factor of equal standing with the Army and the Navy. If I may compare front line strength at the beginning of this war and now, we had at the beginning of the war a total of 4,208 planes at the front ...' This figure of Milch's is considerably in excess of the Harris 1936 estimate of 2,500 first line aircraft backed by 100 per cent reserves. It is clear, however, that Germany reduced reserves and put more into the front line. The medium range offensive force of 1,500 bombers is correct—the German Air Force had, in addition, a vast number of close support aircraft operating with the Army, as well as a considerable escort fighter force.

Holland, Belgium and Northern France and, when operating from bases in Holland, Belgium and Northern France, was within striking distance of London, the south coast of England and the Midlands.

It was this situation that made Harris admit that in the course of his lifetime he had rarely been so depressed.

But the miracle happened. Germany did not attack Belgium, Holland and France, and she did not hurl an aerial blitzkrieg at Britain immediately war was declared. Instead, there was a peaceful movement of the British Expeditionary Force to France in the autumn of 1939, together with its supporting air contingents, and some attempted bombing of German warships at sea and at Wilhelmshaven, and a great deal of leaflet dropping which went by the comic code name of 'Nickelling'. All this without any counter move by the enemy, except to shoot down a number of British planes.

Then in April 1940, Germany invaded Norway and Denmark. On 10 May she opened the blitzkrieg against the Lowlands and France, and the war began in earnest.

Those months of phoney war proved vital to Bomber Command and they were well utilized, more particularly, perhaps, by Harris than by any other group commander. Within days of taking over command of 5 Group he had made a detailed study of his crews, his aircraft and their equipment and the quality of his staff. As a practical airman, he quickly assessed the capabilities of the Handley Page Hampden, with which his Group was armed, and equally quickly he was aware of its shortcomings which he placed into two categories, those which were fundamental and could not be cured, and those which could be remedied, or at least alleviated by modification. On 23 September he wrote his first letter to his C-in-C, Ludlow-Hewitt. It began 'Herewith a digest of matters which will be of interest to you,' and continued with a survey of problems, covering items such as windscreens, cockpit heating, draught in rear gunner's cockpit, armour plating, bomb doors, navigator's compasses, aircraft fittings, bombs, operational speeds and an extensive run-down on personnel. It was comprehensive in that it covered what needed to be done to improve the aircraft, what was being done and what more he planned to do. It was written in the technical fashion of the practical airman, because Harris knew he was sending it to a practical airman who would understand what he was talking about.

Then, on 2 October, he wrote on the subject of the Hampden's rear armament, which consisted of a single K gun, a light machine-gun with ammunition fed from a drum. 'I spent some time yesterday at Hemswell on the range going into the question of K gun and armament troubles,' he reported.

> ... I don't want to be depressing, but I am really quite amazed at the apparent lack of any serious consideration of the rear armament problem as applied to the Hampden. The K gun in its present form on the

Hampden seems to be hopeless. Here are some of the more obvious shortcomings:

(i)   It is a single-handed gun, held by three fingers and a thumb!

(ii)   The top mounting in the Hampden is so gimcrack that there is no hope of getting a steady shot from it.

(iii) The gun gives no indication of the number of rounds left in the magazine.

(iv) The only indication that the drum is empty is when the gun refuses to fire after being repeatedly re-cocked.

(v)   The drums must be wound to the proper tension, yet no means is provided for telling if they are so wound.

(vi) The draught discomfort and oil leakage round the gun positions gravely handicap accurate shooting.

The above considerations alone are quite sufficient to militate against successful defence ... With regard to the lack of any indication of the number of rounds left in the magazine, we learnt in the last war that it was fatal to be caught with nearly empty belts and drums. At my instigation—I made the first one myself—the Vickers guns were eventually fitted with a round counter. With a high rate of fire and lack of provision for showing or seeing what is left in the drum, the gunner in any long drawn-out action must repeatedly be caught at a critical moment of attack with inadequate ammunition ...

Harris finished this letter with a recommendation to double up the K guns in both the top and bottom rear positions and undertake certain modifications to improve handling. But this was in order to produce a speedy palliative to inadequate defence of this bomber against the fighter. His longer term recommendation was to fit rear gun turrets to all bomber aircraft.

It was only a short while after this letter, which Ludlow-Hewitt acted upon promptly, that Harris learnt that consideration was being given to the deletion of the rear turret in the Halifax, one of the four-engined bombers for which he, with Saundby, had set down the specifications when he was at Air Ministry in 1936. The four-engined types were not expected to be available before the beginning of 1942, but Harris was determined that they should be properly equipped for operations when they did arrive on the scene. He therefore immediately took this matter up with Ludlow-Hewitt, writing on 31 January 1940:

I am horrified to note in the minutes of a DOR [Directorate of Operational Requirements] meeting that the Mark II Halifax is to have no tail turret. For years I fought a lone battle for the tail turret and its justification is proved to the hilt by the Wellington's prowess. At night it is normally impossible to see in time a fighter approaching from astern from any position except the tail turret; the gunner's eyes in midship turret are irresistibly attracted into near focus by the empennage and he literally cannot keep them focused out into 'nothingness' astern.

Ludlow-Hewitt, however, had not missed the threat to turrets and had already ensured that the tail turrets were sacrosanct to all the new types which were due to come into service in the near future.

But Harris's vigilance at this time was of the utmost importance to the success of those bombing operations which later in the war were to bring Germany to her knees. In these early months he concentrated on criticising, improving and revolutionising every aspect of the bomber and its application to modern warfare, and he was backed wholeheartedly by Ludlow-Hewitt. Harris covered everything: improved gun alignment, armour plating for crew protection, bombsights and size of bombs, navigational aids and a mass of other items. He also showed great concern for his crews and his men, and pressed for the provision of proper amenities. He was relentless in attacking peacetime bureaucratic practices which were useless in wartime and yet were being foisted upon operational units with precedence over operational requirements. On the subject of auditors, he wrote a scathing letter to Air Vice-Marshal F. J. Linnell,* who was the Air Officer Administration (A O A) at Headquarters Bomber Command. It was dated 11 December 1939 and in it he said:

I was amazed to find auditors still prowling around operational stations. Unreal as this war is, surely this is the most astounding unreality of all . . . Without Station Staffs, Squadron and Flight Commanders working day and night in a sometimes almost despairing effort to compete with operational requirements, the presence of auditors, and the keeping up of the system which requires them, is really too fantastic. I suggest that if we are to persevere in so unreal an appreciation of the urgencies of our situation, then auditing staffs should be put into uniform and sent permanently to the Stations with the idea of themselves looking after and being responsible for the materials and expenditure which they now purport to check and supervise . . . Some of our crews are shortly going to die because their Flight Commander or Flight Sergeant or other essential personnel were distracted from their work by the necessity of discovering and proving to the auditors what has happened to 1·750 of a pennyworth of cat's meat by-product from the Corporals' Mess—or some such inanity! . . . I found the Officer Commanding Finningley running around trying to pacify the auditors on a matter of whether the Army or R A F should pay for the occasional use of a Ford Ten van for running Army Guards out to dispersal points! God help us!

Harris's complaint received sympathy from Linnell and something was promptly done.

Probably the most important action Harris took as A O C 5 Group was, however, the setting up of a comprehensive training organisation for

* Air Vice-Marshal F. J. Linnell, OBE, Air Officer Administration Headquarters Bomber Command until 4 February 1941, when he became Assistant Chief of the Air Staff (Technical Requirements) at the Air Ministry. On 5 June 1941, as Air Marshal F. J. Linnell, CB, OBE, he became Controller of Research and Development.

aircrews, which was to become the blueprint for the later Bomber Command Operational Training Units (OTUs) and Heavy Conversion Units (HCUs). With his fetish for training, which stemmed from his early night flying experience in the RFC and his development of No 45 Squadron in Iraq from a troop carrier to the first real day and night bomber squadron of the Royal Air Force, this action was predictable. On 17 January 1940 he wrote to Ludlow-Hewitt:

> I am ever more profoundly impressed with the hopeless failure of our training organisation to turn out operational crews, or anything remotely resembling them.
>
> There is not so much a gulf as an abyss between the product of the training side and the article required, ready for use, by the operational side. So here is yet another thing which has got to be achieved before we shall get essentials. As usual, it apparently has to be done by the operational squadrons ...

His main criticism was that after teaching pilots to fly, and other categories that formed an air crew to perform their basic functions, the training organisation neglected to instruct crews, as a unit, in the performance of their duties under simulated operational conditions. He therefore proposed to start his own Group training organisation at Finningley, one of the stations under his command.

Harris described how he intended to proceed. After procuring the necessary ground equipment, he planned to produce a complete scenario of procedure for pilots, navigators, air gunners, and W/T (wireless) operators, and, with the aid of schoolmaster-type instructors, to put all the incoming crews through their own particular procedures under realistic conditions on the ground, with 'like-as-life' material, first as individuals, and then as complete crews. He emphasised that they would be put through this training over and over again, until they were really proficient in their duties and thus had some hope of being able to perform as a team in the air under the stress of operational conditions.

He then went on to explain that he was pirating three dummy fuselages, to represent a formation on operations, and that each fuselage was being broken apart—nose, middle and tail—for instructional convenience. Each part was to be manned by full crews, except that the pilot of the formation leader's aircraft would occupy the Link Trainer.* All the intercommunication, navigational, wireless and other equipment used on operations would be made to operate realistically, so that the crews could be sent off on a synthetic two-hour—or more—operational flight. Blind take-offs and landings would be included and special situations created such as icing conditions, tactical problems, aircraft and ship recognition problems,

---

* This was a synthetic pilot's trainer which mechanically simulated flying conditions, responding to the pupil's use of the controls as an aircraft would respond. It was an American invention.

emergency landings, etcetera. Accurate courses would have to be steered and navigators would have their information fed to them at the tempo normally experienced in operational flying, including the bombing run-up, bomb aiming and release of bombs. Similarly the wireless operators and gunners would have to perform their tasks, the gunners even getting surprise attacks from model German fighters.

Harris wrote: 'The individuals, and finally the whole crews, will be put through this "hoop" time and time again, ad nauseam if necessary, until they are procedure perfect.'

On the following day, he again wrote to Ludlow-Hewitt suggesting that the brains of the cine-photography industry and its trick cameramen should be co-opted to develop operational training material that would simulate the flying and associated operational conditions visually, in order to make the synthetic training truly realistic. 'The Pilot or Gunner,' he wrote,

> would be seated in a fuselage in a hangar, or some such similar suitable building. He would have all the normal equipment and controls realistically to hand as in the actual aircraft. A cinema film would be projected on to a screen showing the complete development of an attack by an enemy aircraft. Attached to the pupil's guns would be a second cinema projector arranged so as to superimpose on the film the flight of tracer from his guns. The pupil's gun sights would also be harmonised with a dual control set of sights in front of the Instructor, who could then follow exactly what the pupil was doing and explain and correct his errors.

He went on to suggest, in some detail, similar uses of cine film to teach practical navigation with more realism.

Ludlow-Hewitt backed the scheme to the hilt and Harris was given every bit of support that the C-in-C was able to raise to ensure that the synthetic crew training programme prospered as fast as possible. Air Commodore W. F. MacNeece-Foster who was commanding No 6 Group,* which was at that time the operational training group for Bomber Command which Ludlow-Hewitt had set up at the outbreak of war, was immediately advised to make contact with Harris to view the work of Finningley. By coincidence, Group Captain R. A. Cochrane had joined No 6 Group as Station Commander of RAF Abingdon, which was also the headquarters of the Group as well as being one of the flying training centres. At the time of the birth of the Finningley enterprise he was just taking over as Senior Air Staff Officer (SASO) of the Group and as such it was he who was deputed to look into the Harris scheme. Thus one of Harris's 1922–24 flight commanders in No 45 Squadron, Iraq, was once more to become associated with him in an endeavour to train crews for bombing operations; this time, however, on a much vaster scale and, with the modernisation of aircraft and

---

* In 1942 No 6 Group became an operational Group for the Canadian Air Force and was renamed No 6 Group Royal Canadian Air Force.

their associated equipment emanating from the passing of the years, in far greater technical detail.

Harris kept Ludlow-Hewitt informed of progress with the Finningley crew training plans which he had nicknamed the 'Allez! Allez!' scheme after the principles of the pre-war French Ecole de Guerre. Due to the C-in-C's keen interest, visits to Finningley were made not only by MacNeece-Foster and Cochrane, but also by the Director of Training from the Air Ministry, Air Marshal E. L. Gossage the Inspector-General, and various other persons who were interested in crew training techniques for other commands of the Royal Air Force. Ludlow-Hewitt, the C-in-C, came himself at the beginning of March, a visit which had an amusing sequel. Unintentionally, he left Harris with the impression that Cochrane might be leaving No 6 Group in the near future. Harris, never one to look 'a gift horse in the mouth,' was quick to react. He immediately wrote to Ludlow-Hewitt on 5 March 1940:

> You made a remark at Finningley the other day which gave me the impression that owing to a conflict of personalities in No 6 Group, Cochrane might be going spare. If this is indeed the case I hope you will let me have him. I regard him as an outstanding executive for the purpose of getting the practical details of the synthetic training going with the greatest possible despatch and on the most practical and useful lines. He holds, furthermore, in common with me, some revolutionary ideas in regard to getting more work, and less useless paper maintenance, out of the men and aircraft which we possess. These, also, I should like to put into practice with his assistance.

Ludlow-Hewitt replied to this letter on 11 March. He told Harris that Cochrane was doing very well where he was and was proving most useful in this post. He then added: 'Isolated radicals are most valuable people, but if you get too many of them together they become dangerous!! And so I think perhaps for the moment things are better as they are.'

But if Harris was thwarted at this stage, he had his own way two and a half years later when he was himself C-in-C, Bomber Command, and gained Cochrane as one of his group commanders.

At this period of the war there was very little real bombing, as the Government was not at all anxious to commence a Blitz and thereby encourage swift retaliation from the Germans. The Air Staff were just as reluctant, but for a different reason. They knew that Bomber Command had neither enough aircraft nor an adequate supply of operationally trained crews to sustain a strategic offensive—and this was known best of all by Ludlow-Hewitt and Harris. From the political viewpoint, however, the British Cabinet were anxious that the RAF be seen to be operating with impunity against the enemy and so leaflet dropping became of major importance, although it was looked upon as a complete waste of time by Bomber Command itself. 'Nickelling', as it was called, whilst of doubtful value as propaganda warfare, did, however, provide some training for the crews under operational conditions. Harris was far from impressed by the propaganda claims. 'It was nonsensical, absolutely nonsensical,' he derides. 'I always said that the only thing leaflet raids would achieve would be to supply Germany with toilet paper for the rest of the war! You couldn't propaganda to a nation like Germany that was enthusiastic over its mounting victories and which thought it was getting its own back after its defeat in the First World War.'

Whilst Harris was bitterly opposed to leaflet dropping, he was in favour of some kind of operation which would develop operational skills, after training, under warlike conditions. He therefore concentrated his attention on an earlier idea of his which had been born in the middle of 1936: the employment of aircraft for dropping sea mines, in particular magnetic mines. Pressurising Ludlow-Hewitt, who needed no pressure anyway, and the Air Ministry, he soon had everything working for him. On this occasion there was no Admiralty opposition and HMS *Vernon*, the Admiralty weapons research centre, quickly turned out a selection of mines, continually designing variations in fusing to defeat the enemy's anti-mining efforts. With poetic justice it was found that the Hampden was the most suitable aircraft for laying these early mines, and so No 5 Group landed the major part of the mining operations for itself at this time. Almost immediately Harris introduced the code name of 'Gardening' for these operations, areas mined being identified by names of flowers and the mines being known as 'vegetables'.

Harris expresses his feelings about this activity by saying: 'It was a godsend to me that mining suddenly cropped up like this, because I realised that there was something that one could really do towards getting on with the war and at the same time build up the crews' operational experience. And, of course, the crews felt they were doing something really useful and this helped morale enormously.'

From reports, Harris realised that the Group's mining efforts were having a considerable effect on German shipping even in the early stages. This precipitated a letter from him to HQ Bomber Command, pressing for increased supplies of mines, permission for him to allocate more aircraft effort, and a far sighted recommendation to study the soundings round Italian naval bases with a view to prompt aerial mining should Italy enter the war on the side of Germany. This letter was dated 29 April 1940. In it he reported that despite the disappointing lack of information from the Intelligence resources of the services, in particular from the Admiralty, information had been received from other reliable sources that considerable success had attended the initial mining operations of No 5 Group. The Danish State Railways, for instance, had announced the withdrawal of three of their train ferries in the Belt, owing to damage by explosion, and there were reports that the Germans had been suffering losses in the Little Belt and the Great Belt. These were amongst the areas where mines had been sown. He also drew attention to British United Press reports from Malmo in Sweden, that a merchant ship, believed to have been German, had sunk after an explosion on the Danish side of Oresund, north of Dregden lighthouse, this making the 'fifth shipwreck by explosion in the same neighbourhood to be seen during the past three days from the Swedish coast.' Pointing out the difficulty of getting any information out of German occupied territory, Harris reasoned from these results that comparable success had probably been achieved in the remaining six areas in German waters where mines had been planted. He also drew attention to the fact that results had been achieved from only 110 mines planted in a period of fourteen days, and said that the planting of 1,000 or more should produce 'really decisive results'. 'Strategically,' he said, 'it seems apparent that this method can be quickly developed to an extent where its effects should greatly exceed those of naval action in more open waters,' but he argued that it was essential to press home the present advantage while the enemy still lacked protective measures. This demanded a greatly increased production of mines. He finished his letter by writing:

> Finally I would express my complete confidence that with six Hampden squadrons, including one long-range squadron for the Eastern Baltic, and an adequate supply of these weapons, given reasonable weather conditions we could close all the ports that Germany is using for her overseas ventures, and keep them closed in a manner which will either defeat these ventures or cause her most tremendous losses in an effort to continue.

By 4 May, the Admiralty were so impressed with the early results of Harris's minelaying efforts that even Their Lordships were constrained to put pen to paper and request the Air Ministry to '... express to the Air Officer Commanding No 5 Group their appreciation of the Group's excellent work and accurate planning ...'

Just prior to these successes, Harris was to experience a great disappointment. It was the posting of Ludlow-Hewitt from C-in-C Bomber Command to become an Inspector-General of the Royal Air Force, an appointment that was close to being a polite way of retiring a very senior officer. Harris was genuinely shocked, for he regarded Ludlow-Hewitt as perhaps the most capable commander that the RAF possessed at that time, and one of the only ones who had maintained his capabilities as a pilot and kept abreast of modern techniques. 'The reason they put him "on the beach" was because of his insistence on the formation of the Operational Training Units and ploughing back into training so much that was in the shop window, thereby necessarily depriving the front line of aircraft and crews. This irritated less knowledgeable authorities. But my God, without this policy of Ludlow's the dog would have eaten its own tail to hurting point within a few weeks, and would have been a dead dog, beyond all hope of recovery, within a few months. Ludlow-Hewitt saved the situation—and the war—at his own expense. He did it, as he does all things, with good grace and without thinking of himself or his career.'

Ludlow-Hewitt in fact acted energetically and effectively as an

Inspector-General, and during the rest of the war had a vital influence on design, production, development and organisation. But before he left Bomber Command he demonstrated his high opinion of Harris in a personal letter, dated 2 April 1940, which he wrote to him in his own handwriting:

My Dear Harris,

I enclose a farewell letter which you can use as you think best. I was very glad to get you back into The Command, and I have followed with great interest your successful efforts to increase the strength of the Hampden. The new and enterprising scheme which you have started at Finningley for synthetic air training will, I am sure, do for crews what you have already done for the aircraft.

I am of course dreadfully sorry to relinquish The Command, but I know I leave it in very good hands. I have known my successor for 25 years and have the very highest opinion of his great ability and exceptional qualities of leadership.

My best wishes to you

Yours Sincerely

E. R. Ludlow-Hewitt.

Ludlow-Hewitt's successor was Air Marshal C. F. A. Portal.*

---

* Air Marshal C. F. A. Portal, CB, DSO, DFC, who, since February 1939, had been Air Member for Personnel on the Air Council, took up his appointment as C-in-C Bomber Command on 3 April 1940. At the beginning of August 1940 he received the KCB and became Sir Charles Portal. On 25 October 1940, as Air Chief Marshal Sir Charles Portal, he was appointed Chief of the Air Staff.

9

The Portal–Harris axis

Harris first met Portal at Worthy Down, when he was commanding No 58 Squadron. Portal at this time was commanding No 7 Squadron, which had originally been located at Bircham Newton. Like 58 Squadron, 7 Squadron was equipped with Virginias and concentrated on night flying. As has been previously mentioned, Saundby was one of Harris's flight commanders, having followed him home from 45 Squadron in Mesopotamia. Another coincidence was the fact that at that time Cochrane was Training Staff Officer at Wessex Bombing Area. 'When the two famous squadron commanders, Peter Portal and Bert Harris, were at Worthy Down night flying Virginias, I was training officer at Command Headquarters, so I had a fair amount to do with them,' Cochrane says.

Harris and Portal kept in touch with each other after Worthy Down, although they never served closely together again until after the outbreak of war. They had a short contact with each other in 1934 when Harris took over from Portal the appointment of D D Plans.* Cochrane, who had been Portal's number two at Plans, speaks of this period with some bitterness, but with unstinting praise for both Portal and Harris. 'At that time,' he told the author, 'one was writing papers and trying hard to propagate new ideas which were totally opposed by the accepted ideas of the other two services. There were no points of agreement that I can really think of between the other two services and the Air Force—everything was in dispute. Even the very existence of the Air Force was in dispute, with both the other two services ganging up to try to divide it between them. Anyone who was head of Plans at the time was in the forefront of that battle—they couldn't help but be—and it was entirely due to the skill and intelligence of Portal and Harris that the Royal Air Force survived.'

But now, on 3 April 1940, Harris was serving under Portal, and a close

---

* Portal was on the Air Staff from 15 December 1930 until 12 January 1934. He was promoted to Group Captain on 1 July 1931, and made head of Plans Division. Group Captain Harris was posted to the Directorate of Operations and Intelligence on 11 August 1933, as Deputy Director. In April 1934 the Directorate of Operations and Intelligence was divided into three Deputy Directorates: Operations and Intelligence, Plans, and Operational Requirements. Harris was appointed Deputy Director Plans. He therefore effectively took over from Portal.

knit relationship was soon to develop which was to last throughout the war—a relationship which had tremendous strength and was to prove to be of paramount importance.

With the complete defeat of the British Expeditionary Force in France in June 1940, and its evacuation from the Continent back to England minus its arms and equipment, Britain stood very much alone with only the Royal Air Force and Navy left to defend it from invasion. Harris felt at the time that if the Germans had really persevered they could have invaded successfully, particularly if they had followed the retreating British across the Channel immediately after Dunkirk. But he was also of the view that the Germans had made the fundamental mistake of putting their faith in the medium bomber, which would carry a crew of two or three only and a good bomb load, but which sacrificed all defence in the interests of speed, in the belief that it could outpace the fighter. The result was that they had no rear turret defence whatsoever, and as Harris points out: 'They miscalculated their speeds in relation to our fighters, because the Hurricanes and Spitfires were faster and with their devastating fire-power—eight guns, for which we largely have to thank Sandy [Saundby]—the Germans had no chance. Escort fighters certainly helped the Hun, but escorting is always a chancy business. Once the escort is engaged, the bomber force quickly loses contact and is then attacked by other formations of defending fighters. The Yankees discovered this, but at least the Yankee bomber was well armed and could fight back. No, the more I saw of the failure of Germany in 1940 to beat us, because of their air losses, the more convinced I was of the efficacy of the night bomber, well armed with a four-gun tail turret, preferably armed with 0·5 guns.'

The question of whether the Germans could have continued the Battle of Britain beyond September 1940 is a moot point, but it is interesting to note a comment made to the author by General Johannes Steinhoff, then at NATO, who was a fighter pilot in the German Air Force and commanded a squadron of escort fighters in the Battle of Britain. He says that by the middle of September 1940 the strain of continuous operations had become so intense, and this, with the high loss rate, had reduced morale so badly that the German fighters had reached the end of their tether. The same apparently applied to the bomber crews.

With the fall of France and the beginning of the Battle of Britain the role of Bomber Command changed radically. Leaflet dropping ceased and the bomber forces were first employed on attacking communications and enemy troop and armoured concentrations until after the evacuation of France. Then came the anti-invasion tasks with emphasis upon the destruction of the invasion barges, troops and military supplies assembling in the Channel ports ready for the final attack on Britain, which went by the German code name 'Sealion'. Bomber Command's anti-invasion operations were wholly successful, and on 17 September Hitler postponed 'Sealion' indefinitely. On 12 October he postponed it until the spring of 1941, but in fact it went into cold storage, never to be seen or heard of again.

During this time Harris's 5 Group was involved in all these activities, as well as in the somewhat abortive attacks on strategic targets in Germany, which he knew to be a failure because of the complete absence of adequate navigational aids and target finding devices, and because of the ridiculously small bombs available for attack. But one task he was able to maintain successfully was sea mining, and this he extended with further success to the Baltic. His views on the size and type of bomb required in the future were also formulating, although at this period his mind was more upon the destruction of ships in shallow water docks and the destruction of harbour installations. He was triggered off in his thinking by an intelligence report which intimated that the Germans were developing bombs up to about 4,000 pounds in weight. He immediately wrote to Portal on 6 July 1940 pressing for a similar development for Bomber Command, but proposed that the bomb should consist of a light cased canister containing some 2,000 pounds of explosive. His idea was that these could be used with a slight delay action fuse to sink or damage shipping in the Bauhafen at Wilhelmshaven and other basins, docks and shallow water anchorages. Another use of this weapon could also be for the destruction of aqueducts and canal embankments. Portal immediately supported the proposal, and out of this there came, ultimately, the 4,000-lb and 8,000-lb 'blockbusters' that Harris was to use later with such devastating effect.

Harris, looking well ahead of his own nose—and one also wonders whether he had some extraordinary perception of his future as Commander-in-Chief of Bomber Command—took an active interest not only in bigger and better bombs, but also in the aircraft of the future which were to carry them and in the possibilities of equipment which might be developed to enable crews to drop the bomb loads on the right place. No 5 Group was scheduled to replace its Hampdens with the four-engined Handley Page Halifax, and certain squadrons were due to re-equip with the long range twin-engined Avro Manchester. These, with the Short Stirling, were the heavy bombers for which the specifications had been laid down at the end of 1936 when Harris was DD Plans. The Manchester was the most advanced in development in 1940 and the first prototype of this aircraft was initially reported upon on 2 September 1940, after preliminary trials at the Aircraft and Armament Experimental Establishment, Boscombe Down. Harris immediately went down to see the Manchester for himself. This visit provoked him to write a somewhat caustic semi-official letter to Linnell on 10 September 1940, in which he severely criticised many points of design. He wrote:

I have just been looking over the Manchester. The machine I saw was one of the prototypes and is therefore deficient of a good many military requirements. I hear, however, that the first twenty are going to be short of all sorts of things and that the usual no-modification ban has been laid on by Beaverbrook. As matters stand at present, the first twenty can never be used for operations (otherwise than for the purpose of throwing away crews!) and urgent steps must be taken to put right the short-comings. In other words, if the aircraft is required purely for production advertisement it can no doubt remain as it is, but if it is required for operations the following things *have got to be done*.

He then proceeded to criticise the heating arrangements, the navigator's lack of view vertically downwards, the lack of flame damper exhaust pipes which would certainly make the aircraft easily discernible to fighter aircraft and anti-aircraft defences at night, and the lack of anti-balloon gear. Of the parachute exits, bomb aimer's view and rear turret he wrote:

> Parachute Exits. Generally speaking these are not big enough. It is time that the Air Ministry Department concerned realised that in order to make a fully satisfactory exit from an aeroplane it is advisable to take your parachute with you.
>
> Bomb-Aimer's View. For some reason best known to themselves they have almost entirely obstructed the Bomb-Aimer's compartment with an enormous cushioned sofa or ottoman. This will be fine if the machine is parked and used for petting parties, but it is quite useless for operations. The whole of this peculiar piece of upholstery and the cartridge collector box on which it is mounted must go. The empties from the front turret will have to be collected in collector bags, or alternatively disposed of down a re-designed chute. The Bomb-Aimer can then be given a small hassock or a swinging seat which will normally be out of his way. The Bomb-Aimer's view is quite inadequate for night work and this can easily be, and must be, put right by additional perspex between the existing Bomb-Aimer's window and the front edge of the escape hatch.
>
> Rear Turret. The view from the rear turret is quite inadequate for night work; this can easily be put right by replacing the existing metal cheek pieces with perspex cheek pieces.

He finished by telling Linnell that he had discussed all the points with Rowarth of Boscombe Down who would be pushing them along from his end, but in view of the Beaverbrook embargo on modifications strong pressure would be required from Bomber Command.

With regard to armament for the Manchester Harris took the matter even further by writing to Air Vice-Marshal A. W. Tedder,* who was the Director General of Research and Development at the Ministry of Aircraft Production. In this letter, he displayed his conviction that any real bomber offensive would be undertaken almost entirely by night. He wrote:

> I am not at all happy about the armament proposed for the Manchester.
> I understand she is to have some sort of beam guns fitted in lieu of the dustbin turret, and also that there is going to be some arrangement of

---

* Later as Air Chief Marshal Sir Arthur Tedder GCB, he was Deputy Supreme Commander of Allied Forces to General Eisenhower. After the war he became Chief of the Air Staff and was promoted to the rank of Marshal of the Royal Air Force. He was created a Baron in the Victory Honours List in January 1946.

bottom guns with a periscope sight. Any such sight is useless in the dark. At present she has a tail turret out of which nobody could possibly see anything in the dark and not much in daylight.

I think everybody is agreed that the métier of the heavy bomber is night bombing, and that any idea of using them by daylight is now a 'busted flush', even amongst those who were not seized of this childishly obvious fact before the war started. It is therefore essential that all heavy bomber armament should be orientated towards night defence ...

In fact, the Avro Manchester itself turned out to be a 'busted flush' and was dropped before it saw any real service. Whilst this was rather a disaster at the time, it turned into a blessing. Its failure was due to the fact that its two engines were unable to produce sufficient power to meet its operational requirements. A series of crashes due to engine failure and inability of the aircraft to maintain height on one engine, in addition to numerous other mechanical failures, soon gave the aircraft a bad name. But the basic problem was recognised at an early stage to be insufficient power from the two Rolls-Royce Vulture engines. By some redesign and the fitting of four Rolls-Royce Merlin engines, a type which had already been well proven in Spitfires and Hurricanes, Avro created a metamorphosis that became known as the Lancaster, the four-engined heavy bomber which proved to be the greatest and most effective of the war.

In *The Strategic Air Offensive against Germany 1939–1945*, the authors comment on the subject of the Manchester by saying: 'Bomber Command would have been ultimately stronger if the Manchester had never been produced.' Harris holds an entirely different view. As will be seen later, he had every reason to despair at the performance of the Stirling and Halifax four-engined bombers with which, from 1942 to 1945, he would have had to fight the war. A dismal prospect without the Lancaster. In fact, it was the Lancaster that became the predominant bomber of the war because of its vastly superior performance in range, height, speed and bomb carrying capacity. As Harris says, if there had been no Manchester to fail, Bomber Command would never have had the Lancaster.

Harris's efforts to make the Manchester a really efficient night bomber were not wasted, because his ideas were included in the Lancaster. But more than that, they applied equally to the Stirling and Halifax, which therefore also benefited from his vast practical flying knowledge and his aggressive determination to create, ultimately, an immensely powerful strategic bomber force. His attention to the defence armament of the bomber, which started with the Hampden, created a remarkable direct liaison between No 5 Group and Rose Brothers of Gainsborough, a well-known design and manufacturing company of sweet, chocolate, tea and tobacco packaging machinery. This liaison, which was encouraged by Linnell, resulted not only in the rapid development and production of satisfactory gun mountings for the Hampden, which were urgently required, but also of an electrically driven mounting. Then later in the war, through Harris's clandestine association with Rose's, the famous 0·5-inch gun turrets were developed and produced by this company. The association with the company was begun by Harris and one of his station commanders, Group Captain E. A. B. Rice, who later, as Air Vice-Marshal Rice, AOC No 1 Group, when Harris was C-in-C, cooperated with Rose Brothers in the design of the 0·5 turret with which all the Lancaster aircraft of his Group were ultimately equipped.

Harris's constant pressure for the effective equipment and proper performance of the new four-engined bombers resulted in an important decision by the Ministry of Aircraft Production at this time. It appointed Sir Robert Renwick,* with a roving commission to coordinate the modifications required on the new bombers, to clear up teething troubles and to progress production. Harris was apprised of this fact in a letter from Linnell dated 7 November 1940.

Whilst he fought hard for the bomber of the future, Harris never for a moment lost sight of the necessity for continued extension of, and improvement in, the operational training of crews. Throughout his period of command of No 5 Group he maintained a close liaison with Cochrane, who had been promoted to Air Commodore and appointed AOC No 7 (OTU) Group, and between them aircrew drills were developed, handling manuals prepared and training syllabuses drawn up. The correspondence between them was frequent throughout the second half of 1940, and it covered every conceivable angle of operational training, including many that would have been overlooked by any other very senior officer with less practical experience of flying. Unquestionably, Harris's influence on training at this time was fundamental to the excellence of the product from the Operational Training Units in the years to follow. He overlooked nothing. He even wrote to Cochrane on the subject of when and where not to abandon an aircraft. He enjoined him to incorporate in the OTU instruction the question of making crews parachute-minded, emphasising that there were far too many cases of invaluable and irreplaceable crews being killed under circumstances where the captain should have parachuted them, even if he himself remained in the aircraft and attempted to land it. He said he regarded it as an unforgivable stupidity to kill crews by attempting to pull off landings in bad weather, when those crews could have safely parachuted over this country.

It should be impressed on pilots, [he wrote] that they themselves, as trained pilots, are of far more value to the community than either the

---

* Sir Robert Renwick, Bt, formerly Chairman of the London County Electric Supply Company was brought into the Air Ministry and Ministry of Aircraft Production by Lord Beaverbrook, the then Minister of Aircraft Production. Later he became the Controller of Communications, Air Ministry, and the Controller of Communications Equipment, Ministry of Aircraft Production. He had overall responsibility for the development and production of all radar systems and equipment, both ground and airborne. Later Lord Renwick of Coombe, KBE, he died in September 1973.

aircraft itself or even those civilians who, in a million to one chance, may be killed by the aircraft if it came down by itself. In my opinion no pilot should attempt a landing unless there is a 75 per cent chance of his getting away with it, and he should not keep his crew on board unless in his opinion there is a 99 per cent chance of getting away with it. I suppose that the Command as a whole must have lost at least 100 complete crews quite mistakenly under such circumstances, and what could we not do with an extra 100 crews now!

If Harris had his serious problems, and God knows they were legion at this time, he never lost his tremendous sense of humour. This was well evidenced by a small minor incident. The Air Ministry in those days produced a weekly bulletin which gave as much information as it could on the progress of the war for consumption by all ranks at Commands, Groups and Stations. In Bulletin No 54 a reference was made to a suggestion put forward by some dear old lady for the use of bees to help repel any attempted invasion. Naturally, the suggestion was ridiculed. But Harris was quick to spring to the defence with an amusing letter dated 16 October 1940. He wrote to the Editor:

With reference to Bulletin No 54. You must not mock the lady who made the suggestion about the bees. At the battle of Tanga, Tanganyika, in 1915, our Expeditionary Force had achieved a highly successful landing and had almost broken the German resistance. At that juncture Von Lettow-Vorbeck himself arrived on a push bicycle, rallied together a few machine-gunners and the conventional bunch of orderlies, cooks and clerks, and restarted the battle. For some time the final issue was further delayed, but at no time was the situation apprehended by our command to be other than that the landing was successfully completed bar a little mopping up. In that country, and particularly round that part of the coast, the natives are in the habit of hanging up their home-made bee-hives, consisting of short lengths of hollow log, in large numbers in the trees in the bush. There are enormous numbers of these bee-hives. The fire from Von Lettow's machine-guns, designedly or not, smashed hundreds of these hives. The infuriated bees set upon our advanced troops and completely routed them. This gave Von Lettow-Vorbeck time and opportunity to organise a counter-attack with his ridiculous force, with the result that our entire expedition was driven into the sea.*
It was long before a second expedition could be organised and by then the enemy, who at Tanga had been on the verge of unconditional surrender, had raised large native levies and prepared themselves for resistance to the bitter end. And for us a bitter end it was indeed. The intervention of those bees cost us £150,000,000, 250,000 casualties and three years of war in East Africa. So now apologise to the lady who made

---

* The African bee is very poisonous and can be lethal in multiple attack. In military circles, the battle of Tanga is still referred to as the 'Battle of the Bees'.

the suggestion at which you so smugly mock. Have her posted to Air Staff against the apprehended invasion. Meanwhile, we are collecting bees; and not in our bonnets.

On 5 October 1940, Air Marshal Sir Richard Peirse* was appointed C-in-C Bomber Command, and Portal was posted to the Air Ministry to take over from Sir Cyril Newall as Chief of the Air Staff, with effect from 25 October. Before Portal left Bomber Command he visited Harris at No 5 Group Headquarters at Grantham and told him of his impending appointment. He also told him that he was in despair about Britain's prospects as he, like Harris, was convinced that defeat of Germany, as the only alternative to submission to Germany, was dependent upon carrying a bomber offensive right into the heart of the enemy's homeland. But the priority so far given to Bomber Command was so pathetically low that any hopes of an effective offensive against Germany seemed desperately remote. He congratulated Harris on his mining efforts, the cogent action he had taken to make his present and future aircraft war-worthy and his successful endeavours to train crews up to a proper operational standard, and he said he had contributed more than most to the war effort. Then he added that the job of Chief of the Air Staff was going to be a pretty tough row to hoe and he was trying to get together a good team—and he might want Harris as Deputy Chief of the Air Staff.

On 14 November 1940, Portal wrote a personal letter in his own handwriting from the Air Ministry, to the effect that he would probably want him there in the very near future, possibly in a week or two. An official letter from the Air Ministry, four days later, advised Harris that he had been selected by the Air Council to succeed Air Marshal W. S. Douglas† as Deputy Chief of the Air Staff, and that this appointment would take effect on or about 22 November. In fact, he took over this appointment on 25 November.

*Air Marshal Sir Richard Peirse, KCB, DSO, AFC.
† Air Marshal Sholto Douglas, who became Marshal of the RAF Lord Douglas of Kirtleside, KCB, MC, DFC (1893–1969), was appointed C-in-C Fighter Command, replacing Air Chief Marshal Sir Hugh Dowding on 25 November 1940.

10
DCAS

Harris's spell of duty at the Air Ministry as DCAS was shortlived but eventful. Whilst the very nature of his appointment demanded that he should take an interest in all aspects of the Royal Air Force, and therefore consider the requirements and operational plans of Fighter Command, Coastal Command, Army Cooperation Command and a number of smaller units which were verging on private air forces, it was the future of Bomber Command that most exercised his mind. Indeed, the sudden revelation of the priorities which were being accorded to almost every other Command and specialised unit of doubtful parentage, a state of affairs which he had long suspected but not to the degree which he discovered, enabled him to take more action on Bomber Command's behalf than might otherwise have been possible.

His four principal objectives were the training of crews for operations and the retention of these crews in Bomber Command; the development of bigger and more powerful bombs associated with new types of explosives; the speedy progression of the four-engined bombers and their associated armament and navigational equipment; and the development of the strategic bombing of Germany as opposed to the frittering away of effort on peripheral and largely unimportant targets.

His aim was to enable Bomber Command to grow. Whilst lip-service had been paid to its growth and use, it had in fact become the larder for the Admiralty, the Army and organisations such as the Ministry of Economic Warfare to raid in order to supply them with their never ending demands for bomber aircraft and trained crews for purposes which were defensive, instead of offensive, and for the most part contributing little to the main objective—winning the war. Whilst Bomber Command was being forced to divert much of its abysmally small strength to help the Navy against the U-boat and Focke-Wulfe menace to Britain's shipping, Coastal Command, which should have been using its aircraft for this very purpose, was sallying forth to bomb targets such as the Philips factory at Eindhoven—which they did with a complete lack of success. At Harris's behest, these incidents promptly received a rebuff from Portal as CAS.

At no time, however, did Harris underestimate the dangers of a blockade of Britain by the successful German application of her U-boat and Focke-

Wulf Kondor anti-shipping forces. In fact, in a minute to the CAS dated 2 February 1941, on the subject of a Joint Intelligence Sub-Committee Report on the possibility of a German invasion, he wrote:

In the Summary of Conclusions it is stated that Germany's 'only hope of obtaining victory this year is by successful invasion of this country.'

I do not agree with this, and I consider that within the next few months, and certainly before the end of this year, we shall encounter a vast and perhaps vital increase in the extent and effectiveness of air or other attack against shipping. I am convinced that Germany's plan to win the war against us is, as it always has been in my estimation, to blockade these isles with every weapon and resource at her disposal and to bomb us fortissimo crescendo. So far she has only been playing at it, and the construction of large numbers of simplified submarines, the gaining of open sea ports on the coasts of Europe and the Mediterranean, the collusion with Japan for the operation of raiders, and the chances of obtaining something almost approaching naval superiority if she could make proper use of the Italian and French Fleets and finally bring in the Japanese Fleet, are all indications, in my view, as to the broad trend of German strategy. Furthermore, the operations of the Focke-Wulf aircraft have indicated to her the promise and utility of the air weapon at long range for attacking trade, and I have no doubt whatsoever that this will be fully exploited together with the other means referred to above.

Where Harris differed with the Admiralty on the matter of protection of shipping was in the method. He was convinced that patrolling the North-West Approaches and other sea lanes with bomber aircraft, in the hopes of sighting a submarine and attacking it, was a complete waste of time and effort. By studying statistics of the Whitley aircraft of No 502 Squadron over a period of six months from October 1940 to March 1941, he found that on 144 sorties only six submarines had been sighted, four attacked with claims of one or possibly two sunk, for the loss of eleven aircraft and twenty-nine personnel. In the same period there was only one—and that inconclusive—report of a Focke-Wulf sighting. Taking into account the hours flown, he deduced that it had taken 250 flying hours per submarine sighting. In a note to the CAS, giving him these figures, he said:

It all boils down to this—are we going Navy fashion to disperse our entire resources attempting to cope defensively with the problem at its outer fringes—an immense area—or are we going Air War fashion to concentrate upon attacking the kernel of the problem at the centre? There is no possible comparison in effectiveness as between the two methods and, furthermore, if we adopt the first how the Boche will laugh! 20 Submarines and a dozen Focke-Wulfs providing complete anti-aircraft defence for the whole of Germany!

Harris pressed all the time for the proper use of Bomber Command, whether it was to assist the Navy, the Army or to undertake the strategic bombing targets not directly associated with the activities of the other two services—although all strategic targets, as he persistently preached, were essentially associated with the German war effort and therefore their destruction must inevitably contribute towards the success of the operations of the Navy and the Army. He was convinced that sea mining from aircraft around the ports in the occupied zones, direct bombing attacks on dockyards, ports and Focke-Wulf bases and, above all, bombing of industrial areas and the factories involved in the production of submarine parts and their assembly, were the best methods of defeating a blockade. In No 5 Group he had already proved the efficacy of sea mining, even if on a limited scale, and he pressed for its extension as the major weapon against the enemy's naval and mercantile shipping. It is ironical that Harris should have been denigrated by so much naval top brass for his lack of cooperation, when he was, in fact, the man who proposed the use of bomber aircraft for dropping sea mines long before the war and suggested the development of the magnetic mine—and then proceeded to apply his ideas so energetically in No 5 Group and later as C-in-C Bomber Command. Indeed, the Navy should be indebted to him for not falling for their own outdated ideas on warfare.

Trying to build up a bomber force of the size that could take substantial offensive action against Germany was, as Harris recalls, a heartbreaking task. If it was not calls for bomber squadrons to be allocated for the North-West Approaches, or squadrons to be put at the disposal of the C-in-C of the Mediterranean Fleet, the Ministry of Economic Warfare would produce some obscure reason why they should have a squadron or two of bomber aircraft complete with fully trained operational crews to undertake their private Secret Intelligence Service work, the value of which was more than doubtful.

On 26 April 1941 Harris reported to the CAS on the strength of Bomber Command, following a discussion with him on the small effort that the Command was able to put into the air at night. He revealed a staggering state of affairs. The eight Blenheim squadrons of the Command and one flight of Hampden aircraft were being employed on day work, leaving the Command with '... approximately 90 Wellingtons, 50–60 Hampdens and 50–60 Whitleys. 120 sorties is therefore about 50 per cent of his [the C-in-C's] available effort during the dark period wherein he works on the basis of one night on and two nights off.' He went on to report that the few Manchester twin-engined and Halifax four-engined bombers that had been delivered were grounded because of various technical troubles and of the thirty Stirling aircraft, seldom more than two or three were serviceable at any one time due to electrical problems. Referring to the Stirling problems he wrote:

Everything possible is being done to cure it, but Sir Robert Renwick informs me that the super electrical engineers whom he has lent from his organisation* to investigate the trouble sum it up by saying that the electrical equipment in the Stirling should be a power engineering job ... They are taking interim measures to try to improve upon the existing system, but a very complete redesign will apparently be necessary in the future.

As early as December 1940 he drew the attention of the Vice-Chief of the Air Staff, Sir Wilfrid Freeman,† to the poor level of bomber production. On 8 December 1940 he stated that he was unable to discover any policy in regard to the proportion of bombers to fighters in the Air Ministry's production plans. He reminded the VCAS that ever since the last war, and until the commencement of the present, the official policy had been to achieve a proportion of one-third fighters to two-thirds bombers. 'Within a year of war breaking out,' he wrote, 'we appear to have almost precisely reversed this proportion. We appear also to have reached the position where our fighter production, if not excessive, is at any rate apparently adequate, while the comparative bomber production seems to be going steadily from bad to worse.' To emphasise the lack of support being given to the build up of the bomber force he referred to the recent tabling of requirements by the Ministry of Aircraft Production for the proposal of a joint production plan in America. It called for 2,250 fighters against 250 heavy bombers per month, with the intention of pressing for an additional 1,750 fighters and 250 heavy bombers per month making a total of 4,000 fighters and 500 bombers. He suggested that this was ample evidence of a lack of adequate direction in the Air Ministry and Ministry of Aircraft Production in regard to the proportion of fighters to bombers. He finished with his not unusual asperity: 'As the bomber is the only weapon which can win the war—though almost all others could lose it—it would seem to deserve priority, rather than the apparent disregard with which it seems to meet at present.'

In January 1941 the bomber did receive some priority, in that the Prime Minister agreed to the expansion of Bomber Command and this resulted in a review of priorities for aircraft production and an increase in operational training facilities to provide adequate crews for the expansion. It also provided the CAS with a whip to beat off the constant demands from the Navy and Army to make further inroads into the already sadly depleted bomber force. Even so, it remained a long hard struggle to build up Bomber Command.

One problem in connection with the increases in Bomber Command was to find sufficient new squadron and flight commanders. The C-in-C requested postings of senior officer personnel from sources outside the

---

* Sir Robert Renwick frequently loaned experts from his company, the County of London Electric Supply Company, to assist in trouble-shooting production problems. It was a service which the Nation obtained free of charge—as, indeed, it did in the case of Sir Robert's personal services.

† ACM Sir Wilfrid Freeman, KCB, DSO, MC, a member of the Air Council.

Command to fill these appointments, an action which Harris immediately challenged. He had already experienced in No 5 Group the shortcomings of the senior officer, who had had no experience of flying on bomber operations, being expected to command successfully an operational squadron that was full of highly experienced battle trained crews. He considered it too much to expect some old 'war-horse' who had been 'sitting on his tail in an office' for many years suddenly to have to skip through an OTU course, take command of a squadron and proceed on operations. He suggested that the very senior Air Force officers were in danger of employing the wrong type of commanders of squadrons because, 'they imagine that anybody below the age of 25 ought still to be sucking a comforter and to be capable of no proper share in the command of our fighting units.' He deplored this attitude and asserted that squadron commanders must be weaned in battle and capable of exercising leadership and maintaining respect by the example of their own success on operations. He put these views to the CAS on 26 January 1941, and concluded by saying:

> I would assert most strongly that our best Squadron and Flight Commanders today will be found from amongst the youngsters who themselves have done the job, and that was indeed my experience in No 5 Group.
> Furthermore, there are few, if any, of the type of officer C-in-C Bomber Command wishes posted for these purposes available in the Service.
> I therefore suggest his requirements cannot be met for the following reasons:
> (a)   It is inadvisable.
> (b)   It isn't necessary.
> (c)   There ain't no such animal.
> (d)   Bomber Command alone possesses the material from which the Commanders can be found, and they have plenty, especially from their second run captains—Flight Lieutenants and Squadron Leaders—who should not, however, be called upon to do still more operational flying.

At the same time he wrote to the C-in-C Bomber Command saying that it was seldom that he found himself in opposition to his views. On the contrary, he explained, 'I spend most of my time fighting the battle of the bombers in support of your requirements. Consequently, when I find myself in opposition, I like to inform you of the contrary views which I put forward. I am therefore sending to you personally a copy of my minute to CAS on the subject of your letter ...'

During his battle of the bombers and their crews, Harris never lost sight of the need for more powerful bombs. Within a few days of his arrival at the Air Ministry he was pressing the Directorate of Operational Requirements on the question of bomb design, thereby following up on his earlier proposal from No 5 Group for a light cased canister with some 2,000 pounds of explosive, which had been inspired by the report he had read on the German development of 4,000-pound bombs. By November 1940, Britain, in particular London and the Midlands, had experienced the devastation created by the German land-mines and big demolition bombs, when the night Blitz was in full swing. At the end of November Harris pointed out to the DOR that the success of the German approach to bombing indicated that the Air Ministry needed to review its policy on bomb and fuse design and to investigate by what improvements the bomber force could be assured of having the most effective weapons at its disposal. He drew attention to the fact that there were two principal methods for affecting industrial production by bombing: one by destroying plant and machinery by hits with heavy cased fragmentation bombs, requiring a high degree of bombing accuracy, and the other by dislocating and delaying production by damage to structures, windows, roofs, essential services, etc, by the effects of blast from light cased bombs, with a vast weight of explosives, requiring a lower degree of bombing accuracy. His contention was that the second choice, which had been adopted by the Germans against Britain in their night offensive, and which they had combined with incendiary bombs to devastating effect, was the only viable course to take once it was accepted that the bomber offensive must, of necessity, take place in the night hours. This condition he had long since accepted. In a minute to the DOR, dated 28 November, in which he set out the two approaches to bombing, he wrote that the Germans with their higher charge/weight ratio, lighter cased bombs, were achieving their results by the second method, and that this was proving far more destructive in its effects on production than the first. He pointed out that there had been much more disruption to production by structural damage and the interruptions to utility services than by direct destruction of plant and products. In this direction, the near misses of the German bombs, through the cratering of roads, coupled with the effects of blast and flying debris, had proved as disastrous as the direct hits. 'With the less accurate results we must expect by night bombing,' he said, 'and in the face of increasing defences, this aspect of near misses becomes one of first importance and we are becoming increasingly convinced that the essential services, particularly electricity and gas, are the things to go for.' He added that he thought the reports from abroad about the ineffectiveness of our attacks arose from 'the limited and localised effect of our bombs.'

He then called for a meeting of the Bombing Committee to be held on 2 or 3 December to discuss the matter.

In the meantime, however, some action had been taken on his 6 July letter from No 5 Group, and when the Bombing Committee meeting endorsed his views action became swift. On 19 December, Marshal of the RAF Sir John Salmond, an Inspector-General, telephoned Harris to tell him that he urgently wanted to get on with the production of the 4,000- and 2,000-pound blast bombs, which had by then undergone detonation trials satisfactorily. The Director of Armament Production was, however, not prepared to authorise production until the bombs had undergone operational trials on an enemy target. Harris promptly wrote to the Vice-Chief of the Air Staff, Freeman, on the same day, recommending that the Director of Armament Production be instructed to proceed with production immediately, without waiting for operational trials, with an initial order for 250 of each of the 4,000- and 2,000-pound bombs, aiming at a monthly output of fifty of each. The V C A S approved the action and Harris advised the D Arm P and Sir John Salmond accordingly. At the end of May 1941 the first 4,000-pound bomb was used against Emden.

But if Harris had at last got the big blast bombs under way, he did not neglect the general purpose bombs which were designed with heavy casing and relied on fragmentation to destroy their targets. These now ranged from 500 to 1,900 pounds, and he visualised them as being even bigger in the future. But his approach to this problem led him to consider whether the most rewarding avenue of investigation and subsequent development might perhaps be in research for new types of explosives. On 23 February he wrote to Sir Henry Tizard,* the Scientific Adviser to the Air Ministry, saying that he thought a likely source of technical surprise should be sought in the development and production of an explosive of much greater efficiency than those then in use. It was his opinion that this was an area in which the enemy was more than likely exercising his ingenuity in the hopes of springing a surprise on Britain. He went on to state that according to his information all experiment on explosives was within the province of Woolwich Arsenal, and if this was the case he was uneasy. 'I once went over Woolwich with a Staff College tour and gained an impression that, except for the costumes, we had stepped back into the Crimean period.' Assuming that I C I and similar firms experimented along their own lines in explosives for commercial purposes, he asked whether the Air Force had any organisation for co-opting the best explosive experts and chemists in the country on research into more efficient explosives. 'This is butting into your business,' he concluded, 'but then you are always butting into mine—and I like it.'

In Tizard's absence, Air Commodore Huskinson, an expert on his staff, replied that no outside specialists were being co-opted. He went further. He advised Harris that there was in fact a new and much better explosive, giving 15 to 20 per cent greater power than T N T, which was, at that stage, the best available. Moreover, this new explosive, which went by the name of R D X, had satisfactorily passed handling and filling tests for all types of bombs. But the snag was that it was only being produced in penny-packet quantities by the Ministry of Supply because they were pushing for adoption of another explosive called Pentalite. In Huskinson's opinion—and apparently in Tizard's—this was not as good as R D X. On receiving

---

* Sir Henry Tizard, K C B, A F C, F R S, member of the Air Council from June 1941 onwards.

this information Harris minuted the CAS on 25 February 1941, explaining the situation and recommending that the Air Staff should put pressure on the Ministry of Supply, demanding an increase in the supply of RDX to meet the requirements of the RAF, and strongly recommending the employment of the best brains in the country on the future development of explosives.

Harris's intense and detailed interest in the bomber, its defence armament, and its weapons of destruction was largely stimulated at this time by the operational experience of No 5 Group, when he was its AOC, and by the German Blitz. Probably the most frequent figure to be seen on the roof of the Air Ministry at King Charles Street, Whitehall, in the midst of an enemy raid, was that of Harris. There he would observe, with great regularity, the effects of blast bombs, heavy fragmentation bombs and incendiaries. There he would note the effects of the mixture of the three. There he would consider how much more successfully the Germans could create destruction if they could only accomplish greater concentration in time and space and if they paid more attention to the mixtures of high explosives and incendiaries to achieve greater conflagrations. If the Germans were having a modicum of success in destroying British cities and in burning out the heart of London, in which they nearly succeeded on the night of 10 May 1941, they were also helping to guide the hand of retribution that was to strike them so disastrously in the future.

Bomber Command's efforts against Germany had not been entirely without success during this period. Indeed, it is often forgotten that whilst Fighter Command so skilfully and courageously defeated the German daylight attacks on Britain in 1940, they were quite unable to contend with the German night bombing until airborne RDF (radar) began to assist them in April of 1941. Therefore their contribution towards stemming an invasion became largely sterile from October 1940 onwards. Bomber Command, however, played a notable part in completely upsetting the German invasion plans from the time of the fall of France until they were abandoned by Hitler in the middle of 1941, when he suddenly chose to move eastwards against Russia on 22 June. The anti-invasion activities were not the Command's only success. Its contribution to the defeat of the blockade of Britain was a major one, with its impressive attacks on German and occupied Channel ports and its virtually exclusive role in laying sea mines. But whilst the enemy's seaboard towns were attacked with average success, there was mounting evidence that the raids into Germany itself were a failure. The efforts against south-west Germany between May 1940 and May 1941, including the Ruhr, were in the main wasted, with 49 per cent of the bombs falling in open countryside, and much of the remainder, although dropping on built-up areas, doing so in a very scattered pattern, and completely missing the selected aiming points. Inaccurate navigation, inevitably followed by inaccurate bombing, was to blame, and by the middle of 1941 the problem began to be realised by the Air Staff. The truth was that the crews were being expected to perform miracles without the proper tools. And it was Harris and Saundby who recognised the problem long before anyone else, except for a few farsighted scientists at the Telecommunications Research Establishment, who had utilised radio pulse techniques to detect aircraft from the ground. In RDF, later to be renamed radar by the Americans, scientists such as R. J. Dippy, P. I. Dee, A. C. B. Lovell, A. H. Reeves and F. E. Jones* saw the possibilities of producing apparatus to guide the bomber accurately in the night, without the necessity for seeing the ground or the stars, and to release its bombs so that they would fall within the target area with a relatively high degree of accuracy. These ideas were already well advanced in 1940, even though there had been no real indication from the Air Staff of an imperative need for them.

The first member of the Air Staff to recognise the need for greatly improved navigational aids was Saundby, who was Assistant Chief of the Air Staff (Technical) from 22 April 1940 until 21 November 1940, when he was posted to Bomber Command as Senior Air Staff Officer to the C-in-C, Sir Richard Peirse. Prior to his appointment as ACAS(T) he had been Director of Operational Requirements from 28 December 1938. The liaison between Harris and Saundby, stemming from their long-standing friendship, was remarkably close when Harris was at No 5 Group and Saundby was at the Air Ministry. It continued when the positions were more or less reversed and Harris became DCAS and Saundby went to Headquarters Bomber Command. But prior to his move to Bomber Command, Saundby had, amongst other matters, made himself very aware of what was going on at the Telecommunications Research Establishment and what the possibilities were for improving the navigational and bombing aids for the bomber far beyond those available.†

From Bomber Command Saundby pressed with vigour for the requirements of the bomber to be met as a matter of great urgency, thereby strengthening Harris's hand at the Air Ministry. The great bomber team of the future was, in fact, developing. However, the bomber offensive was to remain a very puny effort throughout 1941 for, despite the Prime

---

* R. J. Dippy developed the navigational aid known as Gee. Dr P. I. Dee, later Professor P. I. Dee, CBE, FRS, Professor of Natural Philosophy at Glasgow University, was in charge of centimetric development and application, which included the blind bombing device known as H2S. Dr A. C. B. Lovell, later Professor Sir Bernard Lovell, OBE, FRS, Director of Jodrell Bank, was responsible for the development of H2S under Dee. A. H. Reeves headed the development of the ground controlled bombing device known as Oboe, and Dr F. E. Jones, MBE, FRS, was principally responsible for the development of Oboe.

† Saundby was briefed on these matters by the author, who was posted from flying duties to the Air Ministry Directorate of Operational requirements in October 1940, with responsibility for developing requirements for radio and RDF aids to flying, in particular for the bomber. In December 1941 the author was posted to Headquarters Bomber Command as the first RDF Staff Officer to the Command, then known as Wing Commander RDF.

Minister's priority for Bomber Command in February 1941, a delay set in when Churchill, under pressure from the Admiralty who were obsessed by the danger to Britain's sea communications, issued a directive on 6 March giving absolute priority to the Battle of the Atlantic. Bomber Command was again plundered, and seventeen squadrons consisting of 204 long-range aircraft with crews were diverted for duties with Coastal Command. Whilst they were supposed to be on loan, they in fact never returned. Another blow was that all replacement crews were drawn from Bomber Command's OTUs. With the additional pirating of aircraft and crews for the Middle East, the hopes of mounting an air offensive against Germany in 1941 were damned. But the preparations for a future offensive were, on the contrary, intensified, and a more powerful and effective bomber force emerged as a result.

It was, in fact, this state of affairs that caused Harris's note of 26 April 1941 to the CAS, referred to earlier, on the subject of the pitiful numbers of aircraft available to Bomber Command for night operations.

But by the summer of 1941 the Blitz had come to an end, the Battle of the Atlantic was virtually over, and with Hitler's invasion of Russia in June the threat of an invasion of Britain had passed. As Denis Richards so aptly puts it in Volume One of the official history, *The Royal Air Force 1939–1945*: 'The German onslaught against Britain, so long and so valiantly defied, had faltered to an uneasy pause. The British onslaught against Germany, for many months to come the exclusive privilege of Bomber Command of the Royal Air Force, could at last gather momentum.'

However, right up to the commencement of Hitler's Russian folly on 22 June, the threat of invasion of Britain remained uppermost in the minds of all in Whitehall. Even the Americans were convinced it would happen, but whereas they had no doubts that Britain would be defeated, the British were equally confident that Germany would receive a bloody nose. Harris recalls a visit by General Arnold, early in 1941. 'He came round to my office,' he says, 'and we had a talk for a bit. Then I took him along to see the CAS and as we went down the long deserted passage old Happy* said to me: "You know Bert, it is extraordinary to me—you go up and down this passage and nobody appears to be moving; you go into the offices and everybody seems to be quite happy, working away quietly. Don't you people realise you've lost the war?" I said, "Good Lord no! All we realise is that we haven't started the ruddy war yet!" '

But Harris was deeply concerned about an invasion and very sceptical about the adequacy of the Army. In particular he was disturbed about the lack of effective anti-tank weapons, and this led him to address to the VCAS on 17 April a most scathing appreciation of the situation as at that date. He first of all castigated the Army for its antiquated outlook, which had resulted in its entering the war under the firm impression that the date

* General Arnold, the Commanding General of the US Army Air Forces, was known as 'Hap' Arnold.

was August 1914. He briefly—and bitterly—surveyed the disastrous actions of Sir Thomas Inskip in 1937 when, as Minister for the Coordination of Defence, he almost ensured that Britain would lose the war and certainly never win it. Finally he summed up in his typically blunt fashion:

It is not the smallest use attempting to shift the soldiers from their ways. It is too late to equip them materially, and impossible to equip them mentally, to defeat invasion. The Navy haven't sufficient ships for the purpose and won't in any case bring them near enough to do so. The civils won't release the men and material for building proper defences, because of the obviously more urgent need to employ 30,000 men, and much essential material, in building futile and fatal bomb traps, at 90 bricks per day per man, at Union rates plus war bonus, outside their own homes or favourite pubs. All this leads up to the most obvious facts with which we have ever been or could ever be faced: either the Air Force beats off the invasion and wins the war, or we as a nation lose it. Luckily Geography makes this easier, if time allows. Given time and material the process is simple, because the Boche Army, though fully equipped, is very nearly as stupid as ours. Except for the fact that their tanks won't eat hay and ours won't work, you couldn't tell one from t'other.

He went on to suggest that Bomber Command could decimate the invasion ports and concentration of barges, air mining and torpedo bombers could sink the transports, Fighter Command, Bomber Command and Training Command could deal with air attacks and attempted troop landings on the beaches or at the ports, and Coastal Command could help generally if it could be retrieved from the control of the Admiralty. But he emphasised that all Commands must be equipped with adequate weapons to wreck the enemy tanks, and trained in their use.

'The Army,' Harris wrote, 'can catch parachutists, will neglect the defence of our aerodromes and will, anyhow, be much too busy repairing their tanks and carrying out postures and gestures of real soldiering to do very much about anything. As for the Home Guard. To quote Wellington's remark to the Commanding Officer on concluding the inspection of an Irish officered regiment of Dutch mercenaries just prior to Waterloo: "Well, Sir. I know not what your troops will do to the enemy—but by God they frighten me!"' He concluded: 'You may not think so, but this appreciation is written in all seriousness. We either get on fast enough with tank-destroying aircraft to save the war, and with heavy bombers eventually to win it, or we perish. These are the facts. True and simple facts—and there is no levity about them.'

A few days later, on 21 April, Harris wrote a personal note to Professor Lindemann, Churchill's scientific adviser and great friend. In this he raised the whole question of dealing with tanks:

It appears to me that there are two problems involved where our defence against tanks is concerned. First, to produce a highly mobile weapon which can out-manoeuvre the outflanking tank. The weapon for this is, in my opinion, patently the aircraft. Bombing is too unreliable against a small and highly manoeuvrable target, which must receive a direct hit to incapacitate it. The aircraft must therefore have a gun capable of knocking out the heaviest armoured tank. Nothing short of the 40-mm cannon is likely to achieve this, and we have only three or four handmade examples. We have asked MAP to push on with further supplies—but that is for the future, not for the present emergency. However, please lend your weight to the emergency production of this essential weapon, by hand as long as necessary until production gets going—and outside of all trade union hours and restrictions.

He then suggested to Lindemann the development of some kind of grenade to be fired from a rifle, perhaps using the new explosive, RDX. He reasoned that if the Royal Engineers could clamp a pat of RDX against a steel girder with a lump of clay and a bit of board, and cut the girder like butter, why should the infantryman not have some projectile weapon to lob a pat of RDX from forty to a hundred yards at a tank. He finished by begging Lindemann to use his influence to get this problem of anti-tank weapons solved.

The invasion, as we know, never materialised, but Harris's concern with anti-tank weapons at this time led to the development of airborne weaponry for the destruction of tanks which was to prove so effective in North Africa, Italy, and on the continent of Europe after the Allied invasion of France.

At the end of April Harris learnt from Portal that it had been decided to send a mission to the USA with the object of expediting the delivery of military stores and equipment which the RAF had already ordered or was hoping to acquire from America. It was also proposed that it should establish a kind of military diplomatic liaison. Portal suggested that Harris should lead this mission. The choice was logical, since he had led the peacetime purchasing mission in 1938. Harris himself was reluctant to go because his heart was set on obtaining a command, but that still seemed out of reach. However, staying at the Air Ministry was more depressing than going to America, so he accepted.

On 13 May 1941 Air Vice-Marshal N. H. Bottomley, who had been SASO at Bomber Command from 1938 until November 1940, and the AOC No 5 Group, arrived at the Air Ministry to take over from Harris. On 21 May he completed his takeover.

At the beginning of June, Harris was promoted to the rank of Air Marshal.

11
Washington interlude

It was an unexpected stroke of luck for Harris to be permitted to take his wife and daughter with him when he went to the USA. He had not relished the idea of leaving his family in the 'battle area' whilst he proceeded to the safety of the American continent, and when Admiral Sir Charles Little, the naval member of the mission, told him the Admiralty had agreed to provide a passage for his wife and baby daughter, he was delighted.

They sailed on 3 June, from Greenock on the Clyde in HMS *Rodney*, which was leaving for Boston for a refit under 'Lease-Lend'. She had, in fact, already left for America once, but this was at the time of the sinking of HMS *Hood* by the German battleship *Bismarck* on 24 May, east of Iceland, and the subsequent pursuit of *Bismarck* by British naval and air forces. Although damaged by HMS *Prince of Wales*, *Bismarck* continued to steam southwards with the cruiser *Prinz Eugen* in search of prey. HMS *Rodney* was by then some 500 miles to the south-east, on her way to America, when she was diverted with certain other ships to join in the pursuit. After playing the major part in delivering the *coup de grâce* to *Bismarck*, *Rodney* had to return to the Clyde to refuel, and it was on her second departure for America that she played host to the heads of the Naval, Army and Air Force delegations to Washington.

The Navy, with its usual hospitality, provided the Harris family with magnificent accommodation in the 'Admiral's Flat' at the aft end of the ship. Its only discomfort was the terrific vibration which, as Harris comments, made one feel as if one was executing a perpetual clog dance. The other discomfort was the rolling of the ship which, whilst having little effect upon Harris, who was a good sailor, gave his wife a terrible time.

'Jillie,' he says, 'was the worst sailor in the world, and so I had to take on the duties of nanny and chief laundress to my eighteen-month-old daughter, Jackie. The Navy provided me with a six-foot-four marine to help me, which was much appreciated. Well, I'm not bad as a nanny, but I'm no damned good as a laundress—and there I was, confronted with those dreadful objects known as nappies. The worst cases I used to wrap up in newspaper and, because of a firmly screwed up porthole—we were on the windward side—I would sidle across to Charles Little's cabin, which was on the leeward side of the ship, and say "Nice morning, isn't it Charles?" as

I backed up to his open porthole and pushed the unwanted objects through it unbeknown to him! I remember later on telling Dalrymple-Hamilton, who commanded *Rodney*, about my problems with the nappies. I was up on the bridge with him when we were going into Halifax—our first stop. He professed to be horrified and said: "Don't you know, sir, that in wartime we're not even allowed to throw garbage overboard because submarines could follow it up!" So I said: "Well yes, I've heard that. But I've worked out that I can't see a submarine following up a string of dirty nappies in expectation of finding a first class battleship at the other end of it." '

The voyage was uneventful, and they arrived at Boston on the evening of 12 June in the dark, which proved to be the most exciting part of the journey, for there the Harris family beheld the lights and neon signs of the city shining far out to sea. After months of black-out in Britain, this was a staggering sight.

Harris spent eight months in America and established the RAF Delegation in Washington on efficient lines, quickly providing it with immensely influential contacts. Diplomatically it was no easy task, but he was greatly helped by two of his team in particular, T. D. Weldon,* better known as Harry Weldon, who in World War I had distinguished himself in the Royal Artillery and between the wars had been Dean of Magdalen College, Oxford; and George Cribbet,† an exceptionally able professional civil servant. The greatest problem was the fact that America was not in the war—she was neutral. The American service chiefs were naturally nervous of being seen too much in the company of the British service representatives. They had their eye on Congress where a lot of Congressmen had aired their avowed intentions of not letting America get into the war at any price. The same applied to civil servants. And the Congressmen were looking over their shoulders at the great American electorate, who were not only opposed to any question of active participation in the war but already regarded themselves as being reduced to great hardship because of the effects of the American Government's incredibly generous scheme of Lease-Lend,‡ which was enabling Britain to continue to procure urgent supplies for military requirements when she had virtually spent her last dollar on the original procurement basis of 'Cash and Carry'.

But there was no question of lack of help from President Roosevelt and his close confidant, Harry Hopkins. Churchill said of Hopkins: 'He was the most faithful and perfect channel of communication between the President and me. But far more than that, he was for several years the main prop and animator of Roosevelt himself. Together these two men, the one a

---

* T. D. Weldon was at this time in the civil service, which he had joined as his contribution to war service. Later he was transferred to the Royal Air Force and as a Wing Commander he became Personal Staff Officer to Harris when Harris was C-in-C Bomber Command. At the end of the war he returned to Magdalen College, Oxford.

† Later Sir George Cribbet.

‡ The Lease-Lend Bill received the President's assent on 11 March 1941.

subordinate without public office, the other commanding the mighty Republic, were capable of taking decisions of the highest consequence over the whole area of the English speaking world.' Of his first meeting with Hopkins, Churchill wrote: 'It was evident to me that here was an envoy from the President of supreme importance to our life. With gleaming eye and quiet, constrained passion he said: "The President is determined that we shall win the war together. Make no mistake about it. He has sent me here to tell you that at all costs and by all means he will carry you through, no matter what happens to him—there is nothing that he will not do so far as he has human power." Everyone who came in contact with Harry Hopkins in the long struggle will confirm what I have set down about his remarkable personality.'* And this meeting took place on 10 January 1941, a year before America came into the war.

Harris, immediately on his arrival, established contact with Roosevelt and Harry Hopkins, and with Averell Harriman, General Marshall, General Arnold and Robert Lovett.† In the case of Harry Hopkins, Harriman, Arnold and Lovett this developed into a lasting personal friendship. At this stage Harris had only met Churchill once—a year earlier when he was AOC No 5 Group—and certainly the unusually rare association he established with Hopkins and Roosevelt did not spring from any championing by Churchill. It was not until he became C-in-C of Bomber Command that the close relationship between Churchill and himself developed. Unquestionably it was Harris's dedication to the defeat of Nazi Germany and his realistic approach to achieving this end, with no illusions about the hardships that lay ahead, and his conviction that the war could only be won by offensive action which would bring the brunt of the war to bear directly on the German nation, that won their approbation and gained their confidence. Harris's determination to bring about the defeat of Germany went much further than the professional satisfaction of a general winning a great battle. He had a profound love of liberty and, with a more astute understanding of the situation than many other commanders, recognised the imminent threat that totalitarian Germany represented to democracy. It was this that appealed to Roosevelt and Harry Hopkins—in particular to Harry Hopkins, perhaps, because he too was a man of great comprehension, with a passionate hatred of tyranny, and foresaw the oppression, brutality and degradation that would engulf all of Europe, much of the rest of the world, and finally threaten the United States of America should Germany triumph over Britain, the last bastion of freedom.

According to Harris, Roosevelt and Hopkins 'leant over backwards' to help Britain and urged the US service chiefs to do the same. Indeed

---

* Volume III of *The Second World War* by Winston Churchill.

† Averell Harriman became Roosevelt's special envoy in Europe. General George C. Marshall was Chief of Staff of the US Army and after the war the author of Marshall Aid for Europe. Arnold was Chief of the Army Air Forces. Robert A. Lovett was the Assistant Secretary of War for Air.

Roosevelt, actively encouraged by Hopkins, gave more help than was strictly correct from a neutral country, and certainly more than was popular with a large section of the American population. 'I heard it on very good authority at the time,' Harris recalls, 'that once or twice Roosevelt was on the verge of being impeached for helping Britain to the extent that he did before America was in the war. I would say that he and Hopkins went perilously out of their way to help us, and if America had managed to keep out of the war, it would have been the end of their careers. But the Japs kicked them into the war with Pearl Harbor.'

Harris was a frequent visitor to the White House to see Harry Hopkins and sometimes they would take refuge in Hopkins's bedroom—once Lincoln's—to discuss the progress of the war, what must be done to win it and what further help America could give Britain. On other occasions Hopkins would join Harris and his wife for dinner, or go to the Shoreham Hotel where they lived. But there were a number of times when Roosevelt himself would summon Harris for discussions. 'On one such occasion,' Harris recalls, 'Roosevelt said to me: "Well, Marshal, is there anything else within reason that I can do to help you?" At the time we were pretty short of pilots and we were having to use quite a lot of our meagre supply of fully trained operational pilots for the purpose of ferrying aircraft from manufacturers to squadrons, even across from West Africa, eastwards to our forces in Egypt and the Middle East. So I said: "Well Mr. President, there is one thing you might be able to help us with and that's ferry pilots." and I explained our problem. Well, Roosevelt promised to speak to General Arnold.'

Roosevelt was as good as his word and the very next day Arnold telephoned Harris. 'He was a great friend of mine,' Harris relates, 'but on this occasion he pretended to be damned angry. He said: "What have you been telling the President about me? And saying you want all my pilots." So I said: "No Happy, I don't want all your pilots, because I know you haven't got any! But if you could help me out with some ferry pilots—civilian pilots—I'd be most grateful." And I explained our problem. "Well, I might be able to help," he said. Of course I knew then that he'd already done something. "Look," he went on, "I'll send someone round to see you this afternoon, but don't laugh—don't laugh." That same afternoon the door of my office opened and in burst a blonde bombshell. I sat back and blinked and said: "Well now, what can I do for you?" And she replied: "No. What can I do for you?" That knocked me back a bit! Then she added: "General Arnold sent me here." Well, of course, the penny dropped and I started to laugh, whereupon she informed me that her name was Jacqueline Cochran, she would ferry pilot for me, and she didn't see what there was to laugh at!'

Jacqueline Cochran, at that time, held many of the world's flying records and Harris immediately recognised the name. When he asked what she could fly, she replied 'Anything.' And then she asked Harris: 'How many more pilots do you want?' She told him that there were 600 to 700 women pilots in America of which about sixty could really fly. So Harris engaged her and any more women pilots she could rustle up. Jacqueline Cochran did not waste time. Within a few days, with about another dozen or so girls, she was on her way to Canada for a training course on Atlantic ferrying. The next time Harris saw her was when she called on him at Bomber Command after he took over as C-in-C. 'She was an absolutely top class pilot,' he says, 'but with America in the war we lost her and her girls to the US Army Air Force, where she became head of the USAAF WASPs.'*

One of Harris's tasks was to go round factories in the USA, chasing up deliveries of new orders and those he had placed in 1938. He also had to oversee the activities of the Civilian Flying Training Schools which had been established, with the blessing of Roosevelt and his administration, in Texas and Florida, to provide initial flying training for young British recruits for the RAF. Harris remembers that he was always being warned that the Middle Westerners were bitterly anti-British, but on the contrary he found that they were very pro-British. One of the most pro-British states of the USA he found to be Texas, the centre of much *ab initio* flying training for RAF recruits from Britain. Harris, who developed a great affection for the Texans, still talks of his first visit to Dallas with members of the mission. 'I shall never forget the police ride we were given when we were going to see an ice skating carnival at one of those vast closed rinks they have. We were treated as special guests, and roared through Dallas with screaming sirens and at least half a dozen cars accompanying us—just like a film. But the highlight of the evening came in the middle of the show when somebody announced the presence of the British party, including Marshal Harris—whereupon a spotlight switched across the darkened arena and lit up a poor old drunk who was sprawled over his seat and who looked up with glazed eyes and a sort of surprised leer. Everybody roared with laughter. Then followed a hasty apology and someone explained there'd been a bit of an error. When the spotlight was hurriedly switched onto us we were laughing our heads off.'

The appointment in America was not, however, to last for very long. Harris and his wife had arrived there ten days before Hitler's unexpected invasion of Russia on 22 June 1941. Now, on 7 December they were to be in the USA for the second surprise of the war—Japan's attack on the American Pacific Fleet at Pearl Harbor. On that same day the Japanese bombed Hong Kong and Singapore and attempted a landing on the coast of Malaya—also without any warning or declaration of war. On 8 December, Britain formally declared war on Japan, and on 11 December Germany and Italy declared war on the United States. It was a momentous time. 7 December was a Sunday, and just after the shattering news of Pearl Harbor, when the greater part of the US Pacific Fleet had been sunk in an unprecedented air attack, Henry Stimson, the US Secretary of State for War, asked Harris to see him without delay. Harris recalls the occasion

---

* The friendship between the Harris family and Jacqueline Cochran still flourishes today.

vividly. 'He was almost in tears. He said he hoped he hadn't been a hard taskmaster to me, but now wanted me to help them by forgoing as much as possible of the orders we had placed with them. Happy contacted me shortly afterwards and explained that it was against the Constitution for them to stop supplies I had ordered before the war and which were already on rail or at the docks, but Stimson was hoping I would voluntarily cancel these orders so that America could use them. The Air Ministry was very upset, but left it to me. I cancelled a lot, but by mutual agreement kept those things that were specific to our own requirements. After all, we were now in the same war. It was an incredible sight in the War Department building that day I saw Stimson. There was an absolute milling mass of people struggling through the corridors, roaring up and down, all discussing the latest news—talk about a flat spin, there never was such a spin. General Marshall swept past me waving a file and shouted "See you later." When I got to Bob Lovett's office he told me the latest news. He said he thought the Japs had sunk the whole Pacific Fleet. So I said "So what?" Then, on 10 December, the Japs sank HMS *Prince of Wales* and *Repulse* by air attack off Malaya and, again, I heard this news from Bob Lovett—and once more I said "So what?" and he said: "Gee, Bud, whenever I tell you a fleet's at the bottom of the sea, all you say is, so what?" I explained to him that this was the beginning of things, not the finish, and that things always went wrong at the beginning of a war for those who were not the aggressors, because the other guy always selected his own timing in hitting first.'

Within a few days of the Japanese intervention in the war, which had now categorically settled the line-up of the opposing forces, Winston Churchill left England for Washington with Lord Beaverbrook, the Minister of Aircraft Production, Admiral Sir Dudley Pound, the First Sea Lord, Field-Marshal Sir John Dill,* and Air Chief Marshal Sir Charles Portal, Chief of the Air Staff. They sailed on HMS *Duke of York*, disembarking at Hampton Roads and flying on to Washington to arrive on the evening of 22 December. One of the purposes of the meetings was to persuade Roosevelt and his service chiefs that the defeat of Japan would not mean the defeat of Germany, but that the defeat of Germany would make the finishing off of Japan merely a matter of time. The British fear was that the hurt pride of the American nation, resulting from the virtual destruction of their great Pacific Fleet at a single blow, would result in an overwhelming desire to get at Japan to the exclusion of all else. The British desire was to convince the Americans that the first requirement was victory in Europe and the Mediterranean, with a defensive war against Japan until Germany was defeated. In fact, Roosevelt, Hopkins, Marshall and Arnold were already in favour of this course, and only Admiral Ernest J. King, C-in-C of the US Fleet, was understandably intent upon concentrat-

---

* Field-Marshal Sir John Dill, formerly Chief of the Imperial General Staff, remained in Washington after the Churchill visit as Churchill's personal military representative with President Roosevelt.

ing on Japan. Consequently, the Washington meetings became a matter of resolving strategic issues within this broad plan of action and determining how best Allied cooperation could be achieved in order to conduct the war effort most effectively. One of the highly valuable results emerging from these meetings was the setting up of the Combined Chiefs of Staff Committee with its headquarters in Washington.

Harris attended the first conferences of this Committee, at which Churchill, Roosevelt and Hopkins were also present for some of the time. It was just after the first meeting that Portal took him aside and told him that he wanted him to come back to England to take over as Commander-in-Chief of Bomber Command. He said he proposed to speak to Churchill that night about the matter. This was in the first week in January 1942. The next day Portal told Harris that Churchill had agreed to the appointment and that he would be getting his instructions right away.

This change in Harris's fortunes came out of the blue and, whilst it is clear that Portal already had the greatest respect for his abilities and powers of command, and strongly supported his long-held views on the strategic uses of the bomber, one is left conjecturing whether Portal's hand was strengthened in making this appointment by the high regard which Roosevelt and Hopkins had for Harris.

Churchill and his party departed for England on 14 January via Bermuda, Sir John Dill remaining behind. Shortly after their departure Roosevelt announced that an eight man Combined Chiefs of Staff board had been established to direct British and American war strategy jointly. Representing America's fighting forces were Secretary of War Stimson, Army Chief of Staff General Marshall, Chief of the Army Air Corps General Arnold, Chief of Naval Operations Admiral Stark, and C-in-C of the US Fleet Admiral King. Representing Britain's armed forces were Field-Marshal Sir John Dill, Lieutenant-General Sir Colville Wemyss, Admiral Sir Charles Little and Air Marshal Arthur T. Harris. It was, in fact, this group of officers that had participated in the historic conferences between Roosevelt, Hopkins and Churchill, together with Lord Beaverbrook, Air Chief Marshal Sir Charles Portal and Admiral Sir Dudley Pound.

Harris's participation, as he then knew, was only to be for a few weeks.

A few days before Harris sailed, on 10 February, from Boston in the armed merchant cruiser *Alcantara*, an announcement in the Press commented: 'Heading homeward to England in the next few days will be Air Marshal Arthur T. Harris and Mrs Harris who have made a record number of friends since they came here last year . . .' They had, indeed; friends who were to be of the utmost importance to Britain in the struggle that lay ahead. Harris had in eight months paved the way to the incredibly close cooperation that developed between the British and US Forces as the war progressed in Europe. His close contact with Roosevelt, Hopkins and Generals Marshall and Arnold undoubtedly influenced their thinking about the conduct of the war.

General Arnold expressed his appreciation in a letter dated 4 February. It read:

My Dear Harris,

Upon the eve of your departure from the United States, I desire to express to you my appreciation and that of the United States Army Air Forces for your splendid co-operation and ever present spirit of helpfulness.

Your presence here aided materially in bringing our airplanes up to a combat standard and also in changing our organisation from one of peace time training to one of preparation for war.

In the name of the Army Air Forces I wish you God speed and good luck.

Very sincerely yours,
H. H. Arnold
Lieutenant-General,
Chief of the Army Air Forces, USA

Now the die was cast. Harris was on his way home to prove his theories and, in revolutionising air strategy, to assist materially in bringing about the total defeat of Germany.

12
Bomber Command prior to 1942

The Prime Minister's directive of 6 March 1941, which gave absolute priority to the Battle of the Atlantic, remained in force until July of that year, and during that period more than half the total bombing effort was directed against naval targets. Even before the March directive the effort against naval targets was considerable, with increased demands by the Admiralty for minelaying, requests for the bombing of the German cruiser *Hipper* at Brest and of the Focke-Wulf bases at Bordeaux and Stavanger. On top of this came the requirement to delay the completion of *Tirpitz*, under construction at Wilhelmshaven, which resulted in more than 400 sorties being despatched against this target in January and February 1941—a relatively small effort compared to the size of bomber raids from the middle of 1942 onwards but, taken in conjunction with the other Admiralty demands and the small size of the total force at that time, representing a considerable proportion of the effort available. Finally, it was decided to divert the Blenheim force in Bomber Command to coastal duties in the North Sea, so that Coastal Command could be strengthened in the North-West Approaches. Effectively, therefore, the Prime Minister's March directive was a reinforcement of what had been going on since the beginning of the year.

Some of the weight of the attack under this new priority did, however, fall upon Germany, but instead of the Ruhr, Berlin, or the various oil targets which had theoretically taken precedence, the weight of the offensive was directed against Hamburg, Bremen, Kiel and Wilhelmshaven, which were major ports with dockyards and naval construction facilities. At the same time the Channel ports on the enemy occupied coast came constantly under attack, with Brest receiving the lion's share after *Hipper* was joined there by *Scharnhorst* and *Gneisenau*, two more of Germany's fast modern battle-cruisers that were posing a serious threat to Britain's convoy routes.

The bombing of the North German ports had some success and was unquestionably more profitable than the 1,161 sorties carried out against *Scharnhorst* and *Gneisenau* in Brest over a period of eight weeks from the middle of January. Moreover this bombing was certainly far more successful than the raids deep into Germany. Indeed, evidence was already accumulating to suggest that inland targets were not being found and bombs were being dropped on the open countryside or, at best, in scattered pattern in the built-up areas of the towns where the main target was located. In fact, it was evident by the middle of 1941 that the policy of night bombing, which had by *force majeure* to be adopted because of the strength of the German defences, was only successful in moonlight and against targets easily identifiable by the presence of large stretches of water or relatively adjacent coast-line. The truth was that the existing methods of navigation and navigational equipment were totally inadequate for operating over blacked-out territory in adverse weather conditions, when the ground was obscured by cloud or when poor visibility denied sight of the stars for astro-navigation, or even in clear conditions when there was no moon to illuminate identifiable landmarks. This ineffectiveness of the bomber was not fully recognised, however, until the immediate crisis of the Battle of the Atlantic passed, and the attention of Germany was suddenly directed towards Russia with Hitler's invasion of his erstwhile ally on 22 June 1941.

It was on 9 July that a new directive was sent to Sir Richard Peirse, the then C-in-C of Bomber Command, by the Air Staff, advising him that a comprehensive review had been made of Germany's political, economic and military situation, which had revealed that the weakest points in the enemy's armour lay in the morale of the civilian population and in his inland transportation system, the latter weakness arising from the very considerable extension of his military activities due to his recently launched Russian escapade. The directive then stated: 'I am to request that you will direct the main effort of the bomber force, until further instructions, towards dislocating the German transportation system and to destroying the morale of the civil population as a whole, and of the industrial workers in particular.' The directive was signed by Air Vice-Marshal N. H. Bottomley for the Air Staff. It went on to list the targets selected for attack and to indicate the priorities. It is interesting to note that Bottomley had previously been the Senior Air Staff Officer at Bomber Command, had then taken over as AOC No 5 Group when Harris went to the Air Ministry, and had finally replaced Harris as DCAS when Harris was promoted to the rank of Air Marshal and sent to the USA in June of that year.

It was this new directive, which turned the Bomber Force onto targets deep in Germany, that began to reveal the inability of the bomber to undertake precision bombing by night. Worse still, it was soon to become apparent that Bomber Command was incapable of area bombing with any degree of real success. Inaccurate navigation was the primary cause, closely followed by inaccurate bombing when the target was, on rare occasions, correctly located. But even if these two problems could be resolved, the total bombing effort available was dismally small, aircraft and crews having been diverted to Coastal Command, the Middle East, and the OTUs.

The Air Staff was anxious to build up a force of 4,000 heavy bombers, the number estimated as being that required to maintain a large enough strategic offensive against Germany to bring about its defeat within a year. Even with every possible priority such a force was inconceivable before 1943/44 at the earliest. The lack of success of the bombing effort against Germany throughout the remainder of 1941, however, caused the Government to be reluctant to commit itself to so big a concentration of effort upon one means of winning the war. Even the survival of Bomber Command was now in question, despite the fact that there lay in this force the only means of carrying the war into the heart of Germany for a long time to come, thereby giving some help to our new Russian allies, and providing time for the Navy and Army to recover from their disastrous losses in 1940 and 1941.

Recognition of Bomber Command's problems was essential, and in some quarters the process had begun. A revolutionary device known as Gee, which would enable the navigator of an aircraft to determine his exact position with a high degree of accuracy, easily and quickly, had reached a stage when it was ready for operational trials. The system had originally been developed as an aid to landing an aircraft 'blind', but its greater potential had been rapidly recognised by the scientists developing the system, led by R. J. Dippy. It was simple in theory and ingenious in application, requiring no transmission from the aircraft which would give away its position to the enemy. The system consisted of three radio stations on the ground situated as widely apart as possible, transmitting pulse signals simultaneously. The middle station was known as the master and the other two as the slaves, and the signals from the slaves were synchronised to that of the master. The Gee apparatus in the aircraft received these signals, measured the difference in time of receipt between each slave and the master and thereby determined the difference in its distance from the master and the one slave and from the master and the other slave. This in effect meant that the aircraft lay on a line of constant path difference between the master and one slave and on another between the master and the other slave, and the point of intersection of these two lines was its exact position. Special charts had been designed with many lines of constant path difference drawn upon them so that they looked as if they were covered with a lattice network. Upon these charts the readings from the instrument could be readily plotted. The system could also be used in reverse by setting up the readings on the aircraft instrument of the point to which the aircraft wished to fly and then homing to that point by following the guiding indications on the instrument. The system had one drawback. Its range from the ground stations—and therefore the shores of England—was limited to approximately 350/400 miles. But this brought the Ruhr and many parts of Western Germany within range.

Gee was not the only revolutionary blind navigating device under development at the Telecommunications Research Establishment at this time. There were systems suitable for both navigation and relatively accurate blind bombing, if not actual precision bombing, which were in their early days of conception and development. But by April 1941 Gee was sufficiently far advanced for its installation to be planned into Wellington aircraft for Bomber Command and, by August, for enough aircraft of No 115 Squadron to be equipped to undertake operational trials.

At the time that the Gee trials were taking place in the first half of August 1941, another event of the utmost importance was embarked upon at the instigation of the Prime Minister's scientific adviser, Professor Lindemann, by then Lord Cherwell. Cherwell was a champion of the bomber. He believed that even if a bomber offensive could not on its own bring about the defeat of Germany, a sustained and devastating bombing campaign against German cities of industrial and political importance was an essential prelude to victory. He also believed that the means of production could be destroyed not only by destroying the factories, but also by destroying the morale of the workers—and he regarded the installations for production of military requirements, their associated workers, and their homes as legitimate targets in war. However, by the middle of 1941 he was convinced that the bomber force was not big enough to destroy Germany quickly enough and, in addition, he was suspicious of the fact that if it were big enough it would not succeed in its task because it would be unable to find its targets and deliver its bomb loads with the required accuracy. He decided that he must have evidence of the accuracy of bombing before he could know how to help Bomber Command to become a highly effective weapon of offensive warfare. With all the facilities that were available to him, and with his influence with Churchill, he was able to set in motion a most searching enquiry into the performance of Bomber Command. In the first half of August, Mr Butt, a member of the War Cabinet Secretariat, examined 650 photographs taken by night bombers during June and July on their bombing approach runs to their targets, 50 per cent purporting to be taken at the time of bomb release on the aiming point, and 50 per cent being taken independently of bombing but naming the position which was believed to have been photographed in the target area. In addition, Mr Butt studied summaries of operations, plotting reports and various other pertinent operational documents. His statistical conclusions were shattering:

1. Of those aircraft recorded as attacking their target, only one in three got within five miles.
2. Over the French ports, the proportion was two in three; over Germany as a whole, the proportion was one in four; over the Ruhr, it was only one in ten.
3. In the Full Moon, the proportion was two in five; in the New Moon it was only one in fifteen.
4. In the absence of haze, the proportion is over one half, whereas over thick haze it is only one in fifteen.
5. An increase in the intensity of AA fire reduces the number of aircraft getting within five miles of their target in the ratio three to two.

6. All these figures relate only to aircraft recorded as attacking the target; the proportion of the total sorties which reached within five miles is less by one third. Thus, for example, of the total sorties only one in five got within five miles of the target, ie within the seventy-five square miles surrounding the target.

The 650 photographs which Mr Butt analysed related to twenty-eight targets, forty-eight nights, and 100 separate raids.

In short, many of the aircraft then credited with attacking a target successfully had, in fact, dropped their bombs in open country.

Bomber Command was critical of the Butt report and convinced that it painted a picture that was much too gloomy. Not so Lord Cherwell. He told the Prime Minister that however inaccurate Butt's figures and findings might be, they were sufficiently striking to emphasise the supreme importance of improving the Command's navigational methods. Churchill agreed, and at last there was a real priority given to the development of RDF to meet Bomber Command's navigational and bomb aiming needs. Cherwell had played his cards well and his timing was excellent. The Gee trials had been highly successful and the results, which were known by the middle of August, indicated that the system was remarkably accurate within its limited range of approximately 350/400 miles, and that it could be the means of navigating accurately to targets within this range regardless of visibility conditions. Its ability to be a blind bombing device was questionable, although it seemed likely to produce better results than those indicated in the Butt report. One aircraft had, however, been lost on the operational trials over Germany, and the CAS wisely took the decision to prohibit any more flights over enemy territory until a worthwhile force could be equipped and the crews properly trained in its use. This decision was made known to the C-in-C, Bomber Command, on 18 August 1941.

Cherwell was aware of all these happenings when he spoke to Churchill about the Butt report. He was also aware of other scientific RDF aids to navigation and bombing which, for lack of priority, were languishing in retarded development at TRE. When Churchill backed priority development of these scientific aids, Cherwell moved again, and behind the scenes engineered the appointment of Sir Robert Renwick to coordinate the research, development and production of all RDF aids for aircraft. This responsibility, as Cherwell realised, would tie in well with Renwick's other major task of 'progressing' the production of the four-engined bomber aircraft.

Renwick assumed his new duties late in October, and immediately formed a committee, known as the RDF Chain Executive Committee (B), to progress the production of Gee ground and airborne equipment, the installation and manning of the ground stations, the modification of production line bomber aircraft to take the airborne sets, and the introduction of the system into Bomber Command. At the same time he proceeded to acquaint himself more closely with the other RDF develop-

ments that had an obvious application to bomber operations. He recognised, from the moment that he took over these responsibilities, that he
would need in the Command Headquarters an organisation to plan and
progress the training of servicing personnel for these new systems, together
with the training of navigators to operate the airborne equipments.
Moreover he knew that the successful completion of development of the
future aids to navigation and bombing would require a close liaison
between the Command and TRE, to ensure that operational requirements
were properly understood by the scientists and that development took
proper cognisance of the need for design to be a practical proposition for
efficient production and within the reasonable capabilities of technical
personnel to maintain in serviceable order under operational conditions. He
discussed this matter with Saundby, who was the man, above all others in
the Command, who was trying to improve the capabilities of the bomber,
because he had recognised that it could never undertake its true role in the
war until the most modern aids to night navigation and blind bombing were
developed and made available. As a result of these discussions it was
decided to form an RDF Department at the Headquarters in High
Wycombe under the command of a wing commander. In December 1941,
Wing Commander D. Saward* was appointed to that post.

At about this time the Operational Research Section of Bomber
Command was expanded and Dr B. G. Dickins, a highly experienced
statistician, was appointed as its head.

The last event which should be mentioned here, and which was of the
utmost importance, was that the Prime Minister, only a few weeks before
leaving for the famous Washington conference with Roosevelt, immediately
after Pearl Harbor and America's entry into the war, had instructed that the
bomber force should be conserved until it had been expanded by the new
four-engined bombers, and assisted by better aids to navigation and
bombing. He hoped for a more effective offensive against Germany in the
spring of 1942 by this husbandry.

Clearly Cherwell, together with the Butt report, had performed a major
service for Bomber Command. All it needed now was a highly competent
and dynamic leader.

The new year of 1942 started somewhat inauspiciously for Bomber
Command. On 12 February the German battle-cruisers *Scharnhorst* and
Gneisenau, together with the cruiser *Prinz Eugen*, escaped from Brest and
successfully passed up the Channel and through the Straits of Dover in
daylight. They had in fact left Brest just before midnight on 11 February,
taking the Admiralty completely by surprise—no one had imagined for a
second that the Germans would be so audacious as to run the gauntlet of the
batteries at Dover by day. Torpedo-carrying aircraft, motor torpedo boats
and destroyers all attacked, but to no avail. Finally, Bomber Command was
ordered to despatch a force of bombers, after the ships had successfully

*The author.

Arthur Harris in 1912, when manager of Gibson's tobacco farm, 'Weltevreden', near Salisbury, Rhodesia.

Harris's certificate qualifying him as a pilot for the RFC.

Certificate No. *915*

ROYAL FLYING CORPS.
(Officers.)

CENTRAL FLYING SCHOOL,
UPAVON, WILTS.,

29 January 1916

CERTIFICATE "A."

THIS IS TO CERTIFY that *F/Lt A. T. Harris*

 R.F.6

has completed a *long course at the Central Flying School, and is qualified for service in the Royal Flying Corps.

DO Fletcher Lt Col.

Commandant.

Major Harris, RFC, with a Sopwith Pup at Marham in 1918. Though usually outgunned by German scouts, the Pup was one of the better British aircraft of the First War.

The De Havilland DH9 two-seat day bomber, which remained in service with the RAF for some years after 1918

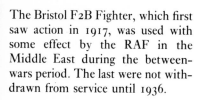
The Bristol F2B Fighter, which first saw action in 1917, was used with some effect by the RAF in the Middle East during the between-wars period. The last were not withdrawn from service until 1936.

A Vickers Vernon bomber of the type used by Harris's squadron, No 45, in Mesopotamia during the Twenties.

A Fairey IIIF, the kind of aircraft used by Harris during the 'East African Cruise' of 1932.

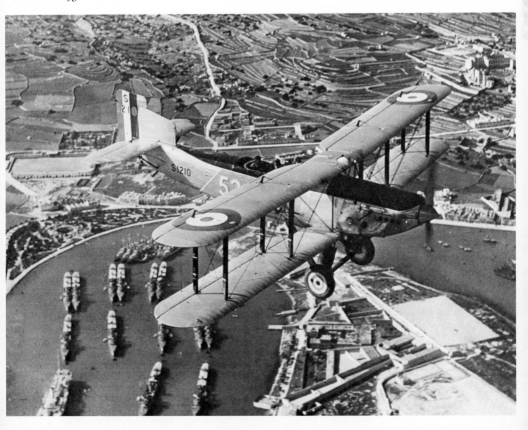

Handley Page Hampdens in flight formation—an aircraft already obsolete by the outbreak of war.

Although, like the Hampden, virtually obsolete by 1939, the Vickers Wellington continued in service throughout the war, largely because of its reliability and range, and the sturdiness of its Barnes Wallis-designed construction. This version is a Mk II, powered by Rolls-Royce Merlins rather than the more usual Bristol radials.

Examining photographic evidence of bomb damage, 1942. Left to right: AVM H. S. P. Walmsley, AVM R. D. Oxland, ACM Sir Arthur Harris, AVM R. H. M. S. Saundby.

General H. H. ('Hap') Arnold, Chief of the US Army Air Force, with ACM Sir Charles Portal, Chief of the Air Staff, during the latter's visit to America in 1941.

The King and Queen with Harris during a visit to Bomber Command HQ, 7 February 1944.

Harris (left) and AVM the Hon. R. A. Cochrane stand listening as one of the crews who bombed the German dams is questioned about the raid.

Left to right: AVM R. Graham with Harris and Saundby examining a map of Bomber Command targets.

1943. Left to right: unidentified, Churchill, his daughter Mary, General Ira C. Eaker, USAAF, General Andrews, USAAF, Commander Thomson, RN (Churchill's ADC), and Harris.

Sir Arthur and Lady Harris with their daughter, Jackie, in the garden of the C-in-C's official residence, 'Springfield', in 1943.

Left to right: Arnold, Harris and Eaker at Springfield in 1944.

The Short Stirling heavy bomber, one of the new generation of strategic aircraft for which Harris had been in part responsible.

passed through the Straits into the North Sea. The weather was appalling and the Command regarded the operation as a waste of effort. The attack was a complete and costly failure. 242 aircraft were despatched, only thirty-nine succeeded in finding the ships in the mist and rain, 188 did not see a thing, and fifteen failed to return to base. However, later that evening *Scharnhorst* and *Gneisenau* were heavily damaged by mines previously laid by Bomber Command in the narrow sea lanes of the North Sea approaches to the Channel. *Gneisenau* just made Wilhelmshaven to beach herself, and *Scharnhorst* limped her way to Kiel.

Churchill judged the escape as 'an episode of minor importance'. But many of the enemies of Bomber Command were pointing a finger of scorn, not because the Command was unable to destroy the ships during their escape through the Channel into the North Sea, but because they were able to move at all from Brest after the much advertised bombing of this port throughout most of 1941. The episode was used, in fact, to attempt to prove that bombing of the more distant targets in Germany could never succeed when a short-range target like Brest had survived numerous attacks. This was grossly unfair, because the ships had been immobilised in Brest for more than ten months by bombing. But if their escape had been an inauspicious occasion for Bomber Command, it was perhaps more inauspicious for Germany, because the new strength of the Command (which was just beginning to grow with the arrival of the four-engined Lancasters, Halifaxes and Stirlings, together with advanced scientific aids to navigation and bombing) would no longer be sapped by the incessant demands of the Admiralty to bomb Brest, to the exclusion of all else. It was an ill wind that blew much good!

By February 1942 the first ten squadrons in Bomber Command to be fitted with Gee were ready for operations, complete with crews trained in the use of the system and with RDF mechanics established at the stations concerned and trained to service this new and revolutionary device. Of these squadrons five were twin-engined Wellington, two were Stirling, two Halifax, and one was a Lancaster squadron. These provided the Command with some 200 Gee equipped bombers. The policy of conserving the bombers, a decision which was taken in November 1941, was now rescinded by an Air Staff directive to the C-in-C Bomber Command dated 14 February 1942. It authorised the Command 'to employ your effort without restriction, until further notice, in accordance with the following directions.' These directions gave the priorities for targets to be attacked in Germany. The introduction of Gee was given as the reason for mounting this offensive:

TR 1335 (Gee) will confer upon your forces the ability to concentrate their effort to an extent which has not hitherto been possible under the operational conditions with which you are faced. It is accordingly considered that the introduction of this equipment on operations should be regarded as a revolutionary advance in bombing technique which, during the period of its effective life as a target-finding device, will enable results to be obtained of a much more effective nature.

The estimated time before the full use of Gee over Germany was impaired by jamming was given as six months. Therefore it was emphasised in the directive that the Command should strike with full force during this period, in order to destroy Germany's capacity and will to make war and to 'enhearten and support the Russians', while they were maintaining so effectively their counter-offensive against the German armies.

Since Air Marshal Sir Richard Peirse had left Bomber Command on the 8 January 1942 to become the Commander-in-Chief of the Air Forces in India and South-East Asia, this directive, which was signed by Bottomley as DCAS, was addressed to Air Vice-Marshal J. E. A. Baldwin, the AOC of No 3 Group, who was acting as C-in-C pending the arrival of Air Marshal A. T. Harris from America. Ten days after the escape of *Scharnhorst* and *Gneisenau* from Brest, Harris assumed command on 22 February 1942, seven weeks before his fiftieth birthday. It was at a time when the fortunes of Britain and her newly won ally, America, were looking more than dismal. The American Pacific Fleet had been destroyed at Pearl Harbor; two great British warships, HMS *Prince of Wales* and HMS *Repulse*, had been sunk off the Malayan coast; on Christmas Day, Hong Kong had surrendered to the Japanese; on 15 February, Singapore had capitulated to the Japanese; in the Western Desert, Rommel with his German Afrika Korps stood triumphant over the British Army in Libya. The Grand Alliance was, in fact, in danger of being stillborn. The only real hope of survival, or of avoiding an ignominious negotiated peace, lay in a successful bomber offensive against the German homeland. In Bomber Command lay the only means by which Britain's strategy could move from the defensive, which spelt ultimate disaster, to the offensive, which offered a chance of eventual victory. Bomber Command had, therefore, been given a new lease of life and a new leader. But its performance in the immediate future would determine its survival, because it was to remain under a constant threat of extinction, not by the enemy, but by the Admiralty, the Army and numerous politicians who had no faith in a bomber offensive or who were opposed to bombing as it conflicted with their so-called ideals.

It was no enviable task that faced Harris. He knew that he had to chalk up successes swiftly, and yet the force at his disposal was lamentable. Excluding five squadrons of light bombers, unsuited for operations over Germany, he had forty-four squadrons of which only thirty-eight were actually operational. This was a far cry from the sixty-eight bomber squadrons, consisting of 990 aircraft, planned in February 1936 to be available by 1937! Of the forty-four squadrons only fourteen were equipped with the new heavy bomber types, the four-engined Stirling, Halifax and Lancaster aircraft and the ailing twin-engined Manchester which was already being replaced by the Lancaster. The rest were equipped with the old Wellingtons, Whitleys and Hampdens which carried a much smaller bomb load, had less range, and were slower. 'On the day I took over,' Harris recalls, 'there were 378 aircraft serviceable with crews, and only sixty-nine of these were heavy bombers. About fifty aircraft in the force were not even medium bombers, but the light bombers of No 2 Group. These, apart from making intruder attacks on the enemy's airfields in Belgium and France, could take no part in the main offensive. In effect this meant that we had an average force of 250 medium and fifty heavy bombers until such time as the Command really began to expand.'

It was therefore with a total force of some 600 aircraft, and a normally available force of only 300 aircraft, that Harris began his long campaign against the industrial cities of Germany.

Ironically, in the same month (February 1942) that Harris assumed command of the bomber force, Fritz Todt, Hitler's Minister of Armaments and Munitions, was killed in an aircraft accident at Rastenburg, Hitler's East Prussian Headquarters. A few hours after his death Hitler appointed Albert Speer to replace him with the urgent task of reorganising German industry, to provide the greatly increased military production demanded by the Russian front and Germany's involvement in the Mediterranean. It was Harris's bomber offensive that was to disrupt Germany's productive capacity so effectively as to prevent it reaching the level that was essential for Germany to maintain its military capability.

13
To bomb or not to bomb

On 25 February 1942, three days after Harris had been installed as C-in-C, Bomber Command, Sir Stafford Cripps, the Lord Privy Seal, made a most extraordinarily damaging speech in the House of Commons when winding up a two day debate on the war situation.

> Another question which has been raised by a great number of Members, [he said] is the question of the policy as to the continued use of heavy bombers and the bombing of Germany. A number of Honourable Members have questioned whether, in the existing circumstances, the continued devotion of a considerable part of our effort to the building up of this Bomber Force is the best use that we can make of our resources. It is obviously a matter which it is almost impossible to debate in public, but, if I may, I would remind the House that this policy was initiated at a time when we were fighting alone against the combined forces of Germany and Italy and it seemed then that it was the most effective way in which we, acting alone, could take the initiative against the enemy. Since that time we have had an enormous access of support from the Russian Armies, who, according to the latest news, have had yet another victory over the Germans, and also from the great potential strength of the United States of America. Naturally, in such circumstances, the original policy has come under review. I can assure the House that the Government are fully aware of the other uses to which our resources could be put, and the moment they arrive at a decision that the circumstances warrant a change, a change in policy will be made.

The Russian victories referred to were nothing more than a greater resistance to the German invasion than had been expected. In fact, the real German offensive, which nearly eliminated Russia, was yet to come. The reference to the American potential was true, but any contribution from America could not be expected for months. Indeed, it was well into 1943 before American help began to make any impression on the fortunes of the Allies. Cripps's speech was therefore ill-informed, if not downright mischievous. The best that can be said is that his pacifist ideals and his intense dislike of exposing civilian populations to a bombing war blinded him to the realities of the true situation and made him forget that civilian populations all over Europe had been and were still being subjected to German bombs, shells, bullets and the ruthless behaviour of their invading armies. Even his own countrymen had had to suffer and were still to suffer.

The Cripps speech transferred the doubts about the wisdom of a strategic offensive from the confines of discussions between the Chiefs of Staff, members of the War Cabinet and the Ministries, to speculation in Parliament, the country at large and, inevitably, the Press. The effect was not only disturbing in Britain but also in America, where the statement had been published in full. In fact, the Royal Air Force delegation in Washington feared that it would be taken to mean that the British Government had lost confidence in the principle of a strategic bomber offensive as a means of weakening the German ability to make war, a view that had been expressed so strongly by Churchill and the British Chiefs of Staff at the Washington conference only a few weeks earlier. The delegation believed that the statement, which had been publicised in the *New York Times*, would strengthen the hands of those Americans who favoured concentrating on the war against Japan, rather than against Germany. In turn, they were apprehensive of the adverse effect it might have upon American production of heavy bombers. In a message to the CAS, the head of the delegation signalled: 'Unless authoritative reaffirmation of our belief in the Bomber Offensive is supplied immediately, effect both on strategic and production planning here may well be irremediable.' It was a quick reaction—dated 26 February, the day after the speech.

The Cripps statement did not pass unnoticed by those serving in Bomber Command and it is true to say that many at all levels read this extraordinary speech with amazement and distress. There was, however, a counter to its effect at Bomber Command HQ, which was rapidly to reach out to groups, stations, squadrons and flights. The arrival of Harris produced a remarkable and pronounced feeling of confidence that was quite inexplicable. Somehow everyone was convinced that this was the turning point. Almost within minutes of stepping into the Operations Room for the first time, the legend of Harris was born. This seemingly remote man, who was in fact so close to every activity and need of his men, whose practical experience spanned over the command of eight squadrons in his service career, as well as operational groups and staff appointments, who could and still did fly aeroplanes, who had developed bombing techniques which were the basis of modern bombing methods as early as 1922, who had introduced the principle of night bombing and who had, in 1936, as DD Plans, laid the foundation of the future Bomber Force, had arrived to lead and direct his own creation. From that moment no one on his Staff had any doubts about the successful outcome. The fears of a successful assassination of Bomber Command by the admirals, generals and politicians began to recede, and within days of 22 February 1942 the Command was to begin to hold its head high.

Harris was deeply conscious of the need to succeed in the offensive immediately. He had in Saundby, his SASO, a man who was keenly aware of the present weaknesses of the Command and the potential of its immediate future with the slow but definite build-up of the four-engined bombers and the introduction of the new and revolutionary RDF blind navigation and blind bombing devices, the first of which, Gee, was now installed in 200 aircraft and which would in future be a part of the equipment of all new and replacement aircraft delivered to the Command. Harris was therefore well briefed at the outset on the capabilities of his aircraft and crews and he adopted the path of caution, seeking certain success for his first major attack.

The Air Staff view was that with Gee the new offensive, which was about to open, would be able to blot out at least four cities in Western Germany during the initial phase. Harris was less sanguine about such success. He did not think he had enough aircraft at his disposal, and therefore enough bomb load, to achieve such dramatic results. Moreover Gee was unproved, except on limited operational trials over Germany in August 1941 and on extensive service trials over the United Kingdom, under the code name 'Crackers', on the 13 and 19 February 1942.

The Directive of 14 February gave Harris four primary targets in the Ruhr area, Essen, Duisburg, Düsseldorf and Cologne; and three alternative targets, also within Gee range, Bremen, Wilhelmshaven and Emden. In addition a list of further alternatives which were outside Gee range were listed—Hamburg, Kiel, Lübeck, Rostock, Berlin, Kassel, Hannover, Frankfurt, Mannheim, Schweinfurt and Stuttgart. All of these targets were important industrial areas; although Berlin was included, according to the Directive, for the purpose of maintaining 'the fear of attack over the city and to impose ARP measures'. An additional commitment was also mentioned. This was the Renault factory at Billancourt, near Paris, which was producing armaments and motorised vehicles for the German military forces.

Harris chose the Renault factory for his first strike and as a testing ground for the new tactical method of attack, which had been tried out in the 'Crackers' exercise with Gee. Gee coverage was not at this stage available over the southern areas of Britain and down into France and so the Bomber Force had to be dependent upon good weather and good visibility, but the principle of using a flare-dropping force to illuminate the target and a liberal load of incendiaries mixed with high explosives, including a maximum quantity of 4,000-pound bombs, was to be employed.

On the night of 3/4 March, just ten days after Sir Stafford Cripps's disturbing statement, Harris delivered the first blow of the new campaign, in entirely favourable weather conditions, against this short-range target. The bombing was concentrated and the devastation impressive, including nearly 25 per cent of the machine tools destroyed or damaged and many others rendered unusable because of the destruction of buildings. Buildings containing designs, blueprints and records were burnt to the ground, 722 vehicles ready for delivery were wrecked, and office buildings and ancillary buildings for stores were damaged or completely demolished. But the death toll was remarkably low—out of 3,000 workmen on duty, only five had been killed. Several others, however, including their families, had unfortunately been killed in neighbouring houses.

Out of 235 bombers despatched, 223 had reached the target as evidenced from photographs taken during the bombing runs, and these had dropped 461 tons of bombs. The raid had lasted just under two hours, achieving a concentration of 121 aircraft per hour over the target, a concentration hitherto unheard of on bombing raids.

It was a notable success and provided a much needed boost to the morale of the bomber force. But Harris was well aware that this attack was no real test of the Command's capacity to destroy the heavily defended targets within Germany itself which were also at much greater range.

He followed this success with the inevitable trial of strength that had to be faced. Using Gee for the first time, three raids were made on the successive nights of 8/9/10/11/12 March against the Ruhr with Essen as the main target. The first attack was undertaken by 211 aircraft, of which eighty-two were equipped with Gee. The Gee force was divided into a flare force dropping flares in sticks of twelve bundles of three flares to light up the target, and an incendiary force of fifty aircraft dropping a full load of incendiaries. This force was followed by a main striking force carrying full loads of high explosive bombs including many 4,000-pounders. Despite the favourable reports of the crews and night photographic evidence that the majority of the Gee aircraft had passed close to their target area, the raid was only a partial success. On the second night, the 9th/10th, the attack went astray because a Stirling aircraft jettisoned its incendiaries over Hamborn after being hit by anti-aircraft fire, with the result that many of the following aircraft released their bombs on the fires that were started in Hamborn instead of proceeding further to Essen where the Krupp armament works was the main aiming point. The third raid, on the 11th/12th, was essentially a failure in that the main bomber force was led astray by an unexpected decoy conflagration near Rheinberg. Nevertheless, damage in Essen resulting from these raids was appreciably greater than anything which had been previously achieved, including damage to engineering works, railway centres and houses; but Krupps was virtually untouched. The Thyssen steel works at Hamborn had, however, received numerous direct hits on the second night from bombs released on the fires caused by the incendiaries jettisoned by the unfortunate Stirling.

Harris had the causes of the failure investigated without delay, not only by Group Staffs but also by his Operational Research Section at Headquarters in conjunction with the RDF Department which consisted of both specialist navigators and signals officers, a number of whom had had experience on operations. It was established that although most of the flares had been dropped with the aid of Gee in the right place, a large proportion of the main bombing force had arrived after the flares had gone out and the first wave, loaded with incendiaries, had dropped their loads over too wide an area to achieve the concentration necessary for real success. The interesting aspect was that the inaccuracy was principally one of bombing short of the target and the pattern of bombing was consistent with the accuracy of the statistical error to be expected with Gee at that range.

On 13 March, Harris despatched his first letter as C-in-C Bomber Command to Churchill. It was to be the beginning of a remarkably close relationship between these two great men, and one which was to secure and maintain the continued existence of Bomber Command throughout the war and to ensure the growth of the strategic bomber offensive against Germany. He wrote:

Prime Minister,
You asked me for a comparison between the weight of attack in the Coventry Blitz and the weight of attack in our first GEE operation on Essen.

Coventry
430 aircraft dropped 400 tons of bombs in 1 night. (It was a 1 night Blitz). Of this total, 220 aircraft dropped 185 tons of bombs on Coventry itself.

Essen
401 aircraft dropped $657\frac{1}{2}$ tons of bombs in 3 nights.
I hope, however, that no official comparisons will be made between these two weights of attack as indicating that Essen has as yet been taking Coventry's medicine.
The analysis of the whole operation, together with the plotting of night photographs, which I have just been able to have completed for a conference with my Group Commanders this afternoon, shows that there was no worthwhile concentration on the exact target of Essen. There were various reasons for this—technical, tactical and training— many of which could possibly not have been anticipated and needed clarification by practical experience to be impressed upon us. These lessons have, I hope, now been absorbed and we are in process of perfecting the method as fast as we can within the limitations of crews, aircraft and weather.
Nevertheless, we are all enthusiastic as to the utility and efficiency of the GEE method. Although, as I have said above, the actual target in Essen did not apparently get it in the neck, there were, so far as we can yet ascertain, great fires in the southern part of Essen, some damage to Krupps Works and I believe, very heavy damage in Hamborn and the Thyssen and Hermann Goering Works alongside Hamborn.
For various reasons the attack was spread and not concentrated. An interesting fact is, however, that the spread of the attack well cor- responded with the expected area of GEE error in that locality.
We are devising methods and means of effecting concentration, and I feel confident that we shall achieve it.
The crews are enthusiastic, especially with the result of the second night's operation on Essen, and the gain so far is not only an excellent

means of navigation and especially of homing, but that the number of aircraft effectively bombing within the immediate neighbourhood of the selected target was far greater than on similar types of operation prior to the coming of G E E.

A. T. Harris

On the same day that this letter was written and despatched, the fourth Gee raid was being planned against Cologne for that very night. The view had been expressed by the R D F Department, supported by the Operational Research Section, that perhaps insufficient reliance had been placed on the Gee equipment when the incendiary force had released their loads in the first Gee attacks, resulting in loads being released by crews when they thought they were over the target, or when they saw the incendiaries mistakenly released by other aircraft, or when they mistook dummy fires for the real thing. The Wing Commander R D F proposed to Saundby that more definite instructions should be given on this matter. This was agreed by Harris after Saundby consulted with him. The attack took place on the night of 13/14 March, the Gee aircraft again being divided into a flare-dropping force and an incendiary force, followed by the main striking force. On this occasion, however, instructions were issued to the Bomber Groups that all Gee aircraft were to approach the target from west to east along a specific Gee path, using the homing technique, and to release their flares 'blind' when the Gee equipment indicated that the bomb release point had been reached. The incendiary aircraft were instructed to approach along the same Gee path, but to drop their load visually if the Rhine, running through the east side of the town, was sighted, or 'blind' on the Gee indications if the river was not sighted. It was, in fact, a moonless night and visual sightings were in any case expected to be difficult.

The raid was far more successful than the first three raids on Essen and substantially more damage was inflicted upon the town than upon any previous raid on targets in the Ruhr or, for that matter, in Germany. On 24 March Harris again wrote to Churchill.

Prime Minister,
On the 13th March I sent at your request a minute in preliminary report on the two first G E E attacks on Essen.
I stated that although we had not achieved our precise object we believed from night photographs and reports that considerable damage had been done in the southern part of Essen and in the Thyssen Works at Hamborn.
We have now obtained photographs of these two areas which confirm those first assumptions. I attach a preliminary interpretation of these photographs made by my own Intelligence Staff ...
I told you (on the telephone) that our G E E attack on Cologne had been highly successful ...
... It seems probable that over fifty per cent of the aircraft claiming to have attacked actually hit Cologne. Evidence over the last seven months

shows that under similar weather conditions with no moon we should normally expect to get only ten per cent of the force on the target. You will note from the attached report on Cologne that day photographs amply confirm the claim that very serious damage was occasioned during the attack. German broadcasts and reports from German sources in Ankara alike confirm that we did a lot of damage and killed plenty of Boche.

We hope that we have further improved the methods and to produce still better results in future.

The crews are enthusiastic over GEE. They increase their skill in using it on every trial. Technical shortcomings in the equipment are being overcome. We are on a good thing.

A. T. Harris.

Concentration in time over the target was still being based on the principle of approximately 100 aircraft per hour. The Renault raid at the beginning of March had achieved a record 121 aircraft per hour. But Harris wanted much more than this. From the initial results in March, which were certainly not unimpressive, he reasoned that he would need to attack a single city with something like 1,000 aircraft in order to achieve real disruption of the industrial working life and truly substantial devastation to factories, services, communications and houses. But even if he had a big enough force to despatch such numbers the question was whether it was physically possible to concentrate such a force over one target in the night hours available. What had been observed with Gee was that the force could be concentrated in time and space because it enabled aircraft to maintain their correct track to the target area accurately and to keep to times along that track, and at the target, as laid down in the overall plan of attack. This both Harris and Saundby believed could open the door to truly mammoth concentrations. The Wing Commander RDF, in a discussion with Harris and Saundby, had already suggested a trial raid on Cologne with 120 Gee aircraft concentrated over the target in a period of fifteen minutes. The idea appealed to Harris and he questioned Saward, his Wing Commander RDF, further, demanding to know how many aircraft he thought could be concentrated into one hour's attack. Saward gave it as his opinion that if the target was within Gee range, and all aircraft were equipped, then because of the tracking and time-keeping accuracy, now made possible by Gee, well over 500 aircraft could be packed into an hour's raid. This was confirmation of the views already forming in the minds of both Harris and Saundby. Moreover they foresaw that such concentrations along the route to the target would provide greater protection against the enemy's defences as well as enabling greater damage to be achieved.

Before the end of March an experiment in concentration was attempted. The target was Cologne. The attack was concentrated into twenty minutes. The number of aircraft was 120. It was a great success and the timing proved to be well nigh perfect. A significant feature was that each aircraft arrived back at its base within a few minutes of its estimated time of arrival. The night photographs taken with bombing showed that Cologne had been attacked and day photographic reconnaissance revealed that quite considerable damage had been inflicted and that this was confined to one area of the town. But the real importance of this experimental raid of Harris's was the proof it provided that with good navigational aids very considerable concentrations of aircraft over the target were possible. Already he was discounting Gee as an adequate blind bombing device, but he was correctly assessing the potential of the system as an aid to accurate navigation, a prerequisite to any successful bombing raid. Moreover, because of the system's exceptional accuracy over England, he knew that aircraft and crew losses due to crashes in England when returning to base had been greatly reduced. Yet another asset of Gee was that when attacking targets beyond its 350/400-mile range, aircraft could navigate accurately to the system's maximum range and then fly the additional distance from a definite plotted position. Without Gee the errors of navigation had invariably been cumulative after passing across the shores of England. An attack on Kiel on the night of 13 March tended to confirm this, the navigators expressing the opinion that the ability to plot their position accurately over the greater part of the route had greatly simplified the problem of navigation over the non-Gee leg to the target. The raid was a great success, with fifty-three out of the force of sixty-eight Wellingtons attacking the target and causing considerable damage to the great shipbuilding yards of the Deutsche Werke.

Churchill, who was under pressure at this time by the Admiralty to divert bomber squadrons to anti-submarine patrolling, was pleased with results of the new offensive as they provided him with a reason to support bombing in preference to submarine patrolling. In addition he had unexpected backing from Roosevelt. In a letter to Harry Hopkins, dated 12 March 1942, Churchill had expressed his deep concern at the extent of tanker sinkings west of the 40th Meridian and in the Caribbean Sea. He went on to suggest some rearrangement of convoy escort duties and hoped that Roosevelt could withdraw a few destroyers from the Pacific to provide additional escort forces until further British anti-submarine corvettes, which were nearly ready, came into service. Roosevelt indicated American cooperation in a cabled reply. But in a follow-up letter, dated 20 March, he wrote:

> Your interest in steps to be taken to combat the Atlantic submarine menace as indicated by your recent message to Mr Hopkins on this subject impels me to request your particular consideration of heavy attacks on submarine bases and building and repair yards, thus checking submarine activities at source and where submarines perforce congregate.

Roosevelt's wording was reminiscent of the Harris approach, when in a minute to the CAS (referred to earlier) dated 20 March 1941, exactly a year before, Harris wrote on the subject of the submarine menace: '... are we going Navy fashion to disperse our entire resources attempting to cope defensively with this problem at its outer fringe—an immense area—or are we going Air War fashion to concentrate upon attacking the kernel of the problem at the centre.' It appeared that the views of Harris, expressed in his private conversations with Harry Hopkins and Roosevelt on the subject of bombing, had taken root!

Churchill's reply to Roosevelt's note, which was dated 29 March, was well timed, for it was written the day after Bomber Command had attacked the Baltic port of Lübeck with enormous success. He wrote: 'In order to cope with U-boat hatchings we are emphasising bombing attacks on U-boat nests, and last night we went to Lübeck with 250 bombers, including 43 heavy. Results are said to be best ever. This is in accordance with your wishes.' He went on to say that in view of the heavy sinkings still occurring in the USA side of the Atlantic, the Admiralty were pressing for the diversion of six bomber squadrons to anti-submarine patrol duties.

> On merits I am most anxious to meet their wish [he said]. On the other hand, the need to bomb Germany is great. Our new method of finding targets is yielding most remarkable results. However, our bombing force has not expanded as we hoped ... Just at the time when the weather is improving, when Germans are drawing away flak from their cities for their offensive against Russia, when you are keen on bombing U-boat nests, when oil targets are especially attractive, I find it very hard to take away these extra six squadrons from Bomber Command, in which Harris is doing so well.

Both Roosevelt's letter and Harris's initial successes with Bomber Command had, in fact, somewhat strengthened Churchill's resolve to give the bombing offensive a fair trial.

The Lübeck raid, which had taken place on the night of 28/29 March, had been so successful that it had even overshadowed the raids on the Ruhr earlier in that month. Lübeck was an old port on the Baltic. At this time the Baltic ice was beginning to break up and the port would soon come into full use for supplying the military requirements of the German armies in North Russia and in Scandinavia. Also it would be open for import of iron ore and other strategic materials from Sweden, a major supplier to Germany. These were important enough considerations to have included the town on the recent list of targets to be attacked, but in addition the town housed industries of importance, military depots and a training centre for submarine crews. The form of attack was similar to those employed against Essen and Cologne except that the incendiary content of the bomb load was much greater as the town consisted of many old wooden buildings and houses and was assessed to be highly vulnerable to fire. The target was well beyond Gee range, but again Gee proved to be a great asset over the major portion of the route. It was a moonlit night and visibility was excellent. The number of aircraft despatched was 234, and not 250 as Churchill had written to Roosevelt with poetic licence, and some 300 tons of bombs were dropped on the target of which 144 tons were incendiaries. The town was literally left ablaze when the last aircraft headed for home.

Daylight photographic reconnaissance revealed that 200 acreas of built-up area in the island city had been completely devastated, including 1,500 houses, the Town Hall and municipal buildings, the gas works, electricity works and tram depot. South-west of the island, in the suburb of St Lorenz, 65 acres of built-up area had been completely destroyed. North-east of the island, in the suburb of Marli, a 4000-pound bomb had destroyed ten large houses and partially destroyed forty-five others over an area of $5\frac{1}{2}$ acres. The Drager works, which made oxygen apparatus for submarines and aircraft, had been obliterated as had numerous other industrial concerns. But the greatest devastation was in the old town and the docks. It was so extensive that no goods could be sent through the town or the port for more than three weeks and the effectiveness of the port was reduced for many months longer.

The German reaction is best summed up in Goebbels' diary. On 30 March he wrote:

This Sunday has been thoroughly spoiled by an exceptionally heavy air raid by the RAF on Lübeck. In the morning I received a very alarming report from our propaganda office there, which I at first assumed to be exaggerated. In the course of the evening, however, I was informed of the seriousness of the situation by a long distance call from Kaufmann. He believes that no German city has ever before been attacked so severely from the air. Conditions in parts of Lübeck are chaotic.

Then again on 4 April he made this entry:

The damage is really enormous. I have been shown a newsreel of the destruction. It is horrible. One can well imagine how such an awful bombardment affects the population. Thank God it is a North German population, which on the whole is much tougher than the Germans in the south or the south-east. Nevertheless we can't get away from the fact that the English air raids have increased in scope and importance; if they can be continued for weeks on these lines, they might conceivably have a demoralising effect on the population.

Harris, himself, did not regard the target as vital, but, as he says, 'It seemed to me better to destroy an industrial town of moderate importance than to fail to destroy a large industrial city.' However, the main object of the attack was to learn to what extent a first wave of aircraft could guide a second wave to the aiming point by starting a conflagration. 'I ordered a half an hour interval between the two waves in order to allow the fires to get a good hold before the second wave arrived ... It was conclusively proved that even the small force I then had at my disposal could destroy the greater part of a town of secondary importance.' Harris was, in fact, already developing his ideas on the principle of the best crews leading the way and marking the target. It was not a new thought to him. He had employed it crudely in Iraq in 1922/24 and then again in No 5 Group at the beginning of the war. For years he had pressed for the development of efficient marker bombs for use by target marking crews.

After more information was available on the Lübeck success Churchill again expressed his satisfaction in another letter to Roosevelt, dated 1 April 1942. In it he wrote:

> Only the weather is holding us back from continuous heavy bombing attacks on Germany. Our new methods are most successful. Essen. Cologne, and above all Lübeck, were all on the Coventry scale. I am sure it is most important to keep this up all through the summer, blasting Hitler from behind while he is grappling with the Bear.

But for all his insistence on giving Bomber Command the opportunity to prove itself, he was concerned about the losses at sea and very conscious of the Admiralty's pressure for diversion of bomber aircraft for anti-submarine patrol. In fact he requested Harris at this juncture to provide him with a note on the Command's past contribution and future intentions in the anti-submarine campaign.

Harris wrote back to Churchill on 3 April, enclosing a brief report. In his letter, he said:

> The note attached has been prepared by my Chief Intelligence Officer from the material available here and in the Air Ministry. The Admiralty would possibly disagree with some of the claims and contentions. But in my view the RAF Intelligence Service is conservative, most careful to obtain and weigh all the confirmation available, while awarding claims only on adequate direct and indirect evidence. On the other hand, the Admiralty are perhaps not over-enthusiastic in their estimation of what the RAF, and particularly the Bomber, has achieved on their behalf. Their organisation and outlook are perhaps not orientated towards the assessment of air intelligence; eg they appreciate a warship blowing up in battle, but find it harder to visualise one that has never materialised, or may have missed the battle, partly because of our bombing of factories and workers, and partly because of the tremendous resources expended by the enemy on Flak and searchlights to prevent us continuing to bomb factories and workers. I am content, therefore, that the picture painted in the attached note is not an exaggerated one.

The note, like the letter, was dated 3 April:

SECRET

NOTE ON

BOMBER COMMAND'S CONTRIBUTION

TO THE ANTI SUBMARINE CAMPAIGN.

INTRODUCTION.

1. In plans drawn up by the Air Staff in collaboration with the Naval Staff at the beginning of the War, it was concluded that the best way that

the bomber force could restrict enemy submarine activity was to bombard the yards where submarines are built. No factors have emerged since then to modify this view, although some lesser but more immediate results have sometimes been achieved by attacking the advanced submarine bases on the West Coast of France.

2. A brief review of the direct effects known to have resulted from attacks on German yards and on the Western bases is given below, but it is emphasised that this is concerned chiefly with assessable results; in addition, submarine building programmes have undoubtedly and seriously been indirectly affected by the delays in production of components caused by bombardment of industrial cities throughout Germany.

REVIEW OF ASSESSABLE RESULTS.

GERMAN YARDS

3. During the first five months of 1941 attacks were concentrated on building yards in NW Germany. The cumulative effect of these attacks was a marked slowing up in the rate of launching and completing submarines, delays varying from two to six months.

4. One raid on Wilhelmshaven in January 1941 was so successful that submarines then building spent 18 months on the slips instead of the normal 8 months.

5. At Emden 3 submarines were reported to be damaged beyond repair and were being dismantled. Moreover, a recent report dated 3rd March 1942 states that the heavy raids on this port during the winter have caused havoc to shipping and particularly mentions the fact that a new submarine was destroyed on the eve of its departure.

6. At Kiel, damage to yards and workers' homes was so heavy that the Deutsche and Germania yards were compelled to close down for a period and the Naval and Administrative Offices had to be evacuated. A 1,000 ton submarine nearing completion on the 7th April, 1941, was still present in August, while two 750 ton submarines were on the slips for 11 months.

7. At Flensburg, the launching of 500 ton submarines was delayed, one in particular occupying the slips for 13 months and at least three others suffering from 2–3 months delay.

8. At Hamburg, where six submarines should have been completed by the end of July, 1941, two were delayed until mid-September.

WESTERN BASES.

9. Up to 15th March 1941, the Command had dropped 130 tons of bombs on the submarine base at Lorient and 47 tons on the base at Bordeaux. Many sources have spoken of the success of these attacks, and although direct results have been difficult to assess, a conservative estimate is that 3 submarines were sunk and 12 damaged at Bordeaux and 4 sunk and 2 damaged at Lorient.

10. Since then, submarine shelters have been built and have come into use in the Western bases indicating the extent of the enemy's fear of bombing and rendering attacks on these bases far less profitable in submarines, but no less provocative of delays due to work-shop damage.

MINING

11. Extensive minefields have been maintained, and are now being greatly increased by the Command in the Bight, the Belts and the Baltic and the approaches to German ports and to the Western bases. Owing to the large number of enemy ships known to have been sunk by these minefields we are confident that they have obtained their quota of submarines sunk and damaged. Interrogation of Prisoners of War tends to confirm this. Unfortunately, whereas trade and insurance sources provide relatively easy and certain confirmation of merchant ship losses, warship losses and perhaps especially submarine sinkings are for obvious reasons much harder to confirm. It is well known that the general dislocation of traffic and necessity for constant sweeping has affected the activities not only of submarines but also of their supply ships.

CONCLUSION

12. The evidence which has been briefly outlined above leaves no doubt that Bomber Command is capable of seriously restricting submarine building and activity, and has in fact achieved this. Now that scientific development has facilitated navigation to isolated targets, and an even greater weight of attack has become possible, it is proposed to extend operations to the factories producing submarine engines and their other major components in conjunction with direct attack on the workers' houses near such factories.

A. T. Harris

Portal, the CAS, had already requested Harris for a note on air mining in a letter dated 23 March, in which he said he was due to have a meeting with the Prime Minister on Friday of that week and would like Harris's views on the mining of the Western French ports. Portal was, of course, as keen as Harris to resist the waste of bombers on useless submarine patrol. Harris sent his note on the 24th. Churchill's direct request to Harris for information had therefore come after Portal's meeting with him. The note to Portal is extremely important in that it shows clearly the effort Harris wished to apply to the submarine war, and that he was only adamantly against the Admiralty's obdurate desire to fritter away the bomber force by having it waltzing around the Atlantic under Naval Command looking for needles in a haystack.

In this memorandum he detailed past results from the beginning of mining operations up to 31 December 1941. 2, 569 mines had been laid, of which 1,757 had been laid by Bomber Command and 812 by Coastal Command. The total number of ships known to have been lost by the enemy was ninety-eight and the total tonnage 211,360 tons. Mines laid per known ship lost were 26·6. But Harris argued that for every known ship lost at least one unknown one had probably been sunk. This assumption he based on over 300 wrecks shown on German wartime charts. Making allowances for losses due to marine risks, our own wrecks resulting from Dunkirk, and direct sinkings from aerial attacks by Coastal Command and other forces, he reckoned it was reasonable to claim 200 ships sunk by Bomber Command's mining efforts. His reckoning, he insisted, was reinforced by a study of the known losses in the sixty minefields laid by air, which showed that the sinkings varied between nil to eight in each minefield, except for one where the known losses were twenty-four. This latter field was under continuous observation from neutral Sweden, and was therefore the only area from which precise results were obtainable.

Harris went on to point out that with the exception of Coastal's 812 mines, all the mines had been laid by Hampdens which could carry only one mine. Now, however, he had put in hand the conversion of all Bomber Command aircraft to carry mines as well as bombs, and since the Stirling and Lancaster could carry six apiece and the Halifax and Wellington two, 'the vast increase in potential effort becomes apparent. With these new facilities in mine-laying,' he reported, 'I anticipate in average weather, which frequently gives opportunities for wholesale mine-laying when nothing else of profit can be done, no particular trouble or serious interference with the bomber effort in laying 800–1,000 mines a month. We laid 306 in February with only a few heavies coming into it.' He continued by stating that the Command would now aim to lay 500 to 1,000 mines in the approaches to Lorient, St Nazaire, La Pallice, the Gironde River, Quiberon and St Jean de Luz, and that these fields would be kept topped up. He argued that the Command's mining activity was far more effective than chasing ships at sea with large numbers of bomber aircraft. Moreover, he emphasised that apart from shipping, this form of attack, together with bombing shipyards and marine factories, would also prove to be the best method of dealing with submarines.

> In view of the very small percentage of submarine sightings by patrolling aircraft [he wrote], and the still smaller, indeed almost infinitesimal, number of kills awarded as a percentage of those sightings, it is apparent that the use of bombers on mine-laying and on direct attacks on submarine building yards and on submarine accessory factories inland, and on the morale of the workers, is beyond doubt the most economical and effective way of employing aircraft in anti-submarine warfare, excepting only in the direct protection of shipping, in which task the aircraft, by forcing submarines to dive, frequently spoils an attack which might otherwise be successful.

He finally warned that the Admiralty would 'be the first to feel, and feel grimly, any diminution of these efforts.' They would regret, he said, the results of misemploying aircraft on the 'profitless task of overseas recon- naissance away from our shipping lanes,' instead of encouraging 'Bomber

Command to assist in the naval war, and particularly the submarine war, by mining, by attacks on dockyards, and on related factories.'

Harris, however, was not content to stave off Admiralty incursions into his force just by arguments on paper. On the 17 April he laid on a daylight attack against the MAN Diesel Engine Works at Augsburg with a raiding force of twelve Lancaster aircraft. This factory produced a large proportion of the German Navy's U-boat engines which was the main reason for selecting it as a target. The attack also provided an opportunity to test the capabilities of the new Lancasters and to experiment with the idea of deep penetration into Germany in daylight to undertake precision bombing of precise objectives. The plan of attack was to fly deep into France and feint for Munich before finally switching course to Augsburg. The operating height was 500 feet until south of Paris in order to be below the German RDF early warning cover. In addition, diversionary attacks were made against targets in Cherbourg, Rouen and the Pas de Calais. The aircraft were selected from Nos 44 and 97 Squadrons and were led by a Rhodesian, Squadron Leader J. D. Nettleton. They set off in the mid-afternoon and the plan allowed for a return from the target under cover of darkness for most of the way.

This attack was both a success and a failure. Five minutes after crossing the French coast they were attacked by some thirty German fighters and four of the Lancasters were shot down. The remaining eight aircraft reached Augsburg and at tree-top level completely surprised the ground defences. They all dropped their bombs, seventeen of which hit the target. Two machine-tool shops, a forging shop and the main assembly shop were severely damaged. But three more aircraft were shot down in the target area. Only five out of the original twelve returned to base and these were all badly shot up. The outstanding courage and skill of the crews was recognised alike in Germany as in England. Squadron Leader Nettleton received the VC, and other decorations for bravery were given to some members of the surviving crews. Churchill sent an immediate note to Harris:

> We must plainly regard the attack of the Lancasters on the U-boat engine factory at Augsburg as an outstanding achievement of the Royal Air Force. Undeterred by heavy losses at the outset 44 and 97 Squadrons pierced in broad daylight into the Heart of Germany and struck a vital point with deadly precision.
>
> Pray convey the thanks of His Majesty's Government to the officers and men who accomplished this memorable feat of arms in which no life was lost in vain.
>
> W.S.C.
> April 18, 1942.

This message was actually written in the Prime Minister's own handwriting, in red ink on Chequers notepaper, and given to Harris when he was reporting to Churchill on the Augsburg raid and discussing other plans he had in mind for the bomber offensive.

Life was, in fact, lost in vain in one sense, and Harris knew it. A very small portion of the plant had been put out of action, but not for long. However, on the success side, the attack, following Lübeck, had began to establish in the minds of the public, Parliament and Ministries that Bomber Command was an effective offensive force after all and, therefore, deserved some backing. Indeed, there was only one sour note at this time, and that came from Lord Selborne, the Minister of Economic Warfare, who wrote a letter of protest to the Prime Minister saying that Augsburg should not have been attacked because it was not on his list of six classes of precision targets recommended by his Ministry. Instead, he said, if Harris was prepared to go to the Augsburg area, then he should have chosen the ball-bearing factory at Schweinfurt. Churchill asked Harris for his comments on Selborne's letter. Harris wrote a very full reply which, in essence, appreciated the Minister's views and at the same time explained how the Minister knew nothing about air operations and was talking nonsense! Schweinfurt had, he said, been considered, but to attack by following a direct route to this target in daylight, and by returning in a similar manner, would have ended in complete disaster as no surprise could have been achieved and the aircraft would have had to fly over densely defended German territory for much of the way. The Augsburg route had been south deep into France, with a feint for Munich, and finally on to Augsburg. To follow similar tactics for Schweinfurt would have put it well out of range, 'unless,' Harris wrote, 'the aircraft returned thence due west across the Rhine. This, however, would have brought them, while still in too much daylight, right across some of the heaviest defences in Germany. They would have had to cross these at high altitude, and the higher you go the longer the daylight persists.' In other words they would have been sitting ducks for both flak and fighters. 'Alternatively,' he continued,

> they would have had to dawdle around, marking time until dark, in a dangerous area. To return by the south about route from Schweinfurt put it right out of range, 200 miles further than Augsburg. Moreover, Schweinfurt, having no such leading landmarks as Augsburg, was extremely difficult, if not impossible to find in a hedge-hopping operation such as that envisaged ... The attack was based and the objective selected on the consideration of a large number of strategical, tactical and technical factors of so overwhelming import that the purely economic factor necessarily fell into minor focus ... The Minister rightly describes the MAN factory at Augsburg as not vital to the enemy war effort in itself, but he is possibly as yet unaware that we are currently, and have been for some time, making a dead set at the whole of the submarine diesel engine capacity in Germany. In this we have been in the closest liaison with his Department ...

Harris's ruthless reply, which was dated 2 May, was a masterpiece of putting a Minister in his place with the maximum of over-politeness. It could easily have annoyed Churchill, but, in fact, it met with his approval. He wrote:

Air Marshal Harris,
Thank you very much for your careful and admirable explanation, which completely satisfies me. I am forwarding it to Lord Selborne, and suggesting that he and you might lunch together one day to talk things over.

W.S.C.

3.5.42

They never did!

Another element of success in this raid was, as Harris himself says: 'It demonstrated beyond all question that daylight attacks on Germany could at that time only be carried out by Bomber Command with a prohibitive casualty rate.' Success, in this case, was knowledge of the Command's limitations at a small cost of crews and aircraft.

But before April was over, Harris was to add another highly successful attack to his growing list of 'winners' as a 'freshman' C-in-C. On the four successive nights of 23/24, 24/25, 25/26 and 26/27 April, the town of Rostock on the Baltic coast, even further away than Lübeck, was, by standards at that time, heavily bombed. It was a target of secondary importance, but rather more important than Lübeck, with a busy port being used for supplies to the Russian front and for importing vital materials from Sweden, submarine building yards and a large Heinkel aircraft assembly plant. The weather was perfect on all four nights with a nearly full moon. Just over 500 sorties were flown and 305 tons of incendiaries and 442 tons of high explosives were dropped. Gee again assisted materially in the navigation over a major portion of the route, enabling crews to be more concentrated in time and space even as far as the target, which was some seventy miles beyond Gee range. The damage was formidable. The Heinkel factory was severely hit—the Turkish Ambassador in Berlin told his Government that 'Neptune Shipbuilding Yard and the Heinkel factory have been completely destroyed from end to end.' More than 70 per cent of the city had been devastated, port installations had been wrecked, all services had been disrupted and over 100,000 people had been rendered homeless. Goebbels was livid. On 26 April he wrote: 'It has been, it must be admitted, pretty disastrous ... The Führer arrived in Berlin at noon ... he is in extremely bad humour about the poor anti-aircraft defence at Rostock which caused him endless worry.' Then, on 27 April: 'Last night the heaviest air attack yet launched had the seaport of Rostock once again as its objective. Tremendous damage is reported. During the morning hours no exact estimate can be made, as all long-distance communication with Rostock has been interrupted.' On 28 April after the fourth successive raid: 'The air raid last night on Rostock was even more devastating than those before. Community life there is practically at an end ... The situation in the city is in some sections catastrophic.' Two days later he received the official reports about conditions in Rostock. He wrote: 'Seven-tenths of the city have been wiped out. More than 100,000 people had to be evacuated ... At Rostock there was, in fact, panic.'

The total cost to Bomber Command was twelve aircraft.

Harris finished April with a small attack on Cologne with ninety-two aircraft on the night of the 27th/28th, one on Kiel with eighty-seven aircraft on the night of the 28th/29th, both of which were successful enough to draw more pained comment from Goebbels and both of which produced quite substantial damage as evidenced by photographic reconnaissance. There had, of course, been other raids during the month, including one in the early hours of 13 April—Harris's fiftieth birthday. That raid was on the Ruhr with Essen as the main target and 327 aircraft attacking.

During the entire period since his takeover as C-in-C on 22 February the activity of the Command had been significantly increased and the effectiveness of the bombing had been so great that, for the first time, the Germans had squealed aloud. Not only had the bombing been stepped up, but so also had the sea-mining. 'Vegetables', as the mines were called, had been sown off the Frisians, in the Bight, in the Belts, at the entrance to Kiel Fiord, off the west coast of France and in the Baltic. Before the end of April a new minefield had been started as far distant as the approaches to the port of Danzig.

But there was one other event which occurred during Harris's first few weeks as C-in-C that was of supreme importance to the successful development of the strategic bombing offensive in the years to come. The advanced echelon of the United States Eighth Air Force, which was in fact the nucleus of its Eighth Bomber Command, arrived in England at the end of February 1942, under the command of Brigadier-General Ira C. Eaker, a Texan and an old acquaintance and firm friend of Harris. The acquaintance had first been made in 1938 when Harris went to America on a buying mission and Eaker was on General H. H. Arnold's Air Staff in Washington. It had been renewed and had developed into a friendship when Harris had again been in Washington in 1941 to head the newly formed RAF Delegation and had worked closely with Arnold, General Carl Spaatz, who was to command the US Eighth Air Force in England, and Eaker. Now, within a few weeks of Harris returning to England to take command of RAF Bomber Command, Eaker had crossed the Atlantic with the advance party of the US Eighth Bomber Command which he was to lead.

The headquarters of the US Eighth Bomber Command were to be established at Wycombe Abbey, a famous girls' school which had been taken over for the purpose and which was situated within a few miles of the RAF Bomber Command HQ. But when Eaker first arrived, Harris insisted that he stay with him at Springfield, his official residence. For the first few months, therefore, whilst the US Eighth Bomber Command Headquarters were being prepared, Eaker stayed with the Harris family, all of whom he knew well. His advance party of officers stayed as guests in the Officers'

Mess of RAF Bomber Command HQ. Also during this period, Eaker spent most of his days working at Bomber Command alongside Harris, attending all operational planning sessions and being brought into close contact with every aspect of the Command's activities. Saundby, who was also living at Springfield, wrote of this period: 'Harris and Eaker were firm friends and they laid the foundations of a cooperation between the two long-range bombardment forces that was both admirable and enduring.'

It was, however, to be some months before the Americans were to be in a position to operate. Indeed, their first Flying Fortresses did not arrive in England until 1 July 1942, and their first operational mission, which was against the marshalling yards at Rouen in France, was not flown until 17 August 1942: their first mission against a German target was as late as 27 January 1943, when they made a daylight attack on Wilhelmshaven. But during the waiting period the links were forged between these two potentially great offensive bombing forces which were to produce that concerted effort of round-the-clock bombing in 1944 and 1945 which made the invasion of Europe by the Allies possible, and which finally brought Germany to her knees. The credit for this powerful link and for the remarkable spirit of cooperation and comradeship that developed between Bomber Command and the US Eighth Air Force must go largely to Harris.

14
To bomb

The first four months of 1942 had seen a profound change in the success of the bombing of Germany as compared with those earlier operations which had been analysed in the Butt Report. But it was clear to Harris that he still needed two vital items before he could produce destruction by bombing on a sufficient scale to be decisive. Gee's accuracy of track and time-keeping enabled him to marshal large forces over England and to concentrate them along the route and over the target, giving greater protection against flak and fighters, and helping to increase damage as a result of concentration in the target area; it also assisted the return to, and landing at, bases with a minimum of crashes over home country. In fact, the advantages gained from Gee were very considerable. But it was not sufficiently accurate for a target-finding or blind-bombing device, nor was its range of 350/400 miles adequate to provide accurate navigation to the more distant targets in Germany, including the important one of Berlin. Therefore one of Harris's needs was for a longer-range system and a more precise target-finding equipment. The other was for enough bomber aircraft to carry the size of bomb load that he knew to be essential to make any real impression on the Ruhr towns, and places like Bremen, Hamburg, Hannover, Frankfurt, Stuttgart, Mannheim, München, Nürnberg and Berlin.

Solving the problems of navigation and blind bombing were now well in hand with the scientists, but defensive-mindedness before and during the war had led to a complete lack of official interest in the needs of the bomber, resulting in it being inadequately equipped for its role. The scientists, however, in their development of RDF radio pulse techniques for detecting aircraft and for enabling the night fighter to 'see' the enemy in the dark, stalk him, and shoot him down, had foreseen applications of these systems which would aid the night bomber in its task. Indeed, the members of the Telecommunications Research Establishment had been discussing what could be done about finding towns at night as early as 1940. Then, on the last Sunday in October 1941, Dr P. I. Dee, who had been experimenting with fighter aircraft air-interception equipment outside the Research Establishment's laboratories above Swanage, suddenly realised that the downward angle at which they were seeing reflection signals in the direction of the Isle of Wight was not appreciably different from the downward angle from an aircraft when viewing towns or coastline at long range. In that moment, an instrument christened 'Home Sweet Home', or H2S for short, by Lord Cherwell, was born. The first working models, which were crude in the extreme, were demonstrated to Wing Commander Saward, head of the Bomber Command RDF Department, and Flight Lieutenant E. J. Dickie, one of his staff, early in January 1942.

The principle of H2S was based on the fact that very high frequency radio waves travel in straight lines and, in the same manner as light, are reflected back to source from suitable surfaces in varying degree. By transmitting these radio waves downwards, the reflections—called echoes—could be picked up on a receiver and displayed in an aircraft on a cathode ray tube. Since built-up area gave strong echoes, open flat land medium echoes, and water no echoes at all, water was represented by a dark shadowy appearance, and land by a lighter response, and a town by a bright area of light roughly in the shape of the built-up area viewed. Effectively, the equipment presented to the navigator a continuous map picture, on a circular cathode ray tube, of the terrain over which the aircraft was flying. It was so displayed that the aircraft's position was always at the centre of the tube, with north at the top. A finger of light constantly indicated the heading of the aircraft. Other features were added to enable the scale of the picture to be altered so that the operator could have a thirty- to forty-mile view of the area all around him, or an enlarged and more detailed view of ten miles for bombing purposes. The system also incorporated a highly accurate RDF altimeter. However, the picture seen was not an exact replica of a map and had to be interpreted, but coastlines did represent an almost perfect pattern of what was indicated on a map.

The potential of the system was considerable and Bomber Command pressed for its introduction immediately after its RDF representatives had received demonstrations. It faced an initial major problem, however, and that was the type of output valve that could be used. The first demonstrations had been given using a klystron, which was too low-powered to provide a strong enough reflected signal to ensure a picture showing enough detail for towns to be identified, and covering enough area around the aircraft's position for purposes of good navigation. What was needed was the very new development known as the magnetron, which was capable of giving much greater output power, resulting in a stronger reflected signal and, therefore, improved range and definition. But it was highly secret and was the real success behind the RAF night fighter's latest air interception (AI) equipment and the ground controlled interception (GCI) system. Therefore there was substantial opposition to its use in any equipment which would be flown over enemy territory and might thus fall into enemy hands.

However, H2S had a firm backer in Lord Cherwell, who exerted his influence on Churchill. This did not bring about a sudden decision on the magnetron, but it did result in an active interest in the system being taken by Churchill and pressure from him to progress its full development with all speed. On 6 May 1942, in a letter to the Secretary of State for Air, Sir Archibald Sinclair, he wrote:

> I hope that a really large order for H2S has been placed and that nothing will be allowed to stand in the way of getting this apparatus punctually ... I have heard Sir Robert Renwick mentioned as a man of drive and business experience who has already rendered valuable service in connection with Gee. Perhaps you might think he is a good man for this purpose ...

In fact, Sinclair had already put Sir Robert Renwick in charge of all RDF aids to bombing and navigation—largely at Cherwell's instigation. Renwick's list now included not only Gee and H2S, but also Oboe and GH. Oboe was a precision system whereby the aircraft could be tracked over a target by two ground stations in England and then instructed when to release its marker bombs so that they would fall within 100 yards of the selected target. Its range was limited to 300 miles, but this was still enough to cover the important Ruhr targets. H2S and Oboe were, however, insufficiently advanced in development by the spring of 1942 for there to be any hope that they would be available for operational use much before the beginning of 1943. GH, which was the reverse of Oboe, in that the aircraft instrument measured its distance from two RDF ground stations in England, tracking itself over the target by measurement from one and determining its bomb release point by its distance from the other, was even further away in development and, because of this, might well have been abandoned. But GH had an important advantage—up to eighty aircraft could operate on the system simultaneously from one pair of stations, and any number of targets could be attacked at the same time. Therefore the system could be used for direct bombing. With Oboe only one aircraft at a time could be operated across the target, using one pair of ground stations. This meant that the system had essentially to be limited to marker tactics.

Harris was well aware of these forthcoming aids, and insisted on being well briefed by his RDF staff through Saundby. He also pressed hard for greater priority to be given to their development, not only by constantly raising the matter with Portal, but also through his regular contacts with Churchill, particularly during the Prime Minister's frequent weekend visits to Chequers which was only a few miles distant from Headquarters Bomber Command. But if he was aware of the new developments, he also knew that they would not help him to improve the effectiveness of the bombing offensive for some time to come. He therefore concentrated at this stage on building up the size of his force. To do this in the face of a very considerable opposition to the policy of strategic bombing, he realised that he needed to stage a dramatic raid that would not only be highly successful in terms of its results, but which would capture the support for Bomber Command from the public at large. Harris also wanted proof for himself that his Command could achieve industrial destruction on a decisive scale, provided he could put sufficient aircraft onto the target in one raid. Lübeck and Rostock had proved that a small relatively undefended town could be seriously disrupted by a concentrated attack of some 200 to 500 aircraft. Lübeck had received the attention of 234 aircraft and 300 tons of bombs in one night, and Rostock 521 aircraft and 747 tons of bombs spread over four nights. But what would be needed for a major Ruhr town, or a large seaport town such as Hamburg?

Harris says: 'I was convinced that a force of 250 to 300 aircraft would be totally inadequate to saturate the defences of a major industrial town of half a million inhabitants. But if we attacked with a much larger force—supposing we had it—could we put many hundreds of aircraft over the target to achieve the desired concentration without danger of collision and chaos in the air—say 600 an hour which was six times greater than concentrations achieved up to the end of 1941?'

By April of 1942, Harris knew the answer. With Gee it was possible to achieve such concentrations. The trial raid on Cologne, late in March, with 120 aircraft concentrated into an attack lasting twenty minutes, had gone a long way towards proving the principle. The problem was that at this stage not all his aircraft had Gee. However, the numbers were increasing and he knew that he could expect to have at least 400 aircraft fitted by the end of May, which would mean that most of his front line strength would have Gee at that date. But this was not a big enough figure for Harris. He had already set his heart on 1,000 aircraft, a figure which he had confided to Saundby.

'At the beginning of May,' he says, 'I did have a force of over 1,000 aircraft in my Command, if I included the aircraft and crews at the Operational Training Units and the Heavy Conversion Units. The OTU crews were, of course, only half trained crews, but the more advanced ones had already had some slight operational experience by dropping leaflets over France. But to use them presented many obvious dangers. I should be committing not only the whole of my front line strength, but absolutely all my reserves in a single battle. And if anything went seriously wrong I knew that the Command's whole programme of training and expansion might conceivably be wrecked. As against the dangers, however, I knew that the advantages of a successful operation with 1,000 aircraft would be very great. It would provide a practical measure of what could be achieved as soon as the bomber force was expanded. The result of using an adequate force against Germany would be there for all to see, and I knew it would enable me to press for more aircraft, crews, and equipment with far more effect than by putting forward theoretical arguments about hitting the enemy where it hurt most. Such a demonstration I knew to be the only way which was likely to prevent our squadrons being snatched away from us by the Navy and the Middle East, or would prevent our efforts being diverted to useless subsidiary targets. Also I reckoned it would help us to extract the radar (RDF) navigational aids, target indicators and other equipment that we desperately needed from the departments that had withheld them from us for so long.'

One evening in the first week in May, Harris discussed the matter again with Saundby in the peace and quiet of Springfield. It was on this occasion that Saundby, who had just made a study of the possible availability of aircraft for a mammoth strike, told Harris that by using aircraft from the OTUs and Heavy Conversion Units with instructor crews and the more experienced pupil crews, it would be possible to raise 700 plus aircraft. This meant that Harris needed outside help to the extent of about 300 aircraft and crews. It was clear to both him and Saundby that the most satisfactory outside help could come from Coastal Command to whom, during the past twelve months, some 200 or more aircraft and crews had been transferred from Bomber Command.

For such a colossal experiment it was obvious that a full moon and good weather would be necessary—and the next full moon period was from 26 to 31 May. If this almost outrageous plan was to be put into action soon, then the choices were limited. The next full moon would be late in June. Then July. Time was running out. With his incredible boldness, Harris decided to plan for the end of May and promptly went to seek support, in the first instance, from Portal. He persuaded Portal that a raid of this magnitude would, if successful, surely bring powerful support from official sources and public alike for the expansion of the bomber force, as it would prove that by bombing, Germany could be effectively attacked and, therefore, Britain's Russian ally could be directly assisted. Furthermore, he emphasised that it would demonstrate how Germany's overall strategic effort could be seriously impaired by industrial disruption and the need to disperse military resources to defend the homeland. Portal, in fact, required no persuasion. He was as great a believer as Harris that a bomber offensive against Germany was the only means by which the enemy could be attacked for months, if not years, to come. But he warned Harris of the opposition that would quickly rear its head unless there was powerful political support.

So Harris visited Chequers the Sunday after seeing Portal, to seek backing from Churchill. The idea was received with enthusiasm and discussed until three o'clock in the morning. Churchill listened to the whole plan, to the fact that the raid would be concentrated into ninety minutes, that the losses should not be greater than 5 per cent because the vast concentration of 1,000 aircraft into so short a space of time would saturate the defences, and that the target would be Hamburg or Cologne, because they had water close by which would help identification, and because they were within Gee range. When Harris left Chequers he had Churchill's blessing and his statement that he was prepared for a loss of 100 aircraft, or 10 per cent, on an operation of such vital importance. Harris recalls that as he drove back to Springfield in his Bentley: 'I found myself humming *Malbrouck s'en va-t'en guerre*. I suddenly realised that that tune always came into my head whenever I had just left him. The spirit of Marlborough did indeed breathe in his descendant, and most emphatically he was going to war. Whether it was coincidence at first and habit thereafter, I do not know. Whatever it was, the mixture of Chequers, moonlight, Winston's

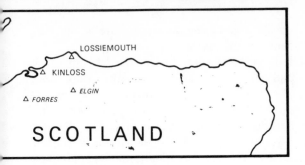

LOSSIEMOUTH

△ KINLOSS

△ ELGIN

△ FORRES

SCOTLAND

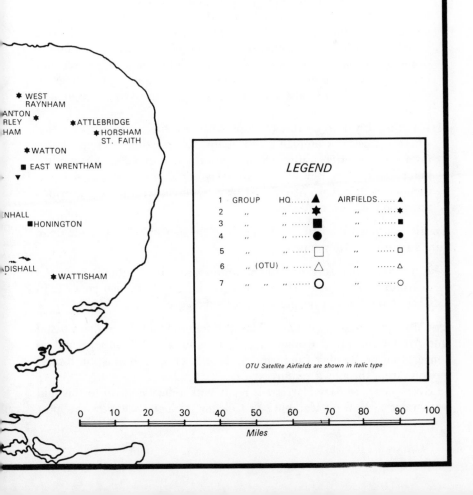

BOMBER COMMAND
5th March 1942

✱ WEST
RAYNHAM

ANTON
RLEY ✱

HAM

✱ ATTLEBRIDGE

✱ HORSHAM
ST. FAITH

✱ WATTON

■ EAST WRENTHAM

▼

NHALL

■ HONINGTON

DISHALL

✱ WATTISHAM

LEGEND

		HQ		AIRFIELDS	
1	GROUP	▲			▲
2	,,	,, ★		,,	★
3	,,	,, ■		,,	■
4	,,	,, ●		,,	●
5	,,	,, ☐		,,	☐
6	,, (OTU)	,, △		,,	△
7	,, ,,	,, ◯		,,	◯

OTU Satellite Airfields are shown in italic type

0   10   20   30   40   50   60   70   80   90   100

Miles

inspiring courage, and my knowledge of the desperate state of the war, always sent me home whistling or singing that old war song.'

The truth was that both these men were alike in that they had the audacity and courage to pull off such a fantastic venture. Both were determined to go to war rather than let it come to them.

Even before the 'Thousand Plan' was finally approved, and before any approach was made for assistance to the other commands, Bomber Command was subjected to yet more demands for transfer of its trained aircrews to Coastal Command and Army Cooperation Command. This at a time when Harris's staff were drawing up preliminary plans and making forward preparations for the great raid. An incensed Harris wrote to Portal on 11 May:

> With your knowledge of the crew position in my Command, and of the constant drains which are inflicted upon my OTU outputs and my operational units, you may agree that there is justification for a rising sense of anger, if not despair, at the way the other Commands (and indeed some departments of the Air Ministry) regard Bomber Command as a milch cow whenever they feel the slightest pangs of hunger or even mere inconvenience within their own organisations.
>
> This robbery has gone on for so long, and is so persistent and rhythmic in its recurrence, that I was wondering whether you would now issue an instruction to other Commands and departments concerned that they are once and for all to disabuse themselves of the idea that Bomber Command is their natural and proper source of revenue, whenever they feel that they would like to increase their own forces or organisations, or get themselves out of some temporary shortage of the type common to all Commands.
>
> I would ask you to do this because it has become apparent to me that whereas Coastal Command and Army Cooperation Command, for instance, are often aware of their future requirements for months beforehand, they never seem to take the slightest steps to equip themselves in advance from their own resources with the crews which they know will be necessary.

Harris continued the letter with details of the demands being made upon him and finished by saying:

> I wonder what sort of outcry would arise if Bomber Command demanded and expected as a matter of course fully trained crews from Coastal and Army Cooperation Commands every time it expanded!

Portal's reply was prompt. On 13 May he wrote and told Harris that Coastal and Army Cooperation Commands had been informed that they could no longer draw on Bomber Command for trained crews and must, in future, provide from their own resources.

By Monday, 18 May Harris was ready with a detailed plan for his raid with 1,000 aircraft on Hamburg or Cologne. Cologne was now the most favoured target, being well within Gee coverage. The advice from Dr B. G. Dickins, the head of the Operational Research Section, strongly supported by Saundby, Air Commodore Harrison* and Group Captain Elworthy,† the three principal planners, was: 'Stay within Gee coverage. Go to Cologne.' Wing Commander Saward had assured for him a total figure of close on 500 aircraft equipped with Gee by installing it in 100 unfitted aircraft of the Heavy Conversion Units to add to the 400 first line aircraft already equipped.

On that Monday morning Harris saw Portal at the Air Ministry and gave him the brief details of the plan, emphasising that to achieve a force of 1,000 aircraft he was looking for 250 to 300 from the other commands. By now, he was also keen on undertaking two raids within the forthcoming moon period, and this idea he also put to Portal, explaining that if the first raid was a success and losses were low then it was arguable that with such a force already marshalled it should be used at least a second time if conditions favoured a further raid.

On 19 May, Portal told Harris by letter that the Prime Minister warmly approved of the Thousand Plan—a fact which Harris already knew—and after speaking to the First Sea Lord about it, thought there would be no objection to the cooperation of Coastal Command in the venture unless they had special operations on hand at the time. Portal therefore suggested that Harris proceed with his arrangements after discussing the matter with the other Commanders-in-Chief concerned, and asked him to let him know if there were any difficulties. He finished by saying: 'Please let me know before the operation is actually staged so that I can tell the Prime Minister.'

The next day, letters prepared by Harris and Saundby in conjunction with the Operations and Intelligence Staffs, setting out the details of the Thousand Plan, were despatched to Coastal, Army Cooperation, Fighter and Training Commands, and to the AOCs of the five operational Bomber Groups and the Bomber Operational Training Groups. In these letters Harris asked for the maximum possible contribution. The intention he expressed in plain blunt terms: '... to annihilate one of Germany's main industrial centres by fire.' With this general letter went a separate one to each individual commander detailing the specific actions required from different Groups. To the Cs-in-C of the other Commands he indicated the special help he needed from them. Under conditions of a full moon the bombers would be easier prey for the night fighters and he therefore requested attacks by Fighter Command, in conjunction with his own light bombers in No 2 Group, on selected German night fighter aerodromes, followed by fighter sweeps over the North Sea to give protection to

---

* Air Commodore R. Harrison was the Deputy Senior Air Staff Officer.

† Group Captain S. C. Elworthy was Group Captain Operations. After the war he became Chief of the Air Staff and then as Marshal of the Royal Air Force Sir Charles Elworthy, GCB, CBE, DSO, MVO, DFC, AFC, MA, he became Chief of the Defence Staff. Later, Marshal of the Royal Air Force Lord Elworthy, Governor of Windsor Castle.

returning aircraft. From Coastal Command he wanted a contribution of 250 aircraft. From Army Cooperation Command and Training Command he expected little but hoped for something.

On 21 May, Joubert of Coastal Command* responded with great enthusiasm and promised the 250 aircraft. This was the major contribution Harris needed to reach his 1,000 figure, but somehow both Harris and Saundby were mistrustful of the Admiralty. Their mistrust was justified. With the attack planned for the night of 27/28 May, or the first night within the moon period thereafter which provided suitable weather conditions, the Admiralty intervened one day beforehand and gave orders to Joubert that under no circumstances were Coastal Command to take part in the operation. It was vicious timing, for it reduced the overall figure to some 800 aircraft. 'Typical Admiralty bloody-mindedness!' Harris commented.

Army Cooperation Command promptly offered nothing, but Air Marshal Sir William Welsh, the C-in-C of Flying Training Command, produced a few aircraft and crews, and Fighter Command stuck by their promise to support the raid with harassing attacks on enemy fighter aerodromes and with North Sea sweeps in protection of returning bombers.

With the figure of aircraft below the 1,000 mark, Harris stubbornly refused to give up his dream and called for a last-minute Herculean effort to raise the extra aircraft and crews from within Bomber Command itself. Weather helped him, for it was not until the night of 30/31 May that it was sufficiently good for the attack to be undertaken. By that time, by dint of tremendous work in the Groups and squadrons, to make more aircraft serviceable and by raising many 'scratch' crews from Group and station staffs, the figure reached 1,046 aircraft of which 1,042 were from Bomber Command alone and four were from Training Command. The Admiralty's bloody-mindedness had proved to be the ill wind that blew plenty of good—the Thousand Plan was now entirely a Bomber Command affair.

The decision for the attack to proceed was taken by Harris on the morning of 30 May, and weather dictated that the target was to be Cologne. The approach was to be made from west to east with the Gee aircraft of Nos 1 and 3 Groups opening the attack, carrying a maximum load of incendiaries, with Neumarkt, in the centre of the old town, as the aiming point. The 367 aircraft of the Operational Training Units were to follow this incendiary attack using the fires started by the Gee aircraft as their guide. The final wave was to consist of all the available four-engined heavy bombers of Nos 4 and 5 Groups, consisting of just over 200 Gee equipped Lancasters and Halifaxes carrying high explosives and incendiaries, packed into a fifteen-minute final crescendo. The total attack over the target was to last precisely ninety minutes.

The raid was an outstanding success. 898 aircraft claimed to have reached and attacked the target, dropping 1,455 tons of bombs of which 915

---

* Air Chief Marshal Sir Philip Joubert de la Ferté, KCB, CMG, DSO, C-in-C Coastal Command.

tons were incendiaries and 540 tons were high explosives. Forty aircraft were lost, representing only 3·8 per cent of the total force despatched. Time keeping en route to and over the target, and back to bases in England, was excellent. The results, compared to any previous attacks against German towns, were prodigious; over 600 acres of built-up area were completely destroyed and more than 250 factories were destroyed or seriously damaged; 200,000 people had to be evacuated from the city; communications, power supplies, gas and water supplies, and travelling facilities were all seriously disrupted. The full extent of the damage could not be assessed by aerial photographic evidence for several days because of the huge pall of smoke that mushroomed over the city to a height of 15,000 feet. For Cologne it was a catastrophic raid.

Before Bomber Command knew the true result of its mammoth attack, which had gone by the code name of 'Operation Millennium', Göring, Hitler's Reichmarschall and head of the German Air Force, was unable to believe the first fantastic reports to come from Cologne. Albert Speer, who was then Minister for Armaments and War Production, was with Göring at the Veldenstein Castle in Franconia when he was told of the reported weight of the attack by his adjutant. Speer said that he shouted: 'Impossible! That many bombs cannot be dropped in a single night! Connect me with the Gauleiter of Cologne.' Speer went on to relate that an incredible conversation then took place on the telephone between Göring and Gauleiter Grohé, in which Göring said the information from the Cologne Police Commissioner was a 'stinking lie'. After Grohé confirmed the bad news, Göring replied: 'I tell you as Reichmarschall that the figures cited are simply too high. How can you dare to report such fantasies to the Führer?' But Göring was quickly to learn the truth and that Cologne was in a state of chaos. His promise that the German Air Force would never let the enemy attack the Fatherland had, overnight, worn remarkably thin. Speer said Göring just could not believe, at first, that such a blow could fall on a German town.

The tremendous success of this raid hit the headlines of the Press on both sides of the Atlantic. Harris had been right in all his assumptions. A major city could be severely devastated and disrupted with a heavy enough attack; with concentration, defences could be saturated; an air raid of this size could capture the public imagination and marshal support from all quarters for an expansion of Bomber Command. The gamble had paid off.

The congratulations on this epic feat of arms, which was perhaps as great as any in the history of Britain, poured in from all quarters. The first came from Churchill himself. It read:

I congratulate you and the whole of the Bomber Command upon the remarkable feat of organisation which enabled you to dispatch over 1,000 bombers to the Cologne area in a single night, and without confusion to concentrate their action over the target into so short a time as one hour and a half. This proof of the growing power of the British Bomber Force is also the herald of what Germany will receive, city by city, from now on.'

W.S.C.

From General Arnold, Harris received the following message:

Dear Air Marshal Harris,
As Commanding general of the US Army Air Forces I desire to extend my congratulations to you, your staff and combat crews for the great raid last night on Cologne. It was bold in conception and superlative in execution.
Please convey to your officers and men my admiration for their courage and skill, and say that our Air Forces hope very soon to fly and fight beside them in these decisive blows against our common enemy.

H. H. Arnold
Lieutenant-General, USA
Commanding General, Army Air Forces.

From Russia, too, came an accolade:

4th June, 1942
In the name of the personnel of the Long Range Bomber Force of the Red Army, I beg you to accept congratulations on the outstandingly successful initiation of massed blows on Hitlerite Germany by the British Bomber Command under your personal direction.
The precision and effectiveness of this immense operation and the valour and skill of the men who took part are highly appreciated by our pilots who beg me to send battle greetings to their British brothers in arms.

A. Golovanov
Lieutenant-General
Commander of the Long Range Bomber
Aviation of the Red Army.

But perhaps of all the messages Harris received, the one that gave him most pleasure was from Colonel Guest, the then Minister of Air for Southern Rhodesia. It read quite simply:

Your old comrades of the First Rhodesia Regiment send you congratulations. Well done.

On 10 June 1942, Harris was made a Knight Commander of the Bath.

15
Preparations for pathfinding

The Thousand Raid on Cologne was followed almost immediately, on the night of 1/2 June, by another major attack; this time with 956 aircraft, including 347 from the Operational Training Units. The target was Essen. The weather was unreliable, and cloud mixed with industrial haze made visual identification of Essen extremely difficult. The result was that the raid was a partial failure in that Essen only received minor damage and Krupps was untouched. The scattered bombing which occurred on this occasion did, however, cause heavy damage to Oberhausen and Mulheim which lay to the north-west and south-west of Essen. The size of the force once again saturated defences and the loss of thirty-one aircraft, or 3·2 per cent, was low for the most strongly defended district of Germany.

Although Harris planned to continue to use the Operational Training Units in order to mount one or two mammoth attacks with 700 to 1,000 aircraft in the full moon period of each month, he was in fact frustrated in his attempts by bad weather. On the night of 25/26 June, however, he managed the third Thousand Raid, when 1,006 aircraft were despatched to attack Bremen. Coastal Command, after the personal intervention of the Prime Minister with the Admiralty, provided 102 aircraft, the other 904 coming from Bomber Command's own resources, including 272 aircraft of the Operational Training Units. In this raid, serious damage was done to the Focke-Wulf works and to the Deutsche Schiffwerke shipbuilding yards, and factories and warehouses all over the city suffered severely. In addition, some 27 acres of the business and residential areas were completely destroyed. But the damage was not on the scale of that achieved at Cologne. Against this, however, it has to be noted that the target was cloud covered and most of the first wave of Gee aircraft had to bomb 'blind' on the indications of their Gee equipment, the rest of the force bombing the glow from the fires started by these aircraft which was reflected vividly in the cloud.

The losses on the Bremen raid proved to be higher than those on the other two big attacks. Forty-nine aircraft, 5 per cent of the force despatched, failed to return.

Apart from these three major raids, only four more operations over Germany, using aircraft and crews from the Operational Training Units, were undertaken in 1942. These were against Düsseldorf on the nights of 31 July/1 August and 10/11 September, and against Bremen on the night of 13/14 September and against Essen on the night of 16/17 September. The Düsseldorf attacks were highly successful, interspersed as they were by a small attack on 15/16 August. The first attack was by 630 aircraft, the second by 131 and the third by 476. 300 acres in the centre of the town were utterly destroyed, a single 8,000-pound bomb totally wrecked the main railway station, a large area of the docks and associated warehouses were devastated, and thirty factories, including the Schiess-Defries and Krieger steel works and two major chemical works were seriously damaged. In fact, the destruction was on a similar scale to that of Cologne.

The raid on Bremen was also a considerable success, but the Essen attack, when the target was again covered by industrial haze and cloud, was effectively a failure. The means of finding Essen and bombing it accurately had not yet come to hand.

These air actions were not the only ones that took place during the period June to the end of September 1942. Harris mounted raids of more than 200 aircraft ten times in June, and in July there were again ten major raids with forces of the order of 300 aircraft on each occasion. Bremen, Hamburg, Kiel, Emden, Frankfurt, Karlsruhe, Munich, Aachen, Osnabrück, as well as the Ruhr towns, all received attention at a level which created a growing fear of the increasing bombing raids amongst the German people. Apart from industrial and town area devastation, the famous battle-cruiser *Gneisenau* was so badly damaged at Kiel by bombing that the First Sea Lord actually conveyed his sincere thanks and congratulations to Harris and confirmed that photographic reconnaissance indicated her condition to be so serious that she was unlikely to put to sea again for a long time. In fact, she remained out of action for the rest of the war.

In addition to the bombing during this period, more than 4,000 mines were laid.

The success of Bomber Command was still, however, insufficient to be decisive in the war against Germany, and Harris knew it. But he had proved, except to those blindly opposed to the strategic air offensive, that with a large enough force at his disposal and with adequate modern navigational and target-finding aids, Bomber Command could bring about a situation whereby an invasion of the continent of Europe could be contemplated without serious losses being sustained by the military and naval forces engaged in such a landing. Harris himself remained confident that a complete defeat of Germany could be achieved by bombing alone, provided he had an adequate night bombing force and the Americans had a big enough day bombing force for the combined forces to produce round-the-clock bombing on a scale similar to that achieved on the Thousand Raids. Portal was of the same opinion.

But the opposition to the build-up of Bomber Command continued to be effective, despite the mounting proof that a large-scale air offensive against Germany was capable of undermining the German will to continue the war and would, in any case, be essential to the success of any invasion venture of the future.

The means for improving navigation and target finding at night were advancing well, so far as scientific RDF aids were concerned at this time. There was, however, a growing feeling at the Air Ministry that a specialised target-finding force should be created by bringing together a number of squadrons under the command of one man and 'creaming off' from the Groups their best crews to man these squadrons and to sustain their losses. This idea was supported by Portal but opposed by Harris. Portal's support was influenced by Mr Justice Singleton's report on 'The Bombing of Germany', dated 20 May 1942, which had been prepared as a result of an instruction from the Prime Minister on 16 April 1942. This report reviewed the effects of the German bombing of England from August 1940 to June 1941 and indicated that its effect had been very serious, and would have been even more serious had it continued beyond that date and had it been intensified; this despite the fact that the offensive had not been well directed, and the tonnage of bombs dropped was small compared to the weights discharged by Bomber Command in the first few months of 1942. It went on to indicate what could be achieved against Germany by an increased weight of attack in the future, giving Lübeck and Rostock as examples. But Singleton was conscious of the difficulties of navigating to and finding targets in the Ruhr and other non-coastal areas, and his examination of attacks on the Ruhr area led him to conclude that the bomber force needed more and better scientific aids to locate difficult target areas if the greater weight of bombs carried was to be of any real value. If the means of getting to and of locating and bombing the industrial inland towns of Germany could be found, then Singleton had no doubts as to the importance of a strategic air offensive against Germany. He concluded his report with a very telling paragraph:

> To sum up, I do not think that great results can be hoped for within six months from 'air attacks on Germany at the greatest possible strength'.* I cannot help feeling that the six month period ought to be looked upon as leading up to, and forming part of, a longer and more sustained effort than as one expected to produce results within that limited time. Much depends on what happens in Russia. The effects of a reverse for Germany, or of lack of success, would be greatly increased by an intensified bombing programme in the autumn and winter. Effect on morale would normally be greater at that time than it would now. And if this was coupled with knowledge in Germany that the bombing would be on an increasing scale until the end, and with the realisation of the fact that the German Air Force could not again achieve equality, I think it

---

* The terms of reference to Mr Justice Singleton asked him, in considering the likely effects of bombing Germany, to assume 'air attacks on Germany at the greatest possible strength', during the next six months.

might well prove the turning point—provided always that greater accuracy can be achieved.

Singleton's emphasis on accuracy was qualified in his report by acceptance of the fact that RDF aids to navigation and bombing were just round the corner and when available, provided they came up to expectations, would greatly increase accuracy and, therefore, the effectiveness of the bomb load dropped on Germany.

Portal saw the Singleton Report as the first outside and impartial support for a large-scale strategic bomber offensive against Germany, but he was conscious of the emphasis on accuracy and aware that the new RDF aids to target finding and bombing, H2S and Oboe, were unlikely to be available even in limited quantities until the winter or early in 1943. Therefore he felt some means of target finding must be found as an interim measure, and a target finding force of the best and most experienced crews in Bomber Command seemed to him to be the best answer. He also went further in his thinking. He believed that the new RDF systems such as H2S would be in such short supply when they first became available that, initially, they should be concentrated in a target-finding force.

Harris was well aware of the problems of accurate bombing and the inadequacy of his then existing scientific aids. He was also more conversant than anyone with the new aids that he was eventually to receive. Moreover, he had already applied the principles of a target-finding force in Bomber Command. Indeed, from the moment that he took over command he had utilised target-finding methods with selected squadrons. But he was opposed to the formation of a *corps d'élite* with its inevitable disadvantage of fostering jealousy and upsetting morale by making the main force Groups feel they were inferior animals. Harris wanted the Groups, however, to have their own target-finding squadrons with the underlying principle that they should be selected for their efficient performance and good record on operations. He also had in mind that when the bomber force was big enough to undertake more than one major raid on the same night, on targets of such different content that they would require different methods of attack, then it would give him greater flexibility if his Groups had their own target-finding forces. They could then operate as separate forces on one particular target. He was even considering the possibility of Groups specialising in the methods of attack required for different categories of targets, but he realised that this was as yet a dream which could only be realised when the bomber force was nearer to twice its present size. But at least he wished to develop in that direction. In fact his opposition to a target-finding force was not in principle, but to the form in which the Air Ministry wished it to be established.

After several meetings with Portal on this contentious subject, Harris wrote a letter to him, dated 12 June 1942, advising him that the Group Commanders were also bitterly opposed to the formation of a separate target-finding force, independent of the Groups and under the command of a senior officer, and therefore constituting, in effect, a target-finding Group. However, he admitted the need for target-finding activities and put forward his own proposals. But Portal was not to be put off a separate target-finding force and he replied swiftly on 14 June:

My Dear Harris,
This is in answer to your letter ATH/DO/6 of the 12th June giving your latest views on our proposal for forming a Target Finding Force. As I read your letter, both you and those of your Command with whom you have discussed the scheme, agree on the urgent need for finding some method of using the best of your crews to identify and mark the target so as to enable the remainder to concentrate their attack on it and thus to avoid the present waste of effort which results from the majority of your attacks being dissipated over a wide area. I take it that you also agree that something must be done to prevent less expert crews from lighting fires in the wrong places during the first stage of an attack.

In the third para of your letter you say that all the Command representatives were utterly opposed to the formation of a Target Finding Force on the lines proposed by the Air Staff. Yet the suggestions which follow all seem to me to imply an admission of the need for such a force and present no reasonable argument against the Air Staff proposal. In fact they seem to me to include those earlier proposals for singling out the best crews and giving them distinctive badges etc to which you formerly objected so strongly on the grounds that this would involve the creation of a 'corps d'élite'. Please do not think that I fail to understand the objections to the 'corps d'élite' idea. To pack one unit with experts at the expense of other units *which have to do the same job* is most unsound and bad for morale. This is emphatically *not* what we are proposing. The TFF would have an entirely different and far more difficult task than the ordinary 'follow up' squadrons and this creates both the need and the justification for having a formation containing none but expert crews.

Over a period of three months your attitude seems to have progressed from the complete rejection of the Target Finding Force proposal, through a Target Finding Squadron phase to this present raid leader suggestion. I cannot feel it is logical that you should now reject the final and essential step of welding the selected crews into one closely knit organisation which, as I see it, is the only way to make their leadership and direction effective.

I cannot believe that your compromise will give equal results. You say that there is nothing particular to be gained from bringing the selected crews into one unit and locating them together on one aerodrome. As we see it, this is the essence of the problem. Without this close association there could be no continuity of technique; there could be no day to day improvement of method; and we could not ensure that the plans and briefing for each individual operation were similarly and clearly interpreted and acted upon by the force as a whole. In effect it would mean perpetuating the present rule-of-thumb tactical methods by segregated crews rather than introducing the finesse and polish which one would expect from a well trained and co-ordinated Target Finding Force. The problem confronting us is clearly so great that nothing less than the best will do.

Portal's reference to a raid leader scheme indicates that there was some confusion in his mind about Harris's ideas. Harris, in his letter 12 June, emphasised that he wanted the best squadron with the best crews to be selected in each Group for raid leadership. His difference with the Air Staff was that he wanted these squadrons to be retained in their Groups rather than that they should be welded into one separate *corps d'élite* or Group. In addition it was his idea that inter-Group conferences, consisting of raid leaders from each Group, should meet regularly to discuss target-finding methods and draw on each other's experience. It was also Harris's suggestion that the crews of the target-finding squadrons formed in the Groups should be called Raid Leaders and be given a special badge.

The advantages of the Harris proposal for a target-finding squadron in each Group were well and truly manifested in 1943, 1944, and 1945, when early in 1943 he began to introduce his own ideas by making No 5 Group an independent Group with No 617 Squadron as its target-finding squadron. It was, in fact, in this squadron that the famous Master Bomber technique was first developed. Later No 3 Group became independent with its own specialised target-finding tactics.

In his letter, Portal made one other statement which indicated a certain lack of understanding of the operational situation. He wrote:

> There is one further point which I particularly desire to emphasise. Your Raid Leader scheme would depend for such success as it might achieve largely upon the assistance of TR 1335 [Gee]. We have already had this equipment in use three months. We cannot expect immunity from interference much longer. When it is denied to us as a target locating device, it is clear that your proposal could not ensure to the Bomber Force the leadership which they must have if the average crews are to overcome their great and increasing difficulties.'

This comment applied equally to any form of target finding force, because the next RDF aids to night navigation and target location, Oboe and H2S, were unlikely to be available until the end of the year.

Portal ended his letter to Harris by saying:

> At the same time, I fully recognise the practical difficulties, and, although I do not consider the proposals which you have so far made go nearly far enough, I am reluctant to impose the Air Staff proposal upon you while you object so strongly to it. I would therefore like to discuss the subject with you tomorrow as a preliminary to holding the conference arranged for next Thursday, and I hope we shall be able to formulate an agreed scheme. The need for early action is increased by the Singleton

report which is now before the Chiefs of Staff. It brings out very clearly the urgent need for an increase in the percentage of bombs on the target, and any failure on our part to effect a radical improvement may well endanger the whole of our bomber policy.

Portal's reference to the susceptibility of Gee to interference was correct. Indeed the Germans commenced jamming the system on the night of 9/10 August 1942. However, the Command RDF staff were quick to react and, in conjunction with the Telecommunications Research Establishment, they had developed and installed in all aircraft an effective anti-jamming circuit by the morning of 21 August. This gave back to aircraft the use of Gee over much of its range.

Following Portal's letter, Harris had a further discussion with him and agreed to set up a target-finding force on the lines proposed by the Air Ministry. After this meeting he wrote to Portal confirming the way in which he intended to implement the decision.   This letter was dated 19 June and, in general, it reiterated his agreement to set up a separate target-finding force, albeit reluctantly, and the fashion in which he would establish this force. After making it clear that it was his opinion that what had already been done in the Command, in relation to target-finding practices, was the best under 'existing conditions with the force at my disposal', he listed the principles which he wished to be approved in connection with the Air Ministry scheme. In short, these were the provision of a special badge for all members of the crews of the target finding force; the name of the force to be the Pathfinder Force and the crews to be known as the Pathfinders; the force to consist of four squadrons initially, and six squadrons ultimately, the squadrons to be provided from the four operational Groups; the establishment of the Pathfinder Force to be in the East Anglia area; the promotion of all crew members to one step up in rank above equivalent ranks in main force squadrons; the manning of the force to be by 'creaming off' the best crews from the Groups initially, and for replacements, with a small proportion of replacement crews coming from the 'top of the class crews from each OTU output.' He completed his letter by saying;

> I am tackling the Group Commanders about setting up the force today, I hope therefore that you will be able to reassure me about the promotion and the badge as soon as possible. Our idea for the badge was the brass eagle, worn on the left hand top pocket flap underneath the wings and medals. There may be difficulty in getting this through, but unless it is insuperable, the use of an existing badge should speed things up . . . I am proceeding on the above lines now in order to avoid delay. Please let me know at once by telephone if I have interpreted your wishes amiss.

Whilst Harris accepted what was now to be known as the Pathfinder Force with good grace, he did not, in fact, abandon his idea of creating separate target-finding forces in some of the Groups at a later date when the total forces at his disposal were sufficiently large to permit major attacks against several targets simultaneously. But for the moment he had insufficient forces to deploy in this manner and therefore he accepted the Pathfinder Force as a satisfactory interim measure, even though he found it less acceptable than his own proposal for the selected pathfinding squadrons to remain within their own Groups. Some historians imply that the principle of pathfinding was conceived by Group Captain S. O. Bufton, who was Deputy Director of Bomber Operations at the Air Ministry in 1942. In fact target-finding and target-marking techniques were being developed by Harris as early as 1922/1924 in Iraq. Moreover, as every member of Harris's staff knew, target-finding and marking techniques had already been applied by Saundby, with the introduction of Gee at the beginning of 1942, just at the time that Harris arrived to take over command. Saundby had served with him, first in Iraq, then in No 58 Squadron at Worthy Down and later at the Air Ministry, and his ideas on target finding were as developed as Harris's. The arrival of Harris in Bomber Command immediately led to a greater application of target-finding and target-marking principles—with the limited facilities then available.

Whether the directorate of Bomber Operations hoped that, as a result of its proposal for the formation of a separate Pathfinder Force winning the day, the opportunity would arise for one of its staff to be appointed to command this force, is not clear. What is clear is that Harris had no intentions of having the name of the commander foisted upon him as well as the force itself. He chose, in fact, a Wing Commander who was in his early thirties and who had served under him in 1932 in No 210 Flying-Boat Squadron at Pembroke Dock. This was D. C. T. Bennett, an Australian who had held a short service commission in the Royal Air Force before the war and had then joined Imperial Airways, where he became a Captain with the remarkable distinction of holding almost every civil licence available in civil aviation, including a first navigator's certificate, a radio operator's licence and an engineer's certificate. When war broke out he had initially taken part in the opening of the transatlantic ferry for the delivery of American aircraft to Great Britain, before joining and commanding a night bomber squadron in 1941. In that same year of 1941 he was shot down in flames over Norway, but escaped by parachute with his crew, whom he led to safety in Sweden after many adventures en route. With his glib tongue he talked his way out of Sweden and back to England. Harris says of him: 'Don Bennett was the obvious man at that time available for the job of head of the Pathfinder Force. He was very young indeed to become a Group Commander, but his technical knowledge and his personal operational ability were altogether exceptional—as also was his courage, both moral and physical.'

Bennett was immediately promoted to group captain. Appropriately enough the formation of the Pathfinder Force coincided with the trials of the new RDF blind navigation and target-finding device known as H2S, to determine whether it should be finally designed with the klystron output valve or the highly secret magnetron. Bennett, whose Pathfinders would be the first to use H2S, was therefore despatched in haste to RAF Defford to take part in these comparative trials. Defford was close to the Telecommunications Research Establishment at Great Malvern and was the experimental flying unit for this establishment. Bennett arrived at Bomber Command HQ on 3 July and on the following day, Sunday, 4 July, Wing Commander Saward, Harris's RDF staff officer, drove him down to TRE and Defford to introduce him to those concerned.

On 14 July, Saward submitted the report of the Command RDF Branch on the magnetron H2S and on 15 July Bennett's preliminary report was available in time for Harris to use at the Secretary of State's meeting, scheduled for the afternoon of the same day. Both Bennett and Saward stated that the magnetron H2S was so superior in performance to the klystron H2S that the utmost pressure should be exerted to secure permission to proceed with the magnetron type and to abandon the klystron version. A few days prior to the 15th, Saundby, in conjunction with Sir Robert Renwick, arranged for Saward to put the case of the magnetron version to Lord Cherwell; it was of importance to a favourable decision that Cherwell should be on Harris's side in his demand for use of the magnetron in equipment which would be used over enemy territory. At the Secretary of State's meeting the opponents of the magnetron H2S used the powerful argument that with the magnetron the enemy could so improve his RDF night fighter equipment and ground warning system that its early revelation to the enemy could prove to be the destruction of our own bomber force. Cherwell and Watson-Watt* were of the opinion that it would take twelve to eighteen months for the Germans to develop the magnetron from the moment one fell into enemy hands. Harris argued that the magnetron, if kept in a glass case, might well be developed by the Germans anyhow, and used against Britain first. Having made it clear that H2S was only viable with the magnetron and that H2S was vitally important to the success of the newly created Pathfinder Force, he emphasised acidly that he was not asking for H2S in order to build Germany but to destroy Germany.

Cherwell's backing of Harris was decisive and the decision to proceed with the magnetron H2S and to abandon the klystron version was taken. Moreover it was agreed that development and production should proceed on the highest priority.

With H2S on its way, with every chance of it being available in sufficient quantities for use by the Pathfinder Force early in 1943, and with the precision marker-bombing device known as Oboe, which was expected to be available by the end of 1942, Harris now foresaw the possibility of a truly successful offensive against Germany. What was missing was enough bombers and crews. With that problem solved Harris knew that he could also develop his ideas on simultaneous attacks on Germany by individual Groups led by their own target-finding squadrons, and this in turn would

---

* Robert Watson-Watt, Scientific Adviser Technical to the Air Ministry. Later Sir Robert Watson-Watt, KBE. He was credited with being the 'Father of RDF'.

put so much pressure on the enemy's defences that it would lead to their dispersion thereby reducing their effectiveness. But equally, with a big enough force and adequate scientific aids, he needed a competent team in the Command Headquarters and at the Groups.

At the end of June it was clear to Harris that he would soon need a replacement for the AOC of No 3 Group, Air Vice-Marshal J. E. A. Baldwin, whom he had been warned was required for another appointment. He discussed the matter with Portal on 11 June and on this occasion Portal recommended that he should consider giving Saundby No 3 Group and then find another SASO. This suggestion did not find favour with Harris because he recognised Saundby's vital importance to the Command in his present appointment. As SASO, Saundby was the brains behind the detailed operational planning; his technical ability was outstanding; and his skill in handling Air Ministry and Ministry of Aircraft Production Departments, the Group Commanders (who could be difficult because of their own individualism), and his own staff at Command Headquarters, was truly remarkable. He was more than SASO. He was truly a Deputy Commander-in-Chief. However, Harris agreed to give Saundby an opportunity to decide for himself.

On 3 July Harris wrote to Portal and said that Saundby wished to remain as SASO. At the same time he expressed a wish for Air Vice-Marshal H. P. Lloyd, who had been in Bomber Command at the beginning of the war as a Group Captain and then, in 1941 and 1942, had made a great name for himself in command of the RAF in Malta. Portal replied promptly with a letter dated 4 July 1942, in which he wrote:

> My Dear Harris,
>
> Thank you for your personal letter of the 3rd July about change of SASO.
>
> The only reason I want to move Saundby is for his own good. Do you realise that he has been on the Staff continuously for 15 years and has never commanded anything bigger than a Flight? Unless he shows soon that he can run a Command I think his future will be seriously prejudiced.
>
> Hugh Lloyd has gone maritime by his own wish, and I think he has earned his right to choose his next job, so I do not propose to interfere. I certainly will not propose anyone for No 3 Group whom you do not wish to have there, so I must ask you to balance Saundby's inclination and your convenience against his future and let me know definitely whether you wish him to go to No 3 Group or to remain with you. I cannot help telling you that I think the latter would be a hard decision for me to justify in view of what I have already said to the Secretary of State in the light of our conversation on the 11th June.
>
> If you elect to keep Saundby would you care to have Baker in command of 3 Group? I think we are agreed about his ability and keenness and you might find him easier to get on with at a distance ...

My personal opinion about all this is that you are making rather a mistake in not having Baker. I am sure you would find him not only energetic and able, but as keen to fight for your ideas as for those of the Senior Officers he has served in the past. Nevertheless, only you can judge about this and I certainly cannot press you.

Equally promptly Harris replied on 5 July 1942. He was quite adamant about Saundby. With the knowledge that Lloyd was not available he and Saundby quickly decided on another candidate whom they knew would greatly strengthen the Bomber Command team. They both knew him well. He had served with both of them in the past. He was of the quality that could, when the time arrived, effectively command a Group that was expected to operate against Germany on its own. Harris wrote:

Dear CAS,
Thank you for your personal letter of the 4th July about Staff and Command changes.
I am sorry indeed that H. P. Lloyd is not now available . . .
As to Saundby. I could not wish for a better SASO. He has served me well for many years, at home and abroad. We understand each other. I have complete confidence in him. In these circumstances, while I should be absolutely content to have him as AOC 3 Group, such a change would be against both my wishes and his, and in my opinion certainly against the best interests of the Country at this juncture.
Where his own future is concerned I can only assure you that it is not a matter which ever enters into his consideration. In view of his strongly expressed desire to remain here as SASO, in full knowledge of the desirability from a career aspect of having held a higher command, neither does that consideration therefore weigh with me.
In these circumstances I would implore you to leave well alone— unless you have other reasons for thinking it not well. It is half the battle to be well suited where one's staff and subordinate commanders are concerned. That, I am sure you will be the first to appreciate . . .
I would prefer Ralph Cochrane above all as AOC 3 Group, and believe that Guy Garrod* would not stand in his way. He has served with me previously in flying and staff appointments and I have complete confidence in him.
Alternatively, Harrison,† my Deputy SASO, would entirely suit me as AOC 3 Group. He is a fine commander, though rather junior. He would be the first AOC in this war with personal operational experience of the war, and that of itself has many attractions . . .

---

* Air Marshal A. G. R. Garrod, CB, OBE, MC, DFC, Air Member for Training.

† Air Commodore R. Harrison, DFC, AFC. Later Air Vice-Marshal R. Harrison, CB, CBE, DFC, AFC.

Harris won Cochrane, who was promoted Air Vice-Marshal and took over as AOC No 3 Group on 14 September 1942. His stay was short, but he gingered up No 3 Group to a pitch of great efficiency during the few months in which he was its AOC. The reason for the curtailment of his command at this Group arose from the posting of Air Vice-Marshal W. A. Coryton from No 5 Group in February 1943. Harris immediately had Cochrane appointed as AOC No 5 Group and Harrison as AOC No 3 Group. These appointments took place on 28 February and the 27 February 1943. Harrison was promoted to Air Vice-Marshal on assuming Command of No 3 Group.

Harris was getting the team he wanted.

Now for the aircraft.

16
The pen and the sword

The strong personal relationship that Harris achieved with Churchill in his first few months as Commander-in-Chief of Bomber Command was quite remarkable and, unquestionably, it had a profound effect upon the conduct of the war. It was a relationship of trust in each other's judgement and respect for each other's capabilities, and it not only grew stronger as the war progressed, but lasted right up to Churchill's death after the war. Headquarters Bomber Command, at Knaphill near High Wycombe, and the C-in-C's residence, Springfield, were both close to Chequers, the Prime Minister's country residence. Churchill, who had a penchant for going behind his Ministers and his Chiefs of Staff, in order to talk directly with his commanders in the field to get the feeling of what was happening and test the opinions of those who were operational in the war on the conduct of the war, took immediate advantage of Harris's close proximity. Undoubtedly he had been impressed by the high regard in which Harris was held by the Americans, in particular Harry Hopkins and Roosevelt. But his own regard for Harris grew because of Harris's dogged determination to fight the Germans on their own ground and because of the bluntness with which he expressed his views. Never did Harris apply the smooth tongue, never did he hesitate to express unpopular opinions when he felt strongly that they were right, never did he hesitate to argue with Churchill when he thought the Prime Minister was wrong. He was perhaps the most outspoken man to have Churchill's ear—and, indeed, his eye, for Harris's letters and memoranda to Churchill are numerous, cogent and not infrequently trenchant. Perhaps there was as much of the spirit of the old Duke of Marlborough in Harris as there was in Churchill, and perhaps it was this that Churchill admired.

Whilst Harris used his special relationship with Churchill to good effect, he was meticulous in keeping Portal informed of his conversations and in showing him copies of his letters and the memoranda he addressed to the Prime Minister. Indeed, the relationship between Harris and Portal was also extremely close and they usually met once a week to discuss the problems and requirements of Bomber Command. Portal was, in fact, very much aware of the influence that Harris could often exert upon Churchill, and therefore encouraged the liaison. He went even further; he planned with Harris how best to approach certain matters with Churchill in order to obtain his support; and then he left Harris to proceed on his own. It was this team work, which they applied after the famous Thousand Raid on Cologne, that ultimately resulted in the growth of Bomber Command at the beginning of 1943 to the powerful force which, in conjunction with the American Eighth Bomber Command, finally brought about the defeat of Germany.

Almost immediately after the outstanding success of the Thousand Raid on Cologne, Bomber Command was again preyed upon by the other Commands and services to provide them with more and more aircraft and crews. It was almost as if Cologne had frightened them into believing that Bomber Command could win the war on its own if it was allowed to become too big, and that this state of affairs must therefore be arrested in case the Navy and Army should become secondary in importance in the grand strategy.

It was time for Harris to drop his first block buster.

On 17 June 1942 he wrote to Churchill enclosing a memorandum on the use of air power: 'Prime Minister, maybe it should not be for me to send you this. It is personal. But of course for you to do as you will with. If it incurs your wrath I shall indeed be sorry, but unrepentant. A. T. Harris.'

He opened his powerful memorandum with a sentence reminiscent of Churchill's own opening sentence in his note on the use of artillery dated August 1941, a copy of which was in Harris's possession. That read: 'Renown awaits the commander who first, in this war, restores the artillery to its prime importance on the battle field from which it has been ousted by heavily armoured tanks.' Harris was, in fact, being more than Churchillian in his own choice of words; he was having a dig at the Prime Minister. He wrote: 'Prime Minister, Victory, speedy and complete, awaits the side which first employs air power as it should be employed.' He went on:

> Germany, entangled in the meshes of vast land campaigns, cannot now disengage her air power for strategically proper application. She missed victory through air power by a hair's breadth in 1940. She missed then only through faulty equipment and training, and the tactical mis-direction of an Air Force barely adequate for the purpose. That is a historical fact. We ourselves are now at the crossroads. We are free, if we will, to employ our rapidly increasing air strength in the proper manner. In such a manner as would avail to knock Germany out of the war in a matter of months, if we decide upon the right course. If we decide upon the wrong course, then our air power will now, and increasingly in the future, become inextricably implicated as a subsidiary weapon in the prosecution of vastly protracted and avoidable land and sea compaigns.

He drew attention to the fact that, in the first half of 1942, a number of important German towns had been largely destroyed, including Lübeck and Rostock, and extensive destruction had been inflicted upon Cologne and Mainz and upon the submarine manufacturing centres at Augsburg,

Deutz, Kiel, Hamburg and Emden. He referred to the successful attacks on six or more other German towns and the fighting vehicle construction centres of Renaults and Matfords in France. For good measure he threw in the fact that the Command had also taken a heavy toll of enemy shipping as a result of its mining activities. 'That, and much more,' he wrote, 'has been done by less than thirty squadrons in six months. It is the only British force that has fetched a squawk out of Germany.' He continued:

... the immediate reaction to the successful Cologne attack is to deprive my Command (which would be 100 per cent stronger today, but for a continual series of similar diversions within the last six months) of a further large part of its striking power for the comparatively futile purposes of carrying a few paratroops on side-shows, to bolster further the already over-swollen establishments of the purely defensive Coastal Command, and further to swell the already over large air contingent in the Middle East.

He then criticised involvement in land campaigns, especially on the Continent, claiming that these merely reduced this country to the level of the 'Horde', whereas it was 'a highly industrialised, under-populated, physically C.3 nation.' Our lead, he said, 'is in science, not in spawn; in brains, not brawn.' He warned of the dangers of becoming embroiled in a Continental war and facing the vast and efficient German Army. This, he avowed, was exactly what Germany wanted, because once we got a footing on the Continent the whole of our air effort would be required to bolster up our land struggle in France, leaving the enemy free to ignore defence measures for the homeland, unless bombing had first been used to reduce Germany to ruins. The outcome of an early invasion of Europe might, he agreed, be in our favour in the very long run, aided as we would be by the massive armies of the Americans and uprisings in the occupied countries, 'but only if Russia maintains an Eastern Front.' At best, however, such a course must lead to 'the easily avoidable immolation of the flower of the youth of this under-populated country in the mud of Flanders and France.' He continued: 'It is imperative, if we hope to win the war, to abandon the disastrous policy of military intervention in the land campaigns of Europe, and to concentrate our air power against the enemy's weakest spots.' What substantial successes we had achieved in the war so far, both on land and sea, had only been possible because of air power. Coastal Command's activities in patrolling the high seas looking for enemy shipping and submarines, Harris likened to 'searching for the needle in the haystack,' whereas Bomber Command had gone to the root of the problem with its mining role and the bombing of shipbuilding facilities and ports—and this had done far more damage to the enemy naval and merchant effort with a fraction of the force.

Given a large enough bombing force by transferring Coastal Command to bombing operations, hastening the contribution from the American Air Force, and stopping the dispersal of bomber aircraft and crews to the

Middle East, there could, he believed, be no doubt of the outcome. Proof of this had already been provided by the success of 'a piddling force of less than thirty bomber squadrons.' A premature landing on the Continent before the bomber had done its work, he warned yet again, could spell disaster. But by increasing the bomber forces and using them against Germany, he was convinced that a sufficiency of the enemy's major cities and resources could be so decimated as to make further prosecution of the war an impossibility. This course, he insisted, was the right course to pursue from all practical and strategical considerations, 'it is the only course offering a quick victory; it is the only course which can bring any ponderable aid to Russia in time.'

He finished his memorandum by stating:

> This war will end as an air war fought on direct lines, and in no other manner, no matter what happens elsewhere, or when, or how. We are now at the crossroads, opportunity knocks at our door; that knock will grow fainter and fainter as the months go by.

On the day before Harris's memorandum was delivered to Churchill, the Prime Minister had, fortuitously, read a report from Sir Stafford Cripps, the then Lord Privy Seal, on a talk he had had with a Mr Nussbaumer, the General Manager of the Schweizerischer Bankverein of Switzerland. This was a very revealing document on the situation in Germany and Italy, and certainly supported Harris's plea for a build-up of the bomber force and an all out bomber offensive against Germany itself. The report, on which Churchill minuted that a copy should be shown to Harris, was in fact sent to Harris on 18 June. It was entitled 'Note of a talk with Mr Nussbaumer.'

Nussbaumer had revealed that there were four main points of difficulty for the Germans—transport, manpower, lubricating oil, and peoples of the occupied territories. As regards transport, the Germans were short of 15,000 locomotives and 250,000 waggons and had been trying to get everything they could from Switzerland. The shortage of waggons was evidenced by the traffic of 120 trains per day which normally passed through Switzerland. Previously these had consisted of fifty to sixty waggons, whereas now they had been reduced to thirty-five to forty per train. Moreover, the time of the journey to Italy had been cut from thirty-seven to seventeen days, resulting in more continuous use of available waggons and therefore faster deterioration. There had been a number of cases of burning axles due to this hard usage and lack of proper lubrication. There was, Nussbaumer reported, an agreement whereby just sufficient oil was put in to carry the waggons across Switzerland to the Italian frontier, from which point they had to be lubricated by the Italians until they got back again to Basel. In view of this waggon and locomotive problem he recommended that special attention should be paid to the bombing of the Henschel works at Kassel where about 10 per cent of German locomotives were built.

On the subject of manpower it was said that despite the use of 2,500,000 prisoners and 1,500,000 workers from the occupied territories, there was a shortage of labour. Moreover, workers had been doing from ten to fourteen hours a day for very long periods and were becoming tired, to an extent which almost amounted to sabotage. These workers were, for one reason or another, not anxious to produce large outputs. They also suffered deficiency in vitamins in their diet which was having its effect. Their morale in the face of bombing, Nussbaumer asserted, was very low. The bombing of Cologne had been most effective in this respect, he declared, and recommended that every effort should be made to annihilate towns rather than merely damage them. This, he explained, was especially effective owing to the division of industry, because, if a factory making parts was destroyed, it might well hold up other factories dealing with other components or assemblies of the final product in other parts of the country. Therefore the destruction of even the smallest factories could disrupt a major production programme. Undoubtedly, he said, there is now an atmosphere of fear in Germany about the bombing raids.

The rest of the report dealt with the conditions in the occupied countries and Italy where the food situation was very bad and from which the manhood had been stripped to meet Germany's wartime requirements.

The net result of Harris's 'victory, speedy and complete' memorandum, and the Nussbaumer talks, was a request to Harris to produce a note on the role and work of Bomber Command and a summary of the contribution of Bomber Command to the anti-submarine campaign. This document Harris completed and submitted to Churchill on 28 June 1942, but not without first letting Portal see it. Churchill's response was prompt. Through his Personal Secretary he asked Harris whether he had any objection to the memorandum being circulated to the War Cabinet as a Cabinet Paper. He stressed, however, that it would need a little editing. This was a reference to some of Harris's caustic remarks about Socialists. It was duly issued on 24 August and predictably had a very mixed reception, with opposition from Army and Navy quarters. But it had its effect, in that the signs of support for Bomber Command slowly began to manifest themselves in political circles. Unquestionably, the Harris report was of the greatest importance. This Paper was, in fact, an unrepentant reiteration of his previous memorandum to Churchill, except that it contained a more detailed review of the strength of the Command, and its successes to date. It also made some pointed comparisons between the effects of Bomber Command's very successful campaign against Germany's maritime power, and the rather mediocre results achieved by Coastal Command. It included appendices detailing the allocation of air resources, the combined bombing and mining effort of the Command, and the effort directed solely against naval targets. The last appendix was an impressive assessment of the contribution of Bomber Command to the anti-submarine campaign.

Harris summed up by saying:

Bomber Command provides our only offensive action yet pressed home directly against Germany. All our other efforts are defensive in their nature, and are not intended to do more, and can never do more, than enable us to exist in the face of the enemy. Bomber Command provides the only means of bringing assistance to Russia in time. The only means of physically weakening and nervously exhausting Germany to an extent which will make subsequent invasion a possible proposition, and is therefore the only force which can, in fact, hurt our enemy in the present, or in the future secure our victory. It is the only type of force which we shall ever be able to bring directly against Japan. Finally, it is apparent that an extraordinary lack of sense of proportion affects outside appreciation of the meaning, extent and results of Bomber Command's operations. What shouts of victory would arise if a Commando wrecked the entire Renault factory in a night, with a loss of seven men! What credible assumptions of an early end to the war would follow upon the destruction of a third of Cologne in an hour and a half by some swift moving mechanised force which, with 200 casualties, withdrew and was ready to repeat the operation 24 hours later! What acclaim would greet the virtual destruction of Rostock and the Heinkel main subsidiary factories by a Naval bombardment! All this, and far more, has been achieved by Bomber Command; yet there are many who still avert their gaze, pass by on the other side, and question whether the 30 squadrons of night bombers make any worth-while contribution to the war.

Both before and after the Harris memorandum was circulated as a Cabinet Paper, inroads into the strength of Bomber Command continued to be made by the Army and Navy with apparent political support, for even though Portal as CAS tried hard to reverse the trend he was constantly thwarted. Harris continued to fight off the demands as best he could, constantly seeking Portal's help. On 7 July he wrote to Portal giving him the state of the five operational Groups at that date:

The constant reduction of my Command, as you are well aware, continues. But it seems to me from various remarks dropped by the PM from time to time that he is deceiving himself into thinking that by occasionally saving us from the giving away of squadrons en bloc he is preserving the position of the Command. The constant dribbling away of just as many squadrons piecemeal is having, and will have, the same effect. We are just approaching the desperate minimum. It is rapidly becoming more and more impossible to put on any sort of a show at adequate strength without biting another piece off the puppy dog's tail.

An attached list indicated that since 15 October 1941, twenty-four squadrons had been taken away from Bomber Command to 'finance' the operations of Middle East, Army Cooperation and Coastal Commands. Some of these squadrons were purported to be on loan, but so far only one had been returned. Fifteen squadrons had been transferred since March

1942. Harris finished his letter by saying: 'No reply. This is only for ammunition.'

On 6 August, in a letter to Portal, Harris was once more on the attack to defend his supply of OTU crews. Again, Middle East, Army Cooperation and Coastal Commands were getting the pick of the crews from Bomber Command's Operational Training Units and, even worse, they were obtaining operationally tour-expired crews, who should normally have gone back to the OTUs as instructors during their 'rest period'. Bitterly he wrote:

> I cannot see what excuse Coastal Command can have for claiming our crews. They have their own OTUs to solve their problems with. As for Army Cooperation Command, they have been sitting on their fannies doing nothing for $2\frac{1}{2}$ years, and with any foresight they could have provided against their own requirements. They make no attempt to. And will make no attempt while the Bomber Command milch cow survives— which should not be long at this rate.

Harris had made his small Bomber Command, together with its own training organisation, so very efficient that the rest of the Royal Air Force, the Army and the Navy wanted to live off the fat of Harris's well-tilled land. The trouble was that their living was at the expense of the ultimate survival of Bomber Command, the only force available that could take offensive action against Germany. On 20 August he again wrote to Portal about the desperate situation. On 22 August Portal replied that he was 'preparing to start, on the Prime Minister's return, a drive for building up the Bomber Command in all possible ways', and that the information contained in Harris's letter was 'valuable ammunition for this'. Portal expected that Slessor* would be approaching Harris before long about the paper which he (Portal) had asked Slessor to prepare for the Prime Minister.

Six days later, Portal again wrote to Harris, this time on the subject of bombing Berlin. Referring to the Prime Minister, he said:

> He has now said he wishes to speak to me about this, and I expect to see him on Monday afternoon when I think he will press for an attack in the near future, or at any rate in the September moon. I think it would be as well, therefore, if you would put down on paper your own views on this question so that I can inform the Prime Minister of them if necessary.

Harris replied on 29 August. He was as keen as anyone to bomb Berlin, But only if the effort could be effective. He pointed out that Berlin was a city of four million inhabitants, five times the size of Cologne, and

---

* Air Vice-Marshal J. C. Slessor, DSO, MC, Assistant Chief of the Air Staff (Policy). Later, Air Marshal Sir John Slessor, C-in-C Coastal Command. After the war he became Marshal of the Royal Air Force Sir John Slessor, GCB, DSO, MC, and Chief of the Air Staff. He died in 1979.

therefore a force of a thousand bombers would be required to inflict serious and impressive damage. Moreover he believed the attack should be sustained; one isolated attack, in his view, would do more harm than good to the Allied cause by playing into the hands of enemy propaganda. In such a large city Harris feared that insufficient damage would be too noticeable; he was also apprehensive of a taunt from Goebbels that the R A F bombers had taken such a beating that they were not prepared to return for more punishment. Harris wrote: 'The time is long past when we could afford to lose valuable aircraft and crews for dubious political advantage of this kind.' Then he said:

As I have frequently pointed out to you, Bomber Command is now quite definitely too small for the tasks it is expected to carry out. Our policy right up to now has been to allot to Bomber Command what is left when the other Commands at home and overseas have been served, and to console ourselves by thinking that, even if the bombing effort is not as big as we would like it to be, we could at least go on hitting Germany with what we have got. The growing power and effectiveness of the German defences have made this conception quite obsolete, and it is now clear that if we are not to fail completely we must increase the first line strength of Bomber Command without delay. If the appalling drain on our resources to overseas and other Commands can be stopped I can compete with war wastage and can begin to increase the strength of my Command. I consider that a daily average of 500 aircraft with crews is the minimum figure to which we should work as a first step. This would require about 50 operationally fit squadrons and would even then require less than 20 per cent of our total [total Royal Air Force] air resources.

Harris, despite all his disappointments, still held firmly to the vision of a decisive victory over Germany by strategic bombing, thereby avoiding vast loss of life to an invading army, which was the alternative course. He had been strengthened in his beliefs by the entry of America into the war and by the realistic outlook of such men as General Arnold and General Eaker. Eaker lived at Springfield with the Harris family for the first few months after his arrival in England in February 1942 until his own headquarters at Wycombe Abbey were ready. A close relationship was established immediately, and Eaker was brought into all Harris's discussions with his staff and took part in all Bomber Command's operational planning as an observer. Asked during the war by a journalist how close the friendship was between himself and Eaker, Harris replied jovially: 'So close that the general even kisses my wife when he leaves for the office in the morning and kisses her again when he arrives back at night!' When Eaker wasn't kissing Harris's lovely wife, he was discussing with Harris and Saundby the sort of combined efforts R A F Bomber Command and the U S Eighth Bomber Command could make against Germany, when the American forces had been built up. As General Eaker told the author: 'When we first discussed cooperative attacks against German towns and industry, Bert [Harris] said he frankly didn't believe that we could bomb by day because our losses would be too high. That had been his experience in the past. But we had trained to operate by daylight. Our aircraft were designed for it and so was their fire power—and we had practised flying in close formation so that we could cover fighter attacks from all angles. Well, Bert always said, and more so as time went on, if we could do it it would be very fortuitous—it would help his effort—it could give us bombing round the clock, keeping the enemy's defences on twenty-four hour alert and holding up work in the factories day and night. He said to me: "Nobody will hope that you succeed more strongly than I do, and I'm going to do everything I can to support your efforts." That was the beginning of the great cooperation that was to develop later.'

However, if Harris still held to the vision of a vast combined aerial assault on Germany of such proportions that it would have a dramatic effect upon the course of the war, he knew well that he and Portal needed first to persuade Churchill that the appropriate priorities must be given to Bomber Command before such a vision could become a reality.

A letter from the Assistant Chief of the Air Staff (Plans), dated 28 August 1942, asked Harris to forward his views on a memorandum circulated by the Vice-Chief of the Imperial General Staff to the Chiefs of Staff Committee. This memorandum proposed that Bomber Command should accept the liability for the parachute training and transport of a complete airborne division for a planned operation at short notice for some date in the future and for some destination unknown. The proposal visualised the provision of 850 heavy and medium bombers, a figure greatly in excess of Bomber Command's existing strength, and it glibly assumed that the modification of the aircraft for direct parachuting and towing gliders could be undertaken easily. No thought was given to what would happen to the bombing effort for months before and months after such an operation. It was a case of the Army saying 'to hell with bombing'. The ACAS (Plans) asked Harris to put forward a paper as to why Bomber Command could not and should not accept such a proposal, which, on 4 September, Harris did in no uncertain terms. But he was so incensed by the absurdity of the idea, and by the fact that Bomber Command could automatically be looked upon as the provider of all and any resources for the fanciful schemes of the Army and the Navy, that he wrote immediately to Churchill. He in fact wrote two letters, one in the form of a paper, dated 3 September, and the other as a covering letter dated 4 September which ran:

Prime Minister.

I take the further liberty of sending you herewith another paper on my view of the existing air situation as affecting the War as a whole.

I am convinced that the time has come, and is indeed passing, wherein we should definitely reassert our intention to carry on the War with the first emphasis on bombing until land operations become mopping-up operations; or, alternatively, decide as definitely on some other method, if any presents itself.

At present we still pay lip service to the Bomber Plan while at the same time every necessary—and a number of avoidable—diversionary withdrawals from the strength of Bomber Command continually impinge upon it. For two years and more have we laboured unceasingly to expand Bomber Command in order to implement the agreed bomber policy. The result of these efforts has been a progressive and continuing reduction.

Today, for instance, I am asked to put forward a paper for the Chiefs of Staff explaining why I should not accept with my Command a liability for the transport and training of the Airborne Division. It would take the effort of three Bomber Commands to transport it. Where?

No matter what efforts we make to build up the force and to produce crews against future expansion, just as fast as results accrue profit is turned into deficit by further demands for dispersion.

We are, in fact, where Bomber Command and the Bomber policy are concerned, facing one way and marching smartly in the reverse direction.

Therefore I appeal to you, on the lines of the attached paper, for a firm and final decision which will enable us to build up Bomber Command to that strength requisite not only for its purpose—but to avoid the unnecessarily high casualty rate now occasioned by the unavoidable employment of too small a force in the face of ever growing defences.

In his paper of 3 September he began by saying:

Prime Minister,
It is urgently necessary that a decision should be arrived at as to the future main strategy of the War, based upon a careful consideration both of the possibilities that are open to the United Nations for the defeat of the Axis and of the actual results up-to-date of the operations that have been undertaken.

Both the future possibilities and the past results point to the inevitable conclusion that no matter what other operations are engaged upon, the final decision, if it is to be in our favour, must come through a direct air war between the United Nations and Germany. This air war must, so far as the United Nations are concerned, be conducted from Great Britain.

The key to German successes, he asserted, had been their policy of always concentrating the maximum force upon a single objective at a time.

They do not undertake any fresh commitment until they have succeeded in the preceding one, and throughout they have maintained the minimum of defensive forces in those areas where they were not actually undertaking offensive operations. The United Nations, on the other hand, have been driven to disperse their forces in such a way as never to have sufficient for a victory in any theatre.

This, he said, had been due to the assumed necessity of maintaining prestige, or of preserving outlying possessions, and because of this the Allies had lost face throughout the world by defeats all over the world. Neither at sea nor on land had we been able to inflict upon the enemy any decisive defeat.

He claimed that there were only three possibilities for the future. One, that Germany might be victorious in the East, and then turn back to the West with a view to attacking Britain with all her strength. Two, that Germany might be semi-defeated and exhausted in the East, but able to stabilise the position there by the use of considerable forces. Her people might then become disheartened, but with the fear of the revenge which might overtake them, be prepared to fight to the last man to prevent invasion of their own country. Three, a condition of stalemate might come about, leading to world-wide war weariness and the danger of a patched-up peace which would become the prelude to a new war. In the event of the first situation, 'it will be out of the question to land or support an army in Western Europe. Our sole means of winning the war will be by air attack on Germany,' he said. In the event of the second situation,

> we might attempt a landing, but our experience of fighting German mechanised armies gives no promise that we could succeed in such a land offensive, in which our losses would be enormous and our shipping decimated. Even if we succeeded in driving the German armies back to their own frontiers, it is most unlikely that we could overcome their defences and successfully invade Germany. We should eventually be thrown back upon the air as the only way by which victory could be won. But by then our air power would have been compromised in an ancillary capacity to our armies. In the last analysis, therefore, the one way in which Germany can be defeated is by air attack.

If Germany could be so devastated and dispirited by bombing, then, he maintained, an invasion 'would be a mopping-up operation.' On the supposition that the ultimate defeat of Germany must come as a result of air power, it was necessary to consider when was the most favourable time to apply this strategy. Harris emphasized that at the present time we had a marked air superiority in Western Europe, both in numbers, quality, and operational devices, and because a major part of the German Air Force was inextricably engaged upon the Russian Front. He warned, however, that as soon as withdrawals could be made by the Germans from the East, Britain's chances of delivering decisive blows against Germany by air would progressively diminish. 'The present is, therefore, the best and, perhaps, the only opportunity that we are likely to have to strike decisive air blows against Germany,' he said.

Harris continued by reiterating his previous claim that the results already secured by less than thirty squadrons, 'prove beyond the possibility of doubt that given a sufficient bomber force it would be possible in the next few months to raze substantially to the ground 30 to 40 of the principal German cities, and it is suggested that the effect upon German morale and

German production of so doing would be fatal to them, and decisive as encouragement and direct assistance to Russia.' He was absolutely convinced that if he possessed an adequate bomber force, of the size which would have been available but for the constant robbing of Bomber Command by other forces, the war could be brought to an end before the next summer. But it had to be made clear that the use over a prolonged period of time of small forces of 200 to 300 aircraft per raid was not the equivalent of the use over a shorter time of large forces of 800 to 1,000 per raid. In the latter case the defences would be saturated, resulting in smaller losses of bombers, and incapacity to deal with the immediate effects of the attacks, leading to much greater damage than was proportional to the numbers bombing.

He summarised the present strength of the Command, which showed that it was less than it was a year earlier. He also drew attention to the situation of the American bombers. 'Six months ago,' he wrote, 'preparations were in hand to receive 100 or more US Bomber Squadrons. The best aerodromes and the best flying counties were given up for their reception. Today there are only some 100 US bomber aircraft in all and plans are apparently on hand to reduce even these to next to nothing.'

He finished by pleading that the whole strategy of the use of air power should be immediately reviewed, because

no matter what happens elsewhere, a decision in the direct air war between the United Nations and Germany must be sought. The war cannot and will not end until that has been decided. That being so, and few would dare gainsay it, why not seek it now when circumstances are in our favour and when the air war decision alone may well decide all. It may end the war in our favour in a year; by no other method can we hope to end it—either way—in years.

Churchill's reply on 13 September 1942, if not a trifle cool, was uncompromising on this occasion. He wrote:

C-in-C Bomber Command.
You must be careful not to spoil a good case by overstating it. I am doing all I can to expand Bomber Command, and I set a high value on your action against Germany. I do not however think Air bombing is going to bring the war to an end by itself, and still less that anything that could be done with our existing resources could produce decisive results in the next twelve months.

However, the same evening, a Sunday, Churchill called Harris over to Chequers. On this occasion he was more amenable to the problems facing Bomber Command, and Harris took the opportunity to impress upon him the fact that the RDF scientific blind-bombing systems of H2S and Oboe were now close at hand and, therefore, it was essential to start the build-up of Bomber Command without delay if full advantage was to be taken of these revolutionary devices initially in the hands of the newly formed

Pathfinder Force, and ultimately, in the case of H2S in the whole of the Bomber Force. Churchill was, of course, well aware of the progress of the new RDF aids from Cherwell, that great scientist and keen protagonist of bombing who was close to Churchill at all times. But, unquestionably, it was the prospect of a devastated Ruhr and the destruction of major industrial seaboard towns, at which Harris confidently hinted, that encouraged Churchill to take a more active interest in priorities for the bombers, even if he was much preoccupied with the plans for Montgomery's imminent assault on the Germans in North Africa from his El Alamein positions, and the American invasion of North Africa at Casablanca, Oran and Algiers.

Harris was also very much aware of these plans, and he knew that they were one of the major causes of Bomber Command's stunted growth, and were soon to be the reason for a cessation of bomber operations against Germany in favour of raids against the North Italian ports of Genoa and Spezia and the industrial towns of Milan and Turin. He feared that this major military operation would result in a protracted diversion of the bomber force away from German targets, and a continuation of the slow dissipation of Bomber Command to meet what he believed to be activities which would never bring about the defeat of Germany. He wanted to pierce the body of the octopus, not dissipate the limited resources of the Allies by trying to cut off each tentacle one by one. He was not alone in his thinking and, apart from Portal, had backing for his ideas from Arnold, Spaatz* and Eaker.

On 3 September 1942, the same date as Harris wrote his paper to Churchill, General Arnold wrote a memorandum, which he sent to Harry Hopkins, on the same basic subject, but from the American viewpoint. It was hardly a coincidence. Indeed, a copy came into the hands of Harris in confidence and unquestionably it was expected that Harris would use it at an appropriate moment. Harris did just that. Two days after seeing Churchill at Chequers on the evening of Sunday, 13 September, he wrote to the Prime Minister as follows:

Prime Minister.

Thank you for your letter of the 13th September on the subject of the last paper I sent you, and for your personal remarks about it on Sunday evening.

I send you herewith, solely for your personal information, a copy of a paper on the same subject which has been sent by General Arnold to Harry Hopkins.

You will see that Airmen think alike on both sides of the world.

I should not officially be in possession of this paper. So far as I know neither the writer nor the recipient is aware that I know of it. That being

* Commanding General of the US Eighth Air Force of which General Eaker's Eighth Bomber Command was a part.

so I am sure you will not quote or refer to it, and I hope you will either destroy it or return it to me after perusal.

The reference to neither the writer nor the recipient being aware that he, Harris, knew of the existence of this paper he repeated to Portal when, on the same date, he also sent him a copy which he requested Portal to return or destroy after perusal. At the same time he advised Portal that he had sent a copy to Churchill.

The Arnold paper was headed 'Plans for Operation Against the Enemy'. Arnold started by referring to the original policy which was agreed immediately upon America's entry into the war—that Germany was the number one enemy and that the major effort should be to defeat her before turning on Japan. He bemoaned, like Harris, the dispersal of air effort against Japan, and in support of other Naval and land ventures, which he regarded as dissipation of vital air power that could otherwise be brought to bear against Germany speedily bringing about her defeat. Then the full force of the Allied air power could finally be launched against Japan. He compared the German and Japanese purposeful strategy with the scattered use of Allied resources.

> Opposing us we find two military nations, each guided by highly skilled staffs which prepare definite objectives on time schedules. Furthermore, nothing is allowed to interfere with those plans. If carrying out of the major plans necessitates weakening their forces in other theaters, they suffer defeats in those other theaters rather than interfere with the successful accomplishment of their major objectives. For that reason, will operations in North Africa cause the diversion of any considerable number of German ground troops or any large German air forces from their apparent primary concentration against Russia? Hitler may send to Africa a holding force, or he may conceivably send an overwhelming land and air force, but the whole operations will be considered and planned as a part of his general strategic scheme.

Arnold continued by criticising the American Naval operations in the South Pacific where, he reported, calls for more and more air support were being met at the expense of the Air Forces required for the central mission. 'These reinforcements,' he said, 'may save our Navy or prevent the recapture of South Pacific Islands occupied by us, but there is a strong possibility that the Navy could withdraw entirely from that theater and we would not lose the war. Furthermore, if we capture all the islands up to and including New Britain, we still would not necessarily win the war. If we beat the Germans we know that we will win the war.' He then referred to the US air effort which was fighting 'in 7 theaters and operating in 13 theaters.' These operations, he pointed out, were tying down 1,000 aeroplanes, distributed between Hawaii and Australia, in wasted effort, because they could not be concentrated for effective use due to lack of geographically close aerodromes from which to operate as a combined force. Then turning to Europe, he wrote: 'Little by little our Air Plan has been torn to pieces and today we find that instead of being able to send 2,000 or 3,000 airplanes against Germany from bases in England, we end up with less than 1,000 bombers if present plans are consummated and if this continued dispersion is not stopped.'

He recommended that the US should prepare a long-range military plan for winning the war, 'a plan that will be religiously and wholeheartedly followed by the Army, the Navy, and the Air Force'. The plan, he asserted, should be based upon the original one, drawn up at the beginning of 1942, which called for the maximum possible British and American air effort against German military and industrial objectives, 'with a view of destroying their productive capacity, causing vital deficiency in her air power, causing confusion and chaos in transportation systems, breaking down the morale of the civilians, and thereby destroying her will to fight.' This plan should be related to a firm date for the invasion of the Continent and the complete elimination of Germany from the war. He foresaw, however, even with immediate planning to this end, no possibility of 'any all-out major attack from England in 1943.' He concluded by saying: 'What we need is a simple, direct plan, tied to a definite date, with united all-out support by all military agencies, and the will to pursue it relentlessly, avoiding like contagion piecemeal and petty diversions all over the world.'

On 16 September, in a letter marked 'Private and Personal', Portal wrote to Harris acknowledging the receipt of his copy of the Arnold document. He said that Harris would be glad to learn that action was being taken on a very high level which it was hoped would result in the necessary priorities being obtained for Bomber Command. This was much more cheerful news than Harris had received before, but Churchill's acknowledgment of receipt of Arnold's paper left him feeling less sanguine about the prospects of an early build up of the Bomber Force. Churchill still seemed to favour the peripheral actions at this stage of the war, and he was highly critical of General Arnold's views. He wrote:

Air Marshal Harris.
Thank you for sending me General Arnold's paper. I agree about strengthening the Air attack on Germany and also that the Pacific should be regarded as a secondary theatre. Apart from this, I think the paper a very weak and sloppy survey of the war, and I am surprised that with his information he cannot produce something better. Both Germany and Japan, completely separated from one another, lie in the centre of large circles and can throw their strength outwards against any part of the circumferences. The Allies have not yet been able to gain the initiative, and are forced to make the best arrangements possible to meet a variety of dangers. However, these evils apply less to Air power than to ground forces because, so long as our Air forces are engaged with the enemy Air force and are reducing the total sum of its strength in daily contact, it does not matter whether the bases from which they operate are dispersed

or not. The wearing down of the enemy's Air forces can be achieved from several different directions, just as batteries are dispersed the better to concentrate their fire.

General Arnold's arguments, if applied to our own case, would have abandoned the Middle East as a major theatre of war, and we should have had the Germans spread over great parts of Asia and Africa today. Nothing that could be done by Anglo-American aircraft bombing Germany would be the slightest compensation for injuries so fearful.

It is a great pity that General Arnold does not try first to send us two or three hundred of his big American bombers to expand our Bomber Command, after they have been adapted to night fighting. Failing this, he should send us as many American squadrons as he can to operate from this country, and teach them to fly by night. So far, his day bombing operations have been on a very petty scale.

I see he does not approve of the important operation which is pending, which certainly shows him lacking in strategic and political sense, as it is the only practical step we can take at the present time, and one which, if successful, will produce profound reactions.

W.S.C.
18.9.42.

Churchill's reference in the last paragraph to the 'important operation which is pending' was to 'Operation Torch', the invasion of North Africa at Casablanca, Oran and Algiers. His remarks in his penultimate paragraph were singularly brutal and rather unfair, as Harris well knew. The Americans had been in the war for only ten months and, and apart from preparing to fight in Europe against Germany, they had a holding action to undertake on their back doorstep against the Japanese. Their bomber force in England was, in the circumstances, a very creditable size, and it had already been operating against the comparatively lightly defended ports of occupied France and was now almost ready to bomb German targets. It had, after all, taken Britain two years to pull together anything approaching a credible bomber force for effective operations against Germany, and even then no real success was achieved until Harris took command in February 1942. The dig about day bombing as opposed to night bombing was a pet hobby horse of Churchill's, even at this late stage when he knew that Harris, who had initially advised Arnold and Eaker against daylight operations, was now supporting the American day bombing policy.

Harris was clearly upset by Churchill's reply, but during his subsequent meetings with him at Chequers he indicated no reaction in favour or against the Prime Minister's views. He just continued to argue for an expanded bomber force. In addition, he worked with Portal on the development of a paper for the Chiefs of Staff Committee of the War Cabinet on the subject of an Anglo-American bomber offensive against Germany.

On 24 October 1942, however, he wrote a plea to Churchill to be more definite about the policy of bombing Germany. He wished to help those of

Britain's friends in the USA who wanted to cooperate in a combined air offensive against Germany, and thus stave off the Navy and Army factions who were determined to thwart this policy. He wrote:

Prime Minister.

My American air friends are despondent.

They foresee the success of efforts by the US Army, and particularly the US Navy, to get them off bombing France and, thereafter, keep them off bombing Germany. They assert that unless the agreement that our War Plan to bomb Germany soft as the first step to victory is reasserted, and thereafter enforced, the US Navy/Army anti-bomber plan school will have their way.

I am informed, and I know this to be true, that there is now a great and growing weight of high public and official opinion in the United States in support of the Bomber Plan.

This opinion gathers weight and momentum.

But the US Navy and, to a lesser extent, the US Army, are almost frantically engaged in doing all they can to scotch this plan.

I am informed also that they are succeeding—so far: but only, I am told, because the Bomber Plan, although so long ago officially agreed, is not sufficiently held to the fore, especially, they say, by our own leaders, as the agreed preliminary move towards victory.

The US Navy/Army faction are, firstly, determined to stop the bombing of the French inland targets by the US Fortresses. If they succeed in this they hope to assert both precedent and preoccupation to keep the bombers off Germany.

To that end the US Navy and Army are engaged in pressing that the whole US Bomber resources now in this country should be switched towards the Atlantic War and the protection of convoys.

It is, moreover, alleged that you, personally, are in favour of this.

Armed with so formidable a stick wherewith to beat the dog, the US Military Authorities on this side are alleged to be quoting—or rather misquoting—you in regard to the futility of continuing to bomb French targets, and as to your leaning towards employing all the US Bombers on the Atlantic War rather than on bombing Germany.

You will please excuse frankness in this matter. My information is that matters have now reached so critical a stage that unless you come down personally and most emphatically on the side of throwing every bomb against Germany, subject only to minimum essential diversions elsewhere, the Bomber Plan, in so far as US assistance is concerned, will be hopelessly and fatally prejudiced within the very near future for an unpredictable period, if not for keeps.

I should be failing in my duty if I did not bring this to your attention. My information comes from sources which must not be compromised, but in which I have complete faith.

I hope therefore that you will see fit to press your previous demand for

US Bombers to get on with the bombing of Germany, if not at once, at least as soon as immediate preoccupations in the Atlantic are cleared. Harris received no reply to this letter.

At the beginning of November 1942, Portal's 'Note by the Chief of the Air Staff—an Estimate of the Effects of an Anglo-American Bomber Offensive against Germany', which was dated 3 November and which had been prepared with assistance from Harris and indirectly from Generals Arnold, Spaatz and Eaker, was distributed as a War Cabinet Paper. It began with the statement:

At the 137th Meeting of the Committee [Chiefs of Staff] held on the 5th October, I was invited to circulate a Note setting out the facts and arguments which support the Air Staff view that a heavy bomber force rising to a peak of between 4,000 and 6,000 heavy bombers in 1944 could shatter the industrial and economic structure of Germany to a point where an Anglo-American force of reasonable strength could enter the Continent from the West.

In conclusion Portal wrote:

I am convinced that an Anglo-American bomber force based in the United Kingdom and building up to a peak of 4,000-6,000 heavy bombers by 1944 would be capable of reducing the German war potential well below the level at which an Anglo-American invasion of the Continent would become practical. Indeed, I see every reason to hope that this result would be achieved well before the combined force had built up to peak strength.

Portal summarised his Note as follows:

(i) The paper assumes that an Anglo-American Heavy Bomber Force would be based in the United Kingdom and built up to a first-line strength of 4,000 to 6,000 by 1944.
(ii) Such a force could deliver a monthly scale of attack amounting to 50,000 tons of bombs by the end of 1943, and to a peak of 90,000 tons by December 1944.
(iii) Under this plan $1\frac{1}{4}$ million tons of bombs would be dropped on Germany between January 1943 and December 1944.
(iv) Assuming that the results attained per ton of bombs equal those realised during the German attacks of 1940–41,* the results would include—

(a) the destruction of 6 million German dwellings, with a proportionate destruction of industrial buildings, sources of power, means of transportation and public utilities;
(b) 25 million Germans rendered homeless;

* This refers to German attacks against Britain.

(c) an additional 60 million 'incidents' of bomb damage to houses;

(d) civilian casualties estimated at about 900,000 killed and 1,000,000 seriously injured.

(v) If the attacks were spread over the main urban areas the result would be to render homeless three-quarters of the inhabitants of all German towns with a population of over 50,000.

(vi) Expressed in other terms, this scale of attack would enable every industrial town in Germany with a population exceeding 50,000 to receive, in proportion to its size, ten attacks of 'Cologne' intensity.

(vii) If the attacks were concentrated on the 58 towns specified in Appendix I, each would receive, in proportion to its size, some 17 attacks of 'Cologne' intensity.

(viii) A concentrated attack of this character would destroy at least one-third of the total German industry.

(ix) A substantial proportion of the total industry of Germany is necessary to maintain a minimum standard of subsistence among the German people. As the German economic structure is now stretched to the limit this proportion cannot be further reduced. Consequently, the loss of one-third of German industry would involve either the sacrifice of almost the entire war potential of Germany in an effort to maintain the internal economy of the country, or else the collapse of the latter.

(x) It is hoped that our bombing efficiency will prove to be substantially better than that achieved in the German attacks of 1940–41. In that case the process of attrition will be much accelerated.

(xi) It is considered that the German defences will be incapable of stopping these attacks.

(xii) It is certain that the diversion of more and more of a waning aircraft production to the defence of Germany will heavily handicap all German operations by land, sea and air in other theatres.

(xiii) It is concluded that an Anglo-American bomber force of the size proposed could reduce the German economic and military strength to a point well below that at which an Anglo-American invasion of the Continent would become possible. This result might well be achieved before the combined force had built up to peak strength.

This note was a document of paramount importance, and was, in fact, the forerunner to the directive which was to emerge from the Roosevelt-Churchill-Combined Chiefs of Staff conference at Casablanca in mid-January 1943. This directive to the Allied bomber forces operating from the United Kingdom was drawn up by the Combined Chiefs of Staff on 21 January, and received the immediate approval of Churchill and Roosevelt. It stated the mission thus:

Your primary object will be the progressive destruction and dislocation of the German military, industrial and economic system, and the undermining of the morale of the German people to the point where their capacity for armed resistance is fatally weakened.

There followed an order of priority of the industries to be attacked. And so the pen fought for the sword.

17

Via Casablanca to the Ruhr

The formation of the Pathfinder Force produced no immediate and dramatic change in the effectiveness of Bomber Command. The Command during the first half of 1942 had, in any case, been spectacularly successful in its bombing of Germany compared to the earlier period of the war. However, during the second half of 1942, Bennett had been using the time well to develop the best methods of attack by ceaseless experiment. His RDF scientific aids were confined during this period to Gee, which was suffering diminution in range due to enemy jamming, and he was therefore gravely limited in his methods of target location in cloud covered conditions. But he knew that early in 1943 he would be in possession of two remarkable RDF systems, H2S and Oboe, which would enable him to locate many targets at differing ranges with great accuracy. Therefore from August 1942, when he started work with his original force consisting of No 7 Squadron with Stirling aircraft, No 35 with Halifax, No 83 with Lancaster and No 156 with Wellington aircraft, he concentrated on developing the most effective marking and target-illuminating techniques for conditions of clear visibility or cloud cover.

By the end of October 1942 the air assault against Germany, with the exception of sea mining, gave way almost entirely to attacks in support of the Allied invasion of North Africa, which commenced on 8 November. The role Harris was given consisted of four tasks: the dropping of leaflets over France to explain the Allies' motives in invading French Colonies; the sea mining of Genoa and Spezia to contain as much of the Italian fleet as possible; the bombing of the Channel targets on the French coast and occasional raids of varying intensity into Germany to keep the German fighters and other defences there; and the major task of the mass bombardment of Genoa, Milan and Turin.

Just prior to the shift of the bomber offensive to Italy, Harris received permission to attack the Schneider armaments factory at Le Creusot in Occupied France. He had, in fact, suggested the attack to Portal in a letter dated 7 April 1942, on the grounds that the company was producing heavy artillery, locomotives and tanks for Germany and was at that time engaged on a large contract for gun barrels and breech blocks. Early in 1942 Harris also wanted some targets in France against which he could operate when weather conditions precluded operations against Germany. Moreover, he was in favour of some geographical diversification of his attacks in order to force dispersion of the German defences. However, when he first contemplated such an attack he had in mind a night operation, but in first class moonlight conditions because the target was in the middle of a small congested town of 22,000 inhabitants and, as always, Harris was opposed to taking unnecessary risks with the lives of the French. The decision to undertake this raid was, in fact, delayed until October, when, on the 17th, a well-planned and brilliantly executed daylight attack was made on the Schneider works by ninety-four Lancasters of No 5 Group flying across France at tree-top level, bombing at dusk and returning under cover of darkness. The damage was devastating and well concentrated. Only one aircraft was lost.

The bombing attacks on the north of Italy commenced a few days later, the first two taking place against Genoa on the nights of 22/23 and 23/24 October, followed by a daylight attack on Milan on the 24th and a night attack on the 24th/25th. In October and November there were six attacks in all against Genoa and two against Milan. These raids were on a scale of between seventy and ninety aircraft on each attack, except for three raids on Genoa when the forces were 112, 122 and 175 aircraft. In November and December there were seven attacks on Turin and, of these, four were with forces of 232, 228, 133 and 227 aircraft. Taken together, this meant that Turin suffered a considerable weight of attack. Indeed, the Fiat and Lancia works were very seriously damaged, as were other smaller factories and built-up areas. Genoa, too, suffered badly in both the port and town area, but Milan was relatively undamaged having received only two raids by eighty-eight and seventy-seven aircraft.

In all, 1,809 sorties were flown against Milan, Turin and Genoa between 22 October and 12 December 1942, for the loss of thirty-six aircraft, or just under 2 per cent. These cities were the only ones open to attack from bases in England which were of any real value to the Axis powers industrially and economically. In the case of Genoa there was also the fact that it was the greatest seaport in Italy. It was for these reasons that priority was given to bombing them. But more importantly there were also the reasons that bombing North Italy would compel the Italians to hold back their fighter aircraft and anti-aircraft guns from Tunisia, at the time of the Allied invasion of North Africa, and would increase the demoralisation of the Italian people, who really had little stomach for this war into which Mussolini and Hitler had led them. After the attacks on Genoa Mussolini even admitted that the people had 'given proof of moral weakness'.

Harris was at no time in favour of his forces being diverted away from the prime target, Germany. Indeed, he expressed his reaction at the time of the North Italy bombing in November 1942, when Portal wrote to him asking him for an appreciation of the advantages and disadvantages of using North Africa and Malta for rearming and refuelling heavy bombers in order to operate a 'shuttle' method of bombing Italy. The idea was to bomb targets such as Rome and Naples, in addition to the northern targets, and then land in Africa or Malta to refuel, rearm and bomb Italian targets again on the way home. This method would, of course, bring more Italian targets within range of Bomber Command. Portal wrote that one of the assumptions for such operations was: 'It is the policy of HMG to attempt to knock out Italy.' He also said: 'It is assumed in high quarters that a great advantage would accrue from the so called shuttle method of operation ...' He finished his letter somewhat cryptically by writing: 'Whether you favour it or not, I should be grateful for an outline plan designed to take advantage of North African facilities.'

Harris's appreciation was dated 13 November, and spelt out the requirements for such a plan in great detail. In fact it was as thorough in its preparation as it was in killing the scheme stone dead. Something approaching a duplication of Bomber Command was going to be required in North Africa for the sake of a few indifferent Italian targets. Harris's covering letter was mild in the extreme for he knew the sting was in the appreciation, but he said he hoped nothing would be done to switch the offensive off Germany. He concluded by saying: 'I am only at present attacking the Italian targets under conditions where it is either impossible to attack Germany, or advisable to keep out of too much moonlight.'

Harris was telling half the truth in his last sentence. The weather over Germany had been impossible from mid-October to mid-November, and continued to be so right through to the end of December. This had precluded any sustained offensive against Germany during this period, and the Italian targets had provided the means of maintaining operational practice with very low losses. This in itself had the salutary effect of enabling the Command to build up its strength in crews and aircraft. But had the weather favoured German targets, Harris would still have been forced to give priority to Italian targets. It was, therefore, with his tongue in his cheek that he pretended his present enforced preoccupation with Italy was the fault of the weather.

'Operation Torch' and the rapid advance into Tunisia combined with Montgomery's drive across the desert from El Alamein, ensured in a perverse sort of way, the start of the combined Anglo-American bomber offensive against Germany in 1943 and its maintenance with growing strength throughout that year and until June 1944. The hope of an invasion of Western Europe in 1943, as had been envisaged earlier under the code name of 'Operation Round-up', was now a dead duck. The forces committed in North Africa and the Western Desert decided the grand strategy of the future. One wonders how much the North African escapade was a sop to Stalin's demands for a Second Front in 1942 or 1943. Stalin, of course, wanted the front in Western Europe, but this could only have been attempted at grave risk, whereas the North African landing was a much safer and easier task. Its value in enabling an ultimate attack against the Axis powers' underbelly was, however, considerable, and this in turn kept

German and Italian forces tied down right up to and after the invasion of the Continent by the Allied forces on 6 June 1944. But it took until June 1944 to build up an Anglo-American military force in England of a size commensurate with the task of landing in the enemy's most heavily defended area and fighting against the enemy's best divisions. It also took until then to batter Germany from the air into a state where her industrial capability was in jeopardy, and supremacy in the air had passed firmly into the hands of the Allies. The North African invasion, therefore, set the time scale for the final assault on Germany by ground forces and this, in turn, provided the demand for the absolutely essential prelude to any invasion of Western Europe if vast losses were to be avoided—a massive bomber offensive against Germany itself by the combined forces of RAF Bomber Command and US Eighth Bomber Command.

As much as Harris would have liked an all out combined bomber offensive to have started in 1942, he knew it was impossible. He himself had neither a big enough force at his disposal nor the necessary scientific navigating and bombing aids available. Nor, indeed, was the US Eighth Bomber Command ready to undertake operations against Germany. In fact, it was not until 27 January 1943 that the Americans struck their first blow against Germany, attacking Wilhelmshaven by day. But by November 1942, Harris knew that the beginning of a serious combined bomber offensive against Germany was in sight, and he was determined that it should under no circumstances be further delayed.

Everything was, in fact, conspiring well to assist him towards a resumption of the offensive against Germany at the beginning of 1943 on a vast and devastating scale. On 26 November permission was granted for two pairs of Oboe ground stations to transmit continuously in readiness for the commencement of operations. This meant that No 109 Squadron, which had been equipped with Mosquito aircraft fitted with the Oboe airborne equipment, could commence concentrated training with the system. This squadron was commanded by Wing Commander H. E. Bufton who, with many of his crews, had been operating as early as 1940 and 1941 on special duties requiring flying skills similar to those needed for the successful use of the Oboe system. On the night of 20/21 December the first attack was made for calibration purposes by six Oboe Mosquitos against a coking plant at Lutterade in East Holland. Further calibration attacks were made during December and January, but it was not until the morning of 16 February 1943, at 03.30, that the first really satisfactory calibration test over enemy territory was made. The attack was directed against the Cadet School at St Trond in Belgium by four Oboe Mosquitos. The success of the test was provided through Intelligence sources; an agent supplied a detailed bomb plot of the result. This indicated that two RDF ground stations in England could accurately direct a Mosquito aircraft, flying at 30,000 feet and more than 250 miles away, over a selected target, and release its bombs with such precision that they would fall within 120 yards of the selected spot. Here, indeed, was the target-finding system that

Harris needed to ensure accurate marking of the vitally important Ruhr targets by the Pathfinder Force.

On 8 December 1942 Harris received good news of the next important RDF device, which was to give the bomber accurate navigational guidance at all ranges without the necessity of seeing the ground, and which would make possible reasonably accurate blind bombing of built-up areas. He was advised that H2S could be used operationally at any time after 1 January 1943. The number of H2S aircraft available to the Pathfinder Force was extremely limited at this stage, and even the hopes that the first two squadrons to be equipped, No 35 Squadron (Halifax aircraft) and No 7 Squadron (Stirling aircraft), would have enough H2S aircraft by that date to commence operations with the system were somewhat forlorn. But at least Oboe and H2S were to hand as the New Year of 1943 dawned.

Certainly Harris could look back on 1942 with some satisfaction. Under his command the capabilities of the Bomber Force had grown immeasurably and the offensive he had mounted had been immensely successful. It had struck a serious blow at the German homeland, which indirectly had helped to slow the progress of the German campaign against the Russians. Defence requirements for German cities grew as more of her industry was threatened by the increasing bombardment, and the direct disruption of some of her military production had added to the problem. All this had been to Russia's advantage. The 1942 bomber offensive had also contributed to the control of the submarine menace, if not its actual neutralisation. Finally it had created a state of exceptionally high morale amongst air and ground crews, Group staffs and the Command staff. Bomber Command was, indeed, ready for the new tasks that lay ahead.

With the dawn of 1943 the whole military situation for the Germans had changed for the worse. Serious reverses were being suffered in North Africa and the Western Desert. They had suffered a major defeat at Stalingrad in November 1942. Their Russian advance had come to a halt in the closing months of 1942 and, into the bargain, the Soviet forces had successfully launched a counter-offensive in the central Caucasus which, in late December, had resulted in considerable advances between the Don and the Donetz. At the beginning of 1943 the offensive was extended over an even greater stretch of the Russian southern front and Soviet gains continued, culminating in February in the capture of Kursk, Krasnodar, Rostov, Voroshilovgrad and Kharkov. In fact, the rot in the Russian defence had been successfully stopped, but this might easily prove to be a temporary development if the supply position to the German army could be quickly improved. The bombing of Germany had undoubtedly helped to cause the sudden interruption of the German onslaught, but it was only too obvious that such a halt would be purely momentary unless the industrial productive capacity of Germany could be more completely disrupted than hitherto.

Harris knew that the time had arrived when the defeat of Germany could and must begin.

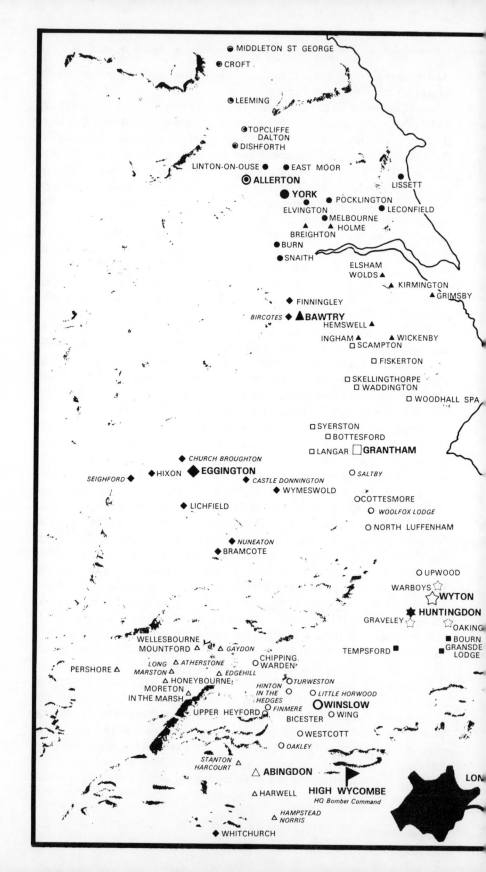

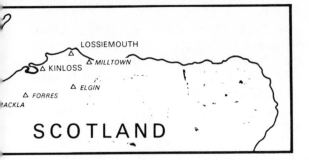

SCOTLAND

LOSSIEMOUTH
△ MILLTOWN
△ KINLOSS
△ ELGIN
△ FORRES
ACKLA

BOMBER COMMAND
5th March 1943

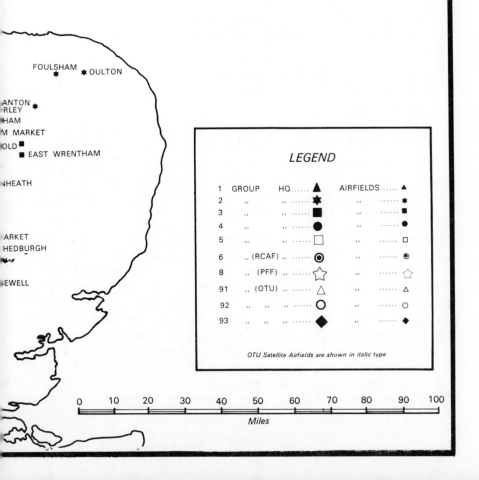

FOULSHAM   ★ OULTON

ANTON
RLEY
HAM
M MARKET
OLD ■
■ EAST WRENTHAM

NHEATH

ARKET
HEDBURGH

EWELL

LEGEND

		HQ		AIRFIELDS	
1	GROUP	HQ...... ▲		AIRFIELDS...... ▲	
2	,,	,, ... ★		,, ... ★	
3	,,	,, ... ■		,, ... ■	
4	,,	,, ... ●		,, ... ●	
5	,,	,, ... ☐		,, ... ☐	
6	,, (RCAF)	,, ... ◉		,, ... ◉	
8	,, (PFF)	,, ... ☆		,, ... ☆	
91	,, (OTU)	,, ... △		,, ... △	
92	,, ,,	,, ... ○		,, ... ○	
93	,, ,,	,, ... ◆		,, ... ◆	

OTU Satellite Airfields are shown in italic type

0   10   20   30   40   50   60   70   80   90   100
Miles

On 4 February 1943 he received his new directive, which had been approved by the Combined Chiefs of Staff at the Casablanca Conference. It was much to his liking and it reflected many of his recommendations over the months of 1942 when he had striven not only to expand Bomber Command to a strength that could prove decisive in the war, but also to preserve it from disintegration at the hands of the Navy, the Army and the politicians. Now its future was assured. Now its role was largely determined.

The directive, which was one of the most important of the war, was addressed to the appropriate British and United States Air Force commanders. The instructions delivered to Air Marshal Sir Arthur Harris and General Ira C. Eaker went under the heading '21st January 1943. Combined Chiefs of Staff Directive for the Bomber Offensive from the United Kingdom.' It went on to say, as has already been mentioned:

> Your primary object will be the progressive destruction and dislo- cation of the German military, industrial and economic system and the undermining of the morale of the German people to a point where their capacity for armed resistance is fatally weakened.

It continued:

Within that general concept, your primary objectives, subject to the exigencies of weather and of tactical feasibility, will for the present be in the following order:

(a) German submarine construction yards.
(b) The German aircraft industry.
(c) Transportation.
(d) Oil plants.
(d) Other targets in enemy war industry.

The above order of priority may be varied from time to time according to developments in the strategical situation. Moreover, other objectives of great importance either from the political or military point of view must be attacked. Examples of these are:

(I) Submarine operating bases on the Biscay coast. If these can be put out of action, a great step forward will have been taken in the U-boat war which the CCS have agreed to be the first charge on our resources. Day and night attacks on these bases have been inaugurated and should be continued so that an assessment of their effects can be made as soon as possible. If it is found that successful results can be achieved, these attacks should continue whenever conditions are favourable for as long and as often as is necessary. These objectives have not been included in the order of priority, which covers long-term operations, particularly as the bases are not situated in Germany.

(II) Berlin, which should be attacked when conditions are suitable for the attainment of specially valuable results unfavourable to the morale of the enemy or favourable to that of Russia.

You may also be required, at the appropriate time, to attack objectives in Northern Italy in connection with amphibious operations in the Mediterranean theatre.

There may be certain objectives of great fleeting importance for the attack of which all necessary plans and preparations should be made. Of these, an example would be the important units of the German Fleet in harbour or at sea.

You should take every opportunity to attack Germany by day, to destroy objectives that are unsuitable for night attack, to sustain continuous pressure on German morale, to impose heavy losses on the German day fighter force and to contain German fighter strength away from the Russian and Mediterranean theatres of war.

Whenever Allied Armies re-enter the Continent, you will afford all possible support in the manner most effective.

In attacking objectives in occupied territories, you will conform to such instructions as may be issued from time to time for political reasons by His Majesty's Government through the British Chiefs of Staff.

In truth, this directive was more a statement of policy than an actual detailed direction of the way in which Harris should use his forces and against which specific targets. It lay open to a certain amount of interpretation, which was more than could be said for the directive he had received three weeks earlier by a letter from Air Vice-Marshal Bottomley, the Assistant Chief of the Air Staff (Operations), dated 14 January 1943. This had instructed him that an increase in enemy U-boat operations demanded a policy of area bombing against U-boat operational bases on the west coast of France. The order of priority was then spelt out—Lorient, St Nazaire, Brest, La Pallice. Whilst this bombing was to take first priority at the earliest possible date, he was advised that the operations were not to prejudice any attacks he might be planning on Berlin or any concentrated attack which suitable weather might enable him to direct against important objectives in Germany or Italy. Harris described this instruction as a misdirection of his force. He was convinced that no damage could be caused to the U-boat pens, which had been constructed by the famous Todt organisation, for by this date they had been completed and were covered by many feet of concrete impenetrable by any bomb available at this juncture of the war. But he followed his orders and made the first raid on the same night of the day on which he received the directive. Between 14 January and 17 February he despatched 1,960 sorties against Lorient, which dropped just over 4,000 tons of HE (high explosive). Between 28 February and 29 March he despatched 1,117 sorties against St Nazaire, dropping just over 2,600 tons of HE.

Grand Admiral Dönitz reported that 'The towns of St Nazaire and Lorient have been rubbed out as main submarine bases. No dog nor cat is left ... Nothing but the submarine shelters remain.' Indeed, Harris was correct; the submarine shelters had remained intact. Admittedly slipways had been severely damaged and services seriously disrupted, but the problem for the Germans was only a temporary one.

Harris would have prefered to drop those 6,600 tons of bombs on Germany, where he was confident they would have done more good. With the Casablanca directive's opening words the way was, however, now open to him to mount his assault on Germany, an assault for which he had struggled from the very beginning. There was no one better qualified, in fact, to interpret and translate this directive into physical action. He had some twenty-seven years of service experience behind him, much of which he had devoted to the idea and development of the aircraft as an offensive weapon of war in the shape of the bomber. He had done more than anyone to develop the concept of the heavy strategic night bomber, even as long ago as 1922 when he took over command of No 45 Squadron in Iraq and converted the Rolls-Royce Vernons from transport aircraft into bombers for both day and night operations. He had spent the major part of his career in the Royal Air Force flying aeroplanes, commanding squadrons, developing night operations, introducing training techniques, and using his technical ingenuity to ensure that aircraft, in particular bombers, should have the necessary instruments, navigation equipment, armament and weapons to make them effective in war. He had a mind of his own which he could express forcibly without fear or favour, but sometimes at inopportune moments which, surprisingly, often proved in the end to be the most fruitful; it was a case of shock tactics. He was not, however, averse to criticism and welcomed the advice and views of others, particularly those of his own staff and his Group commanders; but with a judgement matured by years of practical experience he was impatient of any lack of a considered policy from those above him and of failure to take a firm and consistent line in any strategic policy once it was decided upon. When the politicians or the Air Staff dithered from one policy to another he would persevere tenaciously to secure consistency in strategy, but it has to be admitted that the strategy he sought was that of the bombing of Germany for the purpose of securing a decisive victory. Nonetheless, his training over the years had taught him that he was a man who was as subject to authority as any other serviceman and, therefore, if he was overruled in a matter of policy and ordered to operate in a manner which was against his better judgement, he would obey and operate to the best of his ability—frequently so effectively that he was sometimes the means of proving himself wrong. All his life he had lived under discipline and he knew what it could accomplish; and he knew when it could fail. This enabled him, better than most commanders, to obtain the best from his crews, even during the hardest times in this war which was now to demand so much from Bomber Command and to exact such a heavy toll of life. Hilary St George Saunders said aptly of Harris:*

---

* Volume II of Royal Air Force 1939–1945.

His very ruthlessness, offspring of his fierce honesty of purpose and singleness of mind, drove him to demand the utmost of his crews, not once but again and yet again, while at the same time, with equal vehemence, he strove to move mountains on their behalf. When there was an opportunity to strike the enemy hard, he seized it; but every proposal to make use of them for purposes for which he considered them to be untrained, or which were in his view not such as to produce a result worth the risk, he vigorously opposed.

Harris's concern for his crews went further than his determined protection of them against foolhardy or useless operations. He knew well that risks had to be taken and that in war substantial losses were inevitable if victory was to be won. But he also knew that the contribution which must be made by Bomber Command, if a decisive victory was to be attained, demanded the supply of the best equipment, be it aeroplanes, scientific aids to operating by night, or suitable weapons. Provision of these requirements, moreover, was itself a major protection to his crews, giving them a far greater chance of survival. From early in 1942 it had become apparent that the Short and Harland Stirling aircraft and the Handley-Page Halifax were not meeting their operating height and speed specifications, and were falling short on other performance requirements. This was not the case with the Avro Lancaster which, conversely, exceeded its performance specifications and seemed capable of accepting unending increases in its pay load without serious loss of height, speed, or striking range. The Lancaster, by the latter half of 1942, had proved itself capable of operating at heights between 22,000 and 27,000 feet and capable of carrying a bomb load of some 8,000 pounds to Berlin, or any other distant target in Germany, at a cruising speed of 240 miles per hour. The Stirling was unable to operate at more than about 14,000 feet and the Halifax at barely 18,000 feet, heights which left them well within the lethal ranges of the enemy's anti-aircraft fire. Their slower speeds, a little over 200 miles per hour, made them even more vulnerable. Finally, their bomb load, range for range, was less than half that of the Lancaster. Comparison of bomb load, range for range, is, in fact, injudicious, for the Lancaster was capable of carrying 12,000 pounds well beyond the Ruhr and was also able to carry the enormous 22,000-pound 'Grand Slam' bomb, which became available later, and which no other aircraft in the world was capable of carrying. Neither the Halifax or Stirling could carry anything like 12,000 pounds, let alone 22,000 pounds.

Because the Stirling was unquestionably a failure, and the Halifax was a poor second to the Lancaster, Harris started a campaign in 1942 to have Stirling production facilities switched over to the manufacture of Lancasters, and retrenchment of Halifax production in favour of increased Lancaster production. By the end of 1942 a decision had been taken to stop Stirling production and switch Short and Harlands over to Lancaster production, but Harris had no confidence in a successful switch whilst the management remained. In a condemnatory letter to Sir Archibald Sinclair, the Secretary of State for Air, dated 30 December 1942, he wrote:

> ... the Stirling and the Halifax are now our major worries. They presage disaster unless solutions are found. I understand that the Stirling is to go in favour of the Lancaster as fast as the changeover can be achieved. The Stirling Group has now virtually collapsed. They make no worth while contribution to our war effort in return for their overheads. They are at half strength, and serviceability is such that in spite of the much reduced operational rate and long periods of complete idleness due to weather, I am lucky if I can raise 30 Stirlings from 3 Group for one night's work after a week of doing nothing, or 20 the night after. There should be a wholesale sacking of the incompetents who have turned out approximately 50% rogue aircraft from Short and Harlands, Belfast, and Austins, not forgetting the Supervisories responsible in the parent firm. Much the same applies to the Halifax issue ... nothing whatever ponderable is being done to make this deplorable product worthy for war or fit to meet those jeopardies which confront our gallant crews ... Trivialities are all that they are attempting at present, with the deliberate intent of postponing the main issue until we are irretrievably committed ...
>
> Unless we can get these two vital factors of the heavy bomber programme put right, and with miraculous despatch, we are sunk. We cannot do this by polite negotiation with these ... incompetents. In Russia it would long ago have been arranged with a gun, and to that extent I am a fervid Communist!
>
> If I write strongly it is because I feel strongly, as I know you do, for the jeopardy of my gallant crews and the compromising of our only method of winning the war.

This letter also contained biting criticism of the top management of the two companies concerned, and therefore it was written in great confidence. Sir Archibald Sinclair alluded to this in his reply to Harris, dated 2 January 1943, when he wrote:

> Thank you for your strictly personal and secret letter of the 30th December. You have sent me a bomb full to the brim with RDX, but you tell me I mustn't drop it! I want you to let me show it to Cripps* and Lyttelton,† and, at my discretion—and only if it would clinch an argument—to the Prime Minister. I would not allow copies to be made of it.

Sir Archibald went on to confirm that all the preparations for the changeover of production from Stirlings to Lancasters had been authorised and were in hand, and he promised to look personally into the Halifax fiasco immediately.

* Then Minister of Aircraft Production.

† Mr Oliver Lyttelton, Minister of Production.

Harris replied to Sir Archibald on 5 January, agreeing to Sinclair's making use of the letter in the manner in which he proposed. He also fed him with more detailed information on the repeated failures of Handley-Page to meet their promised performance of the Halifax. Throughout the early months of 1943, Harris continued his fight for pressure to be brought to bear on Handley-Page to improve the Halifax, which he found he had to accept. In the case of the replacement of the Stirling by the Lancaster he had effectively won his battle by the beginning of 1943. But it was not until late in 1943 that he was to feel the first benefits of his struggle for more Lancasters and a greatly improved performance of the Halifax.

On the RDF front, too, he won important concessions. Partly due to a conflict of interests, H2S was being planned for limited production for Bomber Command to permit sufficient production of ASV (Anti-Surface Vessel) for Coastal Command. H2S and ASV were basically the same systems, except that ASV was designed to indicate the position of ships at sea on the cathode ray display tube in the aircraft, and was particularly valuable for hunting down submarines when they were on the surface and allowing an attack with bombs or depth charges. The other reason for the limited production was due to the Air Ministry, in particular the Directorate of Bomber Operations, taking the view that H2S was such a complicated instrument to operate that it should be confined to the Pathfinder Force. In this they were unquestionably encouraged by Bennett, the commander of the Pathfinder Force, now an Air Commodore, who was anxious as a matter of principle to confine to his force all of the new RDF aids to target location and blind bombing. Exceptions which he recognised were Gee, and any device warning of approach and impending attack by night fighters.

H2S was, however, more than a target-finding and blind-bombing device. It was an excellent instrument for night navigation at any range from base, and therefore was complementary to Gee and an essential aid to all aircraft in finding their way to the locality of the target to be pin-pointed and marked by the Pathfinders. Harris was, therefore, not prepared to agree to a limitation of H2S production for Bomber Command. But he had other reasons too. He still clung to his original idea of his Groups being able to operate against targets with their own target-finding and marking force, so that several major operations against German cities could take place simultaneously. Although this could be achieved by the Pathfinder Force marking several targets at the same time, Harris was convinced that better results would be achieved by giving the whole task to one Group on its own, where Group pride of achievement would produce greater cooperation and develop specialist tactics. By February 1943, he could, with the knowledge of the Casablanca directive, foresee the Bomber Force becoming large enough in numbers of aircraft, together with their greatly increased bomb carrying capacity, to justify several attacks of the necessary weight simultaneously. Moreover, he now had certain Group moves impending: Cochrane to No 5 Group as AOC, and Air Commodore R. Harrison from his appointment as D/SASO at HQ Bomber Command to that of AOC No 3 Group with the rank of Air Vice-Marshal. Both of these commanders Harris had chosen because they were highly suited by experience to command Groups which would ultimately operate independently. Either of them would, in fact, like Bennett, have made excellent commanders of the Pathfinder Force.

On 21 February 1943 a letter was despatched to the Air Ministry, signed by Saundby, stating the Command's requirement for the introduction of H2S into all Lancaster and Halifax aircraft, as standard equipment, at the earliest possible date. It was also requested that, to meet this operational requirement, the production of sets be increased substantially beyond the 1,500 already on order. With regard to the Lancaster, there was to be an exception in the case of the Mk II, which was being equipped with the modified bomb bay doors to accommodate the 8,000-pound and other large bombs, as these would not permit installation of the rotating aerial on the underside of the fuselage which was a part of the H2S system. It was Harris's intention to equip No 3 Group with the Lancaster IIs in place of Stirlings and to have these aircraft fitted with G-H, a precision blind-bombing device which was not unlike Oboe, but which could operate with eighty aircraft simultaneously from one pair of stations and therefore could be used for direct bombing of special targets through ten-tenths cloud. Its accuracy was almost as great as that of Oboe. However, G-H was not likely to be available until late in 1943, as was also the case with the Lancaster IIs.

On 15 February, Harris won his battle to have Saundby made Deputy Commander-in-Chief, but it was not until the early autumn of 1943 that he was able to get the post upgraded to that of an Air Marshal and so obtain promotion for Saundby to that rank. Harris himself was promoted Air Chief Marshal on 1 April.

On 28 February, Air Vice-Marshal Cochrane moved from No 3 Group to take command of No 5 Group, and Air Vice-Marshal Harrison moved from HQ Bomber Command to take over command of No 3 Group on 27 February. Air Vice-Marshal Oxland, who had been commanding No 1 Group, was brought into HQ Bomber Command as SASO, and Air Vice-Marshal Rice, who had been, as a Group Captain, one of Harris's best Station Commanders in No 5 Group when Harris was AOC at the beginning of the war, took over command of No 1 Group. With Air Vice-Marshal Carr commanding No 4 Group and Bennett, now an Air Vice-Marshal, commanding the Pathfinder Force, or No 8 Group as it had then been designated in January, Harris had his team together, at last, for the great offensive; a team of senior officers whom he had known personally, off and on, over a number of years and who had served under him previously at some time during their careers. It was a hand picked team and Harris knew their strengths and their weaknesses, their capabilities and their limitations, and above all he knew that there was no better and no more loyal team to carry through the colossal task that lay ahead.

In addition he had No 6 (Royal Canadian Air Force) Group commanded by Air Vice-Marshal G. E. Brookes.

At the beginning of March 1943, Harris had at his disposal an effective operational strength of thirty-seven heavy four-engined bomber squadrons and fourteen and a half medium twin-engined bomber squadrons, giving him a first line strength of some 660 heavies and 300 mediums.

At the same time he had H2S and Oboe available for operations.

'At long last,' he says of this moment, 'we were ready and equipped. Bomber Command's main offensive began at a precise moment, the moment of the first major attack on an objective in Germany by means of Oboe. This was on the night of 5/6 March, when I was at last able to undertake with real hope of success the task which had been given to me when I first took over the Command at the beginning of 1942—the task of destroying the main cities of the Ruhr.'

It was Essen that he chose for the opening of the Ruhr campaign. It was Essen, the largest and most important manufacturing centre in the Ruhr, which was the home of Krupps, perhaps the greatest and most notorious armament manufacturers the world has known, that was to hear Oboe play the opening notes of the 'Ruhr Serenade'.

The first use of the new RDF navigational aids had, however, taken place against Hamburg on the night of the 30/31 January 1943, with a small force of 148 aircraft led by Pathfinders equipped with H2S, but this had been in the nature of an operational trial of H2S, and one which was successful enough to indicate the future promise of this device. Whilst Oboe was to ensure the devastation of much of the Ruhr area over the next twelve months, Harris also had the means with H2S of striking deep into Germany with terrifying effect. These new navigational aids unquestionably revolutionised the tactics of night bombing. Overnight they made the bomber force largely independent of weather conditions en route to and over the target area, and this, in turn, made possible a great expansion in the number of night bombing sorties. Combined with a considerable increase in the first line strength, which consisted almost entirely of four-engined heavies, this expansion was to raise enormously the tonnage of bombs dropped on Germany in 1943. In fact, the increased weight of attack that was now possible was such that the same tonnage of bombs that could be delivered in one month in 1942 could now be dropped in two nights in 1943. With the greatly improved accuracy provided by the new navigational and bombing aids, and with the Pathfinder Force, the rate of devastation was also to be increased. A further implication of the new aids to navigation and the developing Pathfinder techniques was that successful attacks could be made in the dark night periods with no moon, or in relatively bad weather, thereby permitting operations under conditions that were least favourable to the enemy's night fighters. This was to have the double advantage of reducing the casualty rate of the bomber force, thereby providing a larger output of trained crews from the OTUs and HCUs for further expansion of the Force. It was a case of the 'non-vicious circle'.

The new Pathfinding techniques did, however, carry their own limitations. They placed a tremendous responsibility on the Pathfinder Force, for if the marking was scattered no really heavy concentrations of bombing by the main force could develop, and if it was concentrated off target an excellent concentration of bombing was likely to be achieved in open country. But both these limitations proved to be more applicable to targets at long range rather than in the Ruhr, which was within range of the very high precision Oboe system. And it was the Ruhr that Harris had set his heart on attacking and destroying with ruthless determination.

Harris had studied Germany's industrial dispositions with great care, not just as C-in-C Bomber Command, but even before the war when he was entirely convinced that war with Germany was inevitable and that a strategic bomber offensive against Germany, if the war was to be won and not lost, was even more inevitable. He had also assessed the likely capabilities of the bomber and, quite correctly, he had come to the conclusion that if it was to carry an effective destructive load it would have insufficient speed and altitude and be unable to carry adequate armament to be a match for any day fighter. Therefore he had based his thinking on night bombing. Realistically, he had precluded the idea of such high-precision bombing by night that individual industrial complexes could be picked out and bombed in isolation. Even with the new scientific aids coming to hand in 1943 such precise bombing was a forlorn hope. Consequently, before the war, Harris had based his thinking on area bombing of industrial regions, and nothing that had happened by 1943 led him to change his views on his strategy and tactics. He did, however, foresee the possibility of some application of precision tactics as other RDF aids became available in the future, or present aids became more highly developed for greater accuracy.

The Ruhr was now his immediate concern and he knew exactly what force he had at his disposal and the extent of its capabilities. He knew that the Ruhr was Europe's principal producing area for coal, coke, iron and steel, that it was the home of vast metallurgical and chemical industries and above all it was the centre of Krupps, Germany's vitally important armaments complex. The Ruhr was, in fact, a huge concentration of industry which was not only self-sufficing but upon which much of Germany's other industrial areas depended for raw materials, in particular industries associated with war production.

At 21.00 hours the night of 5/6 March 1943, with Essen as the target and the centre of Krupps as the aiming point, the campaign against the Ruhr began. The assault was planned with that attention to detail which was always demanded by Harris, and which was characteristic of the section of the Command Headquarters Staff responsible for operational planning under Saundby. (Indeed, the planning, which remained under Saundby till the end of the war, developed as time went by until it attained a very high degree of complexity and precision, particularly when Nos 3 and 5 Groups formed their own target-finding forces and operated independently of the Pathfinder Force.) A force of 442 aircraft was despatched on this first attack, and of this force 303 were heavies. The attack was led by eight Mosquito aircraft fitted with Oboe; their duty was to put down yellow target-indicator flares along the line of the bombing approach to the target, but finishing fifteen miles short of the target. They then marked the aiming point with salvoes of red target indicator flares in accordance with a closely calculated schedule, the first salvo falling at zero hour, the next three minutes later, the next ten minutes later, and so on up until the last salvo, which fell at zero-plus-thirty-three minutes. A force of twenty-two Pathfinder heavies followed closely on the heels of the Mosquitos. Their job was to maintain the yellow path of flares on the bombing approach to the target, and to drop green target indicators with high-explosive bombs on the red target indicators, followed by a delay of one second before releasing their incendiaries. This bombing technique of HE and incendiary was to get fires going in the target area. The main force, carrying bomb loads of one-third HE and two-thirds incendiaries bombed the red indicators, but if these could not be seen they bombed the green indicators. In all, 1,054 tons of bombs were dropped in thirty-eight minutes.

This raid was a very considerable success and, for the first time in the war, Krupps itself was severely damaged, as were the Goldschmidt Company, the Maschinenbau Union, the power station, gasworks and the municipal tram depot. An area somewhat larger than 160 acres was also laid waste, by far the greater part by fire. 30,000 people, mostly Krupp workers, were rendered homeless.

Further attacks on Essen were made on the nights of 12/13 March, 3/4 April and 30 April/1 May. They continued beyond this last date, but in those two months of March and April 1,552 aircraft bombed Essen in four raids and dropped 3,967 tons of bombs on this vitally important target. The damage by this time was significant and Krupps had suffered so badly that production was gravely impaired.

Following the raid on the night of 5/6 March, Goebbels recorded in his diary:

> During the night Essen suffered an exceptionally severe raid. The city of the Krupps has been hard hit. The number of dead, too, is considerable. If the English continue their raids on this scale, they will make things exceedingly difficult for us. The dangerous thing about this matter, looking at it psychologically, is that the population can see no way of doing anything about it. Our anti-aircraft guns are inadequate. The successes of our night fighters, though notable, are not sufficient to compel the English to desist from their night attacks. As we lack a weapon for attack, we cannot do anything noteworthy in the way of reprisal.

Then again, after the raid on the night of 12/13 March, he wrote:

> Later in the evening the news reached us of another exceedingly heavy air raid on Essen. This time the Krupp plant has been hard hit . . .

Twenty-five major fires were raging on the grounds of the Krupp plant alone. Air warfare is at present our greatest worry. Things simply cannot go on like this. The Führer told Göring what he thought without mincing words. It is to be expected that Göring will now do something decisive.

On 10 April Goebbels visited Essen to inspect the damage. He was greatly shocked. He wrote in his diary:

We arrived in Essen before 7 a.m. Deputy Gauleiter Schlessmann and a large staff called for us at the railway station. We went to the hotel on foot because driving is quite impossible in many parts of Essen. This walk enabled us to make a first-hand estimate of the damage inflicted by the last three raids. It is colossal and indeed ghastly. This city must, for the most part, be written off completely. The city's building experts estimate that it will take twelve years to repair the damage ... Nobody can tell how Krupps can go on. Everyone wants to avoid transplanting Krupps from Essen. There would be no purpose in doing so, for the moment Essen is no longer an industrial centre the English will pounce upon the next city, Bochum, Dortmund or Düsseldorf.

But if Goebbels was depressed, Stalin was, by contrast, elated. In a signal to Churchill on 12 April he said:

I welcome the bombing of Essen, Berlin and other industrial centres of Germany. Every blow delivered by your Air Force to the vital German centres evokes a most lively echo in the hearts of many millions throughout the length and breadth of our country.

Harris's campaign was not just confined to Essen, but concentrated on industrial and other military areas. Berlin, which was largely a political target, was to receive relatively minor attention at this stage of 1943.

Between 1 January and 30 April Essen, Duisberg, Bochum, Düsseldorf and Cologne were heavily attacked. In all 4,219 sorties were flown against them and 10,230 tons of bombs dropped on them, with Essen, Duisberg and Cologne bearing the real brunt of these attacks. The losses to Bomber Command were 163 aircraft or 3·86 per cent, which was well within a supportable loss rate. During the same period, 2,569 sorties were flown on raids against Hamburg, Wilhelmshaven, Kiel, Stettin and Bremen with a total bombdrop of 6,310 tons, for a loss of eighty-four aircraft—3·27 per cent. Hamburg and Wilhelmshaven were the most heavily attacked during this period. Berlin received 2,888 tons from 1,515 sorties spread over five raids; the losses were seventy aircraft, or 4·62 per cent. Nürnberg, München, Stuttgart, Frankfurt, Mannheim and Pilsen also received attention to the extent of 5,797 tons of bombs from 2,812 sorties, Nürnberg, Stuttgart and Frankfurt receiving the bulk of this load. The losses were 133 aircraft, or 4·7 per cent, but they would have been considerably less if it had not been for the loss of thirty-seven aircraft out of 327 attacking the Skoda works at Pilsen on the night of 16/17 April—a loss of 11·3 per cent. In addition, the northern Italian towns of Milan, Turin and Spezia were quite heavily raided.

The total effort of the Command during these four months was 11,910 sorties dropping a total bomb load of 26,269 tons for the loss of 492 aircraft or 4·13 per cent. This was a tremendous increase on the equivalent period in 1942 when 5,435 sorties were flown against Germany and Czechoslovakia dropping only 6,646 tons of bombs. The losses in this 1942 period were 218 aircraft, or 4·01 per cent. A straight comparison of effort is, however, not the only measure of Bomber Command's ascendancy during this period. The 1943 effectiveness was incomparably greater due to the introduction of Oboe and H2S to the Pathfinder Force, and due to the much improved target-marking techniques. The bombs were getting to their targets.

Quite apart from this effort in the first four months of 1943, the Command sowed 5,442 sea mines, flying 2,338 sorties for this purpose and losing ninety-two aircraft or 3·9 per cent. A known toll of some 50,000 tons of shipping was taken, including two U-boats sunk and two damaged.

The attacks on the Ruhr and other important industrial towns continued right through into the summer months, with town after town going down in ruins under the scourge of the Bomber Force. Dortmund and Duisberg were half obliterated, Düsseldorf suffered nearly three-quarters destruction and Hagen, Mulheim and Wuppertal-Barmen were more than 50 per cent devastated. Bochum and Remscheid had 83 per cent of their built-up area destroyed before the summer ended. As a shattering climax, on the night of 24/25 June the small but important industrial town of Wuppertal-Elberfeld was selected for attack. Its position in the Ruhr was such that location by night was almost impossible by normal visual means. Its shape was long and slender, demanding a high degree of bombing accuracy to attain effective concentration. Its size, estimated by population, was slightly greater than that of Coventry, where the Germans in a devastatingly successful attack on the night of 14/15 November 1940, in a raid lasting two hours, had completely destroyed 100 acres in the centre of the town. Wuppertal-Elberfeld was a town of 929 acres when the first Oboe Mosquitos, leading 631 bombers of which 517 were heavies, dropped their target indicators. Twenty minutes later 870 acres of Wuppertal-Elberfeld lay in ruins.

One other major attack on the Ruhr, which was undertaken at this period, must be highlighted because it was exceptional technically and tactically. It introduced the beginning of No 5 Group's break away from dependence upon the Pathfinder Force, and its development as an independent Group with its own target-finding force and techniques.

Barnes Wallis, the leading aircraft designer for Vickers Armstrong, who had designed the Wellington bomber with its unusual geodetic construction, had given much thought to the design of a special bomb to breach the Ruhr dams. The idea of attacking these dams had been considered by the Air Staff before the war as it was recognised that success in breaching them could cause considerable industrial damage to major areas of the Ruhr, but the idea had been shelved because no ordinary bomb or torpedo could hope to collapse a concrete encased wall of the thickness used for such dams as the Möhne and the Eder, or an earth dam such as the Sorpe. Wallis, however, thought up an ingenious bomb, shaped like a cylinder, which could be bounced along the water from a low-level release of about sixty feet, and which could be rotated before release to about 500 rpm in the reverse direction to its line of trajection, so that when it struck the dam wall it would wind itself downwards close to the dam, and detonate at an appropriate depth. Its effect, being that of an underwater earthquake, had been carefully calculated by Wallis to breach a dam such as the Möhne or Eder.

Because Air Ministry interest in his bomb was only faint at first, Wallis suggested to the Admiralty that it might be used against capital ships. Harris says that when he first heard of a proposal to use four-engined bombers to attack ships with such a bomb he was horrified: 'No four-engined aircraft had a hope of surviving an attack at sea level to within point-blank range of a warship's guns. Moreover, the *modus operandi* ensured that it would be useless against moving ships which would be miles away by the time the bomb had completed its cycle of strike, hit, bounce back, crawl forward, under and downwards, and finally explode.' The upshot was that Harris flatly refused to cooperate in this scheme which would gravely risk both his crews and aircraft for no hope of any return. But when it was suggested that this bomb could be developed for attacking the dams Harris, whilst remaining sceptical, was prepared to offer limited cooperation. A proposal late in February 1943, however, to take some thirty Lancasters off the production line to rig them up to take this special weapon appalled him so much that he wrote immediately to Portal deprecating the idea of diverting urgently needed Lancasters for the purpose of being modified to carry a weapon which was neither fully developed nor proven. However, he did agree with Portal to send Group Captain S. C. Elworthy, his Group Captain Operations, down to Vickers to talk with Barnes Wallis. Elworthy admitted to the author that he himself was a bit sceptical of the scheme when he visited Wallis, but that he was entirely convinced of its possibilities against the dams after Wallis had explained his ideas and shown him the films of the laboratory tests and of the half-scale trials from a Wellington at Chesil Bank. He further admitted to the author that having been convinced that the proposition was good enough to pursue, he was pretty nervous at the prospect of telling Harris his views because he felt sure that Harris would blow him apart! He was, in fact, so sure that Harris was of the firm opinion that the scheme was impractical and a waste of time that nothing he, Elworthy, could say would change his mind. Elworthy therefore reported on his visit to Wallis by way of a written memorandum. Harris's first reaction was as Elworthy predicted, but the latter had little difficulty in persuading Harris to see Wallis and hear from him at first hand about his ideas for breaching the dams, and to see the films.

Wallis completely convinced Harris of the credibility of his weapon and, as Elworthy says, once Harris was convinced he acted as he always did, with his full and unqualified support for the project. He immediately gave the task to Cochrane in No 5 Group to undertake trials in direct liaison with Wallis, and he authorised the formation of a special squadron for the job. This squadron was numbered No 617 and was formed under Wing Commander Guy Gibson on 20 March. Within five days of its formation, No 617 Squadron had begun its specialised trials and training for its unique task with Lancasters, with a target date of 10 May for readiness to undertake what was to be known as 'Operation Chastise'.

By 15 May all had been ready for several days and on the night of 16/17 May nineteen Lancasters set off, led by Guy Gibson who was to use the technique of Master Bomber for the first time.

The aircraft left in three waves, the first consisting of nine Lancasters led directly by Guy Gibson to attack the Möhne dam and then the Eder; the second consisting of five aircraft led by Flight Lieutenant J. C. McCarthy to attack the Sorpe dam; and the third consisting of five aircraft to act as reserves should their efforts be required. The attacks on the Möhne and the Eder were wholly successful, and vast walls of water were soon sweeping down the valleys as the pent-up waters of the lakes emptied themselves. The second wave of Lancasters, however, which were allocated to the Sorpe dam, fared badly. One lost its bomb after striking the Zuider Zee through flying too low and had to return to base, one was so damaged by flak en route that it too had to return to base, and two were shot down before they reached the target. The fifth aircraft, piloted by McCarthy, did attack the dam and damaged it in the centre, but just above the water-line. Three reserve aircraft were then called in to follow up this attack, but only one succeeded in locating the target and dropping his bomb. Unfortunately this effort was insufficient to breach the Sorpe dam. Of the two aircraft which failed to locate the target, one went missing, presumably shot down.

The damage resulting from these attacks was considerable, although the emphasis on the destruction of hydro-electric installations which were swept away was out of proportion to their importance to the Ruhr. Whilst physical industrial damage from flooding was severe, the real blow to the Ruhr was the loss of vital water. An ill-informed article on the 'Dam-Busting Raids' in the *Sunday Times Magazine*, of 28 May 1972, suggested that the raids were a failure and a waste of both time and life, because the Sorpe dam was the only one which could have caused any real damage if it had been breached. The losses on the raid were eight aircraft with fifty-four highly trained and gallant men, but according to Albert Speer, Germany's Minister for Armaments Production, their lives were not lost in vain. In an interview with the author he explained that the loss of electric power to the Ruhr as a result of the raid was negligible because hydro-electric power represented only a small percentage of supply needs. In fact, most of Germany's electricity came from coal-fired generating stations and the Ruhr, in common with other parts of Germany, was fed on a grid system.

'What was the harm to us,' he recorded, 'was the water for the coking plants for gas, which was a key to our industrial processes in the Ruhr, and water for the cooling processes in steel production and other industry. We needed a lot of water and the Ruhr wells could not possibly supply sufficient water. If the Sorpe could have been breached as well it would have been a complete disaster. But it was a disaster for us anyway.' Referring to the rebuilding of the dams he said: 'It was urgent to rebuild the dams to be able to conserve the water in the lakes again when the rainfall would be coming in October, November and December and great priority was given to this. My fear was that you would bomb our reconstruction work from high level and so prevent us storing again the water so urgently needed. This was my great fear, because the situation was already a disaster for us for a number of months.'

However, whilst the bombing of the dams was a highly effective raid, seriously damaging to Ruhr industry, it was only one facet of the whole Ruhr campaign. Perhaps the most important outcome of the raid was the formation of No 617 Squadron in No 5 Group and the beginning of Harris's plan to create independence of the Pathfinder Force in certain Groups for specialised attacks, and thus have the best brains and pilot skills of all Groups to work out their solutions to the problems confronting the Bomber Force.

The effectiveness of the Ruhr campaign as a whole was unquestionable. Goebbels admitted it regularly at this period. On 25 May he wrote in his diary:

The night raid by the English on Dortmund was extraordinarily heavy, probably the worst ever directed against a German city ... Reports from Dortmund are horrible. The critical thing about it is that industrial and munitions plants have been hit very hard. One can only repeat about air warfare: we are in a position of almost helpless inferiority and must grin and bear it as we take the blows from the English and Americans.

Then again, on 26 May:

The fact is that the Royal Air Force is taking on one industrial city after another and one does not need to be a great mathematician to prophesy when a large part of the industry of the Ruhr will be out of commission.

On 28 May 1943, he wrote:

The English wrested air supremacy from us not only as the result of tremendous energy on the part of the RAF and the British aircraft industry but also thanks to unfortunate circumstances and our own negligence ... It seems to me that the air situation should be considered one of the most critical phases of the war and that it should be conducted quite independently of developments in the East.

Harris had at least convinced Goebbels that British air power, in the shape of Bomber Command, was the most likely instrument of war to bring about the total defeat of Germany—even if he had as yet failed to convince some of his own leading countrymen.

18
The offensive grows

The 'Combined Bomber Offensive', which was the essence of the Casablanca Directive of January 1943, and which envisaged night attacks by R A F Bomber Command and daylight attacks by U S Eighth Bomber Command, had, up to June 1943, largely resulted in the major offensive being undertaken by R A F Bomber Command, alone, against the Ruhr and other inland German targets.

The failure of the Americans to play their part was twofold. When they began operations the Americans had been confident that their aircraft, flying in close formation and armed with 0·5-inch guns, would be more than a match for the German day fighters. The first few months of 1943 proved this thinking to be sadly incorrect, and losses made it clear that without fighter escort the U S bomber formations were vulnerable to almost unsustainable losses. As long-range escort fighters were not at this stage available, and as it was evident that the German fighter force was being rapidly equipped with 20-mm cannon which could outrange the 0·5-inch guns, the U S Eighth Bomber Command had to confine much of its activity to French targets, primarily coastal ones, and to targets in Germany which were at such short range as to permit fighter escort.

The second reason for the limited American effort at that time was the constant pillaging of Eaker's Eighth Bomber Command for requirements in North Africa, and a reluctance on the part of many sections of the U S A to build up the Eighth Bomber Command in preference to sending available American resources to fight the war against the Japanese.

This second reason was the subject of much discussion between a number of leading Americans and Harris. They hoped he would use his close association with Churchill to persuade him (Churchill) to use his influence with Roosevelt to reverse the growth in the U S A of the 'Japanese first' mentality. The approaches to Harris on these matters took place, as was usual, at Springfield. As Harris's wife says: 'There was a constant stream of official visitors to Springfield, either seeking his help over military and political problems, or to see the workings of Bomber Command and examine the bomb damage photographs through stereoscopes in a special room set aside at Springfield and known as the 'Conversion Chamber'. Its purpose was to demonstrate to disbelieving politicians, admirals, generals and foreign potentates that bombing really was destroying German industrial areas; or to occupy the time of difficult Allied leaders such as General de Gaulle to get them off the backs of Churchill and Eden.' Lady Harris goes on to say: 'He never really had a moment of relaxation, except for brief moments with Jackie [his small daughter] who could bring him down to earth and whom he adored. Of course, Sandy [Saundby], who lived with us, shared his problems, and being able to discuss things with him at any time was a great help to Bud [Harris]. Then again, he never really had any nights of clear sleep. He had a low-ringing 'phone by his bed so as not to wake me—and because of his instructions to his Group Commanders and the Operations Staff at Command Headquarters, they would call him to give him results of raids and the extent of casualties. He always wanted to know immediately about losses—and he always took them to heart so personally—he regarded every loss as his personal responsibility. No, he never really had any time off from 1942 to 1945—and all that time he was also suffering badly from his wretched duodenal ulcer. But he never complained.'

The approaches made to Harris by Americans to persuade him to insist upon the expansion of Eighth Bomber Command came in April 1943, when Harris's Ruhr campaign was well under way and producing excellent results. As a result of these visits he was extremely disturbed about the future of the planned 'Combined Bomber Offensive' and therefore dispatched a personal letter to Churchill, dated 22 April, in which he spoke with great frankness:

Prime Minister,

Mr Harriman,* General Eaker, General Longfellow and General Stratemeyer [General Arnold's Chief of Staff] have all lately stayed at my house. We had discussions on the 'Air War'. They strongly urged me to bring the following to your notice.

Official and unofficial criticisms of American daylight bombing which have been overheard or taken from the Press on this side have been distorted and exaggerated in the States to such an extent that there is now widespread publicity to the effect that the British have no faith in an American Bomber Offensive against German targets and that it is no good per se.

This propaganda, much of which is no doubt enemy inspired, is being exploited by Anglophobes (especially ex-Isolationists), and other interested parties, to encourage the despatch of United States bombers to the Pacific, China, North Africa, or anywhere rather than Britain. The slogan is, 'If they don't want us in England, let's go where we are wanted'. Much telling weight has been added to this appeal by the public

---

* William Averell Harriman, a special representative of Roosevelt in England, who in 1943 became the US Ambassador to the USSR.

utterances of Evatt,* MacArthur,† Kenny (MacArthur's airman) and Madame Chiang Kai-Shek.‡

It falls on eager American ears. They hate the Japs. They urgently desire to give all the air backing possible to such heroes as the Marines of Guadal Canar [Guadalcanal]. They would sooner fly a howitzer to Port Moresby than a ton of bombs to Berlin. They are disappointed with the performance of their troops in North Africa, and tend to soft pedal the war there to the glorification of '100% American' deeds in the Far East. They think that the Royal Air Force can and will do most of the North Africa job. But they prefer even North Africa to bombing from Britain. They have a shrewd idea that it is easier.

The Admirals and land Generals do not want the Bomber to emerge as a Prima Donna in this war's offensive. They try to forestall this by asserting that the Bomber Offensive is useless anyhow, and that the European Theatre must therefore wait until a distant and improbable future when ships become available to transport immense invasion armies.

The majority public opinion has, by such means, been switched to a 'Japan first' mentality.

Out of all this clearly emerged one demand—urgent and reiterated. My guests all emphatically claimed that neither you, the Secretary of State, nor the Chief of the Air Staff, have ever come out with a resounding declaration as to the need for really strong American Bomber Forces to complement the Bomber Command offensive from Britain. It has never been put across to America publicly or officially.

I protested that various Chiefs of Staff papers had stressed this time and again in no uncertain manner, and that it had been officially agreed. This produced a definite reaction (by no means unexpected to me) that Chiefs of Staff and Combined Chiefs of Staff papers and plans are not available to the Press or public and, in any case, seldom get translated into practice in the USA. A normal habit with such agreements, as I found to my cost in Washington. They are regarded as some sort of necessary, though largely futile, by-play. What really matters in the USA is a resounding declaration, or personal approaches, secret or otherwise, by the highest in the land. Hence the effect of propaganda by MacArthur, Madame Chiang Kai-Shek, etc.

All impressed upon me the vital need for you, or failing that, for the Secretary of State or Chief of the Air Staff to voice a loud and urgent demand. An appeal to the President from yourself would, of course, be effective. But if that is ruled out, public pronouncements in the House or elsewhere would carry great weight if they were of the 'they have promised they are coming' order.

---

* The Rt Hon H. V. Evatt, Australian Minister for External Affairs.
† General D. MacArthur, US Supreme Commander, South-West Pacific.
‡ Wife of Generalissimo Chiang Kai-Shek, President of China.

I am assured most earnestly that failing some such action neither official circles in America nor public opinion would be convinced as to the Bomber's part in our strategy. Neither would the aircraft and air personnel be forthcoming in the numbers expected or required as long as there was any reasonable or unreasoned excuse for diverting them ad hoc into more popular and more highly publicised channels.

I therefore give you this account of what transpired. You may see fit to discuss it with Mr Harriman, if he has not already raised it with you.

This letter, which reached Churchill less than two weeks before he sailed for the USA on 5 May for the Washington Conference of May 1943, was promptly acknowledged by the Prime Minister; but he made no comment. Harris, however, followed it up indirectly with a letter on the 15th to Portal who had with the other British Chiefs of Staff, accompanied Churchill to Washington. This letter was addressed care of the Air Attaché in Washington and included a number of excellent reconnaissance photographs showing extensive damage to certain German towns. He wrote:

Dear CAS,

I enclose the first photographs of damage in Duisburg, Dortmund and Bochum. The cover is nothing like complete yet and we shall have plenty more to show later. The night plot of the Duisburg attack, however, is especially good and the damage to the Bochum steelworks is obviously very serious. This sample of what has been happening on an enormous scale in the big Ruhr cities combined with excellent photos the Americans have taken at Kiel should at least be enough to make it clear that if the USAAF gets its reinforcements quickly, the Germans cannot take it for very long.

In a cypher signal earlier that day Harris had referred to the Kiel raid in these words: 'US bombing of Kiel magnificent.'

His pleas did not go unheeded. In the overall strategic concept of the prosecution of the war which emerged from Washington, there appeared high on the list this item: 'Intensify the air offensive against the Axis Powers in Europe.' Admittedly, within a few days of the completion of the conference, Eaker told Harris that two more B24 groups were under orders to move to North Africa, ostensibly for only two weeks; but since the last two groups went there for a promised duration of two weeks, and had remained for two and a half months, he placed little faith in the promises. As Eaker pointed out to Harris, he could not attack Germany with greater frequency because his force was too small to 'stand the racket', particularly without the support of long-range fighters. But from the autumn of 1943 things did begin to improve, and it was Harris's championing of the American effort in Europe that slowly won support from the USA for the expansion of the US Eighth Bomber Command to that strength which was to prove to be of such paramount importance to the Allies in 1944 and 1945. Contrary to the statements of some commentators and writers on the subject of the bombing offensive in World War II, Harris never for one moment doubted the vital contribution that could be made by the US Eighth Bomber Command towards rendering Germany incapable of continuing the war. This is emphatically evidenced in one of his last pleas for the strengthening of the US Air Forces in Britain, which was stimulated by discussions with Eaker and Major-General Fred L. Anderson, who succeeded Eaker as Commander of the US Eighth Bomber Command. The plea took the form of an 'immediate' cypher signal to Portal and was dated 12 August 1943. It read:

Most secret and personal. It is my firm belief that we are on the verge of a final showdown in the bombing war and that the next few months will be vital. Opportunity does not knock repeatedly or continuously and if we let this present one slide the enemy here, and then in the Far East, will find counter-measures and even means of retaliation. I am certain that given average weather and concentration on the main job we can push Germany over by bombing this year. But to do so we must keep diversions cut to the bone. On every front but this one the United States and ourselves now regard it as reasonable, as well as necessary, that we should vastly outnumber our opponents locally in the air. We even brag about complete air supremacy amounting to the virtual elimination of enemy activity on these fronts. But here we and the US Eighth Bomber Command still remain as residuary legatees in air resources while charged with the execution of first, most difficult and most strenuous item of inter-Allied strategy. United States are still making no adequate effort to implement their agreed bomber reinforcement of Eighth Bomber Command. Situation now as follows. Against their force planned for June 30th of 944 [bombers] they received only 741, and by August 4th 796 against 1,192 planned for September 30th. Allocations at present only 850. Their bomber plan, agreed by Combined Chiefs of Staff, asked only for minimum estimated as essential, and if they fall down like this then the plan will not work and opportunity may be gone forever with only alternative vast, long drawn-out land campaign with millions of casualties and most uncertain outcome. I hope you will do your utmost to make them keep their allocations to Eighth Bomber Command up to plan and to make up present leeway. I have found the best approach to leading Americans here to be an expression of astonishment that, while boasting of complete air supremacy everywhere else, they continually leave their Eighth Bomber Command in this prime theatre always far below planned strength fighting the enemy at his point of greatest concentration of defence and hopelessly outnumbered. Outnumbered is a true and, to these people, a startling expression. It is impossible either to justify or to understand this bewildering situation which results also in leaving the enemy free to concentrate against Bomber Command a weight of defence which Eighth Bomber Command's operations would have by now largely reduced had their reinforcements been kept up as planned. There is no doubt in my mind that had Eighth Bomber Command been increased as planned they would have knocked out almost whole German fighter force in the air and most of their fighter factories by Autumn and that between us we could then have had a clear run and rapidly knocked Germany stiff. But the opportunity will be lost within six months if United States persist in their continued neglect of Eighth Bomber Command. Eaker and Anderson wish particularly to get these facts put over at this juncture.

With the growing strength of his own Command, Harris had himself been pounding Germany in no uncertain terms and his highly successful Ruhr campaign had forced the Germans to deploy increasing numbers of fighter aircraft on their western front. Albert Speer referred (in a speech at a conference of Gauleiters in June 1943) to the serious losses in production of coal, iron, steel, crankshafts and other vital war requirements, caused by the RAF bombing. Because of this he explained that a decision had been taken to double the anti-aircraft defences of the Ruhr and draft in 100,000 men for repair duties. These increases in defences in the west, particularly by day and night fighters, made it necessary to reconsider the Casablanca Directive of 21 January 1943. As a result a new directive was issued to Harris and Eaker on 10 June 1943, which came to be known as 'Pointblank'.

After the preliminaries, the directive said:

> The increasing scale of destruction which is being inflicted by our night bomber forces and the development of the day bomber offensive by the Eighth Air Force have forced the enemy to deploy day and night fighters in increasing numbers on the Western Front. Unless this increase in fighter strength is checked we may find our bomber forces unable to fulfil the tasks allotted to them by the Combined Chiefs of Staff.
>
> In these circumstances it has become essential to check the growth and to reduce the strength of the day and night fighter forces which the enemy can concentrate against us in this theatre. To this end the Combined Chiefs of Staff have decided that first priority in the operation of British and American bombers based in the United Kingdom shall be accorded to the attack of German fighter forces and the industry upon which they depend.

The directive went on to say that the primary object of the bomber forces, as laid down in the first paragraph of the Casablanca Directive, was to remain. Then came the division of duties between the Eighth Air Force and RAF Bomber Command. Essentially, Eighth Air Force was given the task of destroying the German airframe, engine and component factories, and the ball-bearing industry, upon which the strength of the German fighter force depended. In addition its tasks included the destruction of enemy fighters in the air and on the ground. Two other items were actually listed, although one was largely complementary to the first. These were the general disorganisation of those industrial areas associated with the aircraft industry, and the destruction of fighter aircraft repair depots and storage parks. Bomber Command's task was in less precise terms. The directive said:

> While the forces of the British Bomber Command will be employed in accordance with their main aim in the general disorganisation of German industry their action will be designed, as far as practicable, to be complementary to the operations of the Eighth Air Force.

In addition to the British and US bombing forces, the directive prescribed activities for RAF Fighter Command and the American fighter forces of the Eighth Air Force. These were: 'The attack of enemy aircraft in the air and on the ground', and 'The provision of support necessary to pass bomber forces through the enemy defensive system with the minimum cost.'

As has already been said, long-range fighters were not available at this stage of the war and therefore fighter escorts could not offer cover for more than marginal penetration into Germany.

To destroy the German aircraft industry required precision bombing of selected factories, and in this the Americans had specialised, having trained themselves to bomb in formation by day, using the most accurate bombsights which could be devised. And it was thus that they interpreted their part of the directive, even though they faced appalling opposition from the German fighter force right up to the end of 1943, when the North American P51 Mustang, fitted with the Rolls-Royce Merlin engine and its derivatives, began to make its appearance in England with the Eighth Air Force for long-range fighter escort duties.

Harris interpreted his part of the Pointblank Directive as requiring him to attack those industrial towns in which there were large numbers of aircraft component factories. Due to the short June nights, and as these targets were to the east and to the south of the Ruhr, he was not at first able to undertake his new task and had to concentrate on such targets as Krefeld, Aachen, Cologne, Mulheim and the closer Ruhr targets as well as Italian targets and some French targets, including a 'topping up' attack against the Schneider Armament Works at Le Creusot by 290 aircraft on the night of 19/20 June, and a raid on the Peugeot Works at Montbéliard. The results of all these raids were highly successful, and by the middle of July the Ruhr was in a desperate condition. One attack was made by Harris, however, on the night of 20/21 June, against a target which might be described as falling into the Pointblank category. This was the former Zeppelin works at Friedrichshaven on the Bodensee (Lake Constance) which was producing RDF apparatus for the use of German night fighters. The raid was undertaken by sixty Lancasters of No 5 Group and was a considerable success. No Pathfinder Force aircraft were used, No 5 Group operating entirely on its own and using its own target-finding and target-marking techniques. The aircraft flew on to North Africa after the attack, where they refuelled and bombed-up again for an attack on the Italian naval base at Spezia on the way back to England. Harris's purpose behind this operation was not just to bomb a target which fitted into the Pointblank priority, but also to create German demand for dispersion of defences away from the Ruhr and other major centres, where the concentration was great, to other areas regarded as less vulnerable in the summer months.

Although the Pointblank Directive gave priority to the destruction of the German aircraft industry, naval targets, particularly those associated with U-boat construction, remained well to the fore and, in July 1943, Hamburg became an urgent target to attack, with much pressure for its elimination from the Admiralty. Hamburg was the second largest city in Germany, with a population in excess of a million and a half. Its shipyards were the most extensive in Europe, housing many ships and U-boats under construction. The greater part of its shipbuilding yards, including the famous Blohm und Voss yards, had been given over to the building and assembly of U-boats, and they were responsible for some 45 per cent of the total output of German submarines. Hamburg was also the largest and most important port in Germany. It contained 3,000 industrial establishments and 5,000 commercial companies, most of which were engaged in the transport and shipping industries. In addition there were major oil and petroleum refineries, the second largest manufacturer of ships' screws, the largest wool-combing plant in Germany, and various manufacturers of precision instruments, electrical instruments, machinery and aircraft components. Quite apart from its extensive shipbuilding factories it was, in fact, a town of the utmost industrial importance to Germany, and, as such, it was one of the most heavily defended. Indeed, next to Berlin, it was the most heavily defended city in Germany and Occupied Europe.

Many attacks had already been made against Hamburg in varying degrees of strength, but the damage remained scattered and insignificant. It had been just outside Gee range and although it had been the target for the first Pathfinder H2S attacks at the beginning of the year, which had proved to be reasonably successful, these had been on a comparatively limited scale. But in July, when Harris was called upon to undertake the obliteration of Hamburg, he planned, with the aid of Saundby and the Operations Staff, not a raid, but a campaign against this second largest city of Hitler's Reich. Whilst Hamburg was outside Oboe range and therefore the Pathfinders could not take advantage of this very precise marking device, Harris now had at his disposal excellent RDF aids for the plan of attack. H2S was, at this stage, fitted to a considerable portion of the main bomber force as well as to the Pathfinders, and since Hamburg was an ideal H2S target, being a seaboard town and therefore easily identifiable from the map-like display of coastlines and rivers provided by H2S on its cathode ray screen, not only could there be certainty of exceptionally accurate marking, but the main force could be sure of following up the Pathfinders with equal accuracy. Quite apart from H2S, the entire Bomber Force was now equipped with the Mk II Gee which could use frequencies additional to those available to Mk I Gee, including some frequencies which greatly extended Gee range to well beyond that at which Hamburg lay. These were easy frequencies to be jammed, but they had been preserved from being compromised until a suitable occasion arose to demand their use. Lastly, a device known as 'Window' was to be used. This consisted of bundles of metallised strips of paper cut in such lengths that when scattered in large quantities they would create so many signal responses to the enemy's RDF aircraft detection and gun-sighting systems that these would be unable to detect the approaching aircraft.

The operation, which went by the ominous code name of 'Gomorrah', was planned to take place over a period of four nights. As Harris told his crews, when issuing his message of good luck to them just before the first assault on the night of 24/25 July:

> The Battle of Hamburg cannot be won in a single night. It is estimated that at least 10,000 tons of bombs will have to be dropped to complete the process of elimination. To achieve the maximum effect of air bombardment this city should be subjected to sustained attack. On the first attack a large number of incendiaries are to be carried in order to saturate the Fire Services.

The route was out over the North Sea to a position exactly fifteen miles north-east of Heligoland, which was the point at which the bomber force was to turn in towards its target. With Gee working perfectly up to these distances the accuracy of navigation was excellent, timing perfect and concentration maximal. Both Pathfinder and main force aircraft then had the aid of their H2S to identify the coast in the neighbourhood of Cuxhaven and the River Elbe as it unfolded itself on the screen as far as Hamburg, and finally as it revealed the bright fingers of light of the dock area. Within thirty minutes, 740 aircraft, out of 791 despatched, rained down 2,396 tons of bombs of which some 980 tons were incendiary, the remainder being HE.

Window worked to perfection. The RDF-controlled searchlights waved aimlessly in all directions, the anti-aircraft gunfire was inaccurate, and German night fighter controllers were thrown into complete confusion—one was heard to shout over the R/T: 'I cannot follow any of the hostiles; they are very cunning!'

The results of the raid were disastrous and Goebbels described it as 'a real catastrophe', and '... an exceptionally heavy raid with most serious consequences for the civil population and for armaments production'. But there was more to come. With the defences of Hamburg in tatters, the US Eighth Bomber Command made precision bombing attacks with sixty-eight bombers against the port and district of Wilhelmsburg on the morning of the 25th, and with fifty-three aircraft against the Neuhoff power works on the 26th. Then, on the night of the 27th/28th, Harris struck again in force, with 739 bombers dropping 2,417 tons, of which 50 per cent were incendiary and the rest HE. This was followed by yet another attack on the night of the 29th/30th, when 726 aircraft dropped 2,382 tons of bombs into the third quarter of the reeling city. Again the mixture was approximately 50 per cent incendiary and 50 per cent HE. The final onslaught was delivered on the night of 3 August, when out of 740 aircraft despatched, 462 attacked and dropped a further 1,462 tons of bombs into what was now a blazing inferno. In these four raids 8,621 tons of bombs had been dropped, 4,309 tons being incendiaries.

It was more than a week before the true extent of the damage could be assessed, photographic reconnaissance being impossible for the first six days after the last attack due to the continuous presence of a vast pall of smoke over the entire city. But reports coming out of Europe were talking about fire storms which raged through the town with immense force and temperatures approaching 1,000°C. When photographic evidence was available it showed that 75 per cent of the city had been razed to the ground. More than ten square miles of built-up area had been eradicated. Shipyards, industrial enterprises, commerical areas and residential areas had been wiped out, and city services were no longer able to operate.

Goebbels wrote in his diary on 29 July, the day after the third raid:

Kaufmann, in a first report, spoke of a catastrophe the extent of which simply staggers the imagination. A city of a million inhabitants has been destroyed in a manner unparalleled in history. We are faced with problems that are almost impossible of solution. Food must be found for this population of a million. Shelter must be secured. The people must be evacuated as far as possible. They must be given clothing . . . He spoke of about 800,000 homeless people wandering up and down the streets not knowing what to do.

Albert Speer wrote in *Inside the Third Reich*: 'The devastation of this series of air raids could be compared only with the effects of a major earthquake. Gauleiter Kaufmann teletyped Hitler repeatedly, begging him to visit the stricken city. When these pleas proved fruitless, he asked Hitler at least to receive a delegation of some of the more heroic rescue crews. But Hitler refused even that.' He went on: 'Hamburg had suffered the fate Göring and Hitler had conceived for London in 1940.' And again on the same subject:

Hamburg put the fear of God in me. At the meeting of Central Planning on July 29 I pointed out: 'If the air raids continue on the present scale, within three months we shall be relieved of a number of questions we are at present discussing. We shall simply be coasting downhill, smoothly and relatively swiftly . . . We might just as well hold the final meeting of Central Planning in that case'. Three days later I informed Hitler that armaments production was collapsing and threw in the further warning that a series of attacks of this sort, extended to six more major cities, would bring Germany's armaments production to a total halt.

In March 1972, when the author talked with Albert Speer at his home in

Heidelberg, he asked him if he had changed his mind about this matter of six towns. Speer replied: 'No, no, attacks like that on six such towns and we would have been finished!' It is interesting, therefore, to conjecture whether, if Harris's views on the build-up of the British and American bomber forces had been accepted earlier and the necessary priorities had been given (which they could well have been, albeit at the expense of some other military or naval priorities), the war might have been successfully won by the end of 1943.

The casualties in Hamburg were high. 41,800 lost their lives and 37,439 were injured, some so seriously that they died. To these figures must be added several thousands who were reported missing. The Police President of Hamburg, in his report on the raids,* described the scenes which took place in the fire storms in the city and told of streets which were covered with hundreds of corpses. 'No flight of imagination,' he wrote, 'will ever succeed in measuring and describing the gruesome scenes of horror in the many buried air raid shelters. Posterity can only bow its head in honour of the fate of these innocents, sacrificed by the murderous lust of a sadistic enemy.' Conveniently forgotten was the fate that had already overtaken millions of innocent Jewish men, women and children in the gas ovens and furnaces of the German homeland. By comparison, the total civilian non-Jewish German casualties in the war, estimated at 800,000, are very small indeed. Posterity should remember to bow its head even lower in honour of the innocents sacrificed by the murderous lust of a sadistic Nazi régime.

Harris had not been content with the mammoth Hamburg operation alone. To add to the German confusion he struck at Essen on the night of 25/26 July, immediately after the first Hamburg raid. 627 aircraft, out of a force of 705 despatched, dropped 2,032 tons of bombs on the city. The attack was Oboe-led and was spectacularly successful. Goebbels recorded on 28 July that: 'The last raid on Essen caused complete stoppage of production in the Krupp works. Speer is much concerned and worried.' Goebbels was not the only one to be affected. Doctor Gustav Krupp von Bohlen und Halbach took one look at the blazing remnants of his works on the morning after the raid and promptly fell down in a fit from which he never recovered.

By August, with the nights lengthening, Harris was able to undertake his interpretation of Pointblank. He turned his attention to Mannheim, Nürnberg, München, and in September and October he added Hannover, Kassel, Stuttgart, Frankfurt and others to his list. During the whole of this period he also kept up heavy attacks against the Ruhr towns to prevent them from achieving any major recovery from the devastating campaign of the first six months of the year. There was one major diversion from this programme, occasioned by Intelligence information to the effect that the Germans were developing rockets carrying warheads of up to a ton of high explosive and capable of travelling considerable distances. This was

* Hamburg Police Records.

evidence of Hitler's secret weapon which had been suspected as early as April 1943, and which by June was believed to be under development at a secret experimental station at Peenemünde on the Baltic coast. Photographic reconnaissance in June revealed that Peenemünde was indeed a centre of rocket development, and specific photographs showed what appeared to be two very large rockets of at least forty feet in length and six or seven feet in diameter. Shortly afterwards Intelligence sources also reported development of a pilotless aircraft which was, in effect, an air mine with wings. This too was confirmed by photographic reconnaissance, which then exposed what was evidently a pilotless aircraft launcher complete with aircraft mounted on it ready for catapulting into the air.

Harris was requested to attack this target as a matter of urgency, which he did on the night of 17/18 August. The raid was led by Group Captain John Searby of No 83 (Pathfinder Force) Squadron, who acted as the Master Bomber. Out of 597 heavy bombers despatched, 571 attacked, dropping 1,937 tons of bombs. When the raid was over, the bombing had been so accurate that the experimental station looked like a giant solitaire board. Over six hundred persons working there were killed, including Dr Spiel who was in charge of development. Unquestionably the effectiveness of this raid greatly delayed the progress of the V1 pilotless air mine, and the V2 rocket bomb, with the result that the V1 could not be used until 1944, just after the Allied invasion of France, and the V2 even later. Since both weapons required bases in Belgium and Northern France to bring Southern England within range, the period of their usefulness was limited by Allied bombing followed by the elimination of the bases by the advancing Allied armies. Consequently the use of V1 and V2 against England, although unpleasant, was of little military significance.

Three other raids which should be mentioned here were attacks delivered against Berlin on the night of 23/24 August, with 617 aircraft out of 727 despatched dropping 1,762 tons of bombs; the night of 31 August/1 September, when 507 aircraft out of 621 attacked and dropped 1,463 tons; and on the night of 3/4 September, when 289 aircraft out of 320 despatched dropped 980 tons of bombs on the capital of the Third Reich. These attacks, though not unsuccessful, were not spectacular. Berliners had certainly begun to regard themselves as relatively immune to the RAF's heavy night raids, but these attacks quickly disillusioned them and demands for better defences followed, which was another embarrassment to the already heavily overstretched anti-aircraft defence forces of Germany.

One of the most important things to emerge from the Berlin raids was that the existing H2S equipment, which operated on a wavelength of 10 centimetres, provided insufficient clarity of picture to distinguish aiming points in such a vast built-up area as Berlin. What was required was the much higher resolution of an H2S operating on 3 centimetres, which was under development by Drs Dee and Lovell at the Telecommunications Research Establishment. Harris and Saundby knew of the state of development of this equipment from Saward, now Group Captain RDF since the Command's R D F Staff had been upgraded in May. With his eye on a major Berlin campaign before the turn of the year, Harris now pressed hard for 3-centimetre H 2 S to be available by November for the Pathfinder Force, if only in small numbers.

From 1 June 1943 to 30 September, a period of only four months, Harris had attacked Germany and its occupied territories with 23,153 sorties, dropping 67,105 tons of bombs. The losses were 838 aircraft, or just 3·7 per cent. Of this tonnage more than 55,000 tons had been dropped on German targets. From 1 January to 30 September 1943, a period of nine months, Bomber Command had dropped 117,387 tons of bombs on Germany and laid 11,000 sea mines. Against these figures the total tonnage of bombs dropped on Germany from September 1939 to the end of 1942, a period of twenty-eight months, was 90,329 tons, and of this tonnage 45,000 tons were dropped in 1942. The number of sea mines laid in that period was 11,391. From these figures, the growth of the power of Bomber Command in 1943 is readily apparent. Harris had certainly taken the Casablanca Directive of January 1943 to heart. But the first nine months of 1943 were only a prelude to what was to come.

19
Berlin

In his speech to a conference of Gauleiters on 6 October 1943, Generalfeldmarschall Erhard Milch referred to the aircraft situation in Germany, resulting from British and American bombing attacks in 1943.

Our supply position [he said] should be approximately 2,400 to 2,500 planes per month—the figures for various types fluctuate slightly. Unfortunately we had to suffer a decrease in the last two months due to the strong attacks of the enemy on our aircraft production centres. The greater part of our factories producing fighters have been attacked by day as well as by night. The enemy has attacked, in preference, the most important supply factories so that in September we constructed 200 fighter planes less than, for example, in July, when we achieved a peak production of 1,050 fighters. This month of September we should have reached 1,300 aircraft and we would have achieved this if the destruction had not taken place. Not only has the direct destruction of aircraft factories affected us, but so also has that of aircraft components. I assume Minister Speer, as the responsible person, has already reported in detail on this question. The worries we have in this field are extremely great.

Referring to all aircraft production he said:

... a total of 1,800 planes were produced in September. In the previous month, however, the number was 1,900 and in the month before that, more than 3,000. We hope, however, that we can make up for this loss providing there are no big attacks which inflict new damage.

On the subject of components he said:

How severely our supply position can at times be affected by what seems minor things, can for instance be seen from the attacks on ... [this word is indecipherable but could be Hannover] and on Hamburg. In both cases our metal variable pitch propellers were badly hit. We produced during this month [September] 52 of our most important types of planes, but when everything should have been according to plan in this month we were only able to deliver 4 to the front because propellers for the others were not available until ten days later. Particularly in Hamburg our production has suffered very severely; because of the loss to these factories of 3,000 skilled workers who are still missing.

Later he referred to the fact that in view of the bombing raids, priority was now being given to the defence of the home country.

This was strong evidence of the initial success of Pointblank and it confirmed that the night bombing, as well as the day bombing, was taking its toll of aircraft production. But more than this, the 1943 bombing under the original Casablanca Directive, as well as the change in target priorities under Pointblank, had caused the Germans to disperse weapons away from the Russian and Mediterranean fronts for the purpose of defending the homeland. Speer wrote in *Inside the Third Reich*:

> In Russia our 8·8 centimetre anti-aircraft gun with its precision sight had proved to be one of the most feared and effective anti-tank weapons. From 1941 to 1943 we produced 11,957 heavy anti-aircraft guns (8·8 to 12·8 centimetre), but most of them had to be deployed for anti-aircraft purposes within Germany or in rear positions ... Fourteen million rounds of 8·8 or higher calibre flak (anti-aircraft) ammunition were used for purposes other than anti-tank ammunition, for which only 12,900,000 rounds were provided.

Talking with the author in March 1972, Speer said: 'The Russians were wrong in complaining at the lack of a second front, because the second front was there by your air attacks, because if we would have had at the Russian front all these anti-tank guns—and the 8·8 was a wonderful anti-tank gun— then the losses of the Russians in their tank attacks would have been disastrous for them. The production of 8·8- to 12·8-centimetre anti-tank guns, from 1942 to the end of 1944 was 19,713 guns, but only 3,172 of these went to the Army, the rest, 75 per cent, had to be diverted to anti-aircraft defence against your bombing. It is a most interesting point, because I think the damage you did by bombing was very heavy, but the damage you did by weakening the German Army was much more. This applied also to the optical industry and the electronics industry which were working largely for defence needs at the expense of the urgent requirements of the Army. Admittedly, the production of 7·5-centimetre anti-tank guns was the greatest, but these guns were not so effective against the heavy armoured Russian tanks as the 8·8-centimetre gun which was highly effective.'

However, whilst Germany had become acutely conscious of the effect of the bombing of the aircraft industry, Eaker's Eighth Bomber Command, penetrating deeper into enemy territory, had suffered terrible losses, and these had been mostly at the hands of the German day fighters. Two disastrous raids were those against Schweinfurt, where a large percentage of the ball-bearing industry was concentrated, an industry that was of the utmost importance to aircraft, tank and other armaments production. The other centres of production were Steyr, Erkner in Berlin, and Cannstatt. Supplies of ball-bearings also came from France and Italy, and there were imports from Sweden and Switzerland. Schweinfurt was a small town some forty miles due east of Frankfurt and, therefore, at some considerable range from bases in England. Its size was such as to make it difficult to locate and hit with a night bombing assault, and consequently it had been included in Eaker's list of targets as it was essentially a target for daylight precision bombing. The first attack was mounted on 17 August 1943, when 376 Fortresses of the US Eighth Bomber Command made a split raid on Schweinfurt and on an aircraft assembly plant in Regensburg, which was some fifty miles south-east of Schweinfurt. In the case of both targets the results of the bombing were excellent and Schweinfurt, in particular, was badly hit. Speer says: 'After this attack the production of ball bearings dropped by thirty-eight per cent. Despite the peril to Schweinfurt we had to patch up our facilities there, for to relocate our ball-bearing industry would have held up production for three or four months.' But the cost of the attack to the Americans was disastrous—sixty of the 376 Fortresses despatched were shot down—16 per cent. Eighth Bomber Command was largely out of action for several weeks as a result.

Then, on 14 October, a second attack was made by Eaker's forces on Schweinfurt, with catastrophic consequences for his bombers. As soon as the Thunderbolt escorting fighters withdrew near Aachen, the German fighters engaged the American bombers in a ruthless and running combat all the way to and from the target. Out of 291 Fortresses despatched, sixty were shot down, seventeen were heavily damaged but reached base, and another 121 were seriously damaged. The attack was, however, successful. Speer says: 'This time we had lost 67 per cent of our ball-bearing production.' On the other hand, the catastrophe to the US Eighth Bomber Command, which had lost in one week 148 bombers and crews in four attempts to penetrate deep into Germany without fighter escort, was such that it was virtually grounded for many weeks.

Speer contends that if concerted attacks had been made on the ball-bearing industry, 'armaments production would have been crucially weakened after two months, and after four months would have been brought completely to a standstill.' But he qualifies this view by saying:

This to be sure would have meant:
1. All our ball-bearing factories (in Schweinfurt, Steyr, Erkner, Cannstatt, and in France and Italy) had been attacked simultaneously.
2. These attacks had been repeated three or four times, every two weeks, no matter what the picture of the target area showed.
3. Any attempt at rebuilding these factories had been thwarted by further attacks, spaced at two month intervals.

And Harris comments on this statement: 'Judging from the catastrophic losses of the Americans on the two Schweinfurt raids, there would have been no Eighth Bomber Command left after the first few weeks of such a programme, and R A F Bomber Command would have been totally occupied on a bombing plan of doubtful effect, to the exclusion of all other industrial targets which were being attacked in 1943 with immense success.' The author asked Speer whether he would have reconsidered his statement if he had been told that the American losses would have been unsustainable within a few weeks, and if Bomber Command had had to cut back its Ruhr and other industrial attacks, almost completely, in order to attack the ball-bearing plants so continuously. Speer replied that it would have been possible to bring armaments production to a standstill if his suggestions had been practicable but, equally, the bombing of other industrial targets was weakening Germany, and if this could not have been maintained, and the bombing of the ball-bearing plants had proved to be only partially effective due to aircraft losses by day and doubtful accuracy by night, then the advantage would have been lost. He also agreed that decentralisation of German ball-bearing production was ordered after the American October raid, with the aim of distributing some facilities in the surrounding villages in the Schweinfurt area and housing others in small towns which were unlikely to be regarded as targets for bombing. In fact it was not until 1944 that this was done. Speer says: 'You overestimated the efficiency of the totalitarian system. The public, by this time, opposed transfers of production to their areas if they thought it would attract bombing, and this induced the Gauleiters to resist such transfers. In the same way, in 1944 and 1945, they wanted the Army to stay out of their towns for fear of their presence attracting your bombs.'

The heavy losses of the Americans during their deeper penetration raids into Germany confirmed the need for long-range fighter escort if precision daylight attacks were to succeed with sustainable losses. More than this, however, the success of the German fighter force was creating doubts about the success of the Pointblank operation. This was a matter for much concern because the destruction of the German fighter force, or at least the considerable reduction of its effectiveness, was a prerequisite to any hopes of a successful invasion of the continent of Europe in the summer of 1944, a date which was now a part of the general strategy. Harris, however, held the opinion that Pointblank had achieved much more than expected, but this was a view held only by those directly involved in controlling bomber operations. At that time he believed that if the forces employed were increased and protected from diversions to other targets then the plan would succeed. In fact, he said,

> The reason why the Pointblank attacks have not achieved the desired result as yet, is because they have been carried out by too small a force and because the targets chosen have been changed too often as the result of vacillations of policy.

In particular at this time he criticised, as he had done on previous occasions, the constant depletion of Eighth Bomber Command for diversions of doubtful value to the Middle East, such as the bombing of the Ploesti oilfields in Rumania. In a letter to Churchill, dated 3 November 1943, he gave the Prime Minister a brief survey of what had been accomplished by bombing up to date. He wrote:

> From the above you will see that the Ruhr is largely 'out' and that much progress has been made towards the elimination of the remaining essentials of German war power. Most of this damage has been done since March this year, when the 'Heavies' came into full production and Oboe, H2S, and the Pathfinders served to concentrate the effort.

He then gave an order of priority of targets yet to be destroyed, or where further bombing was required, and this list was headed by Berlin against which he wrote:

> I await promised USAAF help in this, the greatest of air battles. But I would not propose to wait for ever, or for long if opportunity serves.

Following Berlin came Leipzig, Chemnitz, Dresden and the 'Little Ruhr'—Eisenach, Gotha, Erfurt, Weimar and Schweinfurt. Then came a number of towns already seriously damaged but requiring further attention, and these included Bremen, Hannover, Brunswick, Magdeburg, Frankfurt, Karlsruhe, Darmstadt, Stuttgart, Munich, Nürnberg, Kiel and Stettin. Referring to this programme he then went on to say:

> We have not far to go. But we must get the USAAF to wade in in greater force. If they will only get going according to plan and avoid such disastrous diversions as Ploesti, and getting 'nearer' to Germany from the Plains of Lombardy (which are further from 9/10th of war productive Germany than is Norfolk) we can get through with it quickly. We can wreck Berlin from end to end if the USA will come in on it. It will cost between us 400–500 aircraft. It will cost Germany the war.

In truth, the Americans could not have attacked Berlin at that stage without suffering disastrous losses, unless adequate long range fighter escorts could have been provided. These were not then available. But Eaker, in general, agreed with Harris's views. He felt it was not just fighter protection that would make all the difference. In fact, he pointed out most emphatically that the forces allotted to him had not been large enough to undertake the tasks assigned to him in the Pointblank Directive. Finally he was opposed to diverting more of his forces to operate against Germany from Foggia in Italy, a proposal which had been put forward by the American Chiefs of Staff, now that Foggia was available to the US Air Forces.

In October and November of 1943, Harris continued to operate within the principles set down in the Casablanca and Pointblank Directives, but his eye was beginning to centre on Berlin with the rapid approach of the longest nights of the year. Moreover, Harris and Saundby knew of the clandestine operation to equip six Pathfinder Lancasters with experimental

3-centimetre H2S sets which were being made by the Telecommunications Research Establishment. This was the new H2S, operating on a much shorter wavelength and capable of providing a far more detailed picture of vast built-up areas such as Berlin and thus permitting more accurate location of aiming points. The hope of having some 3-centimetre H2S in November/December through official sources was, by September, a forlorn hope, and Bennett of the Pathfinders, now an Air Vice-Marshal, and Saward, had hatched a desperate plan with Drs Dee and Lovell to build six 3-centimetre sets at TRE and to install them in six Pathfinder Lancasters by the middle of November. Harris and Saundby, when told of the situation, had given their blessing. The only other person in the picture was Sir Robert Renwick, whose unofficial help Saward had sought. This support by Harris of what was clearly a private venture being conducted outside the official channels, was typical of his approach when he needed something urgently for his plans and had no hope of getting what he wanted by following the normal procedures. Once he had approved such a course of action his attitude was: 'If you need my help use my name, but tell me immediately afterwards.'

This 3-centimetre H2S project started on 14 September. By early October Dee and Lovell were safely on the way with the programme, and the Command RDF Staff were already running special training courses for the Pathfinder RDF mechanics in the maintenance of the new equipment. In the second week in October, in response to an official request from Harris for 3-centimetre H2S to be installed in at least part of the Pathfinder Force before the end of the year, Renwick called a meeting at the Air Ministry to discuss ways and means of complying with that request. The most humorous feature of this meeting was that Renwick, Dee, Lovell, Bennett and Saward were the only ones who knew that a programme was already well under way to provide the Pathfinder Force with six equipped Lancasters by the middle of November, regardless of the outcome of the meeting! But with Renwick's usual skill the meeting was led to give its official approval to such a plan.

On 13 November 1943, the first three Lancasters equipped with 3-centimetre H2S, JB 352, JB 355 and JB 356, were delivered to the Pathfinder Force, and by 17 November the remaining three had been delivered.

On the night of 18/19 November, the first attack in the Berlin campaign was made by 402 aircraft out of 444 despatched, dropping 1,590·7 tons of bombs on the city. At the same time, 352 aircraft out of 395 despatched attacked Mannheim, dropping 847·4 tons of bombs, making this the first occasion on which two major attacks were made deep into Germany in one night. On the night of 22/23 November 764 bombers attacked Berlin, dropping 2,450 tons of bombs of which approximately 46 per cent were HE and 54 per cent were incendiary. On the 23rd/24th 382 aircraft attacked, dropping 1,326·3 tons and on the 26th/27th 450 attacked, dropping 1,454·6 tons; three major night raids in one week. Then, on 2/3 December, 400 aircraft bombed the city, dropping 1,673 tons; on the night of the 16th/17th 496 aircraft dropped 1,703·1 tons, and on the 23rd/24th 378 aircraft dropped 1,270·2 tons. During this December period a devastating raid was made on Leipzig with 449 aircraft dropping 1,446 tons of bombs on the town, and another was made against Frankfurt with 650 aircraft dropping 2,196 tons of bombs. In nearly all cases the bomb loads were split approximately in the ratio of 50 per cent incendiary and 50 per cent HE. On 29/30 December 632 aircraft out of 712 despatched again attacked Berlin, dropping 2,314·4 tons of incendiary and HE, and on 1/2 January 1944, 421 attacked and dropped 1,200 tons. On 2nd/3rd 383 aircraft attacked, dropping 1,125·1 tons. Four more assaults followed in January; on the night of 20th/21st 769 aircraft dropped 2,402·4 tons, on the 27th/28th 536 aircraft dropped 1,738·4 tons, on the 28th/29th 678 aircraft dropped 1,932·9 tons, and on the 30th/31st 540 aircraft dropped 1,960·3 tons. The last-but-one major attack on Berlin took place on the night of 15/16 February 1944, when 806 aircraft out of 891 despatched attacked the city and dropped 2,610·1 tons of HE and incendiaries in thirty-nine minutes. This raid was made through thick cloud and the attack was remarkable for its accuracy, considering that no glimpse of the city was possible. The last attack was made on 24/25 March, when 716 aircraft out of 810 despatched dropped 2,590 tons of bombs to close the campaign.

Further substantial raids during this period of January, February and March were also made on other targets in great force, including Stettin, Brunswick, Magdeburg, Leipzig, Stuttgart, Schweinfurt, Frankfurt, Essen and Nürnberg.

The campaign against Berlin was immensely successful, although it did not finish the war then and there. Had Harris and Eaker had enough aircraft to 'wreck Berlin from end to end,' as Harris put it in his letter to Churchill of 3 November 1943, then the rapid collapse of Germany might well have occurred. But as it was, Eaker had neither sufficient aircraft nor adequate fighter escort to risk going to Berlin at all, and Harris, on his own, had insufficient strength to create the damage that was necessary to produce surrender. But, in fact, Harris did not claim immediate collapse if Berlin could be wrecked. He had said it would cost Germany the war. Indeed, what Bomber Command did to Berlin from November 1943 to the middle of February 1944 went a long way towards costing Germany the war.

In sixteen major attacks against Berlin from 18/19 November 1943 to 24/25 March 1944, 9,112 sorties were despatched, all four-engined heavies except for 162 Pathfinder Mosquitos, and over 90 per cent attacked, dropping 29,341·5 tons of bombs. The total losses were 492 aircraft which represented 5·4 per cent of those despatched and 6·2 per cent of those attacking. From the beginning of November 1943 to the end of March 1944 26,297 sorties were flown against Germany and enemy occupied territory, more than 90 per cent being against Germany. The total losses, which include the Berlin losses, were 1,108 aircraft, or 4·2 per cent, a figure well within the sustainable losses of the Command.

The Strategic Air Offensive Against Germany, 1939–1945, an official history of the bomber offensive by the late Sir Charles Webster* and Dr Noble Frankland†, states in emphatic terms that the Berlin campaign was a failure, and that losses were at a level that made it impossible to continue the campaign. This is incorrect. The reasons for the cessation were twofold: by the end of March the nights were becoming too short for operations against such distant targets as Berlin and, secondly, the requirements for the preparation for the invasion of France, which went by the code name of 'Operation Overlord', took precedence over the strategic bombing offensive which had been dictated by the Casablanca and Pointblank Directives.

The suggestion that the Berlin campaign was a failure is not supported by the facts. An examination of the results reveals not failure but success, but as Harris himself admits, judged by the standards of the attacks on Hamburg, the Battle of Berlin was not an overwhelming success. However, for Germany it was an unprecedented disaster. It was the German capital; it was at great distance from the enemy's bomber bases, more than 600 miles, and therefore presumed out of range of continuous attacks in force; it was both a major industrial and commercial area; and it was the centre of government. Moreover, the sixteen attacks had been made in very poor weather conditions and for the most part when the city was protected by complete cloud cover. The myth of immunity from bombing, exploded elsewhere in the Reich, had now been exploded in Berlin.

The campaign resulted in the devastation of 2,180 acres of built-up area, or rather more than four square miles. This was in addition to the 480 acres devastated in earlier raids. These 2,180 acres of damage did not include the considerable additional damage inflicted in the outlying suburbs. These figures, which were estimated from photographic reconnaissance completed a short while after the March 1944 attack, have subsequently been proved to be conservative. Final assessments at the end of the war revealed that 6,427 acres had been devastated in Berlin of which 750 to 1,000 acres is credited to American bombing. Since no further major RAF attacks were made against Berlin during the rest of the war it is certain that the major portion of, say, 5,427 acres of devastation was achieved during the November 1943 to March 1944 campaign.

Goebbels' diary from 24 November 1943 through to the end of the month is a continuous cry of horror at what was happening. He describes the destruction in the government administrative area—the damage to the Reich Chancellery, the utter desolation in the Wilhelmsplatz and the Potsdamer Platz.

Devastation is again appalling in the government section as well as in the western and northern suburbs ... The State Playhouse and the

---

* Emeritus Professor of International History in the University of London.

† A wartime Flight Lieutenant navigator who completed a tour in Bomber Command and was awarded the DFC. After the war he obtained a Doctorate of Philosophy.

Reichstag are ablaze ... Hell itself seems to have broken loose over us. Mines and bombs keep hurtling down on the government quarter ...

A day later, on 25 November, referring to a further raid he wrote: 'Conditions in the city are pretty hopeless ... About 400,000 people in Berlin are without shelter.' On the 26th he said: 'I visited the Reich Chancellery. It looks terrible.' On the 27th he recorded: 'At noon I had a long talk with Speer. The punishment Berlin took has shaken Speer considerably.' That same day, in the late evening, he described a major attack which had just started and he showed great concern about the news he received to the effect that one of the most important armament factories was on fire. This was Alkett, a major producer of guns and tanks. On the 28th he wrote of the previous night:

> This time the munitions industry was especially hard hit. The Alkett works received a blow from which they won't recover easily. At Borsig's too, there was tremendous destruction. It must be remembered that Borsig produces a large percentage of our gun output and has 18,000 employees.

On the 29 November he wrote:

> The Berlin munitions industry is still in bad shape. Alkett is almost completely destroyed and, worst of all, valuable and irreplaceable tools and machines have been put out of commission. The English aimed so accurately that one might think spies had pointed their way.

Speer also described the scenes in Berlin at this time, including the fierce fires that consumed his own Ministry. But his real concern was with the disruption to military production.

> On November 26, 1943 [he wrote], four days after the destruction of my Ministry, another major raid on Berlin started huge fires in our most important tank factory, Alkett. The Berlin central telephone exchange had been destroyed. My colleague Saur hit on the idea of reaching the Berlin fire department by way of our still intact direct line to the Führer's headquarters ... Meanwhile I had arrived at Alkett. The greater part of the main workshop had burned out, but the Berlin fire department had already extinguished the fire.

He also referred to the fact that on the 23 December the Erkner ball-bearing plant in Berlin had been heavily hit. This was the next most important ball-bearing plant to Schweinfurt. In conversations with the author, Speer also emphasised the disruption to many other industrial plants engaged on war production in the capital and its suburbs, and to the serious dislocation to all forms of communications—road, rail, and telephone. In referring to the destruction of the administrative and government buildings, offices and associated archives, Speer confirmed that this was a grave embarrassment although, with his rather droll sense of humour, not unlike that of Harris, he said: 'It could be you did us a favour by disrupting our central bureaucracy! But, no, no, it was, of course, very serious for us.' Speer, however, does not believe that the bombing of Berlin alone could have resulted in a sudden collapse. On the other hand he agrees that it contributed to the downfall of Germany and made yet another demand for defences which detracted from meeting the needs of the Army on its various fronts.

One of the most interesting studies to be made of the bombing of Berlin from November 1943 to March 1944 is by examination of Swiss intelligence reports* prepared during this period by Swiss diplomatic and intelligence sources in Germany. The detailed reports of damage indicated the unquestionable success of the campaign, and much of the reporting was confined to industrial and commercial destruction. An example is the report for 5 December 1943, which describes the disastrous damage to Siemens Werke, Siemens und Halske, and Siemens und Schuckert-Fabrik in Siemensstadt, and to the Spandau factory of Siemens-Schuckert A G. The Siemens electrical combine, the biggest in Germany, manufactured cables, aircraft instruments, electrodes and carbons for searchlights, and various military electronic components and equipment. On 17 December, a report concludes that the damage to Siemens und Halske and Siemens-Schuckert was calamitous: 'The war economic significance of the exceptionally disastrous destruction can hardly be overlooked. The Berlin factories have unfinished armament orders valued at nearly 300 million Reichsmarks.' In the 27 December report there are listed forty-five factories covering a variety of industrial production, precision engineering, electrical instruments, chemical, locomotives, aero engines, tanks, etc, described as entirely or partially destroyed and as having been employed on the manufacture of war equipment. The report of 30 December adds another eight manufacturing companies to the list. More still are added as the reports continue through January and February of 1944, including such names as Daimler-Benz, A E G, Lorenz, Borsig A G, B M W, Dornier, Heinkel and Telefunken. In addition, the damage to railway stations, rolling stock and marshalling yards, gasworks, electricity power plants, commercial offices, shops, houses and apartment houses is all assessed with Swiss thoroughness and an eye to the economic state of Germany and its ability to continue the war. It is clear that the Swiss did not think that Germany would collapse with the bombing of Berlin. But it is equally clear that they took into account the build-up of the bomber offensive throughout 1943 and regarded the Battle of Berlin, and the rest of the major bombing against other industrial centres that took place at the same time, as the final onslaught that would produce the beginning of the end of Germany and result in an early and successful invasion of the continent of Western Europe by the Allies. In fact the Swiss

* The author obtained access to these reports, covering the period from 22 November 1943, which was report No 1886, through to 31 December, which was report No 2223, and the period 1 January 1944, which was report No 1 for 1944, through to 4 April 1944, which was report No 588.

regarded the Berlin bombing as a necessary climax in the overall bombing of Germany prior to a successful defeat of the German forces on the ground with the minimum of Allied losses. These were important reactions, for they immediately affected the Swiss willingness to deal with Germany in the supply of materials and manufactured goods. A defeated nation would be unable to pay its bills!

It is also known from German reports that in the first six raids alone, forty-six factories were destroyed and 259 damaged. By the end of March 1944 this figure, as witnessed by Swiss reports, had risen astronomically and, in addition, approximately $1\frac{1}{2}$ million people were homeless in Berlin as a result of the raids.

The Allied bombing of 1943 and early 1944, which in 1943 was almost entirely undertaken by RAF Bomber Command under Harris, disrupted much of Germany's production, materially assisted the Russians on the Eastern Front, materially assisted the Allies in the Mediterranean theatre and, most important of all, threw Germany on to the defensive in the air and on the ground in its homeland, which in turn forced it onto the defensive in all its theatres of war. And on the defensive Germany remained. As Hitler said to Grand Admiral Dönitz, when he was demanding 200,000 additional naval ratings in 1944: 'I haven't got the personnel. The anti-aircraft and night fighter forces must be increased to protect the German cities.' He was right. The armies had already been deprived by the bomber offensive of 75 per cent of their most effective anti-tank guns, which had been diverted to anti-aircraft defence of the homeland, together with hundreds of thousands of trained soldiers.

It has been stated in various histories and documents that despite the heavy blows against Berlin, production increased in the city thanks to measures of rationalisation and standardisation introduced by Speer. This is true, and Germany was indeed fortunate to have in charge of its armaments production such a brilliant and able man as Speer, a Minister who stood out head and shoulders above all other German Ministers; a Minister who would have been a great asset to Britain if only he had been on the Allied side. But the fact remains that months of production from a great deal of Berlin industry was lost to Germany during the bombing, and an ultimate increase in production over previous levels was necessary to catch up on what was lost. This applied to industrial areas other than Berlin. Moreover, to catch up on lost production was not enough for Germany. According to Speer, production for defence needs was already well below that required for efficient defence, and to return to the offensive on all fronts, which was essential to survival, needed a vast increase in production. In fact, by the spring of 1944, with yet a new major front about to open with the invasion of France by the Allies, Germany had been forced by Allied bombing into a desperate defence of her own homeland, a defence which a number of her senior men now knew to be unsustainable.

The Battle of Berlin was no failure.

The last word should perhaps be left to Milch, Armaments Chief of the German Air Force. On 23 February 1944 he told his Staff:

> Everyone should pay a visit to Berlin. It would then be realised that experience such as we have undergone in the last few months cannot be endured indefinitely. That is impossible. When the big cities have been demolished it will be the turn of the smaller ones.

A few days later, he said to a meeting of representatives of the aircraft industry:

> The British have calculated exactly how many attacks they need to make an end of Berlin. The total may be twenty-five. They have already made fifteen attacks, leaving ten to come. Furthermore they have announced that when they have finished with Berlin it will be the turn of the Central German industrial area . . . I would like to suggest that you look at Berlin; it will then be obvious that what has happened in the last few months cannot be endured indefinitely.

20
The matter of command

With the virtual end of the Battle of Berlin on the night of 24/25 March 1944, the entire emphasis of bombing was rapidly switched to those targets, both strategic and tactical, which would assist and eventually support the invasion of Western Europe by the Allies. By the end of 1943, the indirect effectiveness of Harris's bomber offensive had already been felt on the Russian and Mediterranean fronts. On 30 December 1943, Portal signalled Harris as follows:

> As we approach the end of another year I would ask you to accept for yourself and pass on to those serving under you an expression of my heartfelt appreciation of the magnificent achievements of Bomber Command in 1943. I know very well the weight of responsibility which you and your Group Commanders bear so well in devising and directing these great operations. I appreciate too the efficiency and devotion of your Staffs and the willing response of all who work on the ground to the frequent calls made upon them for long hours of hard and heavy work, often under most trying conditions. Above all, I regard with heartfelt admiration and thankfulness the unswerving courage and the constant skill and determination of your crews in their long and successful battle with the German Forces. You are laying waste, city by city, the industrial and economic power on which German armed resistance depends and in so doing you are steadily undermining the will of the German people to carry on this war and perhaps altering for good their whole attitude towards aggression in the future. How much you have already crippled Germany only the Germans themselves know, but it is widely recognised that a large share of the successes of Allied arms on all German fronts this year is due to the destruction wrought in the heart of Germany by Bomber Command and that upon your efforts in the future will depend in no small degree the resistance which the Germans will still be able to offer before they are finally defeated. With gratitude for all your past achievements and with confidence in the great and growing power of your Command, I wish you all good fortune and success in 1944.

But if Portal was pleased, and recognised the vital contribution of Bomber Command to date, there were others on his staff who were critical. The principal ones were Air Marshal Bottomley, the DCAS, and Air Commodore S. O. Bufton, the Director of Bomber Operations on Bottomley's staff. Bufton, however sincere his intentions, gave the impression of aspiring to command Bomber Command from the Air Ministry, and his attempts in this direction appeared to be supported by Bottomley. This interference was, however, rigorously opposed by Harris and Saundby. But by creating some animosity between Bomber Command and the Air Staff, it did at times nearly weaken the close relationship that existed between Portal and Harris. It was only their great mutual respect for each other, backed by Harris's successes, that prevented these internal politics from disrupting the important personal liaison which Harris and Portal constantly maintained right up to the end of the war.

As early as July 1943, Bufton had been persuaded by the Ministry of Economic Warfare that the destruction of Schweinfurt would bring Germany to her knees, and he pressed behind the scenes for attacks by day by the US Eighth Bomber Command, followed up by night by RAF Bomber Command. Harris was less sanguine about the success of such a venture. Schweinfurt, as has been previously stated, was a very small target, and extremely difficult to locate at night, being well beyond Oboe range. So far as H2S was concerned, Harris knew that the existing 10-centimetre version would not provide sufficient ground detail to find this difficult target. He therefore regarded Schweinfurt as essentially a daylight precision bombing target for Eaker's forces. Even so, Harris did not believe the destruction of the town and its ball-bearing factories would prove to be a crippling blow to Germany. As has already been related, Eaker's Eighth Bomber Command attacked in August and October 1943, and it was the German Air Force that then struck the crippling blow against the gallant American Bombers. Albert Speer's considered opinion was that the frequency of attacks required against Schweinfurt, and also against the ball-bearing plants of Erkner in Berlin, Steyr, Cannstatt, and those in France and Italy, to bring military production to a standstill would have been three to four times every two weeks simultaneously against all targets. Unquestionably this would have been impossible, for Eighth Bomber Command would have been decimated, and Bomber Command could never have successfully achieved this task by night—the principal targets were out of range much of the year due to the period of short nights. Such a wasted effort would have spared the rest of Germany, and given her the desperate breathing space she needed to regain ascendancy in the air and the time she required to rehabilitate her major industrial towns.

Bufton and Bottomley may have wanted to be the instigators of this operation which appeared to offer a dramatic end to the war. But, unlike Harris and Eaker, they did not have to carry the responsibility for the drastic consequences of failure—a failure which might ultimately have lost the Allies the war, and would certainly have extended its duration with consequent increases in Allied casualties.

In November 1943, the Ministry of Economic Warfare decided again that the Kugelfischer ball-bearing plant in Schweinfurt had become of the utmost importance as a target, despite the American attacks of 17 August and 14 October, and they recommended that it should be given the first priority. Bufton seized on his old favourite and, on 30 November, minuted Air Vice-Marshal Coryton, who was the Assistant Chief of the Air Staff (Operations), and pressed for action to be taken by the Air Staff to 'persuade' Harris to attack this target. To quote Webster and Frankland:

> The importance of Schweinfurt had, Air Commodore Bufton said, 'consistently been impressed' upon Bomber Command, but no attack had been made. Bomber Command had, he complained, 'firmly set their faces against panaceas, but,' he said, 'if one exists it is certainly the Axis ball-bearing industry.' The Americans, he observed, were now reluctant to contemplate a third attack, but he once more appealed for Bomber Command participation. He suggested that the difficulty of finding Schweinfurt at night had been much exaggerated at High Wycombe (Bomber Command Headquarters) and he pointed out that the Commander of the Pathfinder Force, Air Vice-Marshal Bennett, saw no great difficulty in the task.
>
> Air Commodore Bufton did not think that further appeals to Sir Arthur Harris would serve any useful purpose. He thought the matter should now be taken up by the Deputy Chief of the Air Staff and that 'by some means' Bomber Command should be persuaded to place Schweinfurt in the first priority until it was destroyed.

Bottomley, the DCAS, wrote to Harris on 17 December enclosing an Air Staff paper in which the conclusions of the Ministry of Economic Warfare on the importance of Schweinfurt were brought to his attention. In his letter Bottomley requested an early Bomber Command attack on Schweinfurt.

On 20 December Harris replied to Bottomley. He was emphatically opposed to the attack because of the difficulty of locating the target:

> The town is in the very centre—by any angle of approach—of the most highly defended part of Germany. It is extremely small and difficult to find. It is heavily defended, including smoke-screens. In these circumstances it might need up to six or seven full scale attacks before a satisfactory result was secured on the town as a whole. Even then the chances of individual factories being written off are dubious. In consequence, as I have repeatedly stated, if Schweinfurt is as important as it is alleged to be, it is pre-eminently a job for the US Bomber Command rather than for us.

He then went on to point out that he only had six 3 cms. H2S aircraft in the Pathfinder Force and that he needed many more to locate and successfully mark such a small target. There followed a lengthy diatribe on the efforts of the many armchair strategic experts who, if they had their own way, would so disperse Bomber Command from its real strategic role, a role which it was capable of executing to full effect, that it would fail in its task of softening Germany sufficiently for a successful invasion of the Continent of Europe.

But Harris, in his letter, did make a most significant statement which has been deftly ignored in *The Strategic Air Offensive 1939 to 1945*. He wrote in the last paragraph: 'In these circumstances any attack by us on Schweinfurt must at least await not only particularly favourable circumstances but, in addition, the acquisition of many more H2X (3cms. H2S) aircraft. Even then, for reasons I have given above, I do not regard it as a reasonable operation of war for night bombers. If it takes us three attempts under favourable conditions to hit Hanover once, and three in favourable conditions to hit Kassel once, (these were both targets outside Oboe range) I am satisfied it would take us at least half a dozen before we hit Schweinfurt.' He then suggested that if the task was vital, which he did not believe, the US Eighth Bomber Command should make another attack in daylight, and if they could set it alight Bomber Command might have a chance of hitting it in the dark on the same night.

Also on 20 December 1943, Bufton minuted Bottomley through Coryton, suggesting that attacks by Bomber Command on Schweinfurt should again be requested. Coryton concurred and even went as far as to recommend to Bottomley that Harris should be 'ordered' to attack. After consultation with Portal, Bottomley despatched a long and wordy directive to Harris on 14 January 1944, which only came to the point in the penultimate paragraph. This read:

> I am to request, therefore, that early consideration be given to the ways and means of destroying this target [Schweinfurt] in particular and that you attack it in force on the first opportunity when weather and other conditions allow, and that you continue to attack it until it is destroyed or until alternative directions are issued.

The last paragraph of this directive is also of interest because it contained four targets which Harris had already attacked in force. All were, in fact, high on his list for attention. This paragraph read:

> Whilst first priority must now be accorded to the destruction of Schweinfurt, high priority must also be given to the destruction of those towns associated with the assembly of fighter aircraft, particularly, Leipzig, Brunswick, Gotha and Augsburg.

The first Bomber Command attack against Schweinfurt did not take place until the night of 24/25 February, when Harris had more 3-centimetre H2S aircraft at his disposal and when the Americans had agreed to precede the night attack with a daylight attack on the 24th. On the afternoon of the 24th, 266 Flying Fortresses of Eaker's Eighth Bomber Command bombed the target; this time with a loss of only eleven aircraft, largely due to the long-range fighter escort that was now available with the Mustangs. The same night, in almost perfect weather conditions, 734 aircraft of Bomber Command, with a bomb load of 2,263·2 tons, were despatched to follow up the Americans. The Bomber Command attack was a failure. Only seven of the first wave and fifteen of the second were plotted over the target from their night photographs taken at bomb release. 312 aircraft dropped their bombs within three miles, thirty a very long way from the target and the remainder had photographs that were unplottable. Moreover, thirty-three aircraft were lost, or 4·5 per cent. As Harris had predicted, Schweinfurt was no easy target to locate, mark, and attack by night. Harris was right on another score. In his letter to Bottomley of 20 December 1943, he had said:

> The claims as to the actual percentage of Germany's ball-bearing supply manufactured in Schweinfurt have always been exaggerated and have been progressively reduced, even by the authors. At this stage of the war I am confident that the Germans have long ago made every possible effort to disperse so vital a production.

They had, indeed. After the second American daylight attack of 14 October 1943, which had been highly successful from a bombing point of view, but with losses which had virtually grounded the Americans for nearly three months, Speer, backed by Göring, put into effect a speedy dispersal of the ball-bearing industry. Despite successful attacks on other plants, and the millions of pounds sterling spent by the Allies in Sweden to corner so much of that country's production that none would be available to Germany, by the second half of 1944 German production, which by April had lost about 50 per cent of its output, was recovering so fast that no war equipment was held up because of insufficient availability of ball-bearings. By the end of 1944, the number of machines producing ball-bearings had risen from 13,000 to 21,000, the number of workers from 35,000 to 48,000 and the area of production floor space from 5·5 to 6 million square feet—and all of this so well dispersed that it was hard to find and impossible to disrupt extensively. The incredibly efficient Albert Speer had not been caught with his trousers down, as Harris had correctly conjectured! The duel between Harris and Speer, both of whom had been appointed to their posts in February 1942, was to continue. Although this duel was in the end to be won by Harris, with Eaker's invaluable help, it would probably have been won earlier if Germany had been denied the brilliant services of Speer.

Harris did not despatch a force to Schweinfurt again until the night of 26/27 April and then a relatively small force of only 226 heavies was despatched, dropping 742·5 tons of bombs. From the night photographs taken at bomb release it was deduced that the raid was again not a success. In fact, later photographic reconnaissance showed a fair degree of damage, but it was not certain how much was due to American daylight raids and how much to Bomber Command.

From the beginning of 1944 until 14 April, when R A F Bomber Command and the U S Eighth Air Force were placed under the direction of the Supreme Allied Commander, General Dwight D. Eisenhower, Harris continued his onslaught on those targets associated with war production, especially for the German Air Force. This was in accordance with the directions to Bomber Command in the Pointblank Directive. This directive had, however, been amended on 17 February 1944 to include attacks against German installations on the coasts of France and Belgium for launching flying bombs and V 2 rockets at London. These were Hitler's secret weapons, developed at Peenemünde and delayed by Bomber Command's attack on that research centre on the night of 17/18 August 1943. Attacks by both R A F Bomber Command and U S Eighth Bomber Command on these sites, code named 'Crossbow', actually began in December 1943. There were fifty-six of them nominated, but it was not until 17 February 1944 that they received a priority. Then again, on 4 March, came another addition to Pointblank. This was for attacks to be made on railway transportation centres and marshalling yards in France and Belgium in preparation for the invasion of France, which was now planned for the beginning of June.

Many notable attacks against German cities heavily involved with aircraft production or associated equipment, were undertaken during this period with considerable success. Augsburg, Stuttgart, Leipzig, Stettin, Essen, Nürnberg, Brunswick, Magdeburg, Frankfurt and Aachen were amongst those to receive major attention. Frankfurt, for example, was attacked on the night of March by 767 aircraft, out of 846 despatched, which dropped 3,157.5 tons of bombs; it was attacked again four nights later on 22/23 by 769 aircraft out of 816 despatched, dropping 3,249 tons of bombs. Shortly afterwards it was claimed by the Germans to be the worst-destroyed city in Germany, a claim which evidence from photographic reconnaissance was disinclined to dispute.

Bomber Command did have its reverses, and the most tragic one occurred on the night of 30/31 March 1944, when 702 aircraft, out of 795 despatched, attacked Nürnberg, dropping 2,473.4 tons of bombs. Ninety-four aircraft were lost; 11.8 per cent of the force despatched. That night the German fighters were greatly helped by the weather. Conditions over the North Sea were too bad for any large-scale diversion to be practicable and with the light of a half moon on the way to and from the target, and the fact that the German fighter controllers made all the right guesses as to the routing, the German fighters struck successfully and had their only major victory against Bomber Command. By contrast, on the night of 26/27 March 675 aircraft, out of 705 despatched, attacked Essen and dropped 2,798 tons of bombs for the loss of only nine aircraft, or only 1.3 per cent of the force despatched.

Webster and Frankland make this statement:

> ... Moreover, in the operational sense, the Battle of Berlin was more than a failure. It was a defeat. The disastrous Nuremberg [Nürnberg] operation, in which the missing rate was no less than 11.8 per cent, brought the Bomber Command tactics of massed and concentrated

attack against major targets to a dead stop and they were not again resumed until the entire air situation over Germany had been radically altered ...

This is a curious conclusion. The question of success or failure of the Battle of Berlin has already been dealt with in the previous chapter. The reason for a reduction in attacks on major German cities was the fact that on 14 April 1944, Harris's Command was placed under the direction of Eisenhower, and until it was released on 25 September 1944, for reversion to strategic bombing of Germany its employment was concentrated on the preparatory bombing for the invasion of France and, later, in support of the Allied armies to enable them to establish themselves on the Continent with the minimum of losses. In fact, during April and May, despite the enormous number of sorties required by the Supreme Headquarters of the Allied Expeditionary Force (SHAEF) for attacks on transportation targets, 'Crossbow' targets, coastal fortifications, ammunition dumps and other concentrations of military stores, and enemy RDF installations, Harris still managed to maintain a powerful offensive against Germany itself. For example, Bomber Command attacked Aachen on 11/12 April with 350 heavies, dropping 1,928·4 tons of bombs; Cologne on 20/21 April with 379, dropping 1,761·8 tons; Düsseldorf on 22/23 April with 596 heavies dropping 2,107·1 tons and, on the same night, Brunswick with 265 heavies dropping 742·1 tons; Karlsruhe with 637 aircraft, dropping 2,180·3 tons on the night of the 24/25 April and, on the same night, Munich with 260 dropping 706 tons; Essen on 26/27 April with 493 aircraft dropping 1,866·2 tons and, on the same night, Schweinfurt with 226 aircraft dropping 742·5 tons; Duisburg on 21/22 May with 532 heavies dropping 2,202 tons; Dortmund and Brunswick on the 22/23 May with 375 and 235 aircraft respectively, dropping 1,623·1 tons and 620·4 tons. In fact, during April and May, a total of 5,795 sorties were despatched against German industrial targets, dropping 19,062 tons of bombs.

This was hardly bringing Bomber Command to a 'dead stop'.

The losses on the Nürnberg raid must be considered in relation to total operations. They should not be assessed in isolation. On 2 April, General Marshall, Chief of Staff of the US Army, sent a signal to Harris via Eisenhower and Portal. It read:

> The United States Chiefs of Staff wish to express their regret over the heavy loss sustained by the British bombing force in the Nuremberg [Nürnberg] raid, and their admiration for the high courage and determination displayed by the RAF Bombing Force in its battle of destruction against Germany.

Harris replied on the same day through Portal. His signal read:

> Please ask United States Chiefs of Staff to accept my grateful thanks for their message. We have to take the rough with the smooth and US Chiefs of Staff will be glad to know that although in March Bomber

Command far surpassed all previous records for sorties and weight of bombs dropped on all targets and also objectives within Germany, the casualty rate at three per cent was the lowest recorded for thirteen months.

The total tonnage of bombs dropped in March was 27,698 tons. In addition, 1,472 sea mines were laid. The total number of sorties on all operations was 9,878 and the losses were 298 aircraft, or 3 per cent. Not exactly enough to bring Bomber Command to a 'dead stop'.

Nevertheless Harris was concerned about losses. To him, it mattered not that they were at a sustainable level. Losses at any level were, to his way of thinking, unacceptable if there was any chance of reducing them. He was a realist, however, and he recognised that losses in war were inevitable; but he also knew that the lower they were, the better were the quality and experience of his crews. Also, Harris was never one to underestimate the prowess of his enemy and he could put himself in his opponent's shoes and consider how he would fight against his own tactics. As early as 1943 he was convinced that the bomber would need greater defensive support if it were to continue to be effective against any targets in Germany within its operational range which it was called upon to attack. As early as 1942 Harris was pressing for 0·5 guns in turrets to replace 0·303, which were inadequate in range and fire-power against fighters. In 1943 he supported a virtually private development by the Telecommunications Research Establishment and his own RDF department to produce a 'picture' of the aircraft around the bomber on a second H2S cathode ray tube indicator. This showed the other aircraft as spots of light. In the bomber stream, those maintaining their relative positions could be regarded as other bombers, but the spot of light creeping up onto the tail of the bomber could be regarded with suspicion. This device was called 'Fishpond' and with the help of Sir Robert Renwick a crash programme installed it into all H2S aircraft by the end of 1943. He also pressed for the 'Air Gun Layer Turret' or AGLT, which was under development at TRE early in 1943 and which was an RDF device for automatically directing the turret guns onto an approaching enemy fighter, at the same time identifying friend from foe; but this device only became available as the war finished.

However, Harris was successful in forming No 100 Group in his Command by the end of 1943, a special Group which consisted of squadrons of aircraft equipped with radio counter-measures for combating the enemy night defence organisation by jamming the R/T communications between the German ground controllers and fighter pilots. The Group was also given three night fighter squadrons to support the bombers, but since they were re-equipping with the night fighter version of the Mosquito aircraft at the time of their transfer from Fighter Command to Bomber Command, their contribution to the defence of the bombers was hardly effective until May 1944. Moreover, the crews had no experience of long-range navigation by night so they also had a new skill to acquire.

If Harris was convinced early in 1943 that the bomber needed greater protection against the enemy defence organisation, he was even more convinced of this fact early in 1944. He reasoned that the Germans, now that they had been emphatically forced onto the defensive, would make superhuman efforts to defeat the bomber and regain superiority in the air—as, indeed, the British had done in 1940 and 1941. Also, he was concerned that the switch from strategic targets in Germany to tactical targets in support of 'Operation Overlord', the invasion of Europe, targets which had already occupied some of his effort from March 1944, would give the German fighters and ground defences sufficient breathing space to build up their strength and offer a far greater resistance when the switch back to strategic targets followed a successful outcome of 'Overlord'. More than this, he was afraid, too, that the reduction in the bombing of Germany itself would release German fighters for a concentrated effort against the invasion forces. As early as December 1943, when he was requested by Portal to discuss the plans for 'Overlord' with the British and US air commanders, he raised these very points. In a letter to Portal he wrote:

I agree, of course, that since we are committed to 'Overlord' everything must be done to render the execution of it as inexpensive as may be in lives which we can ill afford to lose. I shall therefore be most ready to discuss in detail with the British and US Air Commanders concerned the best method of achieving this result. Before I do this, however, I should like to know that I have your support on two major points

(1) I take it that the general principle of the combined Bomber Offensive still holds good and that the primary objective of the British and US heavy bomber force will continue to be: 'The progressive destruction and dislocation of the German military, economic and industrial system, and the undermining of the morale of the German people to a point where their capacity for armed resistance is fatally weakened.' It is clear from paragraph 7 of Air Ministry letter CMS 268/43/DCAS, dated December 23rd, that the British Air Staff are convinced that area attacks by Bomber Command, complemented by precision bombing of selected targets by the USAAF, are capable of producing this result in a short time, and it is presumably still admitted that any failure of the Combined Bomber Offensive to keep down the enemy's production of fighter aircraft would, in any case, rule out 'Overlord' altogether. Furthermore, it will no doubt be admitted that the only way to keep the whole of the German fighter force from falling upon 'Overlord' is to continue the Bomber Offensive against Germany proper. Hence I am in no doubt as to your reply on this point. To avoid any possibility of misunderstanding, however, I should welcome an explicit assurance, before I enter on discussions of detail, that the directive which I have quoted above is still operative.

Harris's second point was in connection with targets which could be most profitably attacked by his Command before the commencement of

Operation 'Overlord' and at the time of its actual execution. He saw no difficulty in reaching agreement on this issue, but felt that so far as tactical bombing by his Command was concerned, this could only be practicable if suitable weather conditions prevailed and, therefore, full weight should be given to this factor in the final selection of the date for invasion.

This fear of the recovery and fresh build-up of the German fighter and defence forces led Harris to press vigorously for a rapid increase in the newly formed No 100 Group. This Group was under the able command of Air Vice-Marshal E. B. Addison, a signals officer who at the beginning of the war had been responsible for the inception and operation of the extremely efficient and effective radio counter-measures organisation which successfully detected and exposed the German radio beam bombing system, known as Knickebein, and produced ingenious methods of disrupting its use in 1940 and 1941. In fact, the measures taken by this organisation, in conjunction with those of the flying unit known as the Wireless Investigation Development Unit, which was specially formed to cooperate in this work and to bomb the German transmitters, resulted in the Germans abandoning their blind-bombing system. Addison, with his considerable experience and knowledge of counter-measures, was able to brief Harris better than anyone else on his needs in this field to cause the maximum disruption to the German fighter control organisation and RDF defences. But, in addition, Addison had as his Senior Air Staff Officer Air Commodore Roderick Chisholm, one of the most experienced night fighter pilots in the Battle of Britain and during the night battles against the German bombers in 1940 and 1941. Chisholm had flown with the first of the RDF fighter detection equipments—and he had flown with the latest. Also, he had been employed on attacks against German night fighter stations in the Low Countries in what were known as 'Intruder' operations. With Addison and Chisholm, Harris could not have had better technical advisers for his needs.

In April 1944 Harris began to press an urgent claim for the expansion of No 100 Group and for greater priority to be given to the provision of aircraft and the development and supply of specialised equipment for the disruption of the enemy's fighter control system. But at this stage he placed the greatest emphasis on more long-range night fighter squadrons for No 100 Group, where their activities could be properly coordinated to fit in with the bombing plans. In a letter to the Vice Chief of the Air Staff on 7 April, Harris expressed his opinions forcibly on this subject. He said that he had foreseen for a long time that the strength of the German Air defences could eventually reach a level 'at which night bombing attacks by existing methods and types of heavy bomber would involve casualty rates which could not in the long run be sustained'. With his mind set on a long-range night fighter offensive as a major means of containing any increased and effective activity of the German fighters against the night bomber, and knowing that No 100 Group had insufficient night fighters for this purpose, he went on to say:

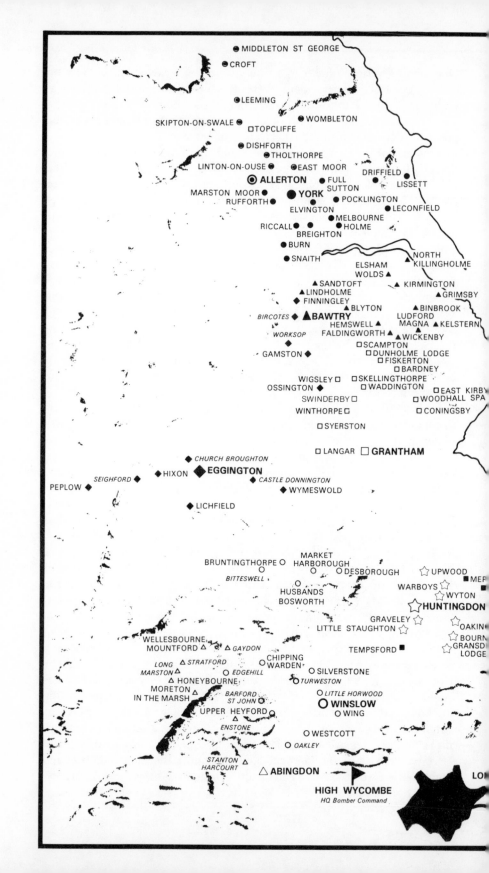

LOSSIEMOUTH
△ MILLTOWN
△ KINLOSS
△ ELGIN
△ FORRES

SCOTLAND

BOMBER COMMAND
25th September 1944

★ NORTH CREAKE
★ LITTLE SNORING
FOULSHAM
★   ★ OULTON
★ WEST
RAYNHAM ★ SWANNINGTON
★ BYLAUGH HALL

M MARKET
OLD

ENHALL
JDDENHAM

CHEDBURGH
ADISHALL
ING
ON

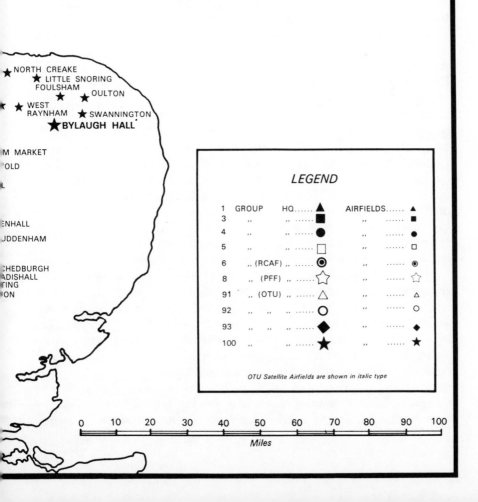

LEGEND

			HQ		AIRFIELDS	
1	GROUP		▲			▲
3	,,	,,	■	,,		■
4	,,	,,	●	,,		●
5	,,	,,	□	,,		□
6	,, (RCAF)	,,	◉	,,		◉
8	,, (PFF)	,,	☆	,,		☆
91	,, (OTU)	,,	△	,,		△
92	,, ,,	,,	○	,,		○
93	,, ,,	,,	◆	,,		◆
100	,, ,,	,,	★	,,		★

OTU Satellite Airfields are shown in italic type

0   10   20   30   40   50   60   70   80   90   100
Miles

We have not yet reached that point, but tactical innovations which have so far postponed it are now practically exhausted. Remedial action is therefore an urgent operational matter which cannot be deferred without grave risk. Already the cost of attacking targets in the Berlin area under weather conditions which give good prospects of accurate and concentrated bombing is too high to be incurred with any frequency.

This reference to Berlin losses was a slight exaggeration, but it was an excusable poetic licence for obtaining what he wanted, particularly when he genuinely believed that such a situation could arise in the future. Continuing, he said:

The only remedy, therefore, is the provision of night fighter support on a substantial scale, and it is considered that a total minimum of ten night fighter Mosquito squadrons should forthwith be placed at the disposal of 100 Group to satisfy this requirement.

In fact Harris only received three additional Mosquito night fighter squadrons against the ten demanded, bringing No 100 Group's strength up to six. But in addition the Group did receive a considerable increase in its radio counter-measures aircraft which greatly improved its effective effort in this important area. However, it should be noted that Harris's fears over losses proved to be pessimistic, but never so pessimistic as to believe that his Command was being brought to a 'dead stop'. Indeed his losses steadily declined, month by month, below the 3 per cent for March 1944. From April to December 1944, Bomber Command despatched 145,190 sorties, dropping 467,338 tons of bombs and laying 13,266 sea mines, for a total loss of 1,945 aircraft, or 1·34 per cent.

As has already been mentioned the demand for attacks on railway transport centres came on 4 March, and at the same time Harris was fully aware that his Command would soon come under the direction of Eisenhower's Supreme Headquarters and would be required, before, during, and immediately after the invasion, to attack precision targets as opposed to bombing German industrial towns. During 1942 and 1943 no precision bombing of any moment had been undertaken by Bomber Command, except for a limited number of special target attacks which Harris had entrusted to Cochrane and his No 5 Group. These attacks included those against the Schneider works at Le Creusot on 17 October 1942, the Ruhr dams on the night of 16/17 May 1943, and the Zeppelin aircraft works at Friedrichshafen on the night of 20/21 June 1943. On these attacks No 5 Group marked and bombed their targets without the assistance of the Pathfinder Force. In fact, with Harris's personal encouragement, the Group had, under Cochrane, been developing its own pathfinding and bombing techniques which were different from those of the Pathfinder Force. The first of these techniques was known as 'offset marking' and was developed by No 5 Group to overcome the problem of the marker bombs becoming obscured by smoke from fires or blown out by blast bombs during the course of a raid, a situation which frequently occurred in the later stages of an attack resulting in much bombing effort being wasted. With this technique, which proved to be highly successful, a Master Bomber was employed to control the attack, and a single marker bomb was dropped by a special crew upwind of the target at a distance of some 400 yards from the aiming point. Its distance and bearing from the aiming point was then estimated by the Master Bomber flying at low level. Other aircraft, specially equipped, had the duty of calculating the wind speed and direction in the target area and passing their calculations by R/T to the Master Bomber, who took an average of these calculations and added a vector to allow for the offset of the marker. He then broadcast the resulting false, or adjusted wind speed and direction to the Main Force crews, who would set up these wind figures on their bombsights and aim at the offset markers in the normal manner, having had their work done for them by the Master Bomber and all therefore using the same calculations for bombing. The advantages of this technique were considerable, for not only did the marker remain clearly visible throughout the attack and unlikely to be blown out or obscured by the bombing, but the Master Bomber could, by adding different vectors to allow for the offset of the marker, direct the Main Force onto more than one aiming point at a time from the same marker. This proved to be a great asset when several industrial aiming points existed in a town or when the target was elongated and required more than one concentration of bombs to saturate the entire area.

No 5 Group's technique, and the others it developed during 1944, with the considerable aid of the now legendary Group Captain Leonard Cheshire,* who became the Master Bomber of all Master Bombers, led Harris to give even more autonomy to Cochrane. This action was entirely in conformity with his long held belief that when his bomber force was large enough, and he was faced with a multitude of demands for its use, he would need his Groups to specialise in the different forms of attacks required for success against different categories of targets. By the beginning of 1944, No 5 Group had already proved its potential capability of precision bombing by night. Because of this, when under Pointblank Harris was charged with the destruction of certain French factories associated with vital production for the German Air Force, he entrusted No 5 Group with the task.

The first of these attacks was undertaken in clear weather on the night of the 8/9 February against the Gnôme et Rhône et Ateliers Industriels de l'Air, a major aero-engine factory at Limoges. On this occasion, the first 12,000-pound bombs were used. The results were spectacular, for the factory was devastated and yet no damage was done to any of the nearby residential areas.

From 8 February to the end of March, a period of seven weeks, twelve small but highly important French targets were attacked by 5 Group, and only one, which happened to be a viaduct, escaped damage. All of the

* Group Captain Leonard Cheshire, VC, DSO and two Bars, DFC.

factories were very severely damaged and, in fact, four were so completely destroyed that no attempt was made to rebuild them. And this had been achieved with only 350 sorties and one missing aircraft!

It was this experience with 5 Group's operations that made Harris say, when considering the inevitable switch to transportation and other precision targets in connection with the invasion; 'In planning to move the whole Command over to precision bombing the first thing to be done was to study our attacks on small targets in the past. We did not have much to go on, but by March 1944 there was a good deal more.' The attacks on 'Crossbow' targets (flying-bomb launching sites), which began in December 1943, had more than confirmed the high degree of accuracy of marking provided by Oboe, in the hands of the Pathfinder Force, on the short-range French and Belgian coastal area targets. No 5 Group's results gave him a clear indication that he now had a Group which could operate independently against a diversity of targets that demanded a high degree of precision bombing. Lastly, No 3 Group, under Harrison, was gaining experience with the RDF precision-bombing device, GH, having first tested it on operations against the Mannesmann steel works in Düsseldorf on the night of 3/4 November 1943. Additionally this Group was fast converting to Lancaster aircraft. Therefore he had yet another Group which was nearly ready to operate independently of the Pathfinder Force. By April 1944, Harris decided to strengthen No 5 Group's target-finding and marking capability by returning to the Group the two Lancaster squadrons from the Pathfinder Force which the Group had originally provided. In addition, he decided to transfer one non-Oboe Mosquito squadron from the Pathfinders to No 5 Group for low-level marking and Master Bombing duties.

To confirm these moves, Harris spoke in the first place to Portal. In the course of these conversations, whilst Portal did not disagree with the proposal, he apparently expressed a hope that Bufton would be kept fully in the picture. This led to some difference of opinion about Bufton's interference in the Command and about the original formation of the Pathfinder Force. The day following their talks, Portal wrote to Harris. The letter was dated 12 April 1944. Referring to the fact that he had looked up the correspondence on the subject of the formation of the Pathfinder Force in 1942, he wrote:

> I cannot find anything to substantiate your contention that the only opposition in your Headquarters to the formation of the PFF was that this would be premature. On the contrary, the arguments used against the scheme were that it would offer no advantage over the then existing procedure and would have serious disadvantages inseparable from the formation of a corps d'élite. It is quite true that the opposition in Bomber Command resulted largely from the attitude of the Group Commanders, who were said to be 'utterly, decisively and adamantly opposed to the Air Ministry proposal'. I quite realise that the success achieved by the PFF

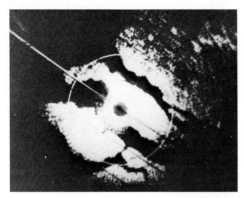

The Scheldt estuary photographed on the indicator tube of a 10-cm H2S set in a Pathfinder aircraft, on the night of 20/21 December 1943. The accompanying map (below) demonstrates the accuracy of the set.

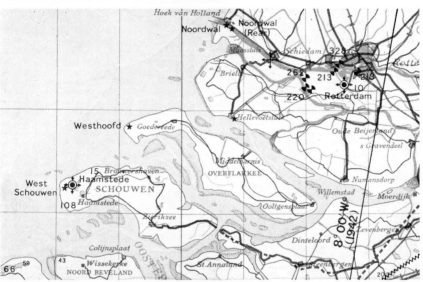

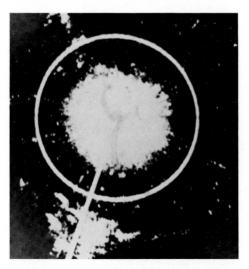

Leipzig at eight miles' range. A photograph of an H2S Mk III indicator tube on the bombing approach during the raid on Leipzig, 3/4 December 1943. The straight thick line shows the aircraft's heading, while the circle is the bombing ring set at the appropriate range for bomb release—when the ring and heading line coincided with the aiming point the bomb aimer released his bombs. This system permitted quite accurate bombing through cloud.

Avro Lancaster bomber, showing the cupola on the underside that housed the H2S rotating aerial.

The Avro Manchester, the inadequately powered aircraft from which the Lancaster was developed.

The Avro Lancaster, mainstay of Bomber Command and probably the most versatile and successful bombing aircraft of all time.

With its larger crew and heavier defensive armament, the Boeing B17 Fortress was better suited to day bombing than the RAF heavies. Despite the American box formations, however, losses to flak and fighters were often grievous.

The pathfinder—the De Havilland Mosquito, used for the precision dropping of marker flares. Its other roles included those of light bomber, day and night fighter, and photographic reconnaissance.

Arnold and Harris in America in 1945, after the German surrender.

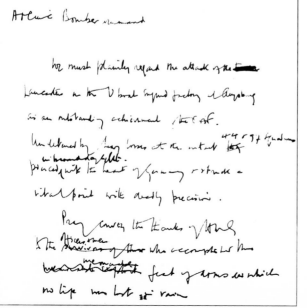

Part of a letter, dated 18 April 1942, from Churchill to Harris, praising the success of the raid on the U-boat engine factory at Augsburg (see page 130).

13 July, 1944

Dear Harris:

Your recent performance in the Caen area was an eye
opener to me, and emphasizes in my mind, again, the
magnitude of the debt that this Allied Command owes
to you and your officers and men. Your long record
of pounding vital targets in Germany, of interrupt-
ing enemy communications, of preparing the way for
our invasion forces and now, literally, becoming an
agent in proper circumstances, of close battle support is one to excite praise and admiration.

I am truly proud to have you and your command in
this Allied Team. We could not possibly get along
without you.

Good luck!

Sincerely,
D wigth at Eisenhower

Air Chief Marshal Sir Arthur T. Harris,
                    KCB, OBE, AFC,
Air Officer Commanding-in-Chief,
Bomber Command,
c/o G.P.O., High Wycombe
Bucks.

These two letters from
Eisenhower, twenty years
apart, tell of his high regard
for Harris

DDE

GETTYSBURG
PENNSYLVANIA

June 5, 1964

Dear Bert—

On this Sixth of June I suspect that your memory
goes back, as mine does, to live over again the
gnawing anxieties, the realization of unavoidable
sacrifices, and the bright hopes that filled us on
D-Day, 1944.

Never, during the two decades that have since
passed, have I ceased to render daily and devout
thanks to a kindly Providence for permitting us
to achieve in eleven months the complete victory
that so many believed would require years.

In the same way, I have always felt a deep sense
of appreciation and gratitude to all who took part
in, or who served in a supporting role for, that
great Allied venture.

To you, one of my close associates in OVERLORD,
I am impelled to send, once more, a special word
of thanks. Your professional skill and selfless
dedication to the cause in which we all served will
be noted by the histories of those dramatic months,
but no historian could possibly be aware of the
depth of my obligation to you.

With warm regard,

as ever
Ike E

Sir Arthur T. Harris
G.C.B., O.B.E.
The Ferry House
Goring-on-Thames
Oxon, England

Albert Speer and the author in the former's study at his home in Heidelberg—researching German production records for evidence of the effectiveness of the bomber offensive.

Speer with Bello in his garden, 1972.

The Installation Service for Knights Grand Cross of the Order of the Bath, Westminster Abbey, 26 October 1972. Left to right: MRAF Sir Arthur Harris, Representative of the Great Master of the Order; HM the Queen; the Very Rev Eric Abbott, Dean of Westminster; ACM Sir Anthony Selway, Registrar of the Order.

The author with Sir Arthur in the summer of 1974.

Left to right: General James Doolittle, USAAF, Harris and Eaker watching a fly-past by a Lancaster and a Fortress at High Wycombe, 8 September 1976, to mark the association between the two air forces.

has been greater through the introduction of Oboe than it could have been without this particular aid, but this was not the point under discussion.

Referring to the 1942 correspondence on the subject, however, Portal could see no reason at all to modify his opinion that the credit for the Air Ministry share in what had been achieved lay with Bufton, and he finished by saying:

I hope you will agree to have a talk some time with Bufton on the subjects on which I touched very briefly when we last met. If you will name a time convenient to you, I will send him down.

Portal's letter touched off a very blunt reply from Harris, dated 14 April, in which he denied that in his conversation he had inferred that the only opposition to the Pathfinder Force in 1942 from Bomber Command was that it would be premature. He agreed that his Group Commanders and his Headquarters Staff had, in the main, been 'utterly opposed to the formation of a corps d'élite on Bufton's lines'. He himself, he averred, had had an open mind, but had favoured a system of pathfinding which would not drain the Groups of their best crews. Referring to his conversation with Portal, he wrote that he recalled two assertions he had made: first, that at the time the PFF was formed he regarded it as premature, and in the event he believed this had proved to be true—it was, he said, the final availability in 1943 of Oboe and H2S that had made the PFF worth while; second, he was not satisfied that the formation of the PFF as a single entity had been the best solution for target-location and marking. His alternative had always been, and still was, to form a Pathfinder element in each Group to meet the Command's requirements without accepting 'the obvious disadvantages of a corps d'élite creaming off the entire Command for one formation.'

Harris then went on to explain that tactically the Command needed to attack multiple objectives on any one night, and to use split routes to each objective to confuse and disperse the enemy's defence system. Into the bargain, the invasion preparations were calling for many such multiple attacks. In such circumstances, the load on Bennett's Pathfinder Force was becoming insupportable, and with 'Overlord' it would soon be impossible for him, or any one commander, to keep pace with the inevitable *ad hoc* demands. Furthermore, 'in Bennett as an individual we have already far too many eggs in one basket.' This was a problem to which, he said, he had devoted much thought.

After examining it at length with my Staff, with Bennett and with Cochrane, I decided some days ago to detach back to 5 Group the two Lancaster PFF Squadrons which 5 Group supported in PFF, plus one Mosquito IV [non-Oboe] Squadron for use as 'lowmarkers'.

Major reasons for this are that 5 Group is the biggest force and Cochrane is the most progressive and technically and tactically expert of my Group Commanders. His Group can therefore form one effective force, or even two, on its own during a combined attack on multiple objectives. He will also be free to use his own initiative in methods of training, pathfinding and marking, which he has exploited with outstanding success on some of the smaller targets in France and Italy in the recent past.

Harris then indicated that he felt it might prove desirable to extend this principle to other Groups, depending upon the personal ability of individual Group Commanders. He had in mind his already explicit intention of making No 3 Group, under Harrison, independent with its special RDF blind-bombing device, GH, which had been confined to this Group alone.

Having dealt with that matter, he proceeded to attack the Directorate of Bomber Operations at the Air Ministry:

Finally, I must say that I am astonished indeed that you should ever have misunderstood me even to infer that the 'credit' for the formation of the Pathfinder Force does not belong to Bufton. So far from that being my opinion, my complaint on that score has always been and still is that Bufton's ideas on Pathfinders, as on some other matters, have always been and still are rammed down our throats whether we like them or not, and that on occasions more weight is given to his opinions as a junior officer two years out of the Command than to the considered opinions of the Commanders on the spot who are responsible for the outcome of events. I have, personally, considerable regard for Bufton's ability and honesty of purpose. I have time and again stressed to Bottomley, who will confirm this, and on occasion—but now long past—to Bufton himself, that he—Bufton—should come and discuss things with me and regard himself as a welcome critic here and a Bomber Command agent in the Air Ministry, in addition to being your personal Bomber Operations Staff Officer, rather than as a sort of shadow C-in-C of the Bomber Offensive.

In that way, Harris emphasized, he could have been of the very greatest assistance to the Command, instead of a thorn in its side.

Nevertheless [he added], if he can rid himself of his idée fixe that he can have the fun of running the Bomber Offensive his way while I take the responsibility, I am still, as I always have been, only too ready to put relations on what I conceive, rightly or wrongly, to be the proper footing. My office or my house here are, as they have always been, open to him as to anybody else who cares to walk in. As to appointments, he has, like anyone else, only to ring up and ask if I will be in ...

Harris concluded:

All that matters is to put these affairs straight with the urgency necessary and regardless of personalities or personal interests. I have always been prepared to seek means of doing that—I have, indeed, repeatedly sought them—but I am not prepared to do so by process of purely unilateral concession amounting to Bufton running my show regardless of the opinion of my Command.

Portal was clearly concerned at the bad feeling that had developed between his Air Staff and Bomber Command Headquarters. Harris had been the only commander who had successfully mounted and maintained an offensive against Germany in the last two years. With his superb leadership and terrific determination he had built up and welded together a very powerful offensive force whose activities in 1942 and 1943 had made it possible to contemplate an invasion of Western Europe in June 1944. With the new, growing strength of the US Eighth Bomber Command there was emerging a gigantic combined bomber force that would be vital to the attainment of ultimate victory. Harris was irreplaceable and Portal knew it. Moreover, Harris had the confidence of the American statesmen directly concerned with the war and of the American air commanders in the European theatre—and, by no means least, he had the confidence of Churchill. There was no other senior commander who had these assets and who, into the bargain was a skilled and practical airman and a first class administrator. Portal could not afford to replace Harris nor to lose him. So he set about the problem of calming the situation. In a private and personal letter to Harris, dated 16 April, he expressed his relief that he, Harris, had regard for Bufton's ability and honesty of purpose and that his sole objection was to Bufton's methods. Therefore, to establish good relations between Bomber Command HQ and the Air Staff, Portal sought to agree with Harris what Bufton's duties should be.

Portal wrote that his first duty was to keep closely in touch with the operational needs, thought and practice of the Command. 'To do this he must have access to it at the level on which he and his officers work, i.e. Air Staff level at Command and Groups, and station and squadron level outside. It would clearly be impracticable to canalise Air Ministry contact entirely through you or your Air Officers Commanding.' The second duty of DB Ops was to use his knowledge of Command requirements to further the efficiency of their operations by action in the Air Ministry or with other departments. 'As you know,' Portal said, 'he has been of considerable value in this way, particularly over the quicker provision of the special pyrotechnics and other aids which you have needed.' The third duty, Portal stated, was that of advising him, when required, in relation to his own responsibility as CAS for the supervision of the operations of the Command. 'I am sure you recognise that I have a direct responsibility to the Secretary of State and to the Minister of Defence in this matter and that I am not only entitled but bound to interfere on high matters of operational policy when I consider it necessary to do so in the discharge of those responsibilities.' He added that the occasions for such interference were likely to be extremely rare, but if they did occur he was bound to seek his Staff's views on matters over which he and Harris might not see eye to eye. This, he said, 'cannot be regarded as improper and it certainly should not poison relations between your Headquarters and the Air Ministry.' He finished by suggesting that if Harris agreed with the three duties of Bufton as set down in his letter, he would instruct Bufton to 'ask to come and see you.'

There was, however, one last paragraph to his letter which gave Harris what he wanted. 'I have read with interest,' he wrote, 'what you say about multiple objectives and the consequential effect of new tactics on the composition of the Pathfinder Force. Naturally I should not wish to interfere in any way over this, particularly as I have for some time been wondering whether some change of this kind would not be forced upon us.'

On 18 April, Harris replied to Portal in a letter also marked 'Private and Personal'. He agreed with the three duties of D B ops as detailed in Portal's letter, but he insisted that access by Bufton and his staff to Groups and lower formations in the Command must be with his (Harris's) knowledge and consent. 'The trouble with Bufton, from my point of view,' he wrote, 'has always been that he has, no doubt with good intentions, short circuited Command Headquarters, thus giving the impression that his real aim was not so much to keep in touch with and assist the Command as to exercise detailed control over it from the Air Ministry.' With regard to the second duty of D B Ops, Harris emphasized that it was for him (Harris) to state these, and for Bufton to do whatever he could to get them met. 'If what I want is inconsistent with Air Ministry policy,' he wrote, 'I should expect him to refer the question to higher authorities and leave it to them to take the matter up with me direct.'

In his final paragraph, Harris agreed, in short, with the three functions of D B Ops as set down by Portal, 'provided that he [Bufton] accepts the condition that he cannot carry them out unless he collaborates closely with Command Headquarters and avoids pressing his own theories on our organisation, operations and requirements without consulting us on their merits.'

At this point Harris and Portal agreed, and relations between Bomber Command Headquarters and the Air Staff improved for a while. The improvement was undoubtedly helped, as well, by Bomber Command being placed under the direction of Eisenhower from the 14 April 1944, for the invasion and its aftermath.

Harris does not recall that Bufton ever contacted him or came down to see him.

21
Under Eisenhower

The planning of the invasion of Western Europe effectively commenced in April 1943, when Lieutenant-General F. E. Morgan was appointed Chief of Staff to the Supreme Commander, who at that date had not been chosen. By July 1943, General Morgan and his staff had drawn up a preliminary plan for invasion which was considered by the Chiefs of Staff at the Chiefs of Staff Conference in Quebec in August. This plan was approved and its further development to cover the detailed plans for the Allied naval, army and air forces was ordered.

The plans for the air forces were to be executed in four phases. The first was the strategic bombing of Germany, which was a confirmation of the Casablanca Directive of January 1943, and the Pointblank Directive of June 1943, wherein the emphasis of strategic bombing was turned onto the German aircraft industry. The second was in connection with the immediate preparation for invasion and included targets such as railway centres, coastal defence batteries, harbours and airfields, particularly those within 150 miles of Caen and in the areas of Brest and Nantes. Flying-bomb and V2 rocket launching sites were not at this stage included, as little of Hitler's secret weapon was known at the time. The third phase was the actual invasion, which included the protection of sea and land forces during their voyage across the Channel and when they were ashore. The fourth was a continuation of attacks on airfields, harbours, railway centres and other communications and a return to the strategic bombing of Germany. These plans covered the requirements of General Montgomery, who was to command all land forces in the initial stages and who had asked for denial of railways to the enemy up to 150 miles from the beach-head and complete air cover during both the landings and the establishment of the beach-head.

On 15 November 1943, Air Chief Marshal Sir Trafford Leigh-Mallory was appointed Air Commander-in-Chief of the Allied Expeditionary Air Force. This force consisted of the Second Tactical Air Force (RAF), Fighter Command, and the US Ninth (Tactical) Air Force, over all of which he had control. Bomber Command and the US Eighth Air Force, with its strategic Eighth Bomber Command, remained at the disposal of the Combined Chiefs of Staff. It was soon apparent to Leigh-Mallory that the air forces available to him for the invasion of Europe were entirely insufficient to undertake phases two and three of the air plan. He had no heavy bombers at his disposal and without them he could not hope to attack and immobilise the large list of targets regarded as essential to success. These views he made known forcibly and, as he was of the opinion that the heavy bombers of Bomber Command and the U S Eighth Bomber Command would have to be used, he planned accordingly.

In January of 1944, when the planning for the use of the air forces was in full swing and Harris, at the request of the Chief of the Air Staff, had begun to attend the planning conferences, Harris wrote a memorandum on 'The Employment of the Night Bomber Force in Connection with the Invasion of the Continent from the UK.' This, dated 13 January, was sent to the CAS, Leigh-Mallory and General Montgomery. His opening paragraph stated:

> Overlord must now presumably be regarded as an inescapable commitment and it is therefore necessary to consider the method by which our most powerful offensive weapon, the heavy bomber force, can be brought to bear most effectively in support of it. This paper gives a summary of the potentialities and limitations of the force from this point of view.

He then went on to explain how the heavy bomber force had developed as an independent strategic weapon and how, for reasons of long-range demands when fighting an enemy occupying a large continental mass, and when long-range fighter escort was out of the question in pre-war days the bomber had been designed essentially for night operations as a means of providing the necessary protection against the enemy's defences. Also the bomber had sacrificed armament in the interests of range and bomb carrying capacity and was therefore unsuitable for daylight operations. Added to this, crews had never been trained for daylight operating, except for a limited number who operated in certain rare circumstances. He continued with a comprehensive survey of the capabilities of the Command by night, the RDF navigational, target-marking and blind-bombing aids in use in the bomber force, and the degrees of accuracy that could be expected on different categories of targets. He covered the problems of weather and tactical restrictions and the relative inflexibility of the bomber force in relation to fleeting targets:

> ... the objective when once selected cannot be changed at will. The time required to refuel, to bomb up, brief crews and marshal the force is such that with maximum efficiency some seven daylight hours are the minimum necessary between the decision to bomb a given target and the take-off of aircraft to attack it—and the target cannot be altered during that period without involving a new start and consequent further delay.

He also drew attention to the limitations which the weather could impose on any strict programme of attacks in support of the ground forces of an invading Army, and he therefore considered that absolute reliance on the bomber force would be unwise. He wrote:

> It is therefore essential for any bombing designed to assist the Army to be planned on the broadest possible lines. As many alternative targets as possible should be included, so that if weather precludes the attack of any one on a given night the desired result may be achieved by the attack of others.

He gave it as his opinion that bombing of such targets as gun emplacements could not be relied upon to destroy them, and he did not believe the heavy bomber force was suitable for cutting railway communications at definite points.

But Harris's major fear, expressed in this paper, was the effect upon Germany of the easing of strategic bombing in favour of an exclusive tactical role for the bomber forces in support of the invasion. He drew attention to German manpower and production locked up in defence measures, and warned of the vast resources of fighters, anti-aircraft guns and other defence material and men that would be released if the bombing of Germany was discontinued. He warned of the effect on German production of a respite from bombing:

> The effects of strategic bombing are cumulative. The more that productive resources are put out of action, the harder it is to maintain output in those that survive. It is easy to forget, however, that the process of rehabilitation if the offensive stops or weakens is similarly cumulative. To put it shortly, the bomber offensive is sound policy only if the rate of *destruction* is greater than the rate of *repair*. It is hard to estimate the extent to which Germany could recoup industrially in say six months' break in bombing. It would certainly be sufficient to enable her to take a very different view of her prospects on land, on sea and in the air. Indeed it is true to say that if the German army survives the present crisis in Russia (and if it fails to do this, Overlord will in any case be superfluous), the cessation of bombing even temporarily would make her military position far from hopeless. What the Russians have done and what we ourselves hope to do on land is fundamentally made possible only by the acute shortage of manpower and munitions which strategic bombing has produced, and by the preoccupation of nearly three-quarters of the enemy fighter force with the defence of Germany proper.

The reference to the Russians was in connection with their tremendous advances over the entire length of their vast front, from Leningrad to the Black Sea, during the second half of 1943.

The conclusion to his paper was as follows:

> It is clear that the best and indeed the only efficient support which Bomber Command can give to Overlord is the intensification of attacks on suitable industrial centres in Germany as and when the opportunity

offers. If we attempt to substitute for this process attacks on gun emplacements, beach defences, communications or dumps in occupied territory we shall commit the irremediable error of diverting our best weapon from the military function for which it has been equipped and trained to tasks which it cannot effectively carry out. Though this might give a specious appearance of supporting the Army, in reality it would be the gravest disservice we could do them. It would lead directly to disaster.

Harris was not alone in his opinions. He was supported by Lieutenant-General Carl Spaatz, now the Commanding General of the US Strategic Air Forces in Europe. But Leigh-Mallory pressed his case for the use of the heavy bombers in the preparation for invasion and, in certain cases, for the support of the Army at the time of the landings and in the course of establishing a beach-head. But, immediately, he wanted to use the heavy bombers for executing a comprehensive plan of disruption and dislocation of those parts of the French and Belgian railway systems which were vital to the military lines of communication of the German armed forces. This plan had been prepared by the Allied Expeditionary Air Forces Bombing Committee under the chairmanship of Air Commodore E. J. Kingston-McCloughry, an Australian. The committee included Professor S. Zuckerman and a Mr R. E. Brant, who had an extensive knowledge of the French railway system acquired before the war. In truth the plan was prepared by Zuckerman and Brant, and the targets listed for attack were selected because of their extensive repair and maintenance facilities. It was Zuckerman's and Brant's contention that destruction of such facilities was the best way of disrupting the railway system. By the beginning of March 1944 the committee had drawn up a list of seventy-five railway targets which were, effectively, the major maintenance and repair centres in Belgium and Northern France.

On 16 January 1944, General Dwight D. Eisenhower took up his post as Supreme Commander Allied Forces in Europe, and on 20 January Air Chief Marshal Sir Arthur Tedder was appointed his Deputy. By March, both were in full support of the railway plan, which had come to be known as the 'Transportation Plan', although Eisenhower, in common with certain high-ranking Government and Service chiefs, was concerned about the possibility of heavy French and Belgian civilian casualties and the effect this might have on their cooperation when the landings took place in France and when the Allied armies pushed through France, Belgium and Holland to the borders of Germany.

The objections of Harris and Spaatz to the Transportation Plan were overruled, but first, at Portal's suggestion, Harris was requested to undertake attacks on six railway targets as a trial. This was, in fact, to be a further test of Bomber Command's ability to undertake precision bombing at night, an ability which had been partially proved by the successful attacks in February by No 5 Group against French factories engaged on production in support of the German Air Force, and by the attacks made against the flying-bomb and rocket launching sites, which had taken place since December 1943. Like the French aircraft industry targets and the launching sites, the railway targets were at short range and mostly in areas of high Oboe accuracy, and where anti-aircraft defences were weak or non-existent.

On 4 March 1944, a directive was issued to Harris headed 'Targets for attack by Bomber Command in moonlight periods prior to Overlord'. After the preliminaries came the statement:

> To provide data for the final detailed planning of Overlord and in order to contribute materially to the requirements of Overlord during periods when Pointblank night operations are not practicable, attacks should be carried out against the following railway objectives using a ground marking technique.

There followed a list of six railway targets—Trappes, Aulnoye, Le Mans, Amiens-Longeau, Courtrai and Laon.

Harris recognised that he was overruled and, as great men do, he set himself and his Command to the task of achieving absolute success in the new tactical role. He spared no effort to ensure that the Command should execute its mission in respect of the Transportation Plan with maximum efficiency and terrifying effect. Within two days of receiving his orders, on the night of 6/7 March, Harris despatched 267 heavies against Trappes, a major railway centre just to the south-west of Paris; 263 aircraft attacked, dropping 1,256 tons of bombs. The results were staggering. Every track in the 'up' reception and the 'down' sidings was put out of action by the concentration of bomb craters, and the western exit was rendered conpletely impassable. In addition, engine sheds and rolling stock were very severely damaged. In fact this rail centre was put completely out of action for one month. On the night of the 7th/8th he attacked Le Mans with 200 aircraft; on the 13th/14th, Le Mans again with 212 aircraft; on the 15th/16th Amiens with 125 aircraft, and again on the night of the 16th/17th with 117 aircraft; on the 23rd/24th Laon with seventy-two aircraft; on the 25th/26th Aulnoye with 182 aircraft; on the 26th/27th Courtrai with 102 aircraft; and on the 29/30 March he attacked the Paris Vaires marshalling yard, which was an additional target. With the exception of Laon all the attacks caused extensive damage and disruption. Vaires, Trappes, Amiens and Courtrai were brought to a complete standstill. With these successes, the Transportation Plan was approved, and on 15 April Tedder issued on behalf of the Supreme Commander a complete list of seventy-nine railway targets to Bomber Command and the US Strategic Air Forces in Europe. Thirty-seven were allotted to Bomber Command and forty-two to the Americans. An eightieth target was added later.

This allotment of railway targets preceded, by a few days, the first official directive by Eisenhower to Bomber Command and the United States Strategic Air Forces. This was dated 17 April 1944, and followed the decision of the Combined Chiefs of Staff to place all the strategic air forces in the European theatre under the direction of Eisenhower with effect from 14 April. The specific instruction to Harris read:

RAF Bomber Command.

In view of the tactical difficulties of destroying precise targets by night, RAF Bomber Command will continue to be employed in accordance with their main aim of disorganising German industry. Their operations will, however, be designed as far as practicable to be complementary to the operations of the USSAF [United States Strategic Air Forces]. In particular, where tactical conditions allow, their targets will be selected so as to give the maximum assistance in the aims of reducing the strength of the German Air Force, and destroying and disrupting enemy rail communications. A list of targets chosen to achieve these objectives, and showing the relative priorities accorded them at present, will be issued separately. These priorities will be adjusted from time to time in accordance with the situation.

The thirty-seven railway targets allotted to Bomber Command, which included the six which were assaulted in March as a trial run, were attacked throughout April and May and by D-Day, 6 June 1944, Harris had bombed all thirty-seven with devastating effect. 8,800 sorties had been flown and 42,000 tons of bombs dropped! When D-Day dawned 21,949 British and American aircraft had attacked eighty railway targets, dropping 66,517 tons of bombs to create a terrible paralysis over the railway network of the Région Nord—and one must underline the fact that 42,000 tons were dropped by Bomber Command. The degree of success was categorised by three classes, 'A', 'B', and 'C'. 'A' class targets were those which had been so badly destroyed that no further attacks were warranted until vital repairs had been undertaken. 'B' class were those which had been severely damaged but still possessed a number of installations which were intact and therefore required a further visitation. 'C' class signified that little or no damage had been inflicted. Of the eighty targets which had been submitted to the onslaught, fifty-one were 'A' class, twenty-five 'B' class and four 'C' class. Bomber Command undoubtedly held the honours, for of the thirty-seven targets it attacked, twenty-two were placed in class 'A' and fifteen in class 'B'.

In addition, the Saumur railway tunnel was completely blocked by nineteen 12,000-pound bombs dropped by No 617 Squadron (No 5 Group) on 8 June, two days after D-Day. So successful was the attack that the Germans never succeeded in clearing the line.

The best indication of the success of the three months' offensive against the railways was, however, the fact that the enemy's major reinforcements reached the battlefront, after the Allied landings, too late to prevent the firm establishment of the Allied forces in Normandy.

Apart from the pre-invasion dislocation of the railway system, Bomber Command attacked coastal defences for many weeks before the actual invasion. In the case of these targets it was not possible to concentrate on the area of the planned landings owing to the need to keep the enemy guessing. Therefore, for every coastal battery or defence work bombed in the intended invasion area, at least two were bombed elsewhere. A total of 14,000 tons of bombs was dropped on these targets. Then, a few hours before the invasion, on the night of 5/6 June, 1,136 aircraft of Bomber Command, mostly heavies, dropped another 5,267 tons of high explosives on the coastal batteries covering the beaches where the Allied Forces were due to land. Opposition was effectively silenced and Allied casualties were unexpectedly low. Also attacked during the pre-invasion period were many purely military objectives, such as military depots. Those at Bourg Leopold and Mailly Le Camp were wrecked by heavy attacks during May, and the success of these raids was regarded as of particular importance, especially so in the case of Mailly Le Camp, a large depot and tank park and one of the chief tank training centres in France. Important ammunition and ordnance depots were also destroyed, including the State Explosive Works at St Medard-en-Jalles.

During April and May, Harris still maintained his offensive against German industrial centres, but on a limited scale. In June, following the successful invasion of France, however, and in July and early August when the demands upon the Command for support of the Allied armies were enormous, Germany was given a complete respite from bombing except for targets associated with transportation, such as Aachen, and small-scale attacks by Mosquito bombers on places as far afield as Berlin.

The use of Bomber Command in a tactical role was an enormous success and if Harris is to be accused, as he has been, of underestimating the capability and necessary flexibility of his Command to achieve success in such a role, then it must be recognised that it was his own prowess in offensive warfare that was the means of proving him wrong. In fact, Harris never doubted that he could hit the railway targets in Northern France and Belgium, because he knew perfectly well that they were all in areas not only of high Oboe accuracy, but also of high Gee accuracy. The author, who was Harris's Chief Radar Officer, can vouch for this, for he, with his staff and in conjunction with Dr B. G. Dickins, the extremely able head of the Bomber Command Operational Research Section, advised Harris and Saundby of the degrees of accuracy that could be expected with Oboe and the southern and eastern Gee chains. The accuracy of these two systems on these short-range targets clearly indicated that success could be achieved, and the same applied to other tactical targets in the invasion areas. What concerned Harris was the degree of concentration of bombing that could be achieved to avoid civilian casualties. If weather was good and ground markers were visible, with the RDF aids available to the main bombing force, tight concentration could be achieved. With cloud cover, however, which had to be expected on many days and nights at that time of the year, the accuracy of bombing might be good enough to hit the targets but not to avoid a great deal of damage being done outside the target area. This is why Harris impressed upon Leigh-Mallory and Montgomery, in January 1944, that 'As many alternative targets as possible should be included, so that if weather precludes the attack of any one on a given night the desired result may be achieved by the attack of others.'

As has already been said, Harris's real concern about his Command being diverted from the strategic bombing of Germany to the tactical support of the invading Allied armies was the breathing space this would give to the German industrial centres to recoup from the bombing to which they had been subjected in 1943 and the first few months of 1944. He, with Carl Spaatz, believed that a cessation of the bombing of Germany, as detailed in the Casablanca and Pointblank Directives, would permit the German Air Force to recover sufficiently to rebuild itself for fighter and bomber offensive action against the Allied front in the west and the Russian front in the east, as well as releasing other forces, equipment and material, tied down for defence purposes, for use against the Allies. Indeed, Harris and Spaatz regarded a period of six months' suspension of the strategic offensive against Germany proper as being capable of exposing the Allies to grave peril in the future.

It was in this assessment that Harris displayed mistaken judgement, for, ironically, he had underestimated the incredibly disastrous effect of his own bombing campaign against Germany and the Occupied Territories in 1942, 1943 and the first few months of 1944, together with that of Eaker's US Eighth Bomber Command, which had begun to get under way in the second half of 1943. The fact is that the German Air Force never was able to recover, nor indeed was German industry, despite six months of almost total abstinence from strategic bombing. Bomber Command losses from April 1944 to the end of the war support this contention. As has been mentioned in the previous chapter, from 1 April to 31 December 1944, Bomber Command despatched 145,190 sorties against all enemy targets of which more than 60 per cent were against targets outside Germany and in support of the Army; during the period 1 May to 30 September 1944, the sorties flown were almost exclusively against tactical targets in support of the Army. Out of the total of 145,190 sorties, only 1,945 aircraft were lost, or 1·34 per cent. Between 1 October 1944 and 31 December 1944, when 42,955 sorties were flown against German industrial targets, consequent upon the return of Bomber Command to its strategic role, only 372 aircraft were lost, or 0·86 per cent. For the rest of the war, from 1 January to the end of May 1945, when hostilities with Germany ceased, 57,583 sorties were flown against Germany for the loss of 608 aircraft, or just over 1 per cent.

There were, of course, losses sustained by the US Strategic Air Forces, the US Ninth Air Force, the Royal Air Force Tactical Air Force and Fighter Command, but they were also negligible. Indeed, the German Air Force was almost non-existent as a weapon of defence or offence from April 1944 until the end of the war. Certainly by May Allied air superiority was overwhelming.

So what of Harris's misjudgement? Inevitably one must conjecture what would have happened if he and Spaatz had had their own way and either the invasion had been delayed to permit the strategic bombing of Germany to continue, or the strategic bombing had been maintained at the expense of support by Bomber Command and the US Strategic Air Forces for the invading Allied armies. The indications are that in both cases Germany would have collapsed under bombing alone, which was what Harris always believed to be a certainty. If, however, the strategic forces had not been fully available to the invading Allied armies and the invasion had gone ahead as planned, that is to say, if it had not been delayed, then the casualties would unquestionably have been substantial. As it was, they were miraculously low. So if Harris misjudged the situation, who else misjudged it to an even greater degree? Or was there a deeper motive in abandoning the idea of bombing Germay into unconditional surrender? Is it possible that the Combined Chiefs of Staff feared that a sudden collapse of Germany, brought about by bombing, would have resulted in the Russians sweeping across Germany with no opposition, and even occupying parts of France, Belgium and Holland, before the British and American occupying forces could gain any worthwhile foothold on the continent of Europe? If this was the case, then Harris believes the decision to invade in June 1944, and to use the strategic air forces almost exclusively as tactical forces at the expense of suspending the bombing of Germany proper for a full five months, was a correct one.

However, whatever Harris's opinions about the use of his forces at the time of the invasion, once the decision was taken to use Bomber Command to support 'Overlord' solely, and once he was placed under the direction of Eisenhower, he cooperated wholeheartedly, and a great mutual respect grew between Eisenhower and Harris which turned into a sincere personal friendship that lasted until Eisenhower's death. Harris has frequently been accused of being uncooperative about the decision to use his forces in a tactical role, but the facts deny this contention. From early in May he regularly attended the Supreme Commander's weekly meetings and, in addition, he attached Air Vice-Marshal R. D. Oxland, his SASO, permanently as Bomber Command's liaison officer with the Supreme Headquarters of the Allied Expeditionary Force. He also withdrew Group Captain S. C. Elworthy, who had previously been Group Captain Operations at Bomber Command until he was given the post of commanding officer of Waddington, a No 5 Group bomber station, and he had him appointed an extra Group Captain Operations to liaise with Oxland on all matters in connection with the requirements for the use of the bomber forces by SHAEF. Between 1 April and 30 September 1944, whilst Bomber Command was under the direction of Eisenhower, Harris despatched 82,411 sorties, of which more than 90 per cent were at the request of Supreme Headquarters, and these aircraft dropped the prodigious total of 304,072 tons of bombs. In addition he despatched 2,923 aircraft on mine-laying sorties and these dropped 10,223 mines in enemy waters.

The deadly effectiveness of the bombing in direct support of the Allied armies is best expressed by Field Marshal Günther von Kluge who, early in July 1944, had been brought from the Russian Front to take command of the German armies facing the Allied invasion. In a letter to Hitler, dated 21 July, he said that there was no form of strategy which could counterbalance the effects of the Allied bombing other than withdrawal from the battlefield.

> The psychological effect [he wrote] of such a mass of bombs coming down with all the power of elemental nature on the fighting forces, especially the infantry, is a factor which has to be taken into very serious consideration. It is immaterial whether such a carpet catches good troops or bad. They are more or less annihilated and, above all, their equipment is shattered.

This letter covered a report by Field Marshal Rommel which expressed the same opinion.

But the period under the direction of Eisenhower was not the only contribution Bomber Command made towards a successful invasion. The bombing of Germany throughout 1943 and early 1944 had a vital effect on success. The 25,249 sea mines laid by the Command from 1 January 1943 to 30 June 1944, which resulted in the loss to German and German controlled shipping of some 175,000 tons, was a further help.

On a visit to Bomber Command on 24 May 1944, just prior to the invasion, Eisenhower, in company with his Naval Aide, Captain Harry C. Butcher, was so impressed with the damage assessment photographs shown to him after dinner in the famous 'Conversion Chamber' at Springfield that he immediately wrote to Harris:

25th May, 1944

Dear Harris,
I have of course been familiar with the overall strategic effort against Germany from the air, but since you showed me last night the photographs and charts portraying the extensive damage inflicted upon the enemy within the boundaries of his own country, I am more impressed than ever.

I would feel derelict in my duty if I did not tell you, and through you every member of your Command, of the appreciation and gratitude which I and all of us hold for the contribution of Bomber Command toward eventual victory.

Now, by combining the efforts of air, sea and ground forces, I hope we can capitalize on the work already done and press on soon to bring the Hun to his knees—and keep him there.

Sincerely,
Eisenhower.

Whilst Harris cooperated to the full with Eisenhower, he did not abandon his belief that it was essential to return to the bombing of Germany at as early a date as possible after the successful Allied landings on the Normandy coast. In a memorandum which he was requested to submit on the effectiveness of attacks on flying-bomb and V2 rocket launching sites in France and Belgium, and his proposed future action, he forcibly voiced these opinions. This memorandum was addressed to Tedder, as Deputy Supreme Commander, and Duncan Sandys, who was Joint Parliamentary Secretary at the Ministry of Supply and Chairman of the 'Crossbow' Committee, which Churchill had formed in 1943 to examine evidence from all sources on the secret German developments of flying-bombs and rockets, and which was now charged with responsibility for reporting on the effects of these rockets and bombs and upon the progress of counter-measures and future precautions to meet them. Harris's memorandum was dated 18 July 1944, and after reporting on what had been achieved so far in bombing attacks against these small sites, which were heavily camouflaged and difficult to locate, he proceeded to draw attention to the diversion of effort they had created for probably largely ineffective results. From the beginning of the year to the middle of July 1944, 9,800 sorties had been undertaken against them and 36,000 tons of bombs dropped.

> I do not believe [he wrote] that apart from the damage to the rocket firing sites and to supply dumps, any of this bombing has had a worthwhile effect in reducing the scale of attack, while it has had the deplorable effect, in conjunction with the invasion targets in France, of taking virtually the whole of Bomber Command and much of the American effort off targets in Germany for $3\frac{1}{2}$ months. It has been conservatively estimated that 5 months virtual freedom from bombing would enable Germany to recover almost entirely her essential war production in her bombed industrial areas. She has already had $3\frac{1}{2}$ months of this freedom and therefore if this continues for another one and a half months the vast national resources and the fighting effort of this Command, which have been put into the progressive destruction of German industrial areas during the last three years will have been largely negatived and a great deal of the work will have to be done all over again.

Harris held the view that the Germans would use any diversion to keep the bombers from returning to Germany proper and therefore he regarded any major extension of the attacks against the rocket sites as a grave mistake. He wrote:

> Therefore all defensive bombing aimed directly against the German offensive measures taken against this country is to be deplored, except that minimum which is essential. In my view, where rockets and flying-bombs are concerned, the essentials are: rocket firing sites and, for the present, the flying-bomb supply dumps, until it has become apparent that the enemy has fully organised other and more direct means of delivery.

This last remark was made in relation to the desire of the Chiefs of Staff to attack every sign of the beginning of construction of new sites by swamping such sites with a massive tonnage of bombs.

The real and only effective way of dealing with the flying-bombs and rockets, which, incidentally, only represented a flea-bite* in terms of real offensive warfare compared to the heavy bombers of Bomber Command, was, Harris believed, to increase the bombing offensive against Germany in every way possible and to destroy Germany's ability to produce the war materials necessary for its offensive and defensive efforts on the ground, in the air, and at sea.

> The aim should be [he wrote] to continue the destruction of all German resources and facilities until their armed forces are disarmed, and the country, as a whole collapses. That this can be achieved there cannot be the least doubt in the minds of anybody who has taken the trouble to study the evidence of past results. Evidence, not opinions. The evidence is available. It should be borne in mind that during the whole of 1943 the American Bomber Force operating from this country dropped only 24,000 tons of bombs on Germany against the 137,000 tons dropped by Bomber Command. But now the picture is vastly altered and the American Bomber Force has been built up until not only does it exceed considerably the first line strength of the forces available to Bomber Command, but it has, for the first time adequate reserves of personnel and material behind it. Therefore a combined and concentrated offensive against Germany by Eighth Bomber Command, Bomber Command and 15th Air Force [US] could produce results so vastly greater than those secured in 1943, when Bomber Command was operating virtually alone, that there could be no doubt whatsoever of the outcome. Furthermore nothing could be calculated to be of greater service to the morale of this country than to have it known that in response to the attacks by flying bombs on this country the combined British and American Bomber

---

* From 12 June 1944, when the first flying-bombs were launched against London and southern England, until 28 March 1945, when the last flying-bomb fell on England, 8,564 were launched against this country, 1,006 crashed soon after launching, and only about 2,400 reached England. Their warhead was approximately 1 ton. They killed 6,184 civilians and seriously injured 17,981. The main flying-bomb attacks actually ceased at the beginning of September 1944, and on 8 September rockets were fired at London. In all, 1,190 rockets, also with a 1-ton warhead, were launched against England, the last falling on 27 March 1945. They killed 2,855 people and seriously injured another 6,268. The average error of the rocket was fifteen miles and that of the flying-bomb much greater. In ten months, the Germans delivered 9,754 tons of HE in an erratically dispersed pattern on England; much less than the tonnage that could be dropped successfully and in concentrated fashion on Ruhr targets by only three Bomber Command raids. The British casualties were regrettable, but never serious. As Speer reports in *Inside the Third Reich*, when referring to Hitler's demand for a stock of 5,000 rockets to be available before using the weapon: even 5,000 long-range rockets, that is more than five months' production, would have delivered only 3,750 tons of explosives; a single attack by the combined British and American Air Forces delivered a good 8,000 tons. The production schedule for rockets was 900 per month.

Force were pouring a weight of attack into the vitals of Germany which was twenty to thirty times greater than anything which the Germans are doing to us. There is no doubt that the Allied heavy bomber forces today could eradicate any German town except Berlin in one combined (though not necessarily simultaneous) attack and that they could repeat that on every occasion when the weather served. In the process they would certainly annihilate the German night fighter force and quickly destroy the remains of his day fighter force, with all that that would mean in giving us a walk-over thereafter.

This constant pressure from Harris, backed by Spaatz, to return as quickly as possible to the strategic bombing of Germany was not popular in all quarters, particularly in the departments of the Assistant Chief of the Air Staff (Operations) and the Directorate of Bomber Operations; but for the moment they were unable to interfere. Harris was under Eisenhower and the Supreme Commander was very conscious of the support Harris was giving him in a tactical task, and was also sympathetic to the desire of the strategic forces to return to their proper role. Eisenhower, in fact, recognised the necessity for such a move. The question was when could he forgo the support of Harris and Spaatz, whose forces he well knew had given him a successful invasion so far, and with such unexpectedly small losses?

Under cover of a personal letter dated 18 July 1944, Harris sent to Eisenhower a copy of the memorandum he had addressed to Tedder and Duncan Sandys. Eisenhower did not lightly dismiss his views. On 27 July he wrote in reply:

I hope I have never left any doubt as to my desire to return all the Strategic Air Forces to the bombing of Germany to the greatest possible extent and at the earliest possible moment. I have been quite pleased, lately, to note the extent to which Bomber Command and the Eighth and Fifteenth Air Forces have been hitting the centers of German production. Of course we always have the emergencies of the battle front, and, most of all, the necessity for beating down Crossbow.

If at any time you believe that we are uselessly neglecting opportunities for striking the German in his home country, do not hesitate to tell me about it. I am quite sure you, Tedder and I are all in complete agreement as to the overall requirements. The only possible question could be the very occasional ones of immediate priority.

Harris in pressing his case for a return to strategic bombing was only doing his duty. He was stressing the need for an early resumption of the bombing, and pointing out the dangers of giving Germany too long a period for industrial recovery to be in the interests of the Allied cause. Eisenhower recognised this and well knew that Harris would obey the orders given to him with vigour and determination, and yet, at the same time, make his views known with absolute honesty of purpose.

By early September Eisenhower's Allied forces had overrun France, reached Brussels on the 3rd, Antwerp on the 4th, Liège on the 8th, crossed the River Meuse and reached Luxembourg on the 10th, pierced the Siegfried Line south of Aachen on the 12th, won bridgeheads over the River Moselle at Nancy and just south of Metz on 16 September, and, a few days earlier, had linked up in south-west France with the Sixth Army Group, which had come up from its landing on the south coast of France in the region of Cannes. By the middle of September the Germans were in retreat; the flying-bomb and rocket sites were in the hands of the Allies, except for those in Holland which were soon to be overrun.

On 14 September the Combined Chiefs of Staff agreed at their conference at Quebec to the withdrawal of the Strategic Bomber Forces from the direction of Eisenhower, and placed Bomber Command once more under the direction of Portal, the Chief of the Air Staff, and the US Strategic Air Forces under the control of Arnold, the Commanding General of the US Army Air Forces. It was at this time that Eisenhower made clear his opinion of Harris. In a letter to Marshall, Chief of Staff of the US Army, which was dated 25 September 1944, he wrote:

> Recently General Anderson came back from Washington giving me two of the major decisions of the Quebec Conference, namely, that Strategic Air Forces were no longer under my command, and that future occupation of Germany would be on strictly nationalistic lines with Allied Headquarters abolished.
>
> The first of these decisions I already knew about, since it was placed into effect immediately the decision was taken. As I wrote you then, we can make the scheme work because of the saving clauses in the Directive regarding support for Overlord and because of the good will of the individuals involved. You might be interested to know, in view of earlier expressed fears that Air Chief Marshal Harris would not willingly devote his command to the support of ground operations, that he actually proved to be one of the most effective and cooperative members of this team. Not only did he meet every request I ever made upon him, but he actually took the lead in discovering new ways and means for his particular types of planes to be of use in the battle field. I am quite sure he was genuinely disappointed to lose his status as an integral part of this organisation. However, he keeps his representative right here in my headquarters, and it is because of the perfection of our past association that I have no real fears for the future. When the great battle occurs for the real entry into Germany, he will be on the job.

Harris was indeed sorry to have the link severed. As soon as he heard that Bomber Command was no longer under the direction of Eisenhower, he wrote him a letter on 21 September assuring him of the Command's support whenever he should call for it. His letter read:

> Dear General of the Army,
> Under the new dispensation I and my Command no longer serve directly under you.

I take the opportunity to assure you, although I feel sure that you will recognise this assurance as superfluous, that our 'continuing commitment' for the support of your forces upon call from you will continue, as before, to be met to the utmost of our skill and the last ounce of our endeavour.

I wish personally and on behalf of my Command to proffer you my thanks and gratitude for your unvarying helpfulness, encouragement and support which has never failed us throughout the good fortunes and occasional emergencies of the campaign.

I speak for my crews as for myself in assuring you of our pride in having served under you through this period of unbroken and brilliant victories which, of our experience, we well recognise to have sprung directly from your leadership.

It has been an honour, as indeed a delight, to serve under you through these historic weeks. We would have asked no better than so to remain. It will be a point of honour to meet your every future requirement and request without question and in fullest measure.

We in Bomber Command proffer you not only our congratulations and our thanks, but our utmost service wherever and whenever the need arises.

I hope, indeed, that we may continue the task together to its completion in our respective spheres.

I hope also that you will realise, however poorly I may express it, the very great admiration, regard and indeed affection that we feel for you personally.

> Yours ever,
> Arthur Harris.

Eisenhower was greatly moved by Harris's letter and he replied on 22 September:

Dear Bert,

Your letter of 21 September crossed in the mails one I recently wrote to you in an attempt to express my appreciation of Bomber Command's spirit and performance during this campaign.

Frankly, I am glad I have already despatched that letter, because yours makes me feel so good that I would feel it necessary to inscribe mine on plates of gold. In these trying days nothing has happened to me that made me feel so proud, and so humble, as your message.

I shall keep it always as a treasured, no matter how undeserved, tribute from a great soldier and a man. I seek no greater reward in this war than a belief that the associates I so greatly admire, both British and American, are convinced I did my best.

> As ever,
> IKE

22
Oil

On the 27 August 1944, Portal, as Chief of the Air Staff, prepared a memorandum on the subject of the direction of the Strategic Air Forces. This he submitted to the Combined Chiefs of Staff on 9 September whilst he was bound for the Allied Conference at Quebec aboard the *Queen Mary* in company with Churchill and his military colleagues. He recommended that the control of the Strategic Bomber Forces should now be removed from the Supreme Commander, as the time had come for them to be used once again for the purpose for which they were originally intended, as defined in the Casablanca Directive of January 1943. He pointed out that the contribution made by the heavy bombers to the various phases of 'Overlord' had been very great, but that the invasion was now over, the Allied forces were firmly established in France and were well on their way to the Rhine and the frontiers of Germany. He pointed out to the Chiefs of Staff that the bomber forces had successfully supported the land battle, attacked the flying-bomb and rocket sites and undertaken the onslaught on the German aircraft industry in accordance with the Pointblank Directive. Now he urged that the assault of the heavy bombers should be directed against oil targets, oil being essential to the continued operation of Germany's armed services.

> It has become abundantly clear over the past few months [he wrote], that the enemy is faced with an increasingly critical situation in regard to his oil supplies. To exploit his difficulties fully it is essential that the attack of his oil resources be pressed home at maximum intensity and on the widest scale possible. Any relaxation in the tempo of our attacks against his oil installations will provide opportunity for rehabilitation and dispersal. On the other hand, a successful campaign against enemy oil at this time may well have repercussions upon the enemy's ability to fight on the French, Italian and Russian fronts which may prove decisive.

Portal, in his note, recognised that rapid changes in the strategic situation were taking place and that it might become desirable at any time 'to apply the whole of the strategic bomber effort to the direct attack of German morale.' He also recognised the probable continuing requirements of Eisenhower for support of the land battles to come, but he believed these calls would be on a much reduced scale as compared to those of previous months. He emphasized, however, that the Supreme Commander must be assured that any emergency requirements of the land battle would be given first priority.

He therefore recommended that Bomber Command should once more be placed under the direction of himself, and that the United States Strategic Air Forces should be placed under the direction of Arnold, thus returning them to the authority of the Combined Chiefs of Staff. In this manner he was confident that the effective cooperation of their future strategic activities would be best accomplished.

Portal's suggestions were adopted at the Quebec Conference and on 14 September he and Arnold issued a directive to Bottomley, the Deputy Chief of the Air Staff, and to Spaatz, on the future control of the Strategic Bomber Forces in Europe. The first two paragraphs of this directive read as follows:

1. The Combined Chiefs of Staff have decided that executive responsibility for the control of the strategic bomber forces in Europe shall be vested in the Chief of the Air Staff, RAF and the Commanding General, United States Army Air Forces, jointly.

2. The Deputy Chief of the Air Staff, RAF, and the Commanding General, United States Strategic Air Forces in Europe, are designated as representatives of the Chief of the Air Staff, RAF, and the Commanding General, United States Army Air Forces, respectively, for the purpose of providing control and local coordination through consultation.

On 25 September 1944, Harris was officially informed of the fact that he no longer served under Eisenhower, a change which in many ways he regretted, for he had developed a tremendous respect for Eisenhower's ability as a commander. The directive of 25 September also advised him that the CAS had designated the DCAS as his representative for the purpose of providing control, on behalf of the CAS, of Bomber Command's activities and their coordination with those of the US Strategic Air Forces in Europe. There followed the instruction that the overall mission would be the progressive destruction and dislocation of the German military, industrial and economic systems and the direct support of land and naval forces. Then came the priorities:

First priority.
  (i) Petroleum industry, with special emphasis on petrol (gasoline) including storage.
Second priority.
  (ii) The German rail and waterborne transportation systems.
  (iii) Tank production plants and depots, ordnance depots.
  (iv) MT production plants and depots.

The directive also stated that as a result of past air action against the German aircraft industry and against the maintenance and operational facilities of the German Air Force, the effectiveness of this Force had been greatly reduced. Since the combined strength and effectiveness of the Allied air forces had increased vastly, it was considered that it was no longer justifiable to regard the German Air Force and its supporting industry as a primary objective for attack.

Included in the directive was a statement to the effect that direct support of the land and naval operations remained a continuing commitment, and that when weather or tactical conditions were unsuitable for operations against specific primary objectives, attacks should be delivered on important industrial areas.

It was this last reference to weather and tactical conditions that exercised the attention of Harris. He did not believe in a concentration of bombing against oil targets to the exclusion of all else. He was not critical of attacks on oil targets, German rail and water-borne transportation systems, tank factories, motor transport factories and ordnance depots, particularly if these were in the Ruhr or other industrial built-up areas. He was critical, however, of a priority that virtually left the question of bombing industrial areas, generally, as an afterthought. The winter months were approaching, weather conditions would be deteriorating, and more and more the Command would be bombing blind, using sky markers dropped by Pathfinder Oboe Mosquitos as guides. And the only targets really suitable for this form of attack were the large industrial towns. Harris was therefore of the opinion that area bombing must enter into any scheme of future strategic bombing. He knew from his vast experience of operations that in the conduct of a bomber offensive it was, particularly in the winter months, seldom a case of being able to bomb exactly what one wanted to bomb, and that what one bombed was generally the target nearest to the top of the priority list that was suitable for attack in the light of weather, tactical and other factors existing at the time of attack.

Harris knew, of course, that the tremendous advances of the Allied armies through France, Belgium and Luxembourg, and the planned drive through Holland, had enabled mobile Gee, Oboe and G-H stations to be set up on the Continent, greatly increasing the number of targets in Germany to come within their highly accurate range. He had pressed for these improved facilities and his RDF staff had seen to it that they were provided and that the coverage was constantly improved by taking advantage of further military gains on the Continent. In addition, he was conscious of the rapidly reducing enemy territory over which his bombers now had to fly and, with refuelling bases on the Continent available to escort fighters, enabling them to escort even deeper into Germany, he was aware of the better chances now available to the Command to carry the bomber offensive to areas which had hitherto largely escaped the scourge of the bomber. In fact, whilst he accepted a list of specific targets such as oil, he also wanted to see an all-out bombing effort against Germany, now that Bomber Command and the US Eighth Bomber Command had the strength, at last, to put into decisive effect the Casablanca Directive of

January 1943: 'The progressive destruction and dislocation of the German military, industrial and economic system, and the undermining of the morale of the German people to a point where their capacity for armed resistance is fatally weakened.'

Just after Harris received his new directive of 25 September, Churchill sent him a paper, referred to as the 'ULTRA paper', which was a Japanese document that had fallen into Allied hands. This was a Japanese survey of the military situation in Europe now that the Allies had successfully landed on the Continent. Churchill asked Harris for his comments, and Harris recognised his chance to press for the return to an all-out bomber offensive against Germany. On 30 September he wrote:

> Of our past experience the Jap diplomats are usually stuffed with Boche propaganda and inclined to swallow it, hook, line and sinker. They seem to have benefited somewhat from experience and I consider that the Jap report now referred to is on the whole a reasonably balanced appreciation. We should, I feel, take a more sober view of what has so far occurred on the Western front. The German Army in Normandy was beleaguered and besieged by our overwhelming Air power at the far end of a long line of communications in a hostile country. The Allied Armies are inclined to turn a blind eye to this indisputable fact. In the circumstances that is human.

He went on:
> That German Army, deprived of transport and of usable transport routes, of reserves, rations, ammunition, and last but by no means least, of air cover and reconnaissance, collapsed in the face of attack by superior and better equipped forces. But it collapsed mainly because it was beleaguered by Air power.

Now that the Allies were near the German frontier, and the German Army's lines of communication had been greatly shortened and no longer ran through hostile country, he suggested that this, as intimated by the Japs, put a very different complexion on the military situation. He acknowledged that the enemy had suffered heavy losses of men and material, but he maintained his opinion that

> no matter how well the Boche has fought outside his own frontiers, we should see him for the first time really fight his damnedest when driven back on his own frontiers, with his rifle in one hand, his essential personal properties in the other, and an awful fear of the wrath and retribution of his victims spurring his final endeavour. His last ditch is indeed his last ditch—and well does the Boche know it.

The Japanese, he said, were of course correct in recognising that the Allied supply problems had increased with their advance, but such problems he dismissed as they would be resolved by the opening of the Channel ports, Antwerp and Rotterdam, and because the Allied lines ran through friendly country. Therefore he rejected the Japanese views on the launching of a successful German counter-attack as unwarranted optimism, but Harris emphasised that it would be the overwhelming Allied air power which would destroy such chances.

> You will note [he wrote] that the whole of the Boche revelation to the Jap centres round retrieving air supremacy. So the Boche and the Jap realise what happened to the German Armies in France—even if our own military minds do not yet quite grasp it. Our armies have had one or two (no more) really tough local battles in France. They have not yet had as many killed as on the first day of the Battle of the Somme. They have not yet had as many killed as Bomber Command in its past efforts to make the invasion practicable. At Le Havre and Boulogne, for instance, we have taken these vital and heavily defended ports with nearly 20,000 prisoners at the cost of less than 150 of our men killed in fierce fighting. Why these extraordinary discrepancies? The answer is Air power. When these facts are hoisted in, the probabilities of the future begin to clear. From now on, as in the past, our fortunes depend on whether we can maintain our Air supremacy. That is what the Boche admits to the Jap in these ULTRA papers. I agree with him.

Harris then reminded Churchill of the final discussion before 'Overlord' when the King, Field-Marshal Smuts and Churchill himself were present. 'You may recall my statement that 5 months cessation of bombing Germany would enable her to reconstitute all her essential war industry.' Whilst the bombing of German industrial cities had not altogether ceased since the invasion, he stressed that Germany had been given a considerable breathing space from all out bombing during the last six months. He added:

> We should now get on and knock Germany finally flat. For the first time we have the force to do it. Opportunities do not last forever and this one is slipping ... If we do not take full advantage now of the vast Allied Air superiority we shall lose the opportunity. With the lost opportunity we shall lose the effect upon the land battles ... We must therefore at any cost nip in the bud any possibility of the German regaining a serious footing in the air ...

Churchill replied the following day:

> I agree with your very good letter, except that I do not think you did it all or can you do it all. I recognise however this is a becoming view for you to take. I am all for cracking everything in now on to Germany that can be spared from the battlefields.

On the same day, 1 October, Churchill minuted General Ismay, his Chief Staff Officer, on the subject of the Harris letter.

> Please see this characteristic letter from Air Chief Marshal Harris. I am sure that he is right in a great deal that he says, though I do not rate the

share of the Air Force as high as he does. It would seem that every effort should be made to crack it on to Germany now and every airplane that can be spared from the battlefield should be at them.

Churchill's reaction had a partial effect and permitted Harris to interpret his directive somewhat broadly; but, nonetheless, Harris met his priorities in a very cogent fashion whilst at the same time mounting a colossal offensive against German towns. But he was inflicted, from the moment of his withdrawal from Eisenhower's direction, with the views of 'every panacea monger and me-too expert,' as he described them, trying to tell him how he should run his Command and what targets he should bomb in order to bring the war to an end in a matter of days. These were, however, interferences of small consequence.

As has already been stated, Portal had committed himself to the support of oil targets as priority number one at the Quebec Chiefs of Staff Conference, where he had won the return of the Strategic Bomber Forces to the control of himself and General Arnold. It was over this subject of oil that Harris was in disagreement with Portal, taking the view that the priority accorded to these targets was disproportionate to their importance *vis-à-vis* all other industrial targets. The divergence of views became readily apparent when Portal criticised a major bombing raid on Cologne on the night of the 30/31 October, when 963 aircraft attacked and dropped 3,937·4 tons of bombs, followed by one on Bochum on the 4/5 November by 703 aircraft dropping 3,323·4 tons of bombs. He asked Harris for an explanation as to why he had made these attacks in preference to raids on synthetic oil or benzol plants in the Ruhr, or other oil or petroleum producing plants in Germany. In a letter to Harris, dated 5 November, Portal stated quite firmly that he believed the air offensive against oil gave the Allies the best hope of complete victory in the next few months. In the same letter he rejected Harris's reasons for attacking Cologne, which had been principally that it was a most important communication centre and industrial area, and as such an attack upon it was of direct value to the Allied armies and generally in line with his directive. The added reasons for selecting it in preference to other priority targets, Harris had explained, were ones of the weather conditions which had been forecast for that night. Portal's letter was, essentially, an initial attempt to convince Harris of the importance of the offensive against oil. This was more clearly evidenced in a further letter from Portal dated 12 November, which was in reply to a letter from Harris dated 6 November, wherein he gave further explanations for the Cologne and Bochum raids, and gave reasons why he had chosen to attack Bochum instead of Gelsenkirchen which harboured two high priority oil production targets. Portal wrote:

> You have been good enough to state in full the factors which influenced you to go to Cologne rather than to the Ruhr, and to Bochum, rather than Gelsenkirchen. I must, of course, accept your decisions in these cases ...
> The issue is a more fundamental one than whether or not you could have

made a better choice in these two individual cases. In the closing paragraphs of your letter of the 1st November* you refer to a plan for the destruction of the 60 leading German cities, and to your efforts to keep up with, and even to exceed, your average of $2\frac{1}{2}$ such cities devastated each month;† I know that you have long felt such a plan to be the most effective way of bringing about the collapse of Germany. Knowing this, I have, I must confess, at times wondered whether the magnetism of the remaining German cities has not in the past tended as much to deflect our bombers from their primary objectives as the tactical and weather difficulties which you described so fully in your letter of 1st November. I would like you to reassure me that this is not so. If I knew you to be as wholehearted in the attack on oil as in the past you have been in the matter of attacking cities I would have very little to worry about.

For a month after this letter the matter lay dormant; but not so Bomber Command. In October, November and December Harris's attacks on oil targets and the Ruhr were unprecedented. Duisburg was fiercely attacked in daylight by 957 aircraft led by No 3 Group G-H Lancasters acting as target locators. 4,401 tons of bombs were dropped. The same night a further 913 aircraft attacked the town dropping another 4,381·9 tons of bombs. In all, only twenty-one aircraft were lost. The raid was highly successful. The Meerbeck synthetic oil plant at Homburg was bombed at the end of October, as also was the synthetic oil plant at Bottrop and the Leverkusen chemical works. These three attacks were daylight attacks, the latter two being undertaken by No 3 Group G-H Lancasters. In the case of Leverkusen, the bombs were released from above ten-tenths cloud, the aircraft relying entirely on their G-H instruments; the accuracy was so great that the chemical works were extensively damaged. In November, the oil plants at Wanne Eickel, Dortmund, Castrop Rauxel, Gelsenkirchen/Nordstern, Kamen, Homberg-Meerbeck, Sterkrade, Bottrop, Wesseling, Harburg and Scholven-Buer were all heavily attacked. By the end of November, attacks against synthetic oil plants in the Ruhr were temporarily suspended as all of them had been rendered inactive. But further attacks were made against certain benzol plants and oil plants outside the Ruhr. Then on the night of 6/7 December, Merseburg/Leuna, one of the two largest synthetic oil plants in Germany was successfully attacked by 460 aircraft dropping 1,841·6 tons of bombs. The full success was difficult to judge because it was subsequently attacked three times by the Americans before photographic cover revealed that it had been put out

---

* This was a letter from Harris to Portal, commenting on a paper entitled 'Notes on Air Policy to be Adopted with a View to Rapid Defeat of Germany', written by Tedder, the Deputy Supreme Commander to Eisenhower.

† In this letter Harris stated: 'In the past 18 months Bomber Command has virtually destroyed 45 out of the leading 60 German cities.' He then went on to refer to keeping up an average of $2\frac{1}{2}$ cities per month.

of action and not before mid-January 1945, could it be expected to return to production, and then only to 25 per cent of its previous production level. Equal in size to Leuna was Pölitz, which was heavily damaged by No 5 Group in a raid on the night of 21/22 December by 182 Lancasters dropping 724 tons of bombs.

But these operations were far from being all of Bomber Command's activities at this time. There were major attacks on Ruhr towns such as Essen, Düsseldorf, Dortmund and Duisburg, and outside the Ruhr on towns such as Münster, Karlsruhe, Ludwigshaven and Munich; there were many attacks in support of the Allied armies, calls which were promptly and effectively answered, such as for the obliteration of Düren, Jülich and Heinsberg for the American Army offensive, and Kleve and Emmerich for the British Second Army, and the reduction of the Walcheren fortress for Montgomery; there were substantial requests from the Navy for attacks on port areas and shipping at Ijmuiden, in Oslo Fjord and at Gdynia in Poland, and on various E-boat and submarine pens; there was the request for the sinking of the *Tirpitz*, which was duly sunk at Tromsö Fjord in Norway on 12 November by twenty-nine Lancasters of Nos 617 and 9 Squadrons from No 5 Group, led by Wing Commander J. B. Tait, dropping 12,000-pound Tallboy bombs from between 13,000 and 16,000 feet—these were the bombs that had been designed by Barnes Wallis, who had developed the dam-busting bomb, and which were used with such success against submarine pens and other targets massively protected by concrete or armour. Finally, on 16 December, when Field-Marshal von Rundstedt mounted his famous counter-attack against the Allies through the Ardennes in weather that completely hampered all air operations, an urgent call went out from Eisenhower's Headquarters for tactical support. Due to extensive and thick fog, which was spreading not only over the battle area but also over the bases in France, Belgium and England, the Allied Air Forces were unable to respond—with the sole exception of Bomber Command. The first priority was for an attack on Trier, which was a centre of concentration of the enemy's supplies and armour. This was called for on the 19th. Harris responded immediately by sending a force of G-H Lancasters from No 3 Group, despite shocking visibility conditions at the Group's bases and the fact that the target was completely covered by fog. Bombing blind on G-H, the attack was an outstanding success, and it drew from Eisenhower his immediate congratulations to Harris in a signal despatched by Tedder:

> The Supreme Commander has asked me to convey his congratulations, to which I add my own, on the magnificent performance of your Command in its attack on Trier on 19th December. The decision to take-off despite increasing fog at Base, and the determination of crews to reach and hit the target, whatever the weather, illustrate once again how ready is the response of the Royal Air Force to the needs of the battle on the ground. Please convey to all who had a part in the planning and execution

of this operation the Supreme Commander's appreciation and congratulations.

Harris replied: 'Very many thanks for the generous message from the Supreme Commander, which has been passed to all concerned. You can count on us in any weather short of the impossible.'

When Eisenhower saw the reply from Harris he wrote against it 'Goddamit, they have already achieved the impossible.'

Despite the atrocious weather conditions Bomber Command continued against fog bound targets with G-H aircraft until the weather cleared on 24 December. Then, in mightier force, the Command loaned its weight to Eisenhower's requirements until Rundstedt's offensive petered out in the middle of January 1945. In *Inside the Third Reich*, under the chapter heading 'The Plunge', Speer describes how he experienced one of the night attacks when he was talking with Sepp Dietrich who was commanding an SS armoured force in the Bastogne area. Speer, who was visiting Dietrich at his headquarters near the Belgian border town of Houffalize, was listening to Dietrich's description of the hopelessness of the situation when, he says:

> As if to illustrate our helplessness our nocturnal talk was interrupted by a low-level attack from huge four-motored bomber formations. Howling and exploding bombs, clouds illuminated in red and yellow hues, droning motors, and no defence anywhere—I was stunned by this scene of military impotence ...

Bomber Command's performance in the last quarter of 1944 was, indeed, remarkable. In October it despatched 17,562 sorties and dropped 61,204 tons of bombs; in November it despatched 15,008 sorties and dropped 53,022 tons of which 14,312 tons were dropped on oil targets; in December, despite weather, 15,333 sorties were despatched, dropping 49,040 tons of bombs of which a considerable tonnage was on oil targets, notwithstanding the heavy priority demands for support of the Allied Armies including attacks against transportation targets.

Portal, however, was still not convinced by late December 1944, that Harris was giving of his best in the battle against German oil and petroleum production. His doubts were perhaps understandable. In a letter dated 12 December, Harris gave him the Bomber Command Operational Research Section's estimate of the effort required to put out of action and keep out of action all the synthetic oil and benzol plants, crude refineries and finishing plants, totalling forty-two, in the western theatre of operations. This amounted to 9,000 sorties per month; 2,600 by day consisting of thirteen raids of 200 aircraft, and 6,400 by night consisting of eighteen raids of 350 aircraft. This estimate took into account the probable number of unsuccessful and partially successful raids and also allowed for repeat attacks necessary to keep the plants out of production. To complete the task, the total effort at this monthly frequency was estimated at 56,500 sorties, dropping 226,000 tons of bombs. The conclusion was that the number of clear days in the remaining winter months would be sufficient for Bomber Command to deal with the twenty-seven oil targets in Western Germany employing 2,600 day sorties per month. The fifteen targets in Central Germany, which if tackled by Bomber Command would have to be attacked by night and would require 6,400 sorties per month, presented a more difficult problem. As Harris explained in the letter, the estimate of three to four nights per month, at this time of the year, on which such operations would be possible, was a fair one; but seasonal weather precluded any hope of undertaking night raids with 350 aircraft at a time at a frequency of eighteen per month—this even if two or three attacks on each clear night were possible, which was unlikely due to the differences in weather over the divergent areas in which these plants were situated. It therefore followed, Harris said, that due to weather and lack of Oboe and G-H cover for these distant targets, the US Eighth Air Force would have to tackle most of them, 'although', he added, 'we will do, and are doing, our best to get at Leuna and Pölitz whenever conditions serve.' The contents of the concluding paragraph of Harris's letter were, however, the cause of Portal's concern:

> You will recall that in the past MEW [Ministry of Economic Warfare] experts have never failed to overstate their case on 'panaceas', e.g., ball-bearings, molybdenum, locomotives etc., in so far as, after the battle has been joined and the original targets attacked, more and more sources of supply or other factors unpredicted by MEW have become revealed. The oil plan has already displayed similar symptons. The benzol plants were an afterthought. I am quite certain that there are dozens more benzol plants of which we are unaware and if and when we knock them all out I am equally certain we shall eventually be told by MEW that German MT [motor transport] is continuing to run sufficiently for their purpose on producer gas, steam, industrial alcohol, etc., etc. However, we should be content if we can deprive them of adequate supplies of aviation fuel. That in itself will take enough doing.

Portal replied on 22 December. He agreed that the US Eighth Bomber Command would have to take on most of the central German plants by day requiring a lower scale of effort per target than would be required by Bomber Command attacking at night. He was also encouraged, he said, that Harris could deal adequately with the twenty-seven targets in Western Germany. 'This, I notice,' he wrote, 'is less than 17% of your average monthly bombing sorties over the last six months, and is a remarkably small price to pay for dealing with so large a part of the primary target system.' He then went on to justify the priority given to the campaign against oil and his conviction that 'if the job can be done this winter, strategic bombing will go down to history as a decisive factor in winning the war.' Referring to the last paragraph of Harris's letter he finally wrote:

7. For these reasons I am profoundly disappointed that you still appear to

feel that the oil plan is just another 'panacea'. Naturally, while you hold this view you will be unable to put your heart into the attack of oil. Your letter gave me the impression that while you have somewhat reluctantly agreed to attack Pölitz and Leuna when occasion offers, you feel that this is all you should be asked to contribute towards the attack of the all-important Central German plants. I must say that I should have hoped that you would on the contrary be eagerly seeking opportunities to attack all or any of them whenever there is a chance of doing so, in order that the RAF might play as large a part as possible in what is by far the most immediately profitable policy we have yet undertaken in this war.

8. Brux, for example, is probably at least as important a producer at the present time as Pölitz and Leuna. Although its attack would normally be undertaken by the Fifteenth Air Force I think it should be well within the capabilities of Bomber Command. Perhaps you would get your ORS and Operational Staff to see whether it is operationally feasible for you to attack it.

9. In your last paragraph you again cast doubt on past estimates by the Ministry of Economic Warfare and by implication on the whole principle of attacking a particular target system. You throw doubt also upon the soundness of our oil policy. If the attack of a particular target system is to be successful, it must be carried out as rapidly as possible and with the object of immobilising as many plants as possible in the system at the same time. Clearly we cannot expect to get very far if only half the plants are out of action at any one time. If we had tried harder in our attack on ball-bearings I have little doubt that the full effects forecast by MEW would have been achieved. I am glad to say that we have shown much more determination in the attack of oil, but if you allow your obvious doubts in this direction to influence your conduct of operations I very much fear that the prize may yet slip through our fingers. Moreover, it is difficult for me to feel that your staff can be devoting its maximum thought and energies to the accomplishment of your first priority task if you yourself are not wholehearted in support of it.

10. I have expressed my views very frankly, but the achievements of your Command in the attack of oil have been so splendid that it would be a tragedy if, through any lack of faith or understanding on your part, the RAF Bomber Command failed to take the greatest possible share in the supreme task of driving home our attacks on enemy oil.

In a lengthy reply to Portal, dated 28 December 1944, Harris indicated quite clearly that he was not convinced of the efficacy of the Oil Plan. In one part of the letter he wrote:

I am afraid that nothing will disillusion me of the view that the oil plan is, for reasons I have given above, and on many occasions elsewhere, another panacea. But you are quite wrong to say that if I hold that view I will be unable to put my heart into the attack on oil. It has always been my custom, and it is one that I will never relinquish, to leave no stone unturned to get my views across, but when the decision is made I carry it out to the utmost and to the best of my ability. I am sorry that you should doubt this, and surprised indeed if you can point to any precedent in support of your statement. I can certainly quote precedent in the opposite sense.

Your remarks re the historical verdict on the oil plan seem tantamount to saying that history will have nothing to record of strategic bombing up to date. I do not share that view. Neither, I am sure, do the Germans.

Your paragraph 9. I throw doubt on the oil policy because, as I say, I put no reliance whatever on any estimate by the Ministry of Economic Warfare. Subsequent discoveries of other sources of fuel and power, and of unsuspected sources of oil such as new plants, coupled with essential diversions in aid of the Army and the Navy, etc., etc., all fill me with doubts as to the possibility of bringing the plan to the conclusion hoped for. Furthermore, it is par excellence a plan which if it fails achieves nothing else whatever. If you miss an oil plant, you hit nothing, and by their nature they are easy enough to miss. Therefore I say that we are forsaking the substance for the shadow. If the Germans were asked today, 'Oil plants or cities?' they would reply, 'Bomb anything you fancy except the cities'—that is the whole tenor of everything we hear from Germany today.

I am sorry indeed that you made the remark that 'if we had tried harder' we might have secured the full effects anticipated by the ball-bearing plan. I am not aware that we lost any feasible opportunity of prosecuting that plan. In fact I am satisfied, and particularly so with regard to the French part of the plan, that we achieved a whole series of brilliantly executed attacks of an effectiveness that nobody would even have thought possible at the time when the ball bearing plan was initiated. Essential plants would have gone underground—and they were and are doing so.

I am sorry that you also imagine my staff cannot be devoting its maximum thought and energy to the oil plan because of my views. I do not give my staff views. I give them orders. They do and always have done exactly what I tell them to. I have told them to miss no opportunity of prosecuting the oil plan, and they have missed no worth while opportunity.

While doing my utmost to push this plan to the conclusion sought, it does not relieve me of my duty to inform you that like all previous panaceas so enthusiastically put forward by MEW the basis of the plan is wrong in the light of all the factors involved, and its pursuance is, and will prove to be, chimerical.

Before ending this letter Harris pointed out that Brux, in Czechoslovakia was not on his list, but now he had added it to those which he had to attack. He finished by writing:

With a vista opening in front of us of bombing nothing but tactical and oil targets—which means a final stopper on bombing Germany in the way that has given her her worst headache—we are finally discarding the substance for the shadow. And an MEW shadow at that.

You may think I feel strongly about it. Indeed I do.

Portal replied yet again in a last and monumental attempt to convince Harris of the vital importance of the Oil Plan, despite the fact that Harris, for all his disbelief in its military virtue as a plan to take precedence over all other offensive bombing plans, was executing the Oil Plan with ruthless efficiency and devastating success. It was an eight-page letter, dated 8 January 1945, and it contained a comprehensive plea to convert Harris, hook, line and sinker, to the Oil Plan. He commenced by saying:

> In your letter of the 28th December you expressed very fully your views upon our present bombing policy. I gather that you are quite convinced that the attack of oil, or for that matter any other particular target system, is unsound and that we would have achieved very much better results if both the RAF and US bomber forces had concentrated throughout on the blitzing of industrial centres.
>
> In view of the tremendous importance of the subject I must reply to you in some detail, particularly as I am sure you have given far too little weight to some of the factors which have played a part in the determination of our present policy.
>
> If the arguments I put to you in the following paragraphs can convince you that the attack of oil is sound, or even that there is considerably more to be said for it than you previously thought, then my letter will have gone some way to achieving its purpose. For in spite of your assertions to the contrary, I believe your attacks on oil would be pressed home harder and more certainly if they were backed not solely by your sense of loyalty but by your enthusiasm as well.

Then followed the arguments for the Oil Plan and a spirited defence of the Ministry of Economic Warfare. Towards the end came Portal's assessment of area attacks as opposed to oil attacks. He wrote:

> Do area attacks hold out a better prospect than oil? There is no doubt whatsoever of the contribution they have made to the general weakening of Germany, and to creating the condition in which we were able to bring all our strength to bear offensively upon her. But such attacks, directed as they are against the entire war machine, can take effect only over a long period unless the rate of attack is very heavy in comparison with the total energy and resources of the enemy. Knowing as we do the energy, resource and resilience of Germany, it would be too big an undertaking to try to defeat her with only a part of our total fighting power. If cities, once attacked, were entirely destroyed, the chances would be better; but, as you yourself admit, cities recover their industrial output—in four or five months. This recovery factor, which has to be reckoned with the attack of every target system, area or precise, must in the case of area

attack limit the proportion of the enemy's total industrial power which a given bomber force can keep neutralized.

In your letter you suggest that on more than one occasion Germany has nearly collapsed under our area blitzing. We know she was seriously alarmed by the impact of the Hamburg and the early Berlin attacks, but, as far as I am aware, there is no evidence to show that she was near collapse. She weathered successfully the storm of the subsequent Berlin attacks.

In view of the doubt which exists as to the point to which area attacks must be carried to be decisive in themselves, it is clearly the sounder policy now to employ the bomber forces so that they may make a calculable contribution to the offensive as a whole. Such a policy has been adopted in the attack of oil and communications. Nevertheless area attacks can throw a very great additional burden upon Germany, and many opportunities for such attacks will arise; the directive makes provision for these.

He finished by saying:

The energy, resource and determination displayed by the enemy in his efforts to maintain his oil production must be more than matched by our own determination to destroy it: and *your* determination matters more than that of all the rest of us together! I am very thankful that you have stated your doubts so frankly and thus given me the chance to try to convince you.

On 18 January 1945, Harris replied to Portal. He was still totally unconvinced that the priority being given to oil targets, at the expense of area attacks on industrial towns, would bring about a speedier end to hostilities. His letter was as powerful an argument against as Portal's was for the Oil Plan; it was as powerful for as Portal's was against an all-out offensive on German industrial towns. It ended on a disturbing note:

You intimate that I have been disloyal in the past in carrying out to the best of my ability (within the limitations of my resources, the climate, and in the press of other calls from the many whom I now serve) policies which have been laid down. That I absolutely and flatly deny.

True, indeed, I have had no faith in some of these policies, as I have none whatever in this present oil policy, or in any panacea. I have always made a point of speaking up about my doubts on such occasions, as I do on this. I regard it as my prime duty, when doubt exists. But I have not failed in any *worth-while* efforts to achieve even those things which I knew from the start to be impracticable, once they had been decided upon. In this decision on oil I was given no prior opportunity to represent my views.

I will not willingly again lay myself open to the charge that the lack of success of a policy, which I have declared at the outset, or when it first came to my knowledge, not to contain the seeds of success is, after the event, due to my personal failure in not having really tried. That situation is simply one of heads I lose tails you win, and it is an intolerable situation.

I therefore ask you to consider whether it is best for the prosecution of the war and the success of our arms, which alone matters, that I should remain in this situation.

Portal replied very promptly to this letter on 20 January. It was the reply of a great man to a great man. He commenced by writing:

I am sorry to see from your letter of the 18th January in reply to mine of the 8th that I have failed to convince you of the soundness of the Oil Plan.

After briefly commenting on a number of points in Harris's letter of the 18th, he wrote:

We must now agree to differ. You apparently believe in putting all your effort into area attacks. We recognise that area attacks have been extremely valuable but we are convinced that in order to be decisive in themselves, or in the near future, they would require a very much larger force than we possess, the main reason for this being that an industrial area recovers much of its productive capacity in 4 or 5 months, as you yourself have stated in the past. We are further convinced that the devotion of a part of your effort to reducing the enemy's supply of a vital commodity of which he is now desperately short, gives the best chance of an early end to the war. A point of major difference between us seems to be that you would apparently regard the Oil Plan as a failure so long as the enemy continued to be able to fight at all, whereas we would regard it as successful as soon as the shortage of oil began to have a really substantial effect on the enemy's power to resist our offensive and that of the Russians. Beyond that point the question is not whether the plan is successful but how great is its success. Judging by the best evidence available to us, the enemy's power of resistance has already been seriously weakened and I cannot believe that the heavier 'blitzing' of industry in general that would result from dropping the Oil Plan now could have any comparable effect during the next few months. I hope, nevertheless, that you will have enough effort left after doing your best on oil to enable you to flatten out some at least of the cities which you name on page 5 of your letter.

I am extremely sorry that you should have stated in your letter that I have attributed disloyalty to you. If you will look again at the last sentence of para. 2 of my previous letter you will see that I assumed your loyalty and sought only to convert you to enthusiasm. It is true that in my para. 7 I said that the facts did not seem to me to bear out your contention as to the amount of effort devoted to ball-bearings in the past, but to question your memory, your judgment or the interpretation which you put upon facts is a very different thing from charging you with disloyalty.

I willingly accept your assurance that you will continue to do your utmost to ensure the successful execution of the policy laid down. I am very sorry that you do not believe in it but it is no use my craving for what is evidently unattainable. We must wait until after the end of the war before we can know for certain who was right and I sincerely hope that until then you will continue in command of the force which has done so much towards defeating the enemy and has brought such credit and renown to yourself and to the Air Force.

Harris immediately told Portal that it was a source of very great personal regret that there should have been any disagreement, and he assured him that despite this disagreement he would continue to do his utmost to carry out the policy which had been decided upon. It was an assurance which he fulfilled so effectively that, once more, as with the Transportation Plan, his prowess as a great offensive commander was to prove him partially wrong in his judgement of the Oil Plan.

By the end of February 1945, Bomber Command had dropped the huge total of 62,339 tons of bombs on oil and benzol targets, to which it was to add in March and April yet another 24,289 tons. Its oil targets had extended far beyond the Ruhr to such targets as Brux and Zeitz in Czechoslovakia. It is also interesting to note that the 62,339 tons of bombs dropped by the end of February had been directed against thirty-six oil and benzol plants in ninety-five attacks. In computing the resultant loss of output to the enemy it is necessary to take into account attacks by the United States Air Forces on the same targets, since it was not always possible to apportion the results between particular attacks. Over the same period, to the end of February 1945, thirty-five attacks were made by the Americans against fifteen of these targets. The total combined output of these thirty-six plants from the date of the first Bomber Command attack until 28 February 1945, assuming no attacks had been made, would have been 1,916,335 tons. As a result of the attacks it was estimated at the time that the overall output had been reduced to 198,430 tons, a reduction of 90 per cent; and these estimates turned out to be close to the actual figures.

In fact, both Portal and Harris could have been right, and if the Oil Plan had been applied to the exclusion of area bombing of industrial targets at that stage of the war, or vice versa, then the timing of the end of the war might well have been the same; but the war might also well have ended later than it did.

The truth is that the combination of executing the Oil Plan and maintaining a powerful area bombing offensive against German cities, in addition to meeting the necessary calls of the Allied armies, is what caused the rapid collapse of Germany, a collapse which would have been far more protracted had any one or other specialist industry been selected for attack to the exclusion of all others. Portal was right to press for oil, and Harris was right to hold out for area bombing. In those winter months of 1944 and 1945, area bombing and, in particular, deeper penetration to those cities which had largely escaped attack and were then, because of their past immunity, becoming more and more vital to Germany's ability to continue the war, were operations best suited to Bomber Command's abilities. Figures provided by Albert Speer to the author are discussed in a later chapter, and they support this contention. To have concentrated the bulk of the Command's effort on oil would not have achieved a greater success than was, in any case, accomplished against oil; but it would have resulted in a great deal of wasted effort by Bomber Command and provided the urgent relief from bombing that the German industrial cities craved.

In the case of the benzol plants, which were small and mostly in the Ruhr and Rhineland, only No 3 Group, with G-H, could find and hit these plants in most weather conditions, particularly in the winter months. To have despatched the whole force against such targets would have been wasteful. The bomb loads which No 3 Group could carry and drop with remarkable accuracy were more than enough to deal with these benzol plants.

Many commanders would have succumbed to the pleadings of the Air Staff and the intervention of the Chief of the Air Staff in the interests of their own careers. Not so Harris. He knew from three years of experience in command, and from many more earlier years of accumulated experience of bombers, what were the capabilities of Bomber Command and how the bomber could best be employed to achieve maximum effect against the enemy. Therefore he fought against what he regarded as the misuse of his forces, even to the extent of giving Portal the opportunity to relieve him of his command. But at the same time he executed those orders with which he disagreed with the most incredible efficiency and devastating effect.

Many Chiefs of the Air Staff, facing views which were held in opposition to those of the Air Staff, and stubbornly upheld by a Commander-in-Chief, would have relieved that Commander-in-Chief of his command. Not so Portal. With his years of experience of the Royal Air Force, his upbringing under the former great Chiefs of the Air Staff, 'Boom' Trenchard and Sir John Salmond, he recognised an exceptional commander and trusted a man who was forthright in his views and formed and held his own opinions honestly and not for personal or political gain. In Harris he knew that he had the greatest commander in the field that the Royal Air Force had ever known, and he conceded that such a man was entitled to his opinions even if they ran counter to his own. Lastly, he knew that a commander of the stature of Harris would support a decision to the utmost of his ability once it was taken, even if it ran counter to his own views.

Historians have hinted that Portal should have rid himself of Harris. It is understandable. They were lesser men than Portal and Harris. Some historians and writers have hinted that Portal regarded himself as let down by Harris over the oil controversy, but that he was unable to dismiss him because of the high regard in which Harris was held by Churchill, the Americans and, indeed, the British public. Because of this, it has been suggested that the close relationship between Portal and Harris was permanently ruptured. The day after the unconditional surrender of Germany, Portal wrote to Harris a personal letter in his own handwriting which gives the lie to such thoughts. It was dated 9 May 1945. It is one of Harris's most treasured possessions:

My Dear Bert,

All official congratulations are going out in the name of the Air Council, but I would like to send you a personal note to tell you how deeply and sincerely grateful to you I feel for all you and your Command have done. It has been truly magnificent.

I also want to thank you for never letting the inevitable differences of opinion in a long war affect our personal relationships, and I would also like to say how tremendously I admired the way you refused to let ill-health affect your grip and mastery of your great 3 year battle.

For the support you have always given me, and for your tremendous personal contributions to the achievements of the R A F in this war I can never adequately thank you, but I do want to send you this short note with all best wishes for the future.

Yours ever,
Peter Portal.

23
Dresden—the truth

Harris was a man quick to give praise when and where it was due, and he did not confine his praise only to those within his Command. When occasion arose he was equally generous to those outside who had given their help. Barnes Wallis, the aircraft designer for Vickers, is an example of this. Wallis had developed the geodetic type of construction and, applying this principle, had designed the important Wellington range of twin-engined bombers upon which Bomber Command had largely had to rely in the first two and a half years of war. Later he had designed the dam-busting bomb, followed by the Tallboy 12,000-pound bombs which had been essential to the success of the Command's attacks against the E-boat and U-boat pens, the rocket sites, certain transportation targets, and the sinking of the *Tirpitz*. Yet, so far, he had received only meagre recognition in the form of the CBE. On 13 November 1944 Harris sought to put this right, and he wrote to Sir Archibald Sinclair, saying that he thought Wallis should be knighted. In his letter he drew attention to the immense personal endeavour by Wallis in bomb design, which was 'no part of his business'. Referring to his successes, including the 22,000-pound bomb known as 'Grand Slam' which was his latest contribution to the war effort, Harris said: 'All this work he had done as an amateur, and he has forced it through to brilliantly successful conclusions in the face of initial opposition and a great deal of unbelief.' Enumerating the bombing results achieved with Wallis's bombs, including the destruction of the Saumur tunnel, which was a key point during one stage of the invasion, he asserted that without Wallis's extraordinary ability, 'amounting to genius,' these successes could not have been accomplished. Therefore, he felt there was an outstanding case 'for an immediate recognition of his brilliant and devoted services, over and above the CBE which was awarded to him after the destruction of the Dams.'

Sir Archibald Sinclair replied on 15 November, agreeing that the country owed Wallis 'a great debt' However, the question of recommending him for a knighthood was 'for Cripps* and I have, therefore, passed on to him your remarks about Wallis.'

Barnes Wallis was not, in fact, knighted until 1968!

* Sir Stafford Cripps was then the Minister of Aircraft Production.

By coincidence, Harris heard at this time from both Sinclair and Portal that Cochrane, his A O C at No 5 Group, was to be promoted to Air Marshal and to take over command of Transport Command. Cochrane had been one of the benefactors of Wallis's bomb developments, his Group having been responsible for the dam-busting raid, many of the raids with 12,000-pounders against E-boat and U-boat pens and rocket sites, the sinking of *Tirpitz* and the demolition of the Saumur tunnel with 12,000-pounders. Cochrane was not, in fact, to leave his duties as A O C until 15 January 1945, but in a letter to Portal dated 18 November 1944, Harris gave another example of his generous praise where he believed it to be due, this time to one of his own commanders. The letter was on the subject of a replacement for Cochrane. This was to be Air Commodore H. A. Constantine, with Group Captain Elworthy as S A S O. Of Cochrane, Harris said:

> He is an absolutely outstanding Commander. His personal value to the war effort in Europe is such that I know you have pondered most seriously before deciding to take him away from Bomber Command at this stage of the war. In the past six months his Group has been twice as effective as any other Group in the Command, although I do not consider that by average or high standards my other Group Commanders are inefficient. Cochrane is a genuis ... As I have told you, I always hoped that Cochrane would replace me here.

With the bombing building up to a crescendo in the early months of 1945, until the unconditional surrender of Germany on 8 May, Cochrane was, indeed, a loss to Harris, but the excellent organisation he left behind him greatly alleviated this loss. Cochrane had developed No 5 Group's target-finding techniques to such a pitch of efficiency, together with the follow-up methods of his own Main Force aircraft, that the Group had achieved successes which from late 1943 to the end of the war were equalling the successes of the official Pathfinder Force under Bennett. No 5 Group's successes were not only confined to their highly effective raids against the German aircraft industry targets in France, which had been a part of the Pointblank programme, nor just against specialist targets like the *Tirpitz*. By 1945, the Group had become the leading force in the attacks on the larger oil targets deep in Germany—Leuna, Politz, Brux and others. It had demonstrated, unequivocally, the original theory of Harris, rejected by the Air Ministry in 1942, that the greatest pathfinding success would come from each Group using its indigenous squadrons to undertake complete operations, from pathfinding to follow-up Main Force bombing, much of this success stemming from Group pride. In No 5 Group the follow-up crews held their target-finding force crews in high regard; the target-finding crews were proud of the skill of the follow-up bomber crews whose part, successfully executed, was essential to total success. There was no attitude, which was unavoidable with a single Pathfinder Force, of 'we the Pathfinders' and 'the others', the others being crews from the other Groups who made up the Main Force. The same spirit of pride in Group efficiency which permeated No 5 Group, also existed in No 3 Group under Harrison when it became independent and operated with outstanding success with G-H. Indeed, it was No 3 Group that undertook the highly effective bombing of the small Ruhr synthetic oil and benzol plants almost entirely on its own, in most cases bombing blind, and frequently from above ten-tenths cloud. As Harris says: 'Without Harrijohn [his name for Harrison] and his Lancasters, we could never have succeeded in putting out of action those oil and chemical plants in the Ruhr, and areas adjacent to the Ruhr, as quickly and as effectively as we did.'

Although oil remained a priority throughout the months of 1945, new demands fell upon Bomber Command from the Army, and some of these were for the destruction of various cities, not just to achieve industrial damage, but to create chaos in those areas which the British, American and Russian armies were soon to overrun. These demands were to be the cause of a great deal of later criticism, in particular the bombing of Dresden, and it was Harris who was made the scapegoat for these decisions of the Chiefs of Staff and the commanders of the Allied armies—American, Russian and British—which were fully supported by their governments. For this reason, the events leading up to these demands, and the perfectly sound reasons for making them, must be studied unemotionally, and in depth.

In January 1945, the war was far from won; certainly not from the point of view of the Allies, for it was considered that once the battle began to rage inside the borders of the Fatherland itself, then the German resistance would be stubborn and the fighting would be fierce. Eisenhower, and the Russian commanders, realised this, and in the interests of minimising casualties in the final onslaught on Germany and in an endeavour to bring about a collapse of the German nation and its armed forces as speedily as possible, Supreme Headquarters, the British and American Chiefs of Staff, and the Russian Chiefs of Staff and their commanding generals began to discuss actively the various means that could be used to achieve a speedy victory, including the use of air power. And it was air power, they decided, that was the key to a swift decisive victory against Germany with minimal Allied losses. The trouble was, however, that there were conflicting views as to how it could be best applied. Spaatz, with bitter memories of how his American bombers had suffered in daylight raids at the hands of the German Air Force in 1943, was now concerned at the appearance of the German jet-engined fighter, the Messerschmitt 262, and wanted the GAF and, in particular, its jet production, training and operational establishments, to become primary objects for attack. The British Navy was concerned about the new Type XXI U-boats, which were speedier under water than their predecessors and were equipped with the ingenious Schnorkel breathing device that enabled them to stay below the surface of the water for much longer periods than previously, and permitted them to charge their batteries whilst submerged. They wanted priority of attack on the production facilities of these U-boats. In fact, the new threat to shipping by the XXIs never materialised. This was due to area bombing by

Bomber Command and precision attacks by the US Eighth and Fifteenth Air Forces, all of which did serious damage to factories making vital components for these U-boats. It was also due to bombing attacks on communication centres and canals which disrupted supplies of pre-fabricated sections to the shipyards for assembly, and to Bomber Command's attacks on these shipyards. Speer, in *Inside the Third Reich*, states: 'We would have been able to keep our promise of delivering forty boats a month by early in 1945, however badly the war was going otherwise, if air raids had not destroyed a third of the submarines at the dockyards.' Finally, Bomber Command's extensive sea mining operations in the Baltic, Kiel Canal and North Sea coastal areas of Germany prevented those U-boats which were completed from becoming operational, except in limited numbers. An indirect consequence of the mining was expressed by the German admiral responsible for training crews, who complained that 'Without trained crews there can be no U-boat offensive, but without a training area free of constantly laid and relaid airborne mines there can be no trained crews.'

In addition to the demands of Spaatz and the Royal Navy, there were others to add to the conflict of views. Portal did not believe that a change in priority in favour of attacks on German Air Force or U-boat targets was justified, unless it was thought that the war would continue until the end of 1945. He himself held the view that victory could be achieved by May, provided the new Russian land offensive was successful, and it was his opinion that priority of attack on oil and communications offered the best chance of ensuring the Russian success. At the same time, he considered that such priorities would offer the greatest assistance to the advancing British and American Armies. If oil and petroleum supplies were denied to Germany's Air Force and mechanised forces, and if military supplies could not be delivered to the fronts, then, he argued, the collapse must inevitably be swift. Bottomley, his DCAS, influenced by his conversations with Spaatz, put the arguments for priority on the German Air Force to Portal. In turn, on 14 January 1945, he also advised Spaatz of Portal's views, but Spaatz largely ignored them and directed his strategic forces to concentrate on the production facilities of the new jet aircraft. Bottomley, who tended to waver from one idea to another, followed Portal's line of thinking, but he now added the idea of a gigantic attack on Berlin, which in the autumn of 1944 had been proposed under the code name of 'Thunderclap', as a means of shattering German morale. At that time 'Thunderclap' had been rejected by Portal because he believed it would only be effective if it was delivered at the crucial moment of an impending collapse of Germany. But who was to judge when this moment had arrived? Bottomley, stimulated by Bufton, his Director of Bomber Operations, who was agile at seeking out war-winning *coups de grâce*, felt that the Russian advances on the Eastern Front might well present that crucial moment. This view was supported by a report dated 25 January 1945, by the Joint Intelligence Committee. It was the opinion of this committee that the devastation of Berlin at a time of a major

Russian advance would not of itself result in the collapse of Germany. Considered in relation to the entire Eastern Front, however, the members believed that a massive flow of refugees from Berlin, coinciding with civilians fleeing westwards in front of the advancing Russian armies, would be bound, to quote from the report, 'to create great confusion, interfere with the orderly movement of troops to the front, and hamper the German military and administrative machine.' An attack on Berlin by the British and American strategic bomber forces dropping some 25,000 tons of bombs over a period of four days and four nights would, the committee concluded, 'materially assist the Russians in the all important battle now raging on the Eastern Front and would justify temporary diversion from attacks against communications or indeed from any targets other than oil plants or tank factories.'

On 26 January Bottomley reported to Portal that he had consulted with Harris on the telephone on the subject of this report. Churchill also now entered the picture. On the night of 25 January, the Prime Minister discussed with Sir Archibald Sinclair, the Secretary of State for Air, the plans for using the Royal Air Force at this critical stage of the war. In particular he wanted to know what plans there were for 'basting the Germans in their retreat from Breslau'. With the forthcoming Crimean Conference at Yalta, timed to begin on 4 February, when Churchill with his Chiefs of Staff would be meeting Stalin and Roosevelt and their Chiefs of Staff, the Prime Minister wanted to know how he could demonstrate to the Russians the contribution that the British strategic air forces, and those of the US, could make to the Russian campaign in the east. On 26 January, Sinclair consulted with Portal, who said that oil should continue to have absolute priority, but after oil he agreed that attacks in support of the Russian advances should have the next priority, and in certain circumstances should have the first. These views were in accordance with the minute he had written to Bottomley in answer to his minute of 26 January, on the subject of the report of the Joint Intelligence Committee and his conversation with Harris. In it Portal expressed the view that after oil and subject to the need to deal with the jet-engine factories and submarine yards:

> We should use available effort in one big attack on Berlin and attacks on Dresden, Leipzig, Chemnitz, or any other cities where a severe blitz will not only cause confusion in the evacuation from the East but will also hamper the movement of troops from the West.

Like Berlin, Dresden, Leipzig and Chemnitz were focal points in the German system of communications behind the Eastern Front and, therefore, confusion which interfered with the orderly movement of German troops in these areas could be just as invaluable to the Russians as in the case of Berlin. But in his minute to Bottomley, Portal emphasised that it would be necessary to obtain the approval not only of Spaatz but of Tedder, as Deputy Supreme Commander of the Allied Forces in Europe, to these proposals. Moreover, he made it clear that the proposals would have to be submitted to the Chiefs of Staff.

On the same day as he consulted with Portal, Sir Archibald Sinclair answered Churchill's query of the night before. In his minute to Churchill the important paragraphs were the last two. After referring to the fact that Churchill had asked him the previous night about plans for harrying the German retreat from Breslau, he said that the retreating German forces were a proper target for Tactical Air Forces rather than for heavy bomber forces bombing from altitude. Then he wrote:

> I feel strongly that the best use of our heavy bombers at the present time lies in maintaining the attack upon German oil plants whenever weather permits. The benefits of these attacks are felt equally by the Russians and by ourselves and nothing should be allowed to interfere with them. There may, however, be occasions when the weather is unsuitable for attacks on the comparatively small targets presented by the oil plants but yet would permit area attacks on Eastern Germany. These opportunities might be used to exploit the present situation by the bombing of Berlin and other large cities in Eastern Germany such as Leipzig, Dresden and Chemnitz, which are not only administrative centres controlling the military and civilian movements but are also the main communications centres through which the bulk of the traffic moves.
>
> To achieve results of real value, a series of attacks would probably be required, and weather conditions at this time of year would certainly prevent these being delivered in quick succession. The possibility of these attacks being delivered on the scale necessary to have a critical effect on the situation in Eastern Germany is now under examination.

Churchill clearly was not satisfied with the urgency being given to the matter of support for the Russians by bombing eastern German towns lying in the path of the Russian advances. In a most peremptory minute to Sir Archibald Sinclair, dated 26 January 1945, he replied:

> I did not ask you last night about plans for harrying the German retreat from Breslau. On the contrary, I asked whether Berlin, and no doubt other large cities in East Germany, should not now be considered especially attractive targets. I am glad that this is 'under examination'. Pray report to me tomorrow what is going to be done.

When Bottomley was apprised of Churchill's minute to Sinclair he immediately wrote to Harris on the subject of attacks against targets in Eastern Germany in support of the Russian offensive. His letter, dated 27 January, was addressed to the Commander-in-Chief, Bomber Command. It read:

> Sir,
> I am directed to refer to a telephone conversation of the 26th January, 1945, between the Air Officer Commanding-in-Chief and the Deputy

Chief of the Air Staff in which the subject of the attack of the industrial areas of Berlin, Dresden, Chemnitz and Leipzig was discussed, in particular reference to the critical situation which confronts the enemy in the Eastern battle zone.

Attached for your personal information and return in due course, is a copy of a J I C Paper dated 25th January, 1945.* This paper has not yet been considered by the Chiefs of Staff. The opinion of the Chief of the Air Staff, however, is that it would not be right to attempt attacks on Berlin on the 'Thunderclap' scale in the near future. He considers that it is very doubtful whether such an attack even if done on the heaviest scale with consequent heavy losses would be decisive. He agrees, however, that subject to the overriding claims of oil and the other approved target systems within the current directive, we should use available effort in one big attack on Berlin and related attacks on Dresden, Leipzig, Chemnitz or any other cities where a severe blitz will not only cause confusion in the evacuation from the East but will also hamper the movement of troops from the West.

I am therefore to request that subject to the qualifications stated above, and as soon as moon and weather conditions allow, you will undertake such attacks with the particular object of exploiting the confused conditions which are likely to exist in the above mentioned cities during the successful Russian advance.

N. H. Bottomley.

On the same day as this formal instruction was sent to Harris, Sir Archibald Sinclair replied to the Prime Minister's minute as follows:

Your minute M.115/5. The Air Staff have now arranged that subject to the overriding claims of attacks on enemy oil production and other approved target systems within the current directive, available effort should be directed against Berlin, Dresden, Chemnitz and Leipzig or against other cities where severe bombing would not only destroy communications vital to the evacuation from the East but would also hamper the movement of troops from the West.

The use of the night bomber force offers the best prospects of destroying these industrial cities without detracting from our offensive on oil targets, which is now in a critical phase. The Air Officer Commanding-in-Chief, Bomber Command, has undertaken to attempt this task as soon as the present moon has waned and favourable weather conditions allow. This is unlikely to be before about 4th February.

Churchill acknowledged receipt of this minute without comment on 28 January, the day before he flew to Malta from Northolt aerodrome for the preliminary meeting with Roosevelt and the British and American Chiefs of

---

* This is the Joint Intelligence Committee's report referred to earlier.

Staff immediately prior to the meeting with Stalin and the Russian Chiefs of Staff at Yalta.

Also on 28 January, Portal and Bottomley discussed the Berlin–Dresden–Chemnitz–Leipzig plan with Spaatz, who was on a visit to England that day; it was agreed that Spaatz and Bottomley should immediately consider the future priorities with Tedder and advise Portal of their findings by signal to Malta, where he would be having preliminary meetings with his British and American colleagues, prior to Yalta, during the next few days. On 31 January, following his meeting with Spaatz and Tedder, Bottomley despatched the following message to Portal in Malta:

> You will wish to know that following your talk with Spaatz and myself and as a result of the discussions with Tedder, we have arrived at following order of priorities for Strategic Air Forces to meet the present situation. You know, however, that these priorities will be primarily determined by weather conditions:
>
> (A) Main Synthetic Oil Plants continue to hold first priority for all Strategic Air Forces. They will be attacked by day whenever visual conditions are anticipated.
>
> (B) Next in order of priority for Air Forces operating in United Kingdom is attack of Berlin, Leipzig, Dresden and associated cities where heavy attack will cause great confusion in civilian evacuation from the East and hamper movement of reinforcements from other fronts. Spaatz has already ordered day attacks to be made on Berlin whenever weather conditions permit. You know the intentions of Bomber Command.
>
> (C) Next in order of priority is attack of communications, particularly as affecting the assembly, entrainment and movement of major re-inforcements to the East and as affecting current and impending land operations. For Strategic Air Forces in United Kingdom attacks are now being directed particularly against targets in Ruhr–Cologne–Kassel. 15th Air Force has been directed to pay particular attention to any signs of transfers of forces and will attack appropriate communication centres as necessary.
>
> (D) Attack of Jet targets and communications in South Germany.
>
> Marginal effort will be directed on tank factories and submarine yards. Marginal effort on tank factories is likely to be substantial since these constitute convenient tactical 'filler' targets in areas of priority oil targets.
>
> In addition, the priority task of the Strategic Day Fighters after the escort of bombers is the attack of rail movement of the main routes of reinforcement to the East.
>
> In view of the rapid Russian advance, particularly towards Berlin, the Russians may wish to know our intentions and plans for attack of targets in Eastern Germany. The Combined Chiefs of Staff will doubtless be considering this situation and we assume will inform Spaatz and myself

as to any limitations on the operations already ordered for USSTAF and Bomber Command.

Spaatz asks that Kuter* be informed of this signal.

On 1 February 1945, the Vice-Chief of the Air Staff, Air Marshal Sir Douglas Evill, who was acting as Chief of the Air Staff in Portal's absence, issued an Air Staff Note on 'Strategic Bombing in Relation to the Present Russian Offensive', which was discussed at a meeting of the Chiefs of Staff Committee on the same day. The representatives at this committee meeting were, in fact, the Vice-Chiefs of Staff, as the Chiefs were all attending the Malta and Yalta Conferences. The Note referred to the discussions between the Commanding General, US Strategic Air Forces in Europe, General Spaatz, the Deputy Supreme Allied Commander, Air Chief Marshal Sir Arthur Tedder, and the Deputy Chief of the Air Staff, Air Marshal Sir Norman Bottomley, and it then detailed the new priorities for bombing with special reference to the Russian offensive. Under a paragraph headed 'Evacuation Areas' it read:

> Evacuees from German and German-Occupied Provinces to the East of Berlin are streaming westward through Berlin itself and through Leipzig, Dresden and other cities in the East of Germany. The administrative problems involved in receiving the refugees and redistributing them are likely to be immense. The strain on the administration and upon communications must be considerably increased by the need for handling military reinforcements on their way to the Eastern Front. A series of heavy attacks by day and night upon these administrative and control centres is likely to create considerable delays in the deployment of troops at the Front, and may well result in establishing a state of chaos in some or all of these centres. It is for these reasons that instructions have been issued for heavy scale attacks to be delivered on these centres at the earliest possible moment, in priority immediately after that of the important oil producers. The justification for the continuance of such attacks would be largely reduced if the enemy succeeded in stabilising his Eastern Front. Successful attacks of this nature delivered at once, however, may well prevent him from achieving this aim.

On 2 February, a signal on 'Strategic Bombing' was sent to the Chiefs of Staff at Malta by the Vice-Chiefs of Staff. It listed the priorities as oil first; communications second, laying emphasis upon 'focal points of communication in the evacuation areas behind the Eastern Front, namely Berlin, Leipzig, Dresden and Chemnitz, or similar areas'; tank factories third; jet fighter production fourth; and U-boat construction and assembly fifth. This signal went out under the code name 'Fleece 75'.

---

* General Kuter was attending the Malta and Yalta Conferences in place of his Chief, General H. H. Arnold, who was suffering from illness at the time.

On the 4th, at a plenary session with the Russians at Yalta, the Chiefs of Staff of the USA, Russia and Britain discussed the coordination of Allied offensive operations. The Russian land offensive had already reached the River Oder and the British and American Armies were fast approaching the Rhine. Soon the armies from the west and from the east would rapidly approach each other and coordination was essential, especially in connection with the policy of strategic bombing. At this plenary session General Antonov, the Deputy Chief of Staff of the Red Army, submitted a note on the present Soviet offensive which included several suggestions as to how the Western Allies might contribute to its success. One way was, he said, by preventing the Germans from moving troops from the Western to the Eastern Front, and he believed this could best be done by strategic bombing. He asked for air attacks against communications and suggested, in particular, that the Western Allied bombers should 'paralyse the centres: Berlin and Leipzig'. There arose a difficulty, however, for General Antonov also wanted to establish a bombline at this stage, which would run from Stettin to Berlin to Dresden to Zagreb. The idea of the bombline was to preclude the danger of accidental bombing attacks by the Strategic Air Forces on Russian troops. Portal felt this bombline was too far to the west as at that date, and would deny attacks by the British and American bombers on certain important targets to the east of that line, although the Russians made it clear that the towns through which their proposed bombline ran should be allotted to the western Air Forces for attack.

As a result of the Antonov bombline request, Portal immediately signalled Bottomley. The message was dated 5 February and it asked him to send, as a matter of urgency, a few good objectives east of the bombline against which it was desirable that attacks were maintained until they became involved in the tactical situation on land.

Bottomley replied the same day as follows:

Following are good objectives against which it is important we maintain attacks until tactical situation on land prevents.

A. *Oil Targets*

Poelitz. Main producer of high octane and mainstay of aviation fuel supply for G.A.F.

Ruhland. Holding second priority among the four major active synthetic plants.

Pardubice, Kralupy, Kolin. Being three crude refineries in Prague area with priorities 17, 18 and 21 respectively.

Moosbirbaum. Vienna-Lobau. Vienna-Schwechat. Vienna-Floridsdorf. Vienna-Kagran. Kornauburg. Vienna-Vosendorf. Being seven refineries in Vienna area holding priorities between 8 and 20 on current list.

B. *Transportation and Industrial Areas.*

Berlin. Dresden.

C. *Tank and Self-Propelled Gun Factories.*
   St. Valentin (East of Linz). Prague-Liben. Berlin-Marienfeld.
D. *Jet Engine Factories.*
   Kakovice. Jinonice and Koniginhof—being three engine component and assembly plants for Jumo 004 jet unit.

In a signal dated 6 February 1945, Portal answered 'Fleece 75', the message from the Vice-Chiefs of Staff, which detailed the proposed priorities for attack by the Strategic Bomber Forces. These were, in fact, the same as those contained in Bottomley's signal quoted above. Portal's message read:

For DCAS from CAS
   The recommendations on strategic bombing priorities contained in Fleece number 75 have been considered by the Chiefs of Staff and approved. Please take these proposals up immediately with Spaatz and if he is in agreement issue a revised directive. The new priorities must of course be kept under constant review during the present critical phase of operations.

But Harris had already received his revised directive from Bottomley in the form of an official letter dated 27 January 1945! This letter is reproduced earlier in this chapter. What is quite clear is that the selection of Berlin, Dresden, Leipzig and Chemnitz as priority targets for Bomber Command and the US Strategic Air Forces was not a personal decision taken by Harris. Indeed, he had not the power to make such decisions. The bombing of these targets, in support of the Russian offensive against the German Eastern Front, was the decision of the combined US, Russian and British Chiefs of Staff fully supported by Churchill, Roosevelt and Stalin. Later, towards the end of March, this decision received further support from Eisenhower, who made known to Stalin and Churchill his intention, after isolating the Ruhr, of making his main thrust from the west along the axis Erfurt-Leipzig-Dresden, thereby joining hands with the Russians and cutting the German forces in two, and making a secondary advance through Regensburg to Linz, also to join up with the Russians, with the intention of preventing, as Eisenhower put it, 'the consolidation of German resistance in the redoubt in Southern Germany.' In this Eisenhower was fully supported by General Marshall.
   Once more the bomber forces were being asked to support the Allied armies in order to achieve victory as swiftly as possible and with a minimum of Allied losses. The bomber forces were to be the long-range artillery, as they had been in the invasion of Normandy, but in this case the targets to be attacked were German towns and not French, Belgian and Dutch towns, which was more to Harris's liking. Unquestionably, the selection of these targets for attack by the Joint Chiefs of Staff and the three heads of government was fully justified by the military situation at that time. The choice lay between the preservation of Allied lives or German lives—and in

these circumstances the decision had to be to preserve Allied lives at the expense of those of the enemy.

The industrial area of Dresden had, in fact, already been bombed by a small force of thirty bombers of the US Eighth Bomber Command on 4 October 1944. Then, on 16 January 1945, the marshalling yards at Dresden were attacked by 133 bombers of the US Eighth Bomber Command. However, the damage to the town was minimal and it effectively remained intact.

Although Harris received his instructions to bomb Dresden, Leipzig and Chemnitz from Bottomley on 27 January, he did not in fact attack Dresden until the night of 13/14 February 1945, and Chemnitz until the night of 14/15 February. Even then he sought, and received, confirmation from Bottomley by telephone that it was in order to attack. In the case of Dresden, 786 heavy bombers out of 804 despatched attacked the target in a split raid dropping 2,647·4 tons of bombs. There was cloud over the target for the first half of the attack, but this cleared for a distance of about ten miles from the target for the second part of the attack. Photographs taken on the morning of the 15th were of poor quality and covered only part of the city on both banks of the River Elbe. A vast cloud of smoke from numerous fires still burning in the city obscured much of the area, but what was visible indicated that there was considerable devastation. This was supported by the German and neutral press with comment to the effect that tremendous damage had been inflicted upon the town. However, the full extent of the damage arising from this night bombing raid was never fully determinable because the US Eighth Bomber Command attacked Dresden with 316 bombers on the morning of 14 February, immediately following Bomber Command's night attack. Then again, on 15 February, they mounted another operation against the city with 211 bombers. The final raid of this series was made by the US Eighth Bomber Command on 2 March with 406 bombers. However, a further raid was made on the marshalling yards of Dresden on 17 April 1945, by 572 bombers of the US Eighth Bomber Command.

The raid on Chemnitz on the night of 14/15 February was undertaken by 663 heavy bombers out of 717 despatched. They dropped 2,108·6 tons of bombs. It was attacked again on the night of 5/6 March by 672 aircraft out of 714 despatched, dropping 1,978·7 tons of bombs. Photographs taken after this second raid indicated major devastation of the town. In fact, in the case of both Dresden and Chemnitz, the bombing by RAF Bomber Command and the US Eighth Bomber Command created just what had been demanded by the Joint Chiefs of Staff, Eisenhower and the Russians—devastation and utter confusion to these German communications and military administrative centres lying in front of the advancing Russian and American armies.

Berlin, which had also been named for attack in support of the Russian advance, was assaulted by the US Eighth Bomber Command on 26 February with a force of more than 1,000 bombers.

Bomber Command undertook no more major raids against Berlin at this time, but from the night of 20/21 February until the night of 24/25 March it attacked Berlin with substantial forces of Mosquito aircraft on thirty-six consecutive nights, dropping many 4,000-pound bombs. Colonel-Divisionnaire* Peter Burckhardt of the Swiss Army, who was the Swiss Military and Air Attaché in Berlin from 1943 until the end of the war in 1945, described these raids to the author as even more demoralising than the great raids of November 1943 to March 1944, because of their frequency which denied all hope of sleep, night after night.

The support of the Eastern Front must not be allowed, however, to assume importance out of proportion to the rest of the great land offensives of 1945, and the colossal contribution to the success of these land offensives made by RAF Bomber Command and the US Strategic Air Forces in Europe. From 1 January to 30 April 1945, Bomber Command alone flew 54,742 sorties, dropping 181,403 tons of bombs on oil targets and targets in support of the Allied armies. In February it dropped 45,889 tons and in March 67,637 tons. The tonnage on Dresden of 2,647·4 tons and on Chemnitz, in two raids, of 4,087·3 tons, represents a relatively small percentage of the total tonnage dropped by Bomber Command in February and March. Even with the tonnage dropped by the US Eighth Bomber Command in their three raids on Dresden, the figure would still be relatively low, for the bomb load of 1,505 sorties of Eighth Bomber Command (three attacks in February and March, and one in April: 316 aircraft, 211 aircraft, 406 and 572 aircraft) was less than 3,000 tons. Such attacks as those on Essen by RAF Bomber Command on 11 March 1945, when 1,053 aircraft attacked dropping 4,783·2 tons of bombs, and on Dortmund on 12 March, when 1,079 aircraft attacked dropping 4,899·3 tons, help to bring the Dresden attack into perspective. Indeed, the battering delivered against the Ruhr and Rhine towns and against other parts of Western Germany in support of the British and American advances was infinitely greater than that meted out to the Southern Redoubt and the Eastern Front.

But the whole question of the Allied bombing policy suddenly came under question, late in March, by Churchill, of all people. This was surprising, for up to this point it was he who had been the greatest protagonist of destroying Germany city by city and who, as late as January 1945, had been pressing for plans to attack targets on the Eastern Front in support of the Russians. In a most astonishing minute to General Ismay, dated 28 March and marked for the Chiefs of Staff Committee, he wrote:

It seems to me that the moment has come when the question of bombing of German cities simply for the sake of increasing the terror, though under other pretexts, should be reviewed. Otherwise we shall

* Equivalent to a Lieutenant-General. General Burckhardt is now the Director of Oerlikon-Bührle Holding SA.

come into control of an utterly ruined land. We shall not, for instance, be able to get housing materials out of Germany for our own needs because some temporary provision would have to be made for the Germans themselves. The destruction of Dresden remains a serious query against the conduct of Allied bombing. I am of the opinion that military objectives must henceforward be more strictly studied in our own interests rather than that of the enemy.

The Foreign Secretary has spoken to me on this subject, and I feel the need for more precise concentration upon military objectives, such as oil and communications behind the immediate battle-zone, rather than on mere acts of terror and wanton destruction, however impressive.

A copy of this minute was also marked for Portal's attention as Chief of the Air Staff. On receipt of it, Portal immediately instructed Bottomley to ask for Harris's comments as a matter of urgency. In a personal letter dated 28 March 1945, Bottomley wrote:

Dear C-in-C.

At the instigation of the Prime Minister we have just been asked to consider whether the time has not come when the question of bombing of German cities 'simply for the sake of increasing the terror, though under other pretexts' should not be reviewed. One of the reasons given is that we shall not for instance be able to get housing material out of Germany for our own needs because some temporary provision would ultimately have to be made for the Germans themselves.

The note comments on the destruction of Dresden as a serious query against the conduct of Allied bombing, and expresses the opinion that military objectives must henceforward be more strictly studied in our own interests rather than that of the enemy. Finally, the note states that there is need for more precise concentration upon military objectives, such as oil and communications behind the immediate battle-zone, rather than on mere acts of terror and wanton destruction.

I am sure you will agree that this note misinterprets the purpose of our attacks on industrial areas in the past, and appears to ignore the aim given by the Combined Chiefs of Staff in their directives which have been blessed by the Heads of Governments. As you know, the overall mission of the Strategic Air Forces in Europe has been given as 'the progressive destruction and dislocation of the German military, industrial and economic systems, and the direct support of land and naval forces.' Our attacks on industrial areas have been ordered with this aim in view. There has never been any instruction issued which gives any foundation to an allegation that German cities have been attacked simply for the sake of increasing terror.

From time to time in the past you have commented on the tremendous contribution which the destruction of German industrial areas has made towards the crippling of the enemy's war economy. There may now be sound political reasons for abandoning our attacks on German cities, but these reasons should be balanced against the contributions which we are making thereby in crippling German war economy and in hastening the military defeat of the enemy.

The CAS feels that before we submit an official reply to the note you should be given an opportunity of commenting on the opinions described above. He would be glad to have your comments both on the allegations which are made as to our efforts in the past, and as to the wisdom of the proposal for discontinuing these attacks and, instead, confining ourselves to what is described as 'more precise concentration upon military objectives such as oil and communications behind the immediate battle-zone'.

Since this subject will be considered early next week by the COS and probably the Defence Committee, the CAS would be glad if we could have your views as early as possible.

Yours sincerely,
Norman Bottomley
PS. Will you please keep this personal at the moment.

Harris's reply was prompt and pungent. He was infuriated by the allegations. In a personal letter dated 29 March, he wrote:

Dear Norman,
It is difficult to answer indictments of which the terms are not fully revealed and for this reason I cannot deal as thoroughly as I should like to with the points raised in your CMS. 608/DCAS of March 28th. I take it, however, that it is unnecessary for me to make any comment on the passages which you quote and which, without the context, are abusive in effect, though doubtless not in intention.

To suggest that we have bombed German cities 'simply for the sake of increasing the terror though under other pretexts' and to speak of our offensive as including 'mere acts of terror and wanton destruction' is an insult both to the bombing policy of the Air Ministry and to the manner in which that policy has been executed by Bomber Command. This sort of thing if it deserves an answer will certainly receive none from me, after three years of implementing official policy.

As regards the specific points raised in your letter, namely the adverse economic effects on ourselves by increasing yet further the material havoc in Germany and the destruction of Dresden in particular the answer is surely very simple. (The feeling, such as there is, over Dresden could be easily explained by any psychiatrist. It is connected with German bands and Dresden shepherdesses. Actually Dresden was a mass of munition works, an intact government centre, and a key transportation point to the East. It is now none of those things.) It is already demonstrated in the liberated countries that what really makes any sort of recovery almost impossible is less the destruction of buildings than the complete dislocation of transportation. If, therefore, this objection is to be taken seriously I suggest that the transportation plan rather than the strategic bombing of cities is what needs to be reconsidered, as I understand it has been, and for precisely that reason. You will remember that Dresden was recommended by the Targets Committee as a transportation target as well as on other grounds.

I do not, however, stress this point since I assume that what is really at issue is (a) whether our strategic bombing policy up to date has been justified (b) whether the time has now come to discontinue this policy. I will therefore confine myself to these questions.

As regards (a) I have on previous occasions discussed this matter very fully in official correspondence with the Air Ministry and to avoid repetition I refer you to the following correspondence ...

I have always held and still maintain that my Directive, which you quote, the progressive destruction and dislocation of the German military, industrial and economic systems, could be carried out only by the elimination of German industrial cities and not merely by attacks on individual factories however important these might be in themselves. This view was also officially confirmed by the Air Ministry in the above correspondence. The overwhelming evidence which is now available to support it makes it quite superfluous for me to argue at length that the destruction of those cities has fatally weakened the German war effort and is now enabling Allied soldiers to advance into the heart of Germany with negligible casualties. Hence the only question which I have to answer is this: would confining ourselves to more precise concentration upon military objectives such as oil and communications behind the immediate battle zone tend to shorten the war more than persistence in attacks on cities. The answer appears to me to be obvious; but even if it is not, I must point out as I have frequently done before that we have by no means always a free choice in this matter. Weather conditions frequently constrain me to decide between attacking cities and not attacking at all. When this happens it is surely evident that it is expedient to attack the cities. I can only find, pinpoint and hit small isolated targets with a small part of my force at a time, and I have not enough fighter escort to do more than two such small attacks daily.

I have thus disposed of point (a). We have never gone in for terror bombing and the attacks which we have made in accordance with my Directive have in fact produced the strategic consequences for which they were designed and from which the Armies now profit.

Point (b) is rather difficult to follow. It can hardly mean that attacks on cities no longer produce dislocation in the German war effort. Quite the contrary is the case. The nearer Germany is to collapse the less capable she is of re-organising to meet disasters of this kind and we ought logically to make a special effort to eliminate the few cities which still remain more or less serviceable.

I therefore assume that the view under consideration is something like this: no doubt in the past we were justified in attacking German cities. But to do so was always repugnant and now that the Germans are beaten anyway we can properly abstain from proceeding with these attacks. This is a doctrine to which I could never subscribe. Attacks on cities like any other act of war are intolerable unless they are strategically justified. But they are strategically justified in so far as they tend to shorten the war and so preserve the lives of Allied soldiers. To my mind we have absolutely no right to give them up unless it is certain that they will not have this effect. I do not personally regard the whole of the remaining cities of Germany as worth the bones of one British Grenadier.

It therefore seems to me that there is one and only one valid argument on which a case for giving up strategic bombing could be based, namely that it has already completed its task and that nothing now remains for the Armies to do except to occupy Germany against unorganised resistance. If this is what is meant I shall no doubt be informed of it. It does not however appear to be the view of the Supreme Commander. Until it is, I submit that the strategic bombing of German cities must go on.

Some final points. As you know Transportation targets are now largely off. Oil has had, and is getting, all we can practically give it in consideration of weather and escort factors. We answer every army support call and, as Monty tells us, in a decisive manner. We have asked for more but there aren't any. All HE [high explosive] is seriously limited in supply. Incendiaries are not. All these factors must therefore also be considered, and the inevitable answer is that either we continue as in the past or we very largely stand down altogether. The last alternative would certainly be welcome. I take little delight in the work and none whatever in risking my crews avoidably.

Japan remains. Are we going to bomb their cities flat—as in Germany—and give the Armies a walk over—as in France and Germany—or are we going to bomb only their outlying factories, largely underground by the time we get going, and subsequently invade at the cost of 3 to 6 million casualties? We should be careful of precedents.

Yours sincerely,
A. T. Harris

At the eighty-third meeting of the Chiefs of Staff Committee, held on 30 March, the Prime Minister withdrew his minute as a result of strong representations by Portal, backed by the letter from Harris. On 1 April 1945, Churchill substituted the following minute:

General Ismay for COS Committee CAS

It seems to me that the moment has come when the question of the so called 'area bombing' of German cities should be reviewed from the point of view of our own interests. If we come into control of an entirely ruined land, there will be a great shortage of accommodation for ourselves and our Allies: and we shall be unable to get housing materials out of Germany for our own needs because some temporary provision would have to be made for the Germans themselves. We must see to it that our attacks do not do more harm to ourselves in the long run than they do to the enemy's immediate war effort. Pray let me have your views.

Resulting from Churchill's revised minute Portal prepared a 'Note by the Air Staff' which he submitted to the Chiefs of Staff Committee on 4 April; in view of its important contents, it is reproduced in full:

COS (45) 238 (O)
4th April, 1945

WAR CABINET
CHIEFS OF STAFF COMMITTEE

AREA BOMBING
(Reference: COS (45) 233 (O))
Note by the Air Staff

The primary object of the Combined Bomber Offensive laid down in the Casablanca directive of the 21st January, 1943, was
'the progressive destruction and dislocation of the German military, industrial and economic systems and the undermining of the morale of the German people to a point where their capacity for armed resistance is fatally weakened.'

The current Combined Chiefs of Staff directive OCTAGON 29 dated 16th September, 1944, states the primary object to be
'the progressive destruction and dislocation of the German military, industrial and economic systems and the direct support of land and naval forces.'

2. In implementing these and other directives which have been issued from time to time, every effort has been made to secure the maximum impact of the heavy bomber forces against the German war effort. It is only in recent months that the development of night bombing technique has enabled us successfully to undertake the night attack of particular industrial plants or other relatively small objectives. By day, the successful bombing of these objectives requires clear skies over the target, conditions which occur on few occasions in the year. For these and other reasons, it has been an essential part of our policy, in order to extract from our bomber forces the maximum continuity and weight of attack of which they were capable, to attack important concentrations of German war industry by means of area attack.

3. The objects of attacking industrial areas have been:

(a) To destroy important industrial plants and to disorganise essential services and labour.

(b) To disrupt communications vital to the maintenance of order and the smooth and efficient working of the military supply organisation to the areas immediately behind the enemy's fighting fronts.

(c) To disorganise and disrupt the Nazi administration.

(d) To force the enemy to employ in defence, repair and re-habilitation measures, resources and manpower which would otherwise be used both in war production and in strengthening the offensive power of his armed forces.

4. In spite of recent advances in our ability to make precise attacks at night, the operational considerations which have in the past necessitated area attacks still exist. Nevertheless, it is recognised that at this advanced stage of the war no great or immediate additional advantage can be expected from the attack of the remaining industrial centres of Germany, because it is improbable that the full effects of further area attacks upon the enemy's war industries will have time to mature before hostilities cease. Moreover, the number of targets suitable for area bombing is now much reduced as a result of our past attacks and the rapid advance of the Allied Armies. For these reasons, and since allied superiority in military resources is already overwhelming, the effort of the Strategical air forces is being directed primarily to secure the most immediate effect upon the enemy's ability to resist the Allies' advance into Germany. This is being achieved by draining the enemy's oil resources to the lowest possible level, by disrupting communications vital to the enemy's resistance and by affording direct support to the armies as necessary.

5. There may still be occasions, however, when the disintegration of enemy resistance can best be brought about through the medium of area bombing. These may arise in the following circumstances.

(a) If resistance should stiffen on the Western Front or fail to disintegrate on the Eastern Front, attacks on built-up areas immediately behind the fronts holding reserves and maintenance organisations, and engaged in handling military supplies, may be as effective in the preparation for an assault as they have proved in the past. Such situations may occur when the Russians approach nearer Berlin and the industrial areas of Saxony, or when we advance into Central Germany from the West.

(b) It may become a military requirement to attack the com-munication systems of Central and Southern Germany, over which the enemy may attempt to move forces between the two fronts, or to withdraw to the redoubt in Southern Germany. The time factor may not always allow us to await precise bombing conditions and area bombing will then prove a necessity.

(c) There is strong evidence that the German High Command, its attendant staffs and Government Departments and the Party Organisation are to be established in a number of Thuringian towns for the purpose of directing continued resistance. The destruction of these towns by means of area attack may then become a military requirement.

(d) The German Navy has been forced by territorial losses to withdraw from the Eastern Baltic and to concentrate in the Western Baltic and North Sea ports, especially at Kiel. Here some eighty commissioned U-boats and a large number of enemy naval vessels are congregated. The attack of this target which is already ordered may well involve widespread devastation in the town of Kiel with results which will approximate to those of an area attack.

6. We appreciate the importance of refraining from the unnecessary destruction of towns and facilities which will be needed by our own troops or for Allied reconstruction purposes. If, however, we were to restrict our bomber forces to visual precision attack we should certainly reduce the contribution which they can make towards hastening the collapse of the enemy. It is considered that area attacks are still justified strategically, insofar as they are calculated to assist in the advance of the Allied Armies into Germany or in shortening the period of the war. Any incidental further destruction of German cities which is likely to be involved in the time remaining will certainly be small in comparison with that already accomplished.

CONCLUSIONS

7. It is concluded that:
  (a) Area bombing designed solely with the object of destroying or disorganising industrial areas should be discontinued;
  (b) There should be no alteration to the current bombing directive such as would exclude area bombing;
  (c) Area attacks may prove necessary against those targets, the destruction of which is calculated best to assist the advance of the Allied Armies into Germany or to have the most immediate effect upon the enemy's ability to continue armed resistance;
  (d) Any ultimate political or economic disadvantages of area bombing necessitated by these operations should be accepted.

C. Portal

Thus Portal and Harris stood together on this great issue of the bombing policy. But the seeds of criticism of this policy had now been sown, and were to flourish in the post-war years. The strange thing is that the policy, so efficiently and effectively put into action by Harris, was one which enabled the British to survive alone, and then, with their Allies, bring about the speediest conclusion to hostilities with the minimum of British and American losses. Indeed, had it been possible to bring to bear the weight of attack achieved by the British and American strategic bomber forces in 1944 in, say, 1942, then the Russian losses, both military and civilian, would unquestionably have been enormously reduced. Moreover, the war in Europe might well have been won as early as the end of 1943.

In this context an examination of casualty figures is very revealing.

In the case of Dresden itself, David Irving, in his book *The Destruction of Dresden* which was published in 1963, spoke of various numbers of persons killed ranging from 35,000 to 220,000. These were estimates arising from his researches into different sources of German statistics. On 7 July 1966, in a letter to *The Times*, he quoted new figures which had come into his possession and which were rather lower. These came from an eleven-page 'final report' by the area police chief, who was responsible for civil defence measures in Dresden. This report was compiled about one month after the February and March Dresden raids, but before the US Eighth Bomber Command attack of 17 April. As Mr Irving states, the crucial paragraph reads:

> Casualties: by 10th March 1945, 18,375 dead, 2,212 seriously injured and 13,918 slightly injured had been registered, with 350,000 homeless and permanently evacuated.

The total expected death roll was given as 25,000, and 35,000 people were reported as missing. These missing persons were in all probability people who had evacuated themselves. This revised figure of 25,000 dead is in line with earlier official British estimates of 25,000 to 32,000 dead based on Russian estimates at the end of the war. The casualties after the Eighth Bomber Command attack on the Dresden marshalling yards on 17 April were presumably insignificant.

It is interesting to compare this figure of 25,000 dead with the death roll in the Siege of Paris in 1870/1871 during the Franco–Prussian war. Between 20,000 and 25,000 were estimated to have been killed or to have died of starvation as a result of the siege. 17,000 are definitely known to have been killed, because their burial costs were paid for by the Municipal Council after the Paris Commune's defeat in May 1871. And not a single bomber flew over Paris at that time!

Heinz G. Konsalik, in his book *Stalingrad*, published in 1968, provides some overall figures of casualties in Germany and Russia arising from World War II. Gerald Reitlinger in his book *The Final Solution*, published in 1968, gives figures of Jews exterminated in Germany and German occupied territory. All these figures are worthy of study for they bring into perspective those figures for individual cities such as Dresden and Hamburg, as well as those for the total number of civilians killed in Germany by air action.

1. *Germany*
   (a) Service personnel (soldiers, sailors and airmen) killed by military action. — 1,809,361
   (b) Service personnel dead by sentence of death, accident, illness and suicide. — 191,338
   (c) Service personnel missing, the majority believed killed — 1,240,629
   (d) Civilians killed in air raids — 500,000
   (e) Allowing for unknown casualties in the chaotic conditions of the last year of war, including soldiers, sailors, airmen and civilians, the total figure for Germans killed is estimated at — 4,000,000

NB Another source quotes the total number of civilians killed in Germany as 800,000, but does not estimate the number killed by air action alone. It is worthy of note that in World War I the British naval blockade of Germany resulted in the deaths of close upon 800,000 civilians from starvation.

2. *Germany*

    (a) Jews exterminated by German authorities   5,700,000

3. *Soviet Union*

    (a) Service personnel (soldiers, sailors and airmen) killed in action   8,500,000

    (b) Service personnel who died from wounds   2,500,000

    (c) Service personnel who died in captivity   2,600,000

    (d) Civilians killed or who died as a result of military action   7,000,000

    (e) Total Russians killed   20,600,000

By comparison, the total British and American casualties in all theatres of war were indeed light:

1. *United States of America**

    (a) Service personnel (soldiers, sailors and airmen) killed in action or died of wounds   291,557

    (b) Service personnel wounded but not mortally   670,846

    (c) Civilians in USA killed or who died as a result of military action   NIL

    (d) Total Americans killed   291,557

2. *British Commonwealth and Empire†*

    (a) Service personnel (soldiers, sailors and airmen) killed in action or died of wounds   353,652

    (b) Service personnel wounded, but not mortally   457,070

    (c) Civilians in Britain killed or who died as a result of military action   63,635

    (d) Civilians in Britain wounded but not mortally as a result of military action   86,182

    (e) Total British killed   417,287

A further analysis reveals that from 6 June 1944, the day that the Allied armies invaded France, until the end of the war with Germany at the beginning of May 1945, the army casualties‡ were as follows:

* The source of these figures was the library of the Embassy of the United States of America in London.

† The sources of these figures are Hansard (Lords) of the 3 August 1961, columns 316 to 320, and *Statistical Digests of the War* published by Her Majesty's Stationery Office. The civilian casualties do not include those of British civilians abroad as there appears to be no reliable figure. However, such casualties were relatively small.

‡ These figures were actually from the 6 June 1944, until midnight on the 22 April 1945. Further casualties between the 22 April and the 9 May 1945, when hostilities with Germany ceased, were negligible. The source of these figures was a message to Sir Arthur Harris from Supreme Headquarters Allied Expeditionary Force, received at 16.30 hours on 27 April 1945.

	Killed	Wounded	Missing	Total
USA	87,107	361,756	39,199	488,062
British Empire	38,670	122,930	18,126	179,726
French	10,155	43,269	3,846	57,270
Polish	1,126	3,806	375	5,307
Others	234	793	69	1,096
Grand Total	**137,292**	**532,554**	**61,615**	**731,461**

Had Harris failed to recognise the vital impact of strategic bombing in 1934, when he became Deputy Director of Plans at the Air Ministry, and had he failed to direct Bomber Command as efficiently and effectively as he did from February 1942, when he assumed command, then these casualties would have been infinitely greater, and the war would have lasted much longer. Indeed, it is questionable whether the Allies would have won the war, and it is without any doubt that many cities of Great Britain would have been devastated by German attack. The frequent utterances of Hitler, during the war, emphasise his avowed intent to burn London from end to end and to lay waste the cities of Britain. Harris denied him the chance to realise his wishes.

The effect of the bombing on the success of the military operations in Europe was perhaps best expressed by Field Marshal Viscount Montgomery who, after the war, referred in public to his 'old friend Sir Arthur Harris' in these words: 'It was a very great pleasure to me, when I came into this room, to see my old friend Sir Arthur Harris—more affectionately known as Bomber Harris—who wielded the mighty weapon of air power to such good purpose that the job of us soldiers on the ground was comparatively simple. And, I would say that few people did so much to win the war as Bomber Harris.' He added: 'I doubt if this is generally realised.'

In fairness, the tremendous contribution of the United States Strategic Air Forces in Europe from early 1944 onwards must also be included in any accolade of recognition of the effect of the bombing offensive on the defeat of Germany with such minimal Allied military and civilian casualties. It was a combined offensive. And it was largely due to Harris that the cooperation between the British and American bombing forces was so close and effective. But it was Bomber Command that alone of the three services carried the offensive into the German homeland from September 1939 until June 1944, being joined in the effort by the US Eighth Bomber Command from the middle of 1943.

Bomber Command's efforts were not without cost. Out of a total of 70,253 officers, non-commissioned officers and airmen of the Royal Air Force killed and missing on operations between the 3 September 1939, and 14 August 1945, 47,268 were killed on Bomber Command operations between 3 September 1939 and May 1945. In addition, 8,090 were killed whilst undertaking non-operational duties and 530 ground staff were killed on active service—a total of 55,888. Over and beyond this number another 9,162 were wounded in action or on active service.

Of these losses, Harris said: 'They will forever lie heavy on my heart.'

24

Taking count

By the time the argument over the bombing policy, and in particular the bombing of Dresden, had reached its climax with Portal's 'Note by the Air Staff' on 'Area Bombing', dated 4 April 1945, the war with Germany was almost over.

Throughout most of March the calls on Harris for bombing support of the Allied armies were legion, and Harris fully honoured his earlier pledge to Eisenhower, made when Bomber Command was removed from the direct control of the Supreme Commander, '... that our continuing commitment for the support of your forces upon call from you will continue, as before, to be met to the utmost of our skill and the last ounce of our endeavour ... It will be a point of honour to meet your every future requirement and request without question and in fullest measure.'

The bombing of the oil targets continued till the end of April, but by March the emphasis shifted to bombing in support of the Allied armies, and once again Bomber Command proved its immense power and skill in this role, one for which it had neither been designed nor trained. One of its most important assignments in March was to prepare for and support the crossing of the Rhine, and this it did with incredible effect. Within this charge was one task which was eminently suited to the Command's skills. The German forces were by this time thinly spread in defence of the Rhine, out Generalfeldmarschall Walther Model, the Commander of Army Group B, which consisted of the German Fifteenth Army and the Fifth Panzer Army, comprising in all twenty-one divisions, had his headquarters in the Ruhr and his divisions available to move as reinforcements to the major points of the Allied attacks across the Rhine once these were revealed. It was Harris's task, in conjunction with the US Eighth and Ninth Air Forces, to prevent Model from moving any of his divisions, and this was to be done by massive bombing of communication centres in the Ruhr, including Essen, Dortmund, Hagen, Bocholt, Barmen and many other targets outside the Ruhr, together with the bombing of military concentrations. The aim was to create chaos and the total disruption of communications. The Ruhr targets were mainly left to Bomber Command, with German airfields, enemy camps and barracks being the charge of the US Eighth Air Force. But in addition to the colossal bombing in the Ruhr, which included such attacks as that on Essen, when, on 11 March, 4,738·2 tons of bombs were rained down on the town by 1,053 heavy bombers, and that on Dortmund when 4,889·3 tons were unloaded on this city by 1,079 heavies on 12 March, other attacks were made on vital targets which required a high degree of precision.

The task of tackling these precision targets went to No 617 Squadron of No 5 Group, which had specialised in bombing small but vital points and which was equipped with those Lancasters that could carry the Barnes Wallis 12,000-pound 'Tallboy' bomb and the 22,000-pound 'Grand Slam'. At this time the squadron was commanded by Group Captain Johnny Fauquier, a Canadian who, late in 1944 had elected to relinquish his rank of Air Commodore in order to take over 617. Fauquier had fully upheld the squadron's traditions for outstanding skill and determination set by its previous illustrious commanders, and he was to continue to demonstrate its exceptional abilities in its last major task in the war. One of the main means of immobilising Model's ability to reinforce points in the German defence of the Rhine was to destroy the railway viaducts at Bielefeld, Altenbeken and Arnsberg which carried the main traffic lines from the Ruhr to the rest of Germany. In addition, a number of major railway bridge targets were allocated for attack which, if destroyed, would paralyse German troop movements in the Rhine and Ruhr area and isolate the Ruhr from North Sea ports such as Hamburg, Bremerhaven, Cuxhaven and Bremen. The Bielefeld and Altenbeken viaducts were attacked on 22 February by eighteen and sixteen aircraft respectively, dropping 12,000-pounders. The Altenbeken viaduct was severed at the north end for a length of 140/150 yards, but the results of the Bielefeld attack were uncertain. However, on 14 March the Bielefeld viaduct was again attacked and, for the first time, the 22,000-pound 'Grand Slam' was used. Fourteen Lancasters made the assault, which was highly successful. The huge bomb shattered two spans of the twin viaduct, destroying a length of more than 100 yards. In addition, thirteen 12,000-pounders dropped by the other aircraft on the by-pass which the Germans had hastily completed to provide an alternative to the viaduct, put it completely out of action. Also on the 14th, fifteen aircraft attacked the Arnsberg railway viaduct which carried the main line traffic eastwards from the Ruhr. One 22,000-pounder and fourteen 12,000-pounders were used, but results were not conclusive. However, on the 19th, this viaduct was again attacked by nineteen Lancasters dropping six 22,000-pounders and thirteen 12,000-pounders. The viaduct was completely severed, more than 100 feet of it collapsing into the river below, with the embankment being cut over a distance of 115 feet at the base of the northern slope. Thus, before 24 March, the day planned for the Allied crossing of the Rhine, the three main routes connecting the Ruhr with the rest of Germany had been rendered unusable.

The immediate and direct support for the crossing of the Rhine by Montgomery's 21st Army Group at Wesel was even more intense than the general preparation over the previous weeks. No less than thirty-two

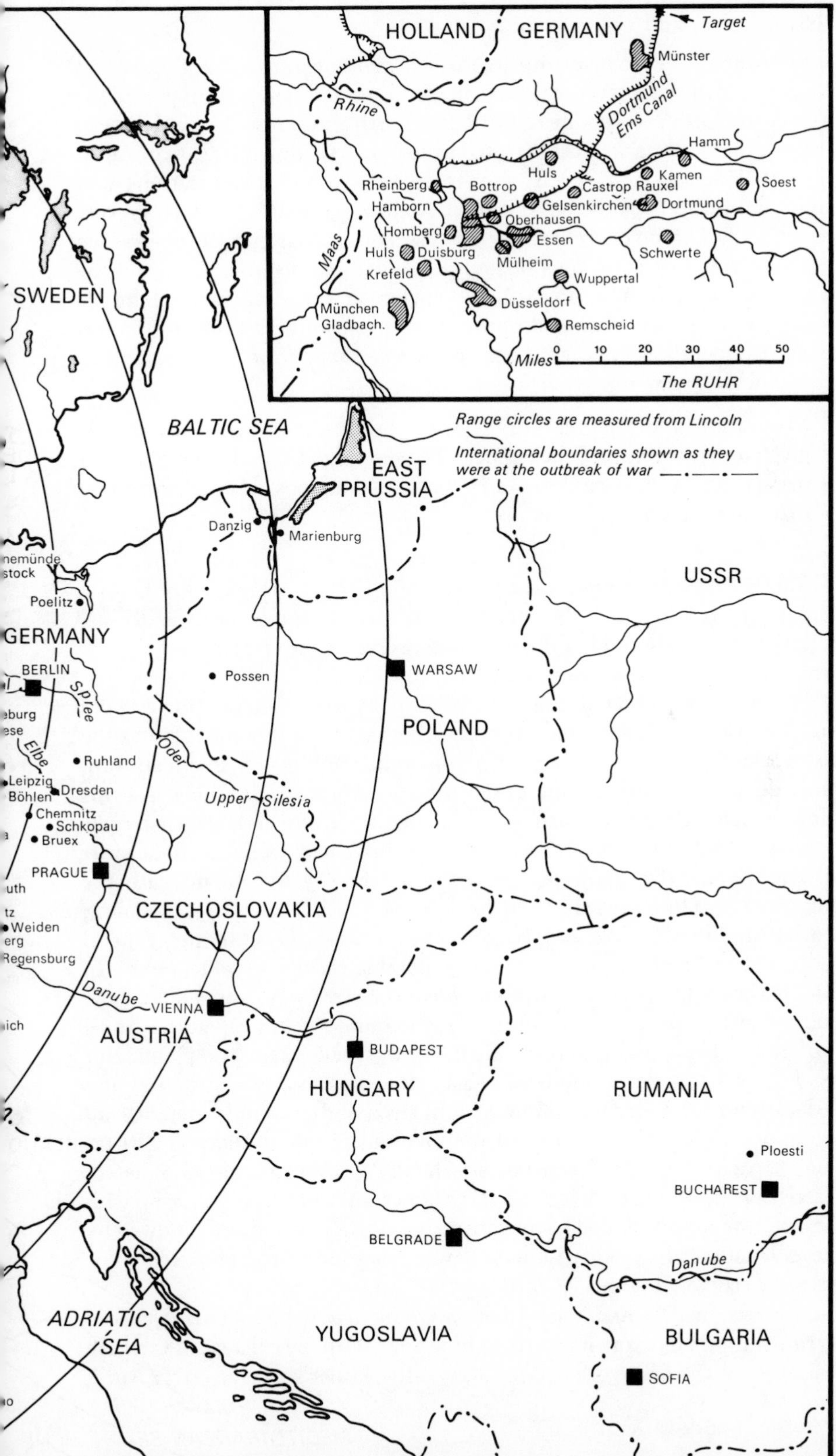

HOLLAND
GERMANY
Target
Münster
Dortmund Ems Canal
Rhine
Hamm
Huls
Kamen
Rheinberg
Bottrop
Castrop Rauxel
Soest
Hamborn
Gelsenkirchen
Dortmund
Oberhausen
Homberg
Essen
Maas
Huls
Duisburg
Schwerte
Mülheim
Krefeld
Wuppertal
München Gladbach.
Düsseldorf
Remscheid
Miles
0
10
20
30
40
50
The RUHR
SWEDEN
BALTIC SEA
Range circles are measured from Lincoln
International boundaries shown as they were at the outbreak of war
EAST PRUSSIA
Danzig
Marienburg
USSR
Poelitz
GERMANY
BERLIN
Possen
WARSAW
Spree
POLAND
Elbe
Oder
Ruhland
Leipzig
Dresden
Böhlen
Upper Silesia
Chemnitz
Schkopau
Bruex
PRAGUE
Weiden
CZECHOSLOVAKIA
Regensburg
Danube
VIENNA
AUSTRIA
BUDAPEST
HUNGARY
RUMANIA
Ploesti
BUCHAREST
BELGRADE
Danube
ADRIATIC SEA
YUGOSLAVIA
BULGARIA
SOFIA

separate attacks were made during the week ending at dawn on Sunday, 25 March, and of these seventeen were in direct preparation and support of the 21st Army Group's crossing of the Rhine north and south of Wesel. Five of these seventeen attacks were directed against marshalling yards, five against railway bridges, and seven against enemy troop concentrations and strongholds. Perhaps the best example of direct support of the Army were the attacks on troop concentrations in Wesel on 23 March by seventy-seven heavies dropping 435·5 tons of high explosive bombs and, again, on the night of 23/24 March, immediately prior to the Army launching its offensive, when 200 heavies dropped 1091·5 tons of high explosive bombs and 7·3 tons of incendiaries. These drew a message from Montgomery to Harris which read:

> My grateful appreciation for the quite magnificent cooperation you have given us in the Battle of the Rhine. The bombing of Wesel last night was a masterpiece and was a decisive factor in making possible our entry into that town before midnight.
>
> Montgomery

Another message from the 1st Commando Brigade which, with the 51st Highland Division, led the attack on Wesel after crossing the Rhine, referred to the bombing raid which had preceded the crossing as: 'A very fine attack. Wesel was taken with only 36 casualties.'

In that week ending at dawn on Sunday, 25 March, 4,327 sorties were flown by Bomber Command, dropping 16,974·6 tons of bombs. It was the last week of massive bombing, for by this time the war was, in effect, won. Only during the week ending at dawn on 15 April was anything like this tonnage again dropped, when 13,274·4 tons were directed against targets deeper in Germany, mainly in support of the Allied armies in their swift advance across the whole of the enemy's territory to join up with the Russians on a line roughly from Kiel and Lübeck, through Magdeburg, Karlsbad, Pilsen, Linz and Salzburg to Trieste. Despite the general reduction in bombing, however, some notable results were achieved. In Kiel harbour, the pocket battleship *Admiral Scheer* was capsized, and the pocket battleship *Lutzow* was sunk at Swinemunde by 617 Squadron, and a further number of highly successful attacks was made against oil plants. But by 29 April Bomber Command's task, 'the progressive destruction and dislocation of the German military, industrial and economic system, and the undermining of the morale of the German people to the point where their capacity for armed resistance is fatally weakened', was completed. Harris was now able to divert his forces to errands of mercy, starting with the airborne supply of food to civilians in Northern Holland and followed by the evacuation of Allied prisoners-of-war from Germany, of which some 75,000 were flown home.

The ease with which the Allies swept across the German occupied territories and Germany itself, from June 1944 until the collapse of German resistance in the first week of May 1945, after Hitler's suicide on 30 April, was unquestionably due to the long and brilliantly executed strategic bomber offensive which was directed by Harris from February 1942 until the end of the war. In this offensive he was assisted enormously in 1944 and 1945 by the powerful strategic offensive of the US Eighth Bomber Command. General Schlatter of the US Army, for example, gave it as his opinion that the American victory at St Lô in July 1944 was not so much due to the bombing in direct support of the Army as it was to the denial of supplies to the Germans by the earlier strategic offensive. This view is supported by the experience of Generalfeldmarschall Model, commanding German Army Group B at the time of the preparation for the Rhine offensive by the Allies in March 1945. When Speer visited him at his headquarters in the Ruhr, 'he was in a state of fury'. He told Speer that Hitler had commanded him to attack the Allies on their flank at Remagen, on the Rhine south of Bonn, using certain specified divisions in order to recapture the bridge. Model said heatedly:

> Those divisions have lost their weapons and have no fighting strength at all. They would be less effective than a Company! It's the same thing all over again. At Headquarters they have no idea what is going on ... Of course, I'll be blamed for the failure.

The truth was that production in Germany had been so effectively and progressively devastated by Bomber Command in 1942 and 1943, and by Bomber Command and the US Eighth Bomber Command in 1944, that German losses of weapons on all fronts were by 1944 and 1945 in excess of replacement rates from production. This, in fact, was Model's problem. Bombing had denied him not the men, but the weapons with which to defend the Fatherland, despite Speer's excellent management of German military production.

From the beginning of the war on 3 September 1939, until 3 May 1945, when the last bombing raid was made on Germany in an attack against enemy shipping at Kiel, Bomber Command despatched 389,809 sorties against enemy targets in Germany, German occupied territory and Italy, for the loss of 8,655 aircraft, a loss rate of just over 2·2 per cent. Of these sorties 336,037 were despatched on bombing raids, dropping a total of 955,044 tons of bombs; 19,025 were despatched on sea-mining missions laying 47,307 mines, a total tonnage in mines of 33,237 tons; the remainder were despatched on radio counter-measure flights, fighter support, decoy flights, intruder activities against enemy aerodromes, meterological flights, reconnaissance and special operations such as agent dropping and pick-up. By far the greatest proportion of this effort was undertaken between February 1942 and May 1945 under the command of Harris. Of the total sorties, 331,001 were despatched at his direction, dropping 906,973 tons of bombs, and laying 45,428 sea-mines. Of the total tonnage of bombs dropped 865,715 tons were dropped in 1943, 1944 and the first four months of 1945. In addition to this prodigious figure the US Eighth Air Force added in 1943, 1944 and 1945 another 621,260 tons.

The effect of this bombing cannot be assessed by simple calculations of destruction, for there were other factors which had as great an effect on disrupting Germany's ability to fight the war; such factors as morale and, more important still, the diversion of production to the needs of defence against the bombing at the expense of production for the Army's offensives on the Eastern Front, in North Africa and in the Mediterranean theatre of war. The necessity to divert more and more production to the defence of the homeland, in itself threw the German Army onto the defensive on all its fronts where previously it had been on the offensive. In 1943 and 1944 the bombing of the German homeland became so intense, heavy and effective that its defence demanded a level of production (production which in any case was being severely hampered by the bombing) so high that the defence needs of the Army on all its fronts had to be drastically curtailed, with the result that the German armies were soon no longer on the offensive but in full retreat on all fronts. With the invasion of Europe by the Allies in June 1944, yet another front was opened which Germany was incapable of defending adequately. The strategic bombing had, in fact, as early as late 1942, created a vicious circle for Germany out of which she was never able to extricate herself.

In *Inside the Third Reich*, Speer commented at the end of the chapter entitled 'Sins of Omission' on the failure of Germany to develop the atom bomb. He wrote: 'But even if Hitler had not had this prejudice against nuclear research'—referring to Hitler's belief that nuclear physics were 'Jewish physics'—'and even if the state of our fundamental research in June, 1942, could have freed several billion instead of several million marks for the production of atom bombs, it would have been impossible—given the strain on our economic resources—to have provided the materials, priorities, and technical workers corresponding to such an investment. For it was not only superior productive capacity that allowed the United States to undertake this gigantic project. The increasing air raids had long since created an armaments emergency in Germany which ruled out any such ambitious enterprise.' This statement is clearly indicative of the effectiveness of Bomber Command's efforts as early as 1942. Moreover, it poses the question: 'Did Harris's bombing policy preserve Britain's cities from annihilation by atomic warheads?'

In November 1972, the author spent several days with Albert Speer examining with him his production records for military equipment from 1942 to 1945, together with those of the allocations of supplies and equipment to defence needs and to the armies in the field. Some of these were not available to the Allies at the end of the war, but came to hand relatively recently and were handed over to the Bundesarchiv by Speer in August 1969.

On the occasion of this visit, Speer said to the author: 'I consider it fair to say that the air attacks in 1943 cost us a loss of 10 per cent of our armaments production.* I should say that this loss of 10 per cent was doubled in 1944 to

* The USA Bombing Survey gave the figure for 1943 as 9 per cent.

20 per cent.' It is essential to note that Harris, with his Bomber Command, was the only one bombing Germany in 1943, with the exception of the two Schweinfurt raids by the US Eighth Bomber Command in August and October 1943, when their losses were so high that they were unable to direct any further significant raids against Germany during that year. During 1943 they did, however, operate with growing strength against French and German coastal ports, but, even so, the scale of these attacks was small compared to the raids executed by Bomber Command. It also has to be remembered that during the first six months of 1944 the scale of the attacks by Bomber Command was still substantially greater than that of the US strategic forces.

Speer, in a further observation to the author, when referring to gun production, said:

In 1943, the total production of all the heavier guns for the Army, that is from 10·5-cm field howitzers upwards, 7·5-cm anti-tank guns and 8·8-cm anti-tank and anti-aircraft guns upwards, came to 23,223; but it should have been 25,000, but for the bombing which lost us in that year 10 per cent, or a loss of about 2,200 guns. In 1944 it was worse. The actual production was 36,746 guns, whereas it should have been about 45,000; so at a loss of 20 per cent we lost some 9,100 guns. Therefore in 1943 and 1944 we lost approximately 11,300 guns due to the bombing. But, really, we lost more, for our production programmes were even higher in 1943 and 1944 and without your bombing they would have been achieved. Another thing, too, you must remember. I told you last time you were here in March that the only guns effective against the heavily armoured Russian tanks were the 8·8-cm onwards to the 12·8-cm anti-tank guns, of which the 8·8-cm, with its precision sight, had proved to be a wonderful anti-tank gun. The production of these 8·8-cm to 12·8cm guns from 1942 up to and including 1944 was 19,713 guns, but only 3,172 were allocated to the Army, despite their desperate need for them against the Russians and, later, against the British and American Armies as well, because the rest were required for anti-aircraft defence against your bombing of the Ruhr, Berlin, and other industrial towns and areas. In fact, we had to divert 75 per cent of the production of them to defence against the bombers. Also hundreds of thousands of trained soldiers were held back from the Russian Front to man these guns.

This example is one which shows not only the effect of bombing on military production alone, which by itself denied the armies on the battlefield the weapons they urgently required, but it also demonstrates the even greater privations precipitated upon the German Army because 75 per cent of what production there was left had to be held back for the defence of the German homeland against the bombing. Studying the production figures one can see why this home defence was so vital. For the period 1 January to 30 September 1944, for example, small-arms production was 3,297,000 weapons against losses on the battlefield, over the same period, of

4,457,000 weapons. The worst case was rifles, where 1,960,000 were produced and 3,470,000 were lost in battle. A similar picture emerges throughout all the figures for all weapons for the Army. This inability of production to meet the needs of the German Army was not just a condition of 1944; it had started in 1942, gathering momentum in 1943, and reaching a state of disaster in 1944. And it was primarily due to Harris's bombing of the Ruhr, Berlin and central Germany.

Another illustration of the state of affairs in 1944 resulting from the bombing in 1942 and 1943, as well as from that undertaken in 1944, is given by the actual production against programme of tanks and aircraft:*

1944	*Production Programme*		*Actual Production*	
	For Year	*Monthly Rate*	*For Year*	*Highest Monthly Rate*
Tanks	38,400	3,200	17,625	1,830 (December)
Day and night fighter aircraft	57,600	4,800	25,822	2,950 (September)
Total all types aircraft	93,600	7,800	39,925	4,219 (July)

Karl Saur, a department head in Speer's Ministry of Armaments and War Production, commented on the seriousness of the production situation in a speech to the Fighter Staff of the Ministry (*Jägerstab*) on 8 April 1944. After referring to the fact that the steel production situation was not entirely satisfactory, because of shortages of manganese, vanadium, chrome, nickel, and so on, but nonetheless was expected to remain at a high level, he said:

> We must be clear about the fact that in addition to our production programme [for steel], the tank production programme must be considerably broadened. Here we have a second task, namely to keep the enemy bombers out of the country until such time as we have built the necessary tanks to be able to win the war with tanks. The war cannot be won with aircraft, but aircraft are our immediate task, so that we can create the possibility of producing tanks. We shall only end the war in the East with tanks. This would create the pre-conditions which yesterday caused the Führer to say: 'If this tank production programme is realised, which is now underpinned in terms of the whole range of models, and all of the initial planning, then this tank programme will decide the war.' However, a pre-condition for this is 100 per cent completion of the Air Force programme, so that we can keep the enemy bombers out of the country in order to be able to continue production.

* Taken from the 'Statistics of Armaments Production of the Technical Office', dated 15 February 1945.

INDEX OF GERMAN ARMAMENTS PRODUCTION (PAGE 256 – JANUARY 1945)

DISTRIBUTION BY TYPES OF ALL AIRCRAFT PRODUCTION

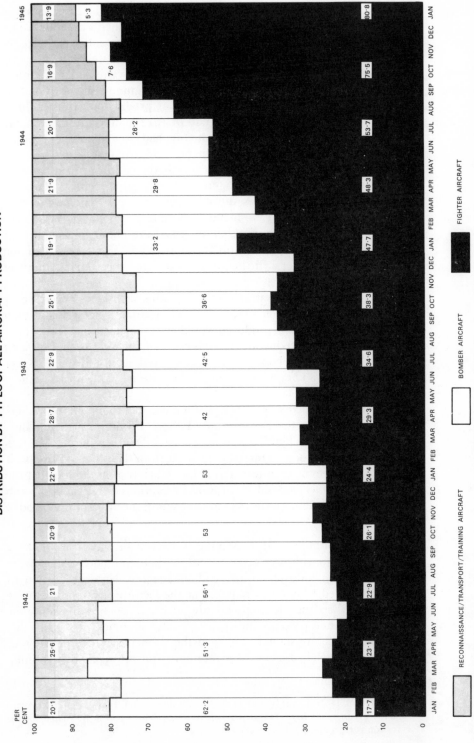

RECONNAISSANCE/TRANSPORT/TRAINING AIRCRAFT   BOMBER AIRCRAFT   FIGHTER AIRCRAFT

In the case of aircraft production, a graph showing the distribution of production by types for 1942, 1943, 1944 and 1945, which was produced for Speer's Ministry,* reveals an incredible state of affairs and is, perhaps, the most telling evidence of the effectiveness and vital importance of the bomber offensive conducted by Harris from 1942 onwards and, in addition, by Eaker and Spaatz in 1944 and 1945. At the beginning of 1942 bombers absorbed 62·6 per cent of all German aircraft production, whilst fighters absorbed only 17·7 per cent. By the end of 1942 bomber production had dropped to 53 per cent and fighter production had risen to 26·1 per cent. By the last quarter of 1943, bomber production had dropped to 36·6 per cent and fighters had advanced to 38.3 per cent. By the middle of 1944 bombers were down to 26·2 per cent and fighters up to 53·7 per cent. By October 1944, bomber production was down to only 7·6 per cent of the total production, whereas fighter production was up to 75·5 per cent! As with the heavy calibre guns, the strategic bombing had not only damaged aircraft production but, more important still, it had forced the Germans to abandon completely any plans for a further air offensive and therefore any hope of winning the war.

When the author was examining these graphs with Herr Speer, Speer remarked: 'If there had been no serious bombing attacks on Germany, then the percentage of bombers produced would have remained at at least 53 per cent—or twice the production of fighters.' In answer to the author's question: 'Would these bombers have been used against Britain?' Speer replied: 'Definitely. They would definitely have been used against Britain—only against Britain.'

Another point made by Speer was that hundreds of thousands of soldiers were held back from the Eastern and Western Fronts to man the anti-aircraft defences. This figure has been estimated by other German sources as being as high as 900,000 men. Quite apart from these trained troops, it was stated by Speer at his interrogation immediately after the war that the number of personnel engaged in Air Raid Precautions (ARP) and in bomb damage repair organisations in 1943 to 1944 was of the order of 1,000,000 to 1,500,000.

> There is no doubt [he said] that in the absence of air raids, it would have been possible to withdraw several hundred thousand more soldiers from the armaments industry at the end of 1943. A large proportion of German skilled labour was required at the factories for bomb damage clearance, where their specialised knowledge and keenness to restore the plants made their presence indispensable after air attacks. If no air raids had taken place, we should have been able to increase the proportion of foreign and unskilled labour. Furthermore, during 1944 Army training

---

* Taken from 'Distribution By Use of all Aircraft Production, Index of German Armaments Production', *Blatt* 256, dated January 1945. The graph in translated English version is reproduced on page 311.

units were increasingly employed on bomb damage clearance work, leading to a reduction in the standard of training and to a lengthening of training schedules.

There are interesting conclusions to be drawn from the situation. Without the strategic bombing, the German Eastern Front would not have been denuded to the extent that Germany's offensive was reversed into a retreat. Indeed, Russia might well have been defeated. The Allied invasion could only have been undertaken, if at all, with an enormous loss of life. The bombing of Britain would have been mounted on a colossal scale and the loss of civilian life would have been considerable, and defeat by the Germans, or a negotiated peace on their terms, almost inevitable.

Whilst the strategic bombing of German and German occupied industrial areas defeated these possibilities, it produced a danger against itself. This was the growth of the German Fighter Defence which might have grown to such proportions that the bomber offensive could have been defeated before the U S and British Armies could overrun occupied Europe and Germany in the west and before the Russian forces could perform the same task in the east. It was a precarious situation, more so than many people realise, for if only the Allied bomber offensive could have been neutralised, then German production would have been resilient enough to recover to that pitch where the German armed forces could have returned to the offensive. This is what Harris feared at all times and this is why he fought so hard for a substantial proportion of his available effort to be directed at all times against German industrial towns. He was right but, in the case of oil, so also was Portal. The question was how much effort from Bomber Command should be diverted to oil, bearing in mind the calls for army support once the British and Americans had invaded France. A study of the figures for oil production and reserves in 1944 leads one to the emphatic conclusion that the effort directed against oil targets by Bomber Command and the U S Strategic Air Forces in Europe was fully adequate, and that an increase in effort, beyond that applied would have been wasted. It was enough, in fact, to keep much of Germany's increasing fighter strength on the ground because of shortage of fuel for both attack and training purposes; and the area bombing of industrial towns remained enough to keep Germany on the defensive; and there was still sufficient effort to spare to give full support to the Allied armies, thereby keeping their casualties to an absolute minimum.

Oil figures for 1944 extracted from Speer's records of reserves and production, including production from occupied countries, such as Poland, Czechoslovakia, France and Norway, but excluding imports from neutral or German allied countries, such as Rumania and Hungary, except where indicated, are given below. It should be noted that imports from neutral or German allied countries had virtually ceased by October 1944.

Oil in metric tons, 1944.

	April	October	November	December	January
1 Aviation fuel reserves	574,000	117,000	22,000		
2 Aviation fuel— monthly production	175,000	20,000	49,000	26,000	12,000
3 Military fuel reserves. (Gasoline and diesel for tanks, MT, etc.)	760,000	79,400	3,000		
4 Military fuel— monthly production	238,000	117,000	114,000	124,000	
5 Total oil production including heating and lubricating oils and all imports	833,000	318,000	325,000	291,000	200,000

The truth is that by January 1945 the production of essential fuel was virtually at a standstill. Figures for February, March and April are not available, but Speer assured the author that what production there was, was totally inadequate to continue the prosecution of the war. He also made the observation that the Bomber Command night attacks against fuel plants and refineries were more effective than those of the US bomber forces because of the heavier weight of bombs used by the RAF mixed with incendiaries.

The examples of production* disrupted by bombing, which have been quoted above, are symptomatic of the entire production capacity of Germany. Wherever you look amongst the records for 1944, the same situation is revealed. Monthly production of motor trucks, including caterpillar trucks, was programmed at 14,000, but the highest monthly figure reached in that year was 8,500 in July; railway waggons were programmed at 2,270 per month, but the highest figure reached was 1,795 in August; infantry munitions were programmed at 800,000,000 rounds per month, but the highest monthly figure achieved was only 484,000,000 rounds; light and heavy field howitzer munitions were planned at a rate of

---

* Fuel reserves have been taken from the 'Personal Statistical Files' of Herr Kehrl, Chief of the Planning Office, dated November 1944. Fuel and oil production figures have been extracted from 'Immediate Reports of War Production (Oil)', dated January 1945.

6,200,000 rounds, but the highest monthly rate reached was 3,923,000 rounds; and so it went on. Moreover, the disruption to production extended even beyond armaments production. All production was disrupted, including production of goods needed for normal life and essential to living. So hard hit were the Germans in their homeland that even the ever powerful Gauleiters (District Leaders) were by late 1943 opposing military production being moved into or added to their areas for fear that even more bombing would be attracted against the towns in their areas. In 1944, after the invasion of France, they were, under public pressure, demanding that the Army should stay clear of their built-up areas for the same reason—an extraordinary state of affairs! Initially, the strategic bombing had caused resentment and created an attitude of 'we'll stand together and revenge will ultimately be ours.' The next stage was fear, coupled with resentment against the authorities and the German Air Force, because they had let the bombing continue by their failure to put up adequate defence against the attacks, though action against the authorities was restrained because of fear of the Gestapo and, to a degree, a feeling of sense of duty. A short period of apathy followed. Finally the public had had enough, and loyalty to Hitler and his Third Reich collapsed. The German public began to display active opposition to the continuance of the war. It was the end.

In taking count there is yet another major contribution made by Harris and his Bomber Command to the winning of the war which has to be considered, one which has been forgotten by too many 'instant history' writers. It is Bomber Command's 'Battle of the Ships'. The greatest success in this battle was achieved by air-laid sea-mines, an original idea that Harris put forward when he was Deputy Director (Plans) at the Air Ministry in 1936. He progressed this idea and put it into practice with considerable effect when he was the Air Officer Commanding No 5 Group from 1939 to the end of 1940. He finally extended air-sea mining to the dimensions of a major campaign when he was the Commander-in-Chief of Bomber Command from February 1942 to the end of the war. The results of this great battle are tabled below.

Enemy vessels sunk in Atlantic and North-West European waters

	Number	Tonnage
Sunk at sea by bombing		
Surface warships	4	1,651
Cargo and other vessels	21	29,503
Submarines (U-boats)	1	
Destroyed by bombing in port		
Surface warships	152	166,576
Cargo and other vessels	127	163,618
Submarines (U-boats)	21	

*Sunk by air-laid mines**	*Number*	*Tonnage*
Surface warships	215	145,743
Cargo and other vessels	544	576,234
Submarines (U–boats)†	17	
GRAND TOTAL	**1,102**	**1,083,325**

The total enemy shipping losses in Atlantic and North-West European waters from all causes, including those sunk by the Navy, Coastal and Fighter Commands, the U S forces and Bomber Command totalled:

All surface vessels	2,340	3,439,270
Captured, confiscated and scuttled	545	1,254,566
Submarines (U–boats)	645	
GRAND TOTAL	**3,530**	**4,693,836**

Of the total number of ships sunk in the Atlantic and North-West European waters, including submarines and vessels captured, confiscated and scuttled, Bomber Command accounted for 31·2 per cent. But if the vessels captured, confiscated and scuttled are excluded, then the percentage accounted for by Bomber Command is just over 36·8 per cent.

Of the total tonnage sunk, excluding the tonnage of submarines which is not known, but including the tonnage of vessels captured, confiscated and scuttled, Bomber Command accounted for 23 per cent. If the tonnage of vessels captured, confiscated and scuttled is excluded, then the percentage of the tonnage sunk by Bomber Command is just over 31 per cent.

The results of Bomber Command attacks on notable enemy warships may be summarised as follows:

Tirpitz, Scheer, Lützow   Sunk
Schlesian   Mined and beached
Gneisenau   Held up in Brest by bombing from March 1941, to February 1942; mined; bombed; partially gutted; finally dismantled
Köln   Damaged by bombs in Oslo Fjord; sunk by U S Eighth Air Force in Wilhelmshaven where she had been forced to return for repairs
Hipper   Severely damaged by bombs in dry dock at Kiel; rendered out of action for rest of war
Scharnhorst   Held up in Brest by bombing from March 1941 to February 1942; mined and severely damaged on return to Kiel; finally sunk by Navy.
Prinz Eugen   Damaged by bombs and kept out of action for a year
Emden   Damaged by bombs at Kiel, beached and burnt out.

---

* Bomber Command laid 47,307 mines between 1939 and 1945, and Coastal Command 936. Losses attributed to Bomber Command under 'Sunk by air-laid mines' includes ships sunk by 936 mines of Coastal Command, an insignificant figure.
† The tonnage of the submarines sunk is not known.

Quite apart from these successes, the *Prinz Eugen* and the *Nürnberg* would undoubtedly have been sunk at Copenhagen during the last week of the war but for the fact that the attacking No 5 Group aircraft were recalled on representations made by the Admiralty. No explanation was given. Copenhagen suffered bombardment by these ships the very next day.

Finally, to complete the analysis of the success of Bomber Command's 'Battle of the Ships', an aspect of the destruction of German U-boats, other than those sinkings which have already been taken into account, must be assessed. As early as the spring of 1943, Grand Admiral Karl Dönitz had come to the conclusion that only the production of a new type of U-boat could save Germany's submarine warfare from failure. He wanted to abandon the principle of a surface ship that occasionally moved under water and switch to a ship with a high underwater speed and greater underwater range which only occasionally sailed above water. Such a U-boat was, in fact, rapidly developed by 1944, together with the Schnorkel breathing device to enable it to recharge its batteries whilst still submerged. Navy trials were undertaken and successfully completed by the middle of 1944 and Speer was able to promise a delivery rate of forty boats a month by the beginning of 1945. These new U-boats were to be built at inland factories where, in addition, engines and electrical equipment were also to be installed. They were then to be transported in sections to the coast to be assembled there and to complete their equipment in the shipyards. Thus the shipyards, which were already heavily overloaded with work, would not be the cause of any hold-up in this bold and ambitious programme, a programme which bore the hall-mark of Speer's incredible ingenuity.

In 1944, Dönitz also formed the opinion that it was essential to regain the initiative in submarine warfare, and then to increase its intensity, in order to draw the Allied bombers off Germany. With this thinking Speer was in agreement. Indeed, anything that offered a chance of diverting the Allied bomber forces away from Germany proper was, by late 1944, the only hope of survival. But it was the Allied bombers that were to defeat the hopes of Dönitz and to negate Speer's highly successful production plans. By late 1944, Speer says, the naval programme was in full swing, but only eighty-three of the new U-boats were delivered to the Navy between January and March 1945. However, the promised forty a month, he says, would certainly have been delivered if it had not been for the bombing of the shipyards. Forty-four of these U-boats were, in fact, destroyed in the shipyards between January and March 1945. If they had not been, the total delivered to the German Navy would have been 127 or forty-two per month. It is to be noted that this bombing was largely undertaken by Bomber Command.

The British Bombing Survey Unit in its report on 'The Effects of Strategic Bombing on the Production of German U-Boats' states that from May 1943 until the end of March 1945, the losses of U-boats caused by the bombing of Germany were:

Production losses   111
Sinkings   42
TOTAL   153

These figures include the forty-four U-boats destroyed between January and March 1945, mentioned above. They also include the twenty-one U-boats destroyed in port by Bomber Command referred to in the earlier table headed 'Enemy vessels sunk in Atlantic and North-West European waters.' The total losses of 153 U-boats reported by the British Bombing Survey Unit as caused by the bombing of Germany cannot, of course, all be credited to Bomber Command. A substantial percentage must certainly be ascribed to the bombing by the US Eighth Bomber Command. Nevertheless, Bomber Command was unquestionably responsible for 50 per cent at the very least; and it is probable that the percentage is a great deal higher than this. In short, Harris's contribution to the defeat of the U-boat was a very major one, as was his contribution to the defeat of the rest of the German Navy.

Taking count of Bomber Command's successes in its 'Battle of the Ships', it is surprising that the Admiralty virtually ignored Harris's efforts and showed little, if indeed any, appreciation.

How did the Allies show their recognition of the immense contribution made by Sir Arthur Harris towards the winning of the war?

On 1 March 1944, the Supreme Soviet of the USSR awarded him The Order of Suverov, First Degree, for 'outstanding successes in the direction of troops, excellent organisation of military operations, and determination and persistence displayed in their execution resulting in victory in battles.'

On 17 October 1944, the President of the United States of America awarded him the Legion of Merit with the degree of Chief Commander. The citation read:

Sir Arthur T. Harris, KCB, OBE, AFC, Air Chief Marshal, Royal Air Force. For exceptionally meritorious conduct in the performance of outstanding services. As Commander-in-Chief, Bomber Command, Royal Air Force, Air Chief Marshal Harris made a noteworthy contribution to the success of the invasion of Europe by the Allied Expeditionary Force. Concurrently with the planning phase of the ground assault, he directed the Royal Air Force bombardment contribution to the Allied aerial assault. His forces lent their weight in tactical support of the ground fighting, assisting the break-through in Normandy and in reducing the Channel Ports, while at the same time continuing the aerial offensive against Germany. He performed his complex task with inspiring leadership and with outstanding cooperation, skill and determination, reflecting great credit upon the service he represents and upon the armed forces of the United Nations.

Approved: Franklin D. Roosevelt
                                                   PRESIDENT ROOSEVELT

On 13 July 1945, on the eve of the termination of the Supreme Headquarters Allied Expeditionary Force, Eisenhower wrote this letter to Harris:

Supreme Headquarters
ALLIED EXPEDITIONARY FORCE
Office of the Supreme Commander

13 July 1945

Dear Harris:

Combined Command terminates at midnight tonight, 13 July 1945, and brings to a close one of the greatest and most successful campaigns ever fought.

History alone will judge the Allied Expeditionary Force in its true perspective, but we, who have worked and struggled together, can feel nothing but pride in the achievements of the men we have been honored to command, and sadness at having to be parted now. Whatever history may relate about the exploits of this Allied Force, and the memory of man is short and fickle, it is only we, at this time, who can fully appreciate the merit and due worth of the accomplishments of this great Allied team.

These accomplishments are not limited to the defeat of the Nazi hordes in battle—a continent has been liberated from all that is an antipathy to the ideal of democracy which is our common heritage. Above all, we have proved to the whole world that the British and American peoples can forever be united in purpose, in deed and in death for the cause of liberty. This great experiment of integrated command, whose venture was cavilled at by some and doubted by many, has achieved unqualified success, and this has only been made possible by the sympathetic, unselfish and unwavering support which you and all other commanders have wholeheartedly given me. Your own brilliant performance is already a matter of history.

My gratitude to you is a small token for the magnificent service which you have rendered, and my simple expression of thanks sounds totally inadequate. Time and opportunity prohibit the chance I should like to shake you and your men by the hand, and thank each one of you personally for all you have done. I can do nothing more than assure you of my lasting appreciation, which I would ask you to convey to all those under your command for their exemplary devotion to duty and for the most magnificent loyalty which has ever been shown to a commander.

Sincerely
Dwight D. Eisenhower

PS Officially you have not been part of us for sometime—but so far as we are concerned you've always been, and will be, one of the 'team'.

The PS was written in Eisenhower's own handwriting.

Harris, who admired Eisenhower greatly, was deeply touched by his message and he wrote in reply a letter which expressed his sincere opinion of this outstanding general.

Dear Eisenhower,

Thank you for your letter of 13 July. All that you say is typical of all that you are, and all that you have been, to all of us who through these heroic months have waited upon your direction and command.

I disagree with you only in one particular:

You say that we have proved to the world that the British and American peoples can forever be united in purpose, in deed and in death, for the cause of liberty. Rather would I say that this past year of war has proved that wherever the life and liberty of our two nations is threatened they can and do forget that there are British or American peoples. With that you will not cavil.

Nevertheless there has been, as there will ever remain, the need on such occasions to find a man in whom can be reposed the confidence and the united strength of our peoples. This past year points yet again the truth of the adage that the occasion finds the man.

It was your direction and yours alone which pointed the road and bypassed every obstacle to Victory. They were many, and they could indeed have been menacing.

Therefore when you express gratitude to us for our share in a combined achievement, it in no sense diminishes in our eyes the credit for the whole—which we in Bomber Command well know to be yours and yours alone.

As the Captains and the Kings depart we bid a last farewell to SHAEF—not without sadness at the dissolution of something of greatness, however sombre the circumstance which gave it birth, and of which we had grown to be and will remain a part.

SHAEF, and all that it meant and always will mean, was yours. It was in fact you. Therefore while needs must we bid a last farewell to SHAEF, you will understand it when I say that Bomber Command will never bid a last goodbye to Dwight Eisenhower.

Yours ever,
Arthur T. Harris.

The tremendous respect that these two men had for each other is clearly evidenced in this correspondence.

Immediately after the cessation of hostilities with Germany Churchill sent the following message to Harris:

Now that Nazi Germany is defeated, I wish to express to you on behalf of His Majesty's Government the deep sense of Gratitude which is felt by all the Nation for the glorious part which has been played by Bomber Command in forging the victory.

For over two years Bomber Command alone, carried the war to the heart of Germany, bringing hope to the peoples of occupied Europe, and to the enemy a foretaste of the mighty power which was rising against him.

As the Command expanded, in partnership with the Air Forces of our American ally, the weight of the attacks was increased, dealing destruction on an unparalleled scale to the German military, industrial and economic system.

Your Command also gave powerful support to the Allied Armies in Europe and made a vital contribution to the war at sea. You destroyed or damaged many of the enemy's ships of war and much of his U-boat organization.

By a prolonged series of mining operations you sank or damaged large quantities of merchant shipping.

All your operations were planned with great care and skill. They were executed in the face of desperate opposition and appalling hazards. They made a decisive contribution to Germany's final defeat. The conduct of these operations demonstrated the fiery gallant spirit which animated your air crews, and the high sense of duty of all ranks under your command. I believe that the massive achievements of Bomber Command will long be remembered as an example of duty nobly done.

Winston S. Churchill

In June 1945, Harris was raised from the rank of Knight Commander of the Order of the Bath (KCB) to that of Knight Grand Cross of the Order of the Bath (GCB).

On 25 July 1945, there was a General Election and a Labour Government, with Clement Attlee as Prime Minister, was elected to replace the Coalition Government under Winston Churchill.

On 1 January 1946, Harris was promoted from the rank of Air Chief Marshal to that of Marshal of the Royal Air Force. In the Victory Honours List, issued under the newly elected Labour Government, the three Chiefs of Staff, who were already Barons, Marshal of the Royal Air Force Lord Portal, Chief of the Air Staff, Field-Marshal Lord Alanbrooke, Chief of the Imperial General Staff, and Admiral of the Fleet Lord Cunningham, were created Viscounts. So also were Field-Marshal Sir Harold Alexander and Field-Marshal Sir Bernard Montgomery. In addition, Admiral Sir Bruce Fraser, Field-Marshal Sir Henry Maitland Wilson and Marshal of the Royal Air Force Sir Arthur Tedder were created Barons. But Harris was ignored. All the British newspapers commented on this petty snub to the greatest British commander to emerge from World War II and, through him, to the only Command in all three fighting services which, alone, carried the offensive to the very heart of the enemy for more than three and a half years. The *Daily Mirror*, in its Editorial of 2 January 1946, put it succinctly:

LEFT OUT!

As we emphasised in our news columns yesterday the name of Sir

Arthur 'Bomber' Harris did not appear in the Honours List. This is a grave omission. Not only is it a slight upon Harris himself, but its effect is that Bomber Command as a whole is deprived of the recognition due to that splendid Arm. Has it so soon been forgotten what a great job the bombers did at a period in the war when there was no other way in which we could strike back at the enemy? Have the incalculable results of strategic bombing in the destruction of German war industries already become a faded memory? Harris may have been in a personal sense, 'difficult'. Possibly he made himself as awkward to the Brass Hats as he did to the Germans. Was that a reason for refusing him a mark of distinction? On the contrary ... !

When Churchill heard of this omission he said to Harris: 'You fought a thousand battles, a record for any Commander, and won most of them. Jellicoe fought one, lost it, and they made him an Earl!' He added that he was going to take the matter up with Attlee. To this Harris said he replied: 'Please don't worry. I am now going back to South Africa where titles are just a joke!'

Although Poland honoured Harris with the Order of Polonia Restituta, France with the Grand Cross of the Légion d'Honneur, and President Vargas personally decorated him with Brazil's Grand Cross of the Southern Cross, the real tribute came from Britain's great American ally. It was, in fact, left to the President of the United States of America to recognise the contribution of this great commander and his indomitable airmen and airwomen of all ranks to the winning of the war, and to express, at this time, the gratitude of a great nation for his exceptionally meritorious service. On the 17th day of September, 1945, President Truman awarded to Harris, on behalf of the United States of America, one of America's highest military honours, The Distinguished Service Medal. It was presented to him at the Pentagon, in person, by Eisenhower early in 1946. The citation read:

THE WHITE HOUSE

WASHINGTON

CITATION FOR DISTINGUISHED SERVICE MEDAL

Air Chief Marshal Sir Arthur Harris, Royal Air Force, performed exceptionally meritorious service in a position of great responsibility as head of the Royal Air Force Bomber Command from 1940, when his Force began the air battle over Germany. Adjusting his strategy so as best to assist the planned invasion of France, he directed his Forces in the spring of 1944 against enemy communication centers in France and the Lowlands. The success of this offensive, achieved at considerable loss, paved the way for the break-through in Normandy. Concurrently with this task, he maintained his offensive over Germany and, in addition, accepted many tactical commitments at the request of the Supreme Commander. The Ground Forces will ever remember with thankfulness the skill and effectiveness of his support, both strategically and tactically, to their own operations. He forged in the Royal Air Force Bomber Command one of the most potent weapons of war which brought about the total destruction of the enemy.

Harry Truman

17th September, 1945.   PRESIDENT TRUMAN

25
Aftermath

With the war in Europe at an end and the war in the Pacific against Japan swiftly terminated by two atom bombs with a minimum of loss of life to the Allies, Harris indicated his desire to retire. Just before the end of the war in Europe he was offered the Governorship of Southern Rhodesia but, despite the attractiveness of such an appointment, he declined the honour because he wished to see the war through to the very end. Shortly after this, Herbert Morrison,* the Home Secretary in Churchill's National Coalition Government, offered him the post of Commissioner of the Metropolitan Police, which he also declined as he could not visualise himself as a policeman. The one offer that he would have accepted, which was made by Churchill just prior to the General Election in July 1945 when the Labour Government under Attlee was returned to power, was that of Governor of Bermuda. Attlee at first agreed with the proposal and, when lunching the Harrises at Chequers, just after becoming Prime Minister, he commented to Harris on his pending appointment. But a few days later he wrote to Harris to say that the appointment had been cancelled!

Admittedly, in January 1946, Harris was promoted to the rank of Marshal of the Royal Air Force, the highest rank that an officer of that service can attain. But, as has already been stated, he was otherwise ignored in the Victory Honours List. Moreover, as soon as the Labour Government indicated its indifference to the contribution of Harris and his Bomber Command to the winning of the war, Harris began to come under attack for his handling of the bomber offensive. A wave of hypocritical condemnation of the bombing policy and the attack of German cities, involving civilians in the ravages of war, swept through the ranks of the left-wing politicians and intellectuals. Sorrow for the Germans, with never a thought for the disaster that would have overtaken their fellow countrymen in Britain if the bomber offensive had not been so effective, seemed to pervade their minds. Swiftly forgotten were the 5,700,000 Jewish men, women and children who had been systematically exterminated in history's greatest and most bestial experiment in wholesale genocide. Quickly out of mind were the millions of Russian civilians killed and mutilated in the fearful land battles on the

* The Rt Hon Herbert Morrison, MP (later Lord Morrison of Lambeth), was a member of the Labour Party.

Eastern Front, whose numbers would have been far greater had the bomber offensive failed or never taken place. Soon forgotten were the millions of families in the German occupied territories which had been disrupted and destroyed by the practice of slave labour in Hitler's Third Reich.

Certainly, elements of the Labour Party have always had a devout belief in pacifism and for this they are not to be censured. But can it be truly said that they were prepared, in defence of their pacifist ideals, to put at risk the freedom of the British nation from the tyranny of Nazism? This is surely unacceptable, and therefore one must look further for the reasons underlying the extraordinary post-war attitude to the bombing policy and to the infamous treatment of Harris and Bomber Command—Harris ignored and the ground staff and personnel of the Command to receive, as Harris bitterly commented at the time, 'only a Home Defence medal whilst every clerk, butcher, baker and candlestick-maker, serving miles behind the fighting fronts on the Continent, in Egypt and the East, were to get a campaign medal.'

The war had been conducted by a National Coalition Government under Churchill, with Clement Attlee as the Deputy Prime Minister and all parties, Conservative, Labour and Liberal, well represented at Cabinet and Ministerial levels. The strategical control of the bomber force had been exercised by the Defence Committee of the War Cabinet taking advice from the Chiefs of Staff. The Defence Committee and the War Cabinet consisted at all times of the leaders and other senior members of the political parties which formed the National Coalition Government, including such names as Winston Churchill, Clement Attlee (Labour), Sir Archibald Sinclair (Liberal), Anthony Eden (Conservative), Sir Stafford Cripps (Labour), Ernest Bevin (Labour), Herbert Morrison (Labour), Sir John Anderson (National Liberal) and Lord Beaverbrook (Independent). The Chiefs of Staff Committee consisted of the heads of three armed services. When America came into the war, the Joint Chiefs of Staff, British and American, would jointly decide on advice to be given to the Heads of State on the conduct of the war, the liaison being remarkably close at all times. There was one temporary exception of this method of exercising control over the bomber forces and that was in 1944 when, immediately prior to and during the invasion of France, the Joint Chiefs of Staff, British and American, made their recommendations to the Supreme Commander-in-Chief of the Allied Expeditionary Force for strategic bombing and the Supreme Commander had prior call on all Allied bomber forces in Europe for his immediate strategical and tactical requirements, a right which he retained until the end of the war. In September 1944, however, after the invasion forces had penetrated deep into France and crossed into Belgium, the British bomber force reverted to control by the Chiefs of Staff and the War Cabinet and the American strategic bomber forces reverted to control by the head of the US Army Air Force and the US equivalent to the War Cabinet. Both Forces were, however, subject to Eisenhower's overruling right mentioned above.

Clearly, therefore, the Labour Party members of the National Coalition Government supported and held as much responsibility for the policy of bombing Germany, much to their credit, as did the other members of the Government and the Chiefs of Staff. Indeed, it was a Labour Government that was in power in August 1945 when, on the 6th, the first atom bomb was dropped on Hiroshima, and on the 9th, the second was dropped on Nagasaki, thereby swiftly ending hostilities with Japan at a probable saving of a million or more Allied lives. The Japanese surrendered on 14 August 1945, and Clement Attlee broadcast the news to the nation at midnight following the surrender.

Harris himself found it difficult to point to the reasons for the shameful treatment of Bomber Command. But one wonders whether it had its roots in a course of action he took in his earlier days as Commander-in-Chief, when he and his staff had serious grounds for doubting the adequacy of the security arrangements for the Command. When investigating these arrangements, it was brought to his attention by one of his staff that a Labour politician with a war-time temporary commission of squadron leader was serving in the Directorate of Bomber Operations, and that this officer had at one time been a member of Sir Oswald Mosley's Fascist party, had later become a Marxist and finally had 'middled out' into socialism. The individual concerned was Squadron Leader John Strachey, who had been a close friend of Sir Oswald Mosley in the 1920s and the early 1930s when Mosley was a member of the Labour Party. When Mosley was Chancellor of the Duchy of Lancaster in 1929, Strachey became his Parliamentary Private Secretary and when Mosley resigned from the Labour Party in May 1930 and launched his New Party in March 1931, Strachey followed him. But Strachey's allegiance to Mosley's New Party, which was quickly to become the British Fascist party, was relatively short lived. After the Ashton-under-Lyme by-election in 1931 when the New Party split the vote and lost Labour the election there was violent reaction from Labour supporters. Mosley's party then began to offer violence back at its meetings around the country with its members dressed in black shirts, breeches and field boots. Mosley wrote* of this time that Strachey '. . . quite suddenly formed the view after this occasion that the mass of the workers were against us, and that we were on the wrong side. From his opinion he never turned back, until his collaboration with the Communist Party. It then took him some time to evolve once more into a pillar of Labour orthodoxy.' Mosley, after referring to Strachey's writings on Marx, said, 'he became excessively preoccupied with Marx and Freud.' This led Mosley to say somewhat cynically to him on one occasion: 'You are governed above the waist by Marx, below the waist by Freud, but no part of you by Strachey!'

Harris, having regard to the possible security risk of employing a person

* *My Life* by Sir Oswald Mosley, published by Nelson in 1968, pages 284–285 and 329–330.

in the Directorate of Bomber Operations with such an unstable political past as that of Strachey, requested the Air Ministry to investigate the matter and to have him removed from the Directorate. Since Strachey stayed, the Air Ministry presumably decided that if he had been a Mosleyite Fascist and later a Communist he was then neither of these things, but just a good ordinary member of the Labour Party. Harris said of this episode that he never believed in the 'exness' of any political extremist, left or right.

In the biography of John Strachey by Hugh Thomas,* it is stated that Strachey, after abandoning Mosley, followed communism and in 1932 expressed the wish to join the Communist Party proper. After talks with Palme Dutt, however, the half-Indian, half-Swede intellectual leader of the British Communist Party, he was persuaded that he could do more for the Party if he were not a paid-up member and therefore not a card-carrying Communist. Strachey accepted the force of Dutt's arguments and followed the dishonest course of becoming a clandestine communist. It is also revealed that in July 1939, he was still a clandestine Communist and in intimate touch with the communist leaders who were no friends of Britain. Indeed he actually helped Dutt with the drafting of the Communist Party programme for the congress due to take place in October of that year. More remarkable is Strachey's admission to Dutt in December 1931, that he had sought the advice of Sokolnikov, the Russian Ambassador in London, as to whether he should join the Communist Party.

Thomas also states that in the winter of 1940 Strachey applied to join the Royal Air Force as an adjutant, but went to his interview with some misgivings as he believed his left-wing past would prevent any chance of his being accepted.

> Two 'fatherly' officers interviewed him. One asked him where he had been at school. 'Eton,' said Strachey. The other asked what games he played. 'Cricket,' was the reply. That went down well. 'Any other games?' 'Tennis and squash,' said Strachey. Finally they both put down their pencils, and one said: 'As a matter of fact, Mr. Strachey, we know all about you.' Strachey thought of his friendship with Dutt, his association with David Springhill (now in gaol for spying) and his old commitment to Mosley. 'Yes, Mr. Strachey,' said the officer, 'your father was the editor of the *Spectator*.' Strachey was saved, not for the last time, by the 'old boy net'.

Harris was clearly right to demand Strachey's removal from such a sensitive department as that of the Directorate of Bomber Operations. The fact that Strachey stayed was presumably due to the existence of other 'fatherly' officers.

At the end of the war, after the Labour Party came into power, Lord

---

*Published by Eyre Methuen in 1973. See pages 122–123, 183 and 204–205.

Stansgate,* formerly William Wedgwood Benn, became Secretary of State for Air, and John Strachey, curiously enough, was appointed Under-Secretary of State for Air.

Certainly Harris was recommended by Portal and Churchill to Attlee for a peerage in the Victory Honours List, as also he was recommended by Churchill for the Governorship of Bermuda. Equally certain is the fact that both recommendations were cancelled by the Labour Government, and one can only assume that this must have been at the instigation in part, if not in whole, of Strachey as Under-Secretary of State for Air and of Lord Stansgate as Secretary of State for Air.

Could it therefore be that there was an element of petty revenge in the treatment of Harris and that Attlee, ill-advisedly, yielded to this ignoble gesture?

One now comes to the second strange episode in this saga of mutilating the memory of one of the British Empire and Commonwealth's greatest commanders. The late Sir Charles Webster, an Emeritus Professor of International History in the University of London and a distinguished scholar of nineteenth- and twentieth-century diplomacy, was appointed to write the official history of Bomber Command under the title of *The Strategic Air Offensive against Germany 1939–1945*, which was published by Her Majesty's Stationery Office in four volumes in 1961. Noble Frankland, an ex-wartime flight lieutenant navigator who completed a tour of bomber operations and was awarded the DFC, and who obtained an MA and a Doctorate of Philosophy after the war, was appointed as assistant to Sir Charles Webster. Although this history concludes that, 'Both cumulatively in largely indirect ways and eventually in a more immediate and direct manner, strategic bombing and, also in other roles strategic bombers, made a contribution to victory which was decisive,' it largely in indirect ways, and not infrequently in a more immediate and direct manner, attacks Harris's views on strategic bombing, his handling of the bomber force and goes as far as to say that much of the bomber effort was a failure and wasted.

The historians certainly had access to all official documents. But did they bother to go further than captured German documents and the records of post-war interrogations of top German personnel? Did they seek to interview such important individuals as Herr Albert Speer in person, to meet and talk with members of the German military forces, or to study Swiss diplomatic and intelligence reports? Or was Webster, perhaps, personally against the principle of the bomber offensive and therefore, unwittingly, ready to find fault with Harris and Bomber Command? Perhaps the Air Ministry should have been more circumspect, at the time,

---

* A Liberal MP in the 1920s who switched to Labour. Secretary of State for India in the Labour Government from 1928 to 1931. In World War II he became Director of Public Relations at the Air Ministry with the rank of Acting Air Commodore.

in its approval of the choice of historians. Certainly the Navy and the Army seem to have been. By contrast the Air Ministry's choice of Denis Richards and Hilary St George Saunders to write the short history *Royal Air Force, 1939–1945*, which was published in 1953, was an excellent one. Denis Richards, as the head of a group of historians and technical experts writing confidential studies for the Air Ministry, and Hilary St George Saunders, as an official diarist for Combined Operations Headquarters and the Allied Expeditionary Force, and the author of such outstanding accounts as *The Battle of Britain* and *Bomber Command*, could not have been more appropriate for that assignment.

What did Sir Charles Webster do to enlist Harris's aid in the writing of his history? He visited him in New York on 18 November 1952, to advise him that he had been entrusted with the task, with Frankland as his assistant. He then made it abundantly clear that he had always been opposed to the policy of the bomber offensive and the way in which it had been conducted. Since Webster displayed a complete indifference to the views of Harris, and since he made no move to seek Harris's cooperation, the reason for his visit remains obscure.

In a letter dated 18 November 1958, Sir Charles Webster wrote to Harris advising him that the draft of the official history of Bomber Command's strategic offensive against Germany was complete. The letter asked Harris 'whether you would be willing to look at the draft, if we sent it to you unofficially'. That Webster and Frankland should offer to send the draft *unofficially* was indeed odd. Odder still was the fact that Harris had not been consulted about the history. Harris replied:

> South Africa,
> 23rd December, 1958
>
> Dear Sir Charles,
> Thank you for your letter of the 18th November which only reached me to-day. While it is kind of you to offer to send me the draft 'unofficially', presumably for my comments, it raises a difficulty, which you will appreciate.
> I should, indeed, be interested, but as Commander-in-Chief for the major part of the war of what was for some of that time the country's major war effort, I find it odd, to say the least of it, that I have received no *official* invitation to consult with the historians concerned in producing what purports to be a historical account of, inter alia, the period of my Command.
> In such circumstances, unusual as they would seem to be to most people, though not apparently to the Government department concerned, I could not accept the idea of playing any 'unofficial' part in the production beyond the chat which we had in my flat in New York.
>
> There is nothing personal in this; but if this is the normal working method of the Historical Branch of the Government then perhaps it is

understandable that amongst others—I suspect— I would not wish to be associated with it.

Yours sincerely,
Arthur T. Harris

It is doubtful whether one will ever know the true reasons for the gross ingratitude displayed by the post-war Labour Government, under Attlee, to Harris and his 'Bomber Boys' for their immense contribution to victory and their undoubted protection of the British nation from the heel of the Nazi boot. But one is bound to conclude that Strachey was primarily responsible.

There was a third incident, immediately post-war, which seemed to indicate that the Government had no desire to establish the effectiveness of the bomber offensive. As the Allied armies entered Germany, and the war in Europe ended, the Americans sent into Germany and the former German-occupied Western European countries a force of men known as the United States Strategic Bombing Survey consisting of 300 civilian experts, 350 officers and 500 enlisted men. Its task was to assess the results of the strategic bombing and to produce an authoritative account of the American contribution for the official history of the United States Army Air Forces. This it did with great efficiency and in considerable detail, but with scant reference to the contribution of Bomber Command. The British Government, for its part, sent a dozen or so observers as the British Bombing Survey Unit, a totally inadequate force, and then failed to publish the reports. From the withholding of these reports one can only conclude that there was a desire on the part of the Government to deny to the British public, firstly, the truth about the contribution of Bomber Command to victory and, secondly, any knowledge of the greatness as a commander of Sir Arthur Harris.

Early in 1946, with the Bermuda appointment cancelled, Harris planned to fulfil his long-held intention to return to Africa with his family to enjoy a life of retirement. But fate was to intervene again in his life. The United States of America had not finished giving him honours and there were certain influential individuals in that country who were not prepared to see his talents go to waste. The USA granted him an honorary diplomatic visa so that he and his family could reside in America whenever he wished. Then, Mr Henry Mercer of the States Marine Corporation, a leading shipping industrialist in the United States and a friend of Harris who had done much to help Britain in the war, invited him to visit New York before going to South Africa as he had a proposition to discuss with him which might be of interest. Henry Mercer had, in fact, decided to launch and develop a new shipping line sailing the route USA–South Africa, and for its Managing Director he had decided upon Sir Arthur Harris if he could be persuaded to accept.

Harris did accept and with the considerable help of Averell Harriman, Secretary for Commerce, who as Roosevelt's special envoy in Europe during the war years had been one of Harris's greatest admirers, he acquired for the new corporation its first three ships, which were ex-United States troopships. These he had converted into cargo liners and re-commissioned as the SS *Constantia*, SS *Morgenster* and SS *Vergelegen* in the service of what was soon to become well known as the South African Marine Corporation Limited, or Safmarine for short. This line quickly extended its operations to world-wide routes and it was Harris who managed this highly successful shipping company from scratch.

But Britain was not entirely to forget its greatest commander. In October 1951, following a General Election, the Labour Party was defeated and the Conservative Party was returned to power with Churchill once more as Prime Minister. In April 1952, Viscount Bracken, who as Brendan Bracken had been Minister of Information and then First Lord of the Admiralty in Churchill's wartime National Coalition Government, contacted Harris, on behalf of Churchill, saying that it was the new Government's opinion that he had been treated abominably by the Labour Government after the war and, now that the Conservatives were back in power, Churchill wished to make amends. Indeed, the choice of a peerage was Harris's for the asking. It was particularly appropriate that the approach to Harris, who was now alternating between his homes in Cape Town and New York, should have been made by Brendan Bracken, for Bracken had long been a great personal friend of the Harris family and frequently stayed with them when he was in Cape Town on business. Harris indicated that the only honour he would accept would be that of a baronetcy which would enable him to retain his present mode of address and which would still be a recognition, through him, of the tremendous contribution made by all ranks of Bomber Command to victory and of the skill, determination and courage of the bomber crews. To become a peer and, therefore, to take upon himself Lord Harris as a mode of address would be, he said, 'as out of place in South Africa as a hippopotamus in Trafalgar Square.'

In a letter to Brendan Bracken dated 28 April 1952, and written from New York, Harris wrote, after indicating his pleasure at Churchill's offer:

It will greatly ease my present lot vis-à-vis the steadily increasing number of people, a few of whom really matter to me, who more and more are inclined to accept the gossip mongers' dictum that I was 'struck out' of the Honours List and forced to resign and leave the country ... However, any such public recognition now from W.S.C., as Prime Minister and Minister of Defence at the time, will certainly put a stopper on this once and for all. Incidentally, it will also make it possible for me to visit England again without the Press, as on previous occasions, invariably greeting my arrival with conjectures on why I was 'left out, resigned, and cleared out' and greeting my true explanation that I retired voluntarily with a disbelieving smirk! Moreover, I well know that should Strachey and Co. ever regain power in my lifetime, they would not hesitate if it suited them, in some foreseeable political circumstances, to hand me over to the Huns and make capital out of the fact that the Government of that day pointedly disassociated themselves in the Honours List from the Bomber Offensive as a whole and myself in particular. This is not a pleasant atmosphere in which to eke out the short while that may remain to me; although I have myself become so hardened to it, and so contemptuous of the authors, that I am personally indifferent to all of it, except the gross insult it implied to my bomber boys ... It has always infuriated me, but never surprised me, that in pursuit of his personal spites and vengeance on my person that turncoat Strachey would willingly smear those fine boys as a whole—after all they suffered, and all they achieved for England.

There were matters of Harris's dual nationality to be cleared before Churchill could put forward his name to Her Majesty the Queen. He had, in the course of his work as Managing Director of the South African Marine Corporation, acquired South African citizenship. This status was, however, about to be rescinded as he was giving up his residence in Cape Town and would only be visiting South Africa for business purposes.* On the 17 May 1952, Churchill wrote to Harris to say that he proposed to put his name forward for a baronetcy in the New Year Honours List. On 28 May, Brendan Bracken also wrote. Addressing him 'My Dear Bert', he said: 'You will have heard long since from the Boss about the modest recognition you wanted for the sake of Bomber Command and as a thistle for Strachey ...'

Sir Arthur Harris was made a baronet in January 1953. And so, at last, the nation, through its greatest Prime Minister in history, and by the gracious consent of Queen Elizabeth the Second of England, recognised and paid tribute to one of the greatest commanders in British history. Harris was in Vancouver when the honour was promulgated and the congratulations poured in from all over the world. Typical of the expressions of delight was one telegram which read: 'Hearty congratulations on your well deserved honor. At last your great achievement has been recognised.'

From Brendan Bracken came this letter:

My Dear Bert,
'Let me tell you, Bert, that W.S.C. was delighted that you should have the comparatively modest honour that has come your way. Had you wished to join the morgue† to which Portal, Tedder and I belong, your desire would have been fulfilled.

The Prime Minister and many of your colleagues are not likely to forget that you held what was probably the most difficult Command in the war and that you, and you alone, as Commander-in-Chief were able

---

* The National Government in South Africa would no longer permit dual citizenship and Harris, as a British officer, could not remain a South African citizen.

† The House of Lords.

to carry the war into Germany when the soldiers and sailors were unable to strike a blow at Hitler's warriors.

And so there is no honour in the gift of the Monarchy that you do not deserve.

Putting aside your remarkable successes as Commander-in-Chief Bomber Command, I shall always remember with gratitude your willingness to look after all the visiting Firemen whether they were neutral, Americans, Turks, Greeks and all the other strange folk inflicted on you by No. 10* or the Ministry of Information. I remember telling you in 1942 that you were the best propagandist Britain possessed. The years that have passed have increased this belief.

> Give my love to Jill and Jackie.†
>
> Yours aye
>
> Brendan.

Included in the messages of congratulation were those from his old colleagues in arms, both British and American, and from many of the members of Churchill's wartime administration, including Churchill himself.

But as the years passed, memories faded and soon the horrors and fears of Nazism receded, to be replaced by a fanatical desire on the part of historians, sensation writers, some journalists, and television writers and producers to degrade and assassinate the character of the commander and the one Command to whom they owe their very liberty, and to pour out, unchallenged and unchecked, their scurrilous and, more frequently than not, inaccurate reports on a war which most of them never knew. Harris harboured no bitterness over this from his own personal point of view, but he felt deeply hurt that those who strived so hard in Bomber Command for victory and the freedom of the nation, many of whom gave their lives, should suffer vilification through his person.

In retirement, Harris remained silent, not wishing to stir up controversy. But at last he agreed to allow one who served with him in Bomber Command during those hard and critical years of World War II, to write his story.

It is difficult to pay an adequate tribute to Sir Arthur Harris. I have, at least, tried to tell the truth, supported by facts, and I hope that this may in some way make clear in history the great debt of gratitude that we as a nation owe to Sir Arthur Harris. Our obligation to him for our freedom is profound indeed.

Perhaps the last word should be left to Dwight D. Eisenhower who, as President of the United States, remembered Harris on the occasion of the twentieth anniversary of D-Day, 1944, when the Allied forces invaded the continent of Europe to liberate France, Belgium, Holland and Luxemburg,

---

* No 10 Downing Street, the Prime Minister's official residence.

† Harris's wife and daughter.

and to complete the final phase of the defeat of Nazi Germany. He wrote:

DDE

Gettysburg
Pennsylvania
June 5, 1964.

Dear Bert,

On the Sixth of June I suspect that your memory goes back, as mine does, to live over again the gnawing anxieties, the realization of unavoidable sacrifices, and the bright hopes that filled us on D-Day, 1944.

Never, during the two decades that have since passed, have I ceased to render daily and devout thanks to a kindly Providence for permitting us to achieve in eleven months the complete victory that so many believed would require years.

In the same way, I have always felt a deep sense of appreciation and gratitude to all who took part in, or who served in a supporting role for, that great Allied venture.

To you, one of my close associates in OVERLORD, I am impelled to send, once more, a special word of thanks. Your professional skill and selfless dedication to the cause in which we all served will be noted by the histories of those dramatic months, but no historian could possibly be aware of the depth of my obligation to you.

With warm regard,
As ever
IKE

Bibliography

DOCUMENTS

Cabinet Office Historical Branch: War Cabinet Minutes, Chief of Staff Minutes, Prime Minister's (Churchill's) files, 1939–45.
Public Record Office and Air Historical Branch: Air Ministry and RAF Bomber Command files 1918–45.
United States of America Strategic Bombing Survey.

BOOKS

Anon. *Der Jüdische Krieg*. Nibelungenverlag, 1944.
Avon, The Right Hon. The Earl of *The Memoirs of Sir Anthony Eden* Vols. I & II. Cassell, 1965.
Boyle, A. *Trenchard—Man of Vision*. Collins, 1962.
Bryant, Sir Arthur. *The Alanbrooke Diaries* Vols. I & II. Collins, 1957 & 1959.
Chisholm, Air Commodore R. *Cover of Darkness*. Chatto & Windus, 1953.
Churchill, W. *The Second World War* Vols. I–VI. Cassell, 1948–54.
Dietrich, Dr O. *Das Buch der Deutschen Gaue*. Gauverlag Bayerische Ostmark, 1938.
Goebbels, J. *Das Eherne Herz, Reden und Aufsätze aus den Jahren 1941–42*. Zentralverlag der NSDAP, 1943.
Harris, Marshal of the Royal Air Force Sir Arthur *Bomber Offensive*. Collins, 1947.
Irving, D. *The Destruction of Dresden*. William Kimber, 1963.
Konsalik, H. G. *Stalingrad*. Hestia Verlag, 1968.
Lochner, L. P. trans. & ed. *The Goebbels Diaries*. Hamish Hamilton, 1948.
Mosley, Sir Oswald *My Life*. Nelson, 1968.
Reitlinger, G. *The Final Solution*. Vallentine Mitchell, 1968.
Richards, D. and St. George Saunders, H. *The Royal Air Force* Vols. I–III. HMSO, 1953 & 1954.
Saward, Group Captain D. *The Bomber's Eye*. Cassell, 1959.
Slessor, Marshal of the Royal Air Force Sir John. *The Central Blue*. Cassell, 1956.
Speer, A. *Inside the Third Reich*. Weidenfeld & Nicolson, 1970.

Thomas, H. *John Strachey*. Eyre Methuen, 1973.

Webster, Sir Charles, and Frankland, N. *The Strategic Air Offensive Against Germany* Vols. I–IV. HMSO, 1961.

Winkelnkemper, Dr T. *Der Grossangriff auf Köln*. Zentralverlag der NSDAP, 1942.

Index